A Multiliteracies Framework for Collegiate Foreign Language Teaching

A Multiliteracies Framework for Collegiate Foreign Language Teaching

Kate Paesani
Wayne State University

Heather Willis Allen
University of Wisconsin–Madison

Beatrice Dupuy
University of Arizona

Series Editors
Judith Liskin-Gasparro
Manel Lacorte

PEARSON

Boston Columbus Indianapolis New York San Francisco Upper Saddle River
Amsterdam Cape Town Dubai London Madrid Milan Munich Paris Montréal Toronto
Delhi Mexico City São Paulo Sydney Hong Kong Seoul Singapore Taipei Tokyo

Editor in Chief: Bob Hemmer
Editorial Assistant: Pauline Kitele
Marketing Director: Steve Debow
Vice President Product Development: Dickson Musslewhite
Team Lead, Project Management: Melissa Feimer
Project Manager: Molly White
Team Lead, Program Management: Amber Mackey
Program Manager: Annemarie Franklin
Full Service Project Management:: Anju Joshi/Lumina Datamatics, Inc.
Art Director: Maria Lange
Cover Art: Mr Twister/Fotolia
Manager, Rights and Permissions: Ben Ferrini
Project Manager, Rights and Permissions: Lee Scher
Printer/Binder: Courier/North Chelmsford

Credits and acknowledgments borrowed from other sources and reproduced, with permission, in this textbook appear on the page number 291.

Library of Congress Cataloging-in-Publication Data

Paesani, Kate, author.

A multiliteracies framework for collegiate foreign language teaching / Kate Paesani, Wayne State University; Heather Willis Allen, University of Wisconsin-Madison; Beatrice Dupuy, University of Arizona.

pages cm

Includes bibliographical references and index.

ISBN 978-0-205-95404-9 — ISBN 0-205-95404-9 1. Language and languages—Study and teaching (Higher) 2. Multilingualism—Study and teaching (Higher) 3. Multilingualism—Psychological aspects. 4. Multicultural education. 5. Literacy programs. 6. Language teachers. I. Paesani, Kate, author. II. Allen, Heather Willis, author. III. Dupuy, Beatrice, author. Title.

P51.P234 2014
418.0071—dc23

2014026299

10 9 8 7 6 5 4 3 2 1 V092 14

ISBN 10: 0-205-95404-9
ISBN 13: 978-0-205-95404-9

CONTENTS

ACKNOWLEDGMENTS

This book is the result of the collaborative research we have been conducting on multiliteracies-based pedagogy and foreign language teacher development over the past several years. Many of the initial ideas arose from Heather and Beatrice's work on the PErCOLATE project—funded by the Center for Educational Resources in Culture, Language, and Literacy (CERCLL), a Title VI Language Resource Center at the University of Arizona—and we wish to thank the CERCLL co-directors, project coordinators, and staff for their support. These ideas have been honed in the courses we have taught, the introductory language programs we have directed, the workshop and conference presentations we have given, and the scholarship we have published. We are thus grateful to the students, instructors, workshop and conference participants, and manuscript reviewers and editors who have helped shaped our ideas. In particular, we want to thank the students who have participated in our foreign language pedagogy courses at the University of Arizona, University of Miami, University of Pittsburgh, University of Wisconsin–Madison, and Wayne State University.

This book would not have been possible without the careful editorial work of our series editors, Judy Liskin-Gasparro and Manel Lacorte, who read numerous iterations of every chapter and made significant contributions to our ideas. Because of their feedback, this book has a coherence that we would never have been able to achieve on our own.

We are also grateful to the colleagues who provided feedback as we completed this project. We especially want to thank Heidi Byrnes, Rick Kern, and Janet Swaffar for providing valuable comments on our prospectus that helped shaped the manuscript into its current form. In addition, Cathy Barrette, Rick Donato, Karen Johnson, and Hiram Maxim were important sounding boards throughout the various stages of this project.

Many people at Pearson deserve recognition for their contributions to this book, including Bob Hemmer, who supported this project from its inception, Molly White, our project manager, and Anju Joshi, the project manager for production.

Finally, we express our deepest gratitude to our family and friends for their patience and support as we saw this project to its completion.

ACKNOWLEDGMENTS

INTRODUCTION

Making the Case for Literacy in Collegiate Foreign Language Programs

Over the past decade, the landscape of U.S. collegiate foreign language (FL) education has changed significantly. This change results from a number of factors, including shifting enrollment trends within FL programs, diversification of course offerings that reflect the rise of critical languages, economic pressures that bring advocacy of FL programs to the forefront, and a general questioning of the role of the humanities within the larger mission of institutions of higher education. As an example of this changing landscape, following increased focus on the need to understand and communicate with other cultures and peoples after 9/11, a survey of the Modern Language Association (MLA) reported that undergraduate FL enrollments increased 6.6% overall between 2006 and 2009; however, enrollments in advanced courses, already dangerously low in 2006, remained unchanged in 2009 (Furman, Goldberg, & Lusin, 2007, 2010). This fact alone suggests that FL programs are in crisis.

The most frequently cited cause of this crisis has been the well-known bifurcation of FL programs, such that there exist fixed lines of demarcation between introductory and intermediate language courses and advanced literature and culture courses, with differing instructional goals and techniques in each level (e.g., Byrnes, Maxim, & Norris, 2010; MLA, 2007; Swaffar & Arens, 2005). The table below lists the typical characteristics of these two parts of the curriculum.

Departmental bifurcation results from a number of factors, and the one most relevant for the purposes of this book is the lack of a unified approach to FL teaching and curriculum design across instructional levels. For instance, in introductory and intermediate language courses, instruction is usually organized around principles of communicative language teaching, whereas in advanced literature and culture courses, individual instructors determine the instructional approach, often with little consistency across courses. Moreover, in neither level of the program does instruction typically include

Characteristics of Bifurcated FL Programs (adapted from Kern, 2000 and Maxim, 2006)

Introductory and Intermediate Language Courses	Advanced Literature and Culture Courses
Development of functional abilities to communicate everyday needs, thoughts	Development of analytical and critical thinking skills
Focus on language forms and conventions	Focus on cultural and literary sensibilities
Expression of personal opinions and familiar ideas	Expression of new ideas, analysis, and synthesis
Reading and writing as support skills for practice of language forms	Reading and writing as integral to learning literary–cultural content
Classroom organized around language	Classroom organized around content
Functional texts (ads, weather reports, menus, etc.)	Literary texts (poetry, prose, drama, etc.)
Collaborative, supportive, small-group environment	Serious, lecture- and discussion-oriented environment

a simultaneous focus on the development of language competencies and on the ability to engage with the content of FL texts. Indeed, constructing curricula with an eye toward individual faculty members rather than to the FL program as a whole, and toward language development in introductory and intermediate courses while ignoring language development at advanced levels are "pernicious assumptions" related to the FL crisis (Swaffar, 2003, p. 20). These assumptions are compounded by a tendency to use teaching practices that separate form from meaning and communication from content (i.e., texts) and context (Swaffar & Arens, 2005).

Our challenge, then, is to develop broader and more coherent curricula, instructional approaches, and assessment practices that respond to the problems caused by FL program bifurcation and to recent changes in the profession. The 2007 MLA report, "Foreign Languages and Higher Education: New Structures for a Changed World," underscored this challenge by advocating reform of the content, goals, and governance structures of collegiate FL programs, as can be seen in the following proposal:

> Replacing the two-tiered language-literature structure with a broader and more coherent curriculum in which language, culture, and literature are taught as a continuous whole . . . will reinvigorate language departments as valuable academic units central to the humanities and to the missions of institutions of higher education. (p. 3)

The report further recommended implementing this curricular reform by developing students' "translingual and transcultural competence" (p. 3), or the ability to operate between languages and cultures, through interaction with target language texts. These suggestions are certainly laudable, yet as Byrnes, Maxim, and Norris (2010) pointed out, the report assumes that students will reach advanced-level language competencies with no consideration of how they achieve that goal.

In this book, we respond to concerns regarding how students reach advanced-level competencies by addressing two interrelated goals. The first goal is to outline a coherent pedagogical framework that responds to the aforementioned calls for change and provides an alternative to the differing instructional goals and techniques that characterize bifurcated programs. The second goal is to present this framework in an accessible manner for novice collegiate FL teachers.

To meet the first goal, we foreground the *multiliteracies framework* (Cope & Kalantzis, 2009; Kern, 2000; New London Group, 1996) and the framing concept of *literacy* which, according to Kern (2003), offers the following benefits:

> It offers a way to narrow the long-standing pedagogical gap that has traditionally divided what we do at the early levels of language teaching and what we do at the advanced levels. That is, it offers a way to reconcile the teaching of 'communication' with the teaching of 'textual analysis.' (p. 43)

This approach extends the more traditional definition of literacy—the ability to read and write—to encompass "dynamic, culturally and historically situated practices of using and interpreting diverse written and spoken texts to fulfill particular social purposes" (Kern, 2000, p. 6), with the goal of preparing FL learners to participate in diverse discourse communities both at home and in the target culture (e.g., with other FL students, target culture youths, online communities). Within this approach, given its priority for engaging students in text-focused literacy events, reading and writing are integral to meaning construction rather than support skills intended for practice of language forms. However, instead of carrying out text-centric literary analysis, learners are encouraged to interpret, transform, and think critically about discourse through a variety of contexts and written, oral, and visual textual genres. Texts are therefore essential to our approach. Not only are they a common element that can unite the language and literary–cultural sides of the FL curriculum, they provide a crucial link to the overall mission of the humanities in institutions of higher education by "highlighting the language-based nature of knowing, the language-based nature of learning in educational settings across the disciplinary spectrum, and the centrality of language in contemporary society" (Byrnes, Maxim, & Norris, 2010, p. 23).

To meet the second goal of presenting the multiliteracies framework in an accessible manner for novice collegiate FL teachers, we focus primarily on pedagogical strategies for integrating the study of language and literary–cultural content at lower levels, given that approximately 92% of FL graduate students' teaching assignments during their first three years of the PhD are in introductory- and intermediate-level language courses (Steward, 2006).[1] Even so, we situate the multiliteracies approach within the context of the entire undergraduate curriculum, and throughout the book care is given to introduce strategies applicable beyond lower-level courses as well as additional references with specific relevance for teaching advanced undergraduate FL courses. Thus, in addition to the primary intended audience of methods instructors and novice FL teachers, this book will appeal to a wide range of readers, including FL faculty members interested in multiliteracies instruction, graduate students enrolled in applied linguistics and FL education courses, and researchers focusing on literacy and the multiliteracies approach in the context of collegiate FL education.

Given its goals, this book serves as a key tool for transforming both what is taught in FL courses and how it is taught. In this Introduction, we lay a foundation to help you understand how the multiliteracies framework can lead to this transformation and why it is a viable alternative to existing approaches to FL curriculum and instruction. We begin with a brief history of communicative language teaching, the predominant approach to teaching FL at lower levels in U.S. institutions of higher education. An understanding of communicative language teaching's most important contributions and limitations serves as an essential backdrop for moving on to address the foundational notion of literacy and how it may serve as an overarching concept for organizing FL curriculum and instruction across undergraduate programs. We conclude the Introduction with an overview of the remaining chapters of the book.

1. COMMUNICATIVE LANGUAGE TEACHING: HISTORY, CONTRIBUTIONS, AND LIMITATIONS

Since the 1970s, communicative language teaching (CLT) has been the predominant approach to teaching FLs in the United States. The origins of CLT are based in research from European linguists with social and functional orientations (e.g., Halliday, 1978; Hymes, 1972) and in shifting priorities in education at the time.

> The growing convergence in social and functional orientations in linguistics, along with the needs of learners seeking practical language skills for social, academic, occupational, and other purposes in the UK and continental Europe, gave rise to a very pragmatic and learner-centered approach to language teaching and learning. (Duff, 2014, p. 18)

---

[1]Throughout this book, we refer to lower-level and advanced-level FL courses. Lower-level courses are the introductory and intermediate language courses that typically comprise the first two years of collegiate FL study; advanced-level courses are the literature, culture, and language (e.g., advanced composition, phonetics) courses that typically comprise the FL major or minor.

At the same time, researchers in the United States were focused on the social aspects of language and the need to use language appropriately in a range of situations with different speakers (e.g., Hymes, 1972; Savignon, 1972). This work led to the notion of *communicative competence*, which characterized "the ability of classroom language learners to interact with other speakers, to make meaning, as distinct from their ability to recite dialogues or perform on discrete-point tests of grammatical knowledge" (Savignon, 1972, p. 2). Canale and Swain (1980), expanded by Canale (1983), further developed the concept of communicative competence to include grammatical, discourse, sociolinguistic, and strategic competencies. They defined grammatical competence as "the knowledge and skill required to understand and express accurately the literal meaning of utterances" (Canale, 1983, p. 7) through mastery of language features and rules. Unlike grammatical competence, discourse competence goes beyond isolated words and phrases to include "mastery of how to combine grammatical forms and meanings to achieve a unified spoken or written text in different genres" (p. 9). As the name implies, sociocultural competence is concerned with using and understanding language appropriately in different social contexts, and is dependent on "the status of participants, purposes of the interaction, and norms or conventions of interaction" (p. 7). Finally, strategic competence includes "mastery of verbal and non-verbal communication strategies" (p. 10) for the purposes of overcoming communication breakdowns and making communication more effective.

Although the Canale and Swain model of communicative competence has predominated in FL teaching, learning, and assessment for decades and is the model we assume throughout this chapter, it is important to summarize two additional influential models of communicative competence to fully understand the importance of the concept. Using Canale and Swain's work as a starting point, Bachman (1990) and Bachman and Palmer (1996) proposed a model of communicative competence based in empirical research in language testing and assessment. They proposed that communicative language ability has two main components: organizational knowledge and pragmatic knowledge. Organizational knowledge entails abilities required to control the formal structures of language in order to use language accurately to understand and produce larger units of discourse. Organizational knowledge can be further subdivided into grammatical knowledge and textual knowledge, which are similar to Canale and Swain's linguistic competence and discourse competence, respectively. The second component of Bachman and Bachman and Palmer's model is pragmatic knowledge, which refers to the ability to relate words and discourse to their meanings, intent, and contextual use. Pragmatic knowledge has three subdivisions: lexical knowledge, or the knowledge of word meanings and figurative language; functional knowledge, or an understanding of relationships between language and its communicative purpose; and sociolinguistic knowledge, similar to Canale and Swain's sociolinguistic competence.

Celce-Murcia (2007), building on past models as well as her previous work on communicative competence (Celce-Murcia, 1995; Celce-Murcia, Dörnyei, & Thurrell, 1995), proposed a third model of communicative competence that includes the familiar notions of linguistic, discourse, sociolinguistic, and strategic competence, as well as the notions of formulaic and interactional competence. Formulaic competence "refers to those fixed and prefabricated chunks of language that speakers use heavily in everyday interactions" (Celce-Murcia, 2007, p. 47). Interactional competence includes three subparts: actional competence, or "knowledge of how to perform common speech acts . . . in the target language involving interactions" (p. 48) with others; conversational competence, which includes the ability to open and close conversations, take turns appropriately, and the like; and non-verbal/paralinguistic competence, which entails reading body language or non-verbal cues such as pauses or silence.

CLT, with its focus on communicating appropriately with others, therefore represented a shift from its predecessor, audiolingualism (and the structuralist and behaviorist theories that informed it), whose focus was on mastering the building blocks of language through drilling, memorization, and reinforcement. Jacobs and Farrell (2003) identified ten key components of this paradigm shift from audiolingualism to CLT:

1. change from teacher-centered to learner-centered pedagogy;
2. focus on the process of language learning rather than its products;
3. greater attention to the social nature of learning;
4. study of individual differences rather than application of a one size fits all approach;
5. greater focus on views of those inside the classroom rather than on theorists outside of the classroom;
6. promotion of holistic learning that extends beyond the classroom;
7. priority given to having students to understand and participate in their own learning;
8. view of language learning as whole-to-part rather than part-to-whole;
9. emphasis on meaning rather than on drills and rote learning; and
10. view of learning as a lifelong process. (p. 8)

Language learning from a CLT perspective, therefore, entails interaction, collaboration, negotiation, attention to input and feedback, focus on meaning, and creative, experiential language use (Jacobs & Farrell, 2003; Richards, 2006).

Of course, as is the case with communicative competence, CLT-oriented pedagogy has evolved since its origination in the 1970s, and some scholars speak of two phases or versions of CLT: the strong version, or classic CLT; and the weak version, or current CLT. The strong or classic version of CLT is more experiential in nature in that students learn by doing and grammar is not taught explicitly. This version of CLT is based on the idea that language is used to carry out specific functions. Attention is given to development of the skills needed to use language tools such as grammar appropriately, fluently, and accurately, and classroom activities are focused on communication for real-world purposes, experimenting with language, and allowing students to discover grammar rules on their own. Practice often follows a mechanical–meaningful–communicative sequence and emphasis is placed on pair or group work and the use of authentic language samples. The weak version of CLT is more analytic in that grammar is sometimes taught explicitly. Instead of referring to specific instructional strategies, such as those listed above, current CLT "refers to a set of generally agreed upon principles that can be applied in different ways" (Richards, 2006, p. 22). These principles (e.g., meaningful communication through interaction, effective strategy use, teacher as facilitator, classroom as community) are intentionally broad so that they may be applied to different contexts via particular strategies as instructors see fit (Littlewood, 2011; Richards, 2006). The result is that there presently exist a number of CLT variants rather than a single model for instructors to follow; indeed, CLT is often considered a cover term for a wide range of approaches to FL teaching (Dörnyei, 2009; Richards, 2006; Richards & Rodgers, 2001; Spada, 2007).

That fact that CLT has evolved into a generalized approach that can be applied in a number of ways attests to its importance and popularity, and it has certainly made a number of significant contributions to FL teaching. First and foremost, CLT reminds us that the purpose of FL teaching is not mastery of grammatical forms, but rather development of students' ability to communicate effectively with others (Littlewood, 2011). Moreover, the concept of communicative competence underscores that grammatical mastery alone is insufficient; competency also has sociolinguistic, discourse, and strategic dimensions. A second important contribution of CLT is the idea that form and meaning are related: To communicate effectively, one must use grammar and vocabulary to carry out meaningful language functions. Finally, CLT opened the door to implementing collaborative, interactive, and student-focused classroom practice activities due to a shift away from the teacher-fronted instruction that typified audiolinguialism.

Despite these contributions, many scholars have argued that CLT's various transformations over the past decades have resulted in a watering down of the concept of communicative competence and of the content of FL instruction. Some have even suggested that "because there have been so many different implementations of CLT since it was introduced, it is no longer a useful concept and should probably be discarded" (Spada, 2007, p. 271). Although we do not advocate a complete abandonment of CLT or communicative competence, we do believe that the role these concepts play in FL programs should be reconsidered, given the problems related to departmental bifurcation, curricular coherence, and pedagogical approaches identified here. We see two main limitations of CLT in its current form: (1) its heavy focus on oral, functional language use; and (2) its superficial treatment of cultural and textual content.

According to Byrnes, "in programmatic and pedagogical practice, the notion of communicative competence has come to be associated primarily with interactive, transactional oral language use" (2006, p. 244). When speaking takes priority over other language modalities, reading and writing typically function as secondary support skills, developed to practice language forms rather than to interpret cultural content. A further result of this practice is that language is used in generic contexts to achieve instrumental goals such as ordering food in a restaurant, asking for directions, or describing a memorable party one attended (e.g., Allen & Paesani, 2010; Byrnes, 2006; Kern, 2000; Kramsch, 2006;

Swaffar, 2006). Additionally, in CLT classrooms, students are encouraged to share their attitudes, opinions, and feelings; however, such sharing rarely extends beyond expression of individual viewpoints. Therefore, learners do not see language used in a range of contexts to express differing cultural practices, values, and perspectives. Kern (2000) presents the situation this way:

> Communicative teaching programs have largely succeeded in their goal of promoting learners' interactive speaking abilities. They have tended to be somewhat less successful, however, in developing learners' extended discourse competence and written communication skills—areas of academic ability that are extraordinarily important in academic settings. (p. 19)

Not only does "interactive, transactional oral language use" fail to develop learners' discourse competence and academic abilities, it is incompatible with the kind of content with which students typically interact outside of the context of lower-level language courses. Pennycook underscored the superficiality of the content studied in CLT classrooms when he wrote of the "empty babble of the communicative language class" (1994, p. 311), in which development of language skills is paramount to critical awareness of the cultural and political contexts in which language is used. Likewise, Swaffar (2006) argued that the current conceptualization of communicative competence encourages learners to recall information rather than interpret and analyze it. Much of this superficiality is due to the fact that the focus in CLT classrooms is on functional communication and, as a result, language is often divorced from cultural content. As such, lower-level learners are ill equipped to intelligently discuss the cultural content with which they interact when moving to advanced-level courses where they must read and discuss literature and other cultural texts. A further consequence of this separation of language and content is that it "may unintentionally sustain the long-standing bifurcation of FL programs into language courses and content courses with all the attendant negative consequences" (Byrnes, 2006, p. 244). Indeed, CLT may not be the best framework for developing the kinds of language competencies and familiarity with FL discourses that university departments must foster to maintain the intellectual integrity of their programs (Byrnes, 2006; Levine, Melin, Crane, Chavez, & Lovik, 2008).

Earlier we highlighted that current CLT reflects "a set of generally agreed upon principles" (Richards, 2006, p. 22). This viewpoint has contributed to the notion of *principled eclecticism* (Kumaravadivelu, 1994), in which teachers apply these principles through conscious reflection about how they best fit the needs of their students and instructional context. However, principled eclecticism may not be the most effective solution to the limitations of CLT outlined here. For instance, it is not clear what CLT-based principles instructors follow or whether their adoption of these principles is grounded in theoretical or classroom-based research about the nature of FL learning. Moreover, principled eclecticism implies that instructors adopt CLT in pieces rather than as a whole, thus compromising its validity as a coherent pedagogical approach. Indeed, CLT appears to mean different things to different people and is thus used as a "generalized umbrella term" (Harmer, 2007, p. 70) to describe any teaching approach with the goal of developing communicative abilities.

In the remainder of this Introduction, we wish to situate the important contributions that CLT brings to the table within a reconceptualized view of FL teaching and learning grounded in the concept of literacy and implemented through multiliteracies pedagogy. These contributions—a focus on effective communication, a broader view of language competencies, connections between form and meaning, and learner-centered instruction—are significant, yet they do not go far enough. The functional and mostly oral nature of communication within current CLT limits the ways in which students can use language as well as their understandings of how language, communication, and culture are interrelated (Kern, 2000). To push the concept of communication further and overcome the shortcomings of CLT and current configurations of FL programs discussed earlier, we argue that curriculum and instruction should be grounded in texts with the aim of developing students' academic literacy.

> It seems clear that learners cannot develop the kind of spoken communication ability required in academic settings without a serious commitment to the study of written communication, because much of the former for academic purposes requires "literate" sensibilities about the particular ways the foreign language can be used in written contexts. Oral communication also requires a familiarity with the cultural premises that underlie communication in another society, which, in the absence of lived experience in that society, are often discovered through texts. (Kern, 2003, p. 42)

In the past decade, literacy has been the predominant framework for curricular and pedagogical reform in collegiate FL programs (e.g., Allen & Paesani, 2010; Byrnes, Maxim, & Norris, 2010; Kern, 2000; Kern & Schultz, 2005; Mantero, 2006; Swaffar & Arens, 2005). Few additional curricular solutions to the problems outlined above, other than the approach suggested in the *Standards for Foreign Language Learning in the 21st Century* (National Standards, 2006), have been proposed (Paesani & Allen, 2012). On the one hand, literacy-based approaches and the Standards are similar. Both suggest curricular goals for FL programs grounded in cultural content and espouse a broad understanding of communication that views the modalities of speaking, listening, reading, and writing as overlapping rather than distinct, as is typical in CLT. Literacy-based approaches envelop communication in the textual, whereas the Standards conceptualize communication as being interpersonal (active negotiation of meaning between two or more speakers/writers), interpretive (one-way comprehension of oral/written texts), and presentational (one-way creation of oral/written texts). On the other hand, these curricular solutions are different in that only the multiliteracies framework outlines a pedagogical approach for putting into practice curricular goals, content, and communication and foregrounds texts, both literary and non-literary, as the core content of FL courses. Literacy is thus an appropriate framing concept to meet the goals of this book, not only because it reflects current thinking about FL curriculum and instruction, but also because it meets the short-term needs of novice instructors teaching introductory and intermediate FL courses as well as the long-term needs of FL programs seeking coherent solutions to departmental bifurcation. Moreover, firmly aligning teaching practices according to one theoretical concept and approach (i.e., literacy and the multiliteracies framework) avoids the pitfalls of principled eclecticism and equips teachers with a coherent foundation for FL teaching and learning that can be applied across curricular levels. In the next section, we provide a brief history of literacy and New Literacy Studies, as well as a summary of sociocultural approaches to language learning (all of which inform the multiliteracies approach) before outlining our definition of the concept literacy.

2. WHAT IS LITERACY?

The concept of literacy has been studied in multiple contexts and through numerous theoretical perspectives. Traditionally, literacy has been defined as the ability to read and write. This definition reflects the autonomous model of literacy, which posits that literacy exists independently of social factors and social practices. It was the predominant view prior to the social turn that took place in the humanities and social sciences in the 1970s and 1980s (Lankshear, 1999; Street, 1984). According to Kern (2003), this traditional view of literacy "tends to limit reading and writing to straightforward acts of information transfer" (p. 44). The result is that "for many foreign language students, the de facto goal of reading is uncovering *the* meaning, *the* theme, *the* point of a text. That is to say, what the teacher reveals in class. Similarly, writing is all too often about capturing in *the* right words *the* summary or *the* analysis of something they have read" (p. 44, emphasis in the original).

In conjunction with the social turn and as a reaction to the autonomous model, ideological models of literacy and New Literacy Studies emerged. The ideological model posits that literacy is a social practice rather than an individual skill; literacy is shaped through interaction, as opposed to residing wholly in the private mind of the individual. Defining literacy as social practice means that literacy varies according to social context and is embedded in cultural practices. In other words, reading, writing, viewing, and other literacy practices can be understood only within the social, political, historical, cultural, and economic contexts within which they take place. Moreover, because these contexts are meaning based, literacy itself is about making meaning (Gee, 2012; Lankshear, 1999; Reder & Davila, 2005; Street, 1997, 2000).

Among the theoretical and research trends that contributed to New Literacy Studies were conversation analysis, ethnography of communication, sociolinguistics, cognitive linguistics, post-structuralism, narrative studies, and Vygotskian sociocultural theory. The result was a sociocultural approach to literacy education that considered various forms of textual engagement carried out within contexts of literacy practice that reflect different values, beliefs, power relations, goals, political conditions, interests, and so on (Lankshear, 1999).

A sociocultural perspective on language learning considers the role of social interaction in human development and thus sees learning as a cultural process in which knowledge is possessed individually but is constructed jointly through involvement in literacy events (Lantolf & Thorne, 2006). According to this perspective, language learning entails learning "structures of language, the conventions for using and interpreting its components, and the social meanings, values, and attitudes attached to those conventions in the process of interaction with others and being aware of the means by which the communication is accomplished" (Hall, 2001, pp. 28–29). Moreover, socioculturally oriented approaches to FL learning "focus on if and how learners develop the ability to mediate (i.e., regulate or control) their mental and communicative activity" (Lantolf, 2011, p. 24). Language learning, therefore, is not a simple act of information transmission, but rather a sociocognitive act that involves using tools like language, symbols, or behavior that mediate interactions with others and facilitate the ability to construct meaning in various culturally dependent discourse contexts.

Grounding this book in theoretical concepts related to literacy and sociocultural views of language learning allows us to reconsider communicative development in a FL from a broader perspective than that of current CLT, whose goal is the development of functional oral language use in generic contexts. This grounding facilitates a more complex and creative understanding of discourse, how it functions in oral, written, and visual texts, and its relation to various social and cultural contexts. Moreover, it creates the potential to expand the intellectual relevance and cultural content of FL instruction at introductory levels and beyond.

For the purposes of this book, we adopt the following definition of literacy, which reflects ideas related to ideological models of literacy and sociocultural views of language learning summarized above:

> Literacy is the use of socially-, historically-, and culturally-situated practices of creating and interpreting meaning through texts. It entails at least a tacit awareness of the relationships between textual conventions and their contexts of use and, ideally, the ability to reflect critically on those relationships. Because it is purpose-sensitive, literacy is dynamic—not static—and variable across and within discourse communities and cultures. It draws on a wide range of cognitive abilities, on knowledge of written and spoken language, on knowledge of genres, and on cultural knowledge. (Kern, 2000, p. 16)

Key to this definition is its focus on texts, which, along with language, are integral to FL instruction across curricular levels. Indeed, given that literacy entails interpreting and creating multiple text types from various perspectives, it is perhaps more appropriate to speak of *multiliteracies* (New London Group,

1996), or the multiple ways of engaging in communication across communities and cultures through a variety of language forms (e.g., dialects, registers, contexts of use) to represent meanings linguistically, visually, spatially, or otherwise. Swaffar and Arens (2005), also working within a multiliteracies framework, argued that this approach contributes to the core purpose of the humanities and the specific mission of FL programs: the development of academic literacy, or the teaching of textuality and genre in cultural contexts.

Inherent in this definition are three dimensions of literacy: linguistic, cognitive, and sociocultural. These overlapping and interrelated dimensions provide a holistic view of oral and written communication that entails not only language use, but also a consideration of how meaning is constructed and negotiated (Kern, 2000). The *linguistic dimension* of literacy has a "text focus" (Kucer, 2009, p. 311) and includes knowledge related to syntactic, morphological, and lexical features of language, as its name suggests. Yet this linguistic dimension goes far beyond these formal features to involve the ability to understand and produce linguistic features of language and to apply conventions that dictate how these linguistic features work together to create phrases, sentences, paragraphs, and so on (Kern, 2000). As a result, this dimension of literacy accounts for relationships between oral and written language and across different genres, language varieties, and styles. Within the linguistic dimension, the learner is seen as a "code breaker and code maker" whose role is to figure out linguistic features and relationships (Kucer, 2009, p. 7). The *cognitive dimension* of literacy focuses on the mind and the mental strategies and processes that go into constructing meaning from texts (Kucer, 2009). It involves the ability to access existing knowledge to establish connections between different pieces of information and to create and transform new knowledge. Moreover, the cognitive dimension entails the use of various mental processes and strategies to construct meaning and overcome difficulties as one interacts with textual content (e.g., inferencing, predicting, evaluating, revising). As a result, the learner is more than a simple decoder and encoder of information (Kern, 2000) and instead is a "meaning maker" (Kucer, 2009, p. 7). Finally, the *sociocultural dimension* of literacy moves us away from a view of the learner as autonomous and toward the idea that literacy is socially constructed; it is shared and changed by members of a society or group (Kern, 2000). The sociocultural dimension of literacy further entails an awareness of the dynamic nature of culture and of the ways in which culture influences how we think. It also includes an understanding of communicative norms, expectations, and values and how these vary within and across social groups. The learner therefore has to navigate and evaluate various cultural perspectives and is seen as a "text user and text critic" (Kucer, 2009, p. 7).

Although not explicitly referenced in our definition of literacy, we can extrapolate a fourth dimension of literacy, as proposed by Kucer (2009). The *developmental dimension* of literacy focuses on growth, how a learner builds his or her understandings of the linguistic, cognitive, and sociocultural dimensions of literacy. This dimension therefore underscores the idea that one becomes literate; literacy is seen as a process rather than a product. Factors that influence this developmental process include observations of and interactions with more proficient language users, the use of strategies to construct the other three dimensions of literacy, and the application of knowledge gained through interpretive literacy events (e.g., reading, listening, and viewing) to assist with interpersonal and presentational literacy events (e.g., speaking and writing). Because the learner has an active role in his or her own literacy development, he or she is a "scientist and construction worker" (p. 7).

To develop FL literacy, including its linguistic, cognitive, and sociocultural dimensions, we follow Kern (2000) and highlight seven principles—language use, conventions, cultural knowledge, interpretation, collaboration, problem solving, and reflection/self-reflection—that can help translate our definition of literacy into the concrete realities of FL teaching, assessment, and curriculum design. Although we discuss the seven principles of literacy in detail in Chapter 1, we provide a brief discussion here to underscore their links with our definition of literacy and the ideas about communication we have already explored.

Language use is always contextualized, and it involves making form–meaning connections through linguistic and sociocultural knowledge. *Conventions* include linguistic resources, such as writing systems, grammar, and vocabulary, as well as schematic, or knowledge-based, resources such as genres and their organizational patterns. *Cultural knowledge* entails the products, practices, and perspectives that characterize a particular society, community, or cultural group. Taken together, these three principles of literacy characterize the content with which learners interact when reading, writing, listening to, or viewing FL texts. The remaining four principles of literacy represent the learning processes in which we wish to engage students to effectively access that content. *Interpretation* involves moving beyond comprehension of surface-level facts to gain deeper understandings of cultural products, practices, and perspectives. *Collaboration* includes interaction on multiple levels: between students and instructor participating in a classroom community, between a writer and his or her audience, and between a reader and the text he or she is interpreting. Collaboration therefore entails collective social engagement with textual content. *Problem solving* is related to how language forms are used to create meaning; it thus involves "figuring out relationships between words, between larger units of meaning, and between texts and real or imagined worlds" (Kern, 2003, p. 49). Finally, *reflection and self-reflection* include thinking about language and culture and how they relate to the world and oneself. They also involve reflecting on one's learning processes and the difficulties encountered and strategies used within that process (Hall, 2001; Kern, 2000, 2003). According to Kern, "this seven-point linkage between literacy and communication has important implications for language teaching, since it provides a bridge to span the gap that all too often separates introductory *communicative* language teaching and advanced *literary* teaching" (2003, pp. 49–50, emphasis in the original).

A final concept essential to understanding this expanded view of literacy is multimodality. *Multimodality* underscores the fact that literacy is not just about written texts, nor is it just about reading and writing. It is instead about the complementary and overlapping nature of language modalities, including reading, writing, speaking, listening, and viewing. One consequence of this viewpoint is that written language is "becoming more closely intertwined with the other modes, and in some respects itself is becoming more like them" (Cope & Kalantzis, 2009, p. 15), in part due to the fact that oral and written language are typically used in conjunction with other resources, such as gestures or images. In addition, modern communication practices, particularly those that are technology enhanced, combine text with image, movement, hypertext, or sound. As a result, "in a profound sense, all meaning-making is multimodal" (New London Group, 1996, p. 81). Multimodal texts are "defined as texts which communicate their message using more than one semiotic mode, or channel of communication" (OpenLearn, 2010). The individual components of multimodal texts (e.g., words, sounds, images) take on new meanings when combined with one another, and the study of multimodality involves looking at these components and how they interact to convey meaning. Our understanding of texts throughout this book is therefore quite broad. In keeping with the multiliteracies approach, we define texts to include written, oral, visual, audiovisual, and digital documents or documents that combine one or more of these modalities.

3. WHY LITERACY?

Now that we have developed a view of communication that goes beyond functional oral language use, is grounded in texts, and includes linguistic, cognitive, and sociocultural dimensions, let us consider some of the benefits of orienting FL curriculum, instruction, and assessment according to the framing concept of literacy and how doing so meets the two main goals of this book: (1) to outline a coherent pedagogical framework that responds to calls for curricular change and provides an alternative to the differing instructional goals and techniques that characterize bifurcated programs; and (2) to present this framework in an accessible manner for novice collegiate FL teachers.

As we have already pointed out, making literacy development the primary goal of FL curriculum, instruction, and assessment creates a way to link the typically bifurcated parts of undergraduate FL programs. The concept of literacy allows the two sides of the curriculum to better communicate with and understand one another because it brings textual analysis to introductory and intermediate courses, as well as language development to advanced courses. As such, the curriculum supports continuous development of communicative abilities in all language modalities across the undergraduate sequence (Kern, 2000).

Related to this first benefit is that a literacy orientation allows us to rethink the role of texts and to prepare learners to interact with textual content at all levels of the undergraduate curriculum. Although the multiliteracies approach does not prescribe the texts appropriate for use at different curricular levels, it does foreground texts of various genres as the core element of instruction. A literacy framework also calls into question the common practice in CLT-oriented textbooks to present students with mostly short, informational texts, many of which are created for the textbook and thus lack authenticity (Allen & Paesani, 2010). As you will see in the remainder of this book, developing FL literacy through interaction with authentic texts allows us to treat language and literary–cultural content as an integrated whole. As a result, texts become "the locus of the thoughtful and creative act of making connections between grammar, discourse, and meaning, between language and content, between language and culture, and between another culture and one's own" (Kern, 2000, p. 46).

A second benefit of adopting a literacy orientation is that it provides a coherent framework for rethinking curriculum, instruction, and assessment across undergraduate FL programs. Street (1997) outlined several proposals for curriculum, instruction, and assessment based on the view of literacy adopted here. Specifically, he argued that "if we want learners to develop and enhance the richness and complexity of literacy practices evident in society at large, then we need curricula and assessment that are themselves rich and complex and based upon research into actual literacy practices" (p. 84). By the same token, to "develop rich and complex curricula and assessment for literacy, we need models of literacy and of pedagogy that capture the richness and complexity of actual literacy practices" (p. 84). The broad view of literacy adopted here accounts for this complexity through its linguistic, cognitive, and sociocultural dimensions, its focus on multimodality, and the seven principles of literacy. The pedagogy and assessment practices necessary to apply our conceptualization of literacy, grounded within the multiliteracies framework, are laid out in subsequent chapters of this book.

Not only does a literacy orientation provide a foundation for reconfiguring the structure of FL programs through instruction, assessment, and texts, it also challenges teachers and learners to rethink their beliefs and assumptions about the teaching of grammar, skills, or culture from a holistic and multimodal perspective. As we saw earlier, CLT tends to tease out the four skills of reading, writing, listening, and speaking and to situate skill development in functional contexts that do not allow deep engagement with cultural content. Kumaravadivelu's (1994) challenge of this approach bears repeating here:

> Skill separation . . . has very little empirical or theoretical justification. It is a pedagogical artifact that has been shown to be inadequate for developing integrated functional skills. . . . Its inadequacy arises because language skills are essentially interrelated and mutually reinforcing. Fragmenting them into manageable, atomistic items runs counter to the parallel and interactive nature of language and language behavior. (p. 39)

A literacy orientation emphasizes the interdependence of language forms, language modalities, and literary–cultural content and how these work in concert with various cognitive processes to develop students' ability to communicate and analyze texts. As Kern (2000) explained, this orientation avoids the typical CLT format, wherein skills development is seen as linear, progressing from reading to writing or listening to speaking and wherein reading and writing are done outside of class to maximize in-class oral language use. Instead, reading and writing are seen as both individual and collaborative acts of communication that often take place inside the classroom context. Moreover, reading, writing, speaking, listening, and viewing are not seen as separate or linear, but rather as overlapping. As a result, "instructional activities . . . focus students' attention on the interactions between linguistic form, situational context, and communicative and expressive functions" (Kern, 2003, p. 51) and thus emphasize the multimodal nature of language use and texts.

A final benefit of orienting FL curriculum, instruction, and assessment according to the framing concept of literacy is that it enables more holistic, consistent, and effective professionalization of collegiate FL teachers. Grounding teacher professional development in a single framework not only challenges us to rethink our beliefs and assumptions about curriculum, instruction, and assessment, it provides novice FL instructors with coherent understandings of teaching and learning that can be applied across the curriculum and throughout their professional development experiences (Lantolf & Johnson, 2007). Specifically, the multiliteracies framework is conducive to establishing a long-term model of FL professional development given that the concept of literacy is consistent with both short-term needs for teaching in lower-level courses and long-term needs for future teaching at more advanced levels. Moreover, because a literacy orientation further challenges us to rethink traditional perceptions of language, literary–cultural content, and skills development, it opens a window of opportunity for educating collegiate FL instructors as teacher–scholars. Finally, grounding teacher development in the concept of literacy means that teaching techniques are linked to a framework rather than to a textbook. FL instructors are therefore equipped with tools for teaching in multiple contexts and for thinking about instruction from course-level and curricular perspectives.

4. HOW IS LITERACY ELABORATED IN THIS BOOK?

To meet our goals of outlining a coherent pedagogical framework grounded in texts and the concept of literacy and of presenting this framework in an accessible manner for novice FL teachers, we have organized the book into eight chapters and an afterword. Each chapter reconsiders traditional components of introductory and intermediate FL instruction (e.g., grammar and vocabulary, speaking, reading) according to a literacy orientation. By organizing the book in this way we do not wish to imply that linguistic forms and language modalities should be treated in isolation. Rather, we start with a discussion of what is familiar to readers and then emphasize how each of these traditional components works in concert to contribute to the development of students' FL literacy.

In Chapter 1, "Understanding the Multiliteracies Framework," we further develop your understanding of the concept of literacy by challenging you to consider how it can be used to organize curriculum, instruction, and assessment. We outline the theoretical and pedagogical framework that underlies a literacy-based approach and lay the foundation for practical applications of this framework in subsequent chapters. Chapter 1 begins by exploring the act of meaning design, which forms the backbone of the multiliteracies framework. We then examine the what (i.e., the content) and the how of multiliteracies pedagogy—Available Designs and learning processes based on Kern's (2000) principles of literacy—and introduce four pedagogical acts that allow instructors to apply the what and the how.

Chapter 2, "Reconsidering Goals, Objectives, and Assessment From a Multiliteracies Perspective," introduces the idea that articulating coherent learning objectives and goals is an essential element of multiliteracies-based teaching. After defining goals and objectives and explaining their relation to instruction and assessment, we encourage you consider how each is important for rethinking courses, instructional units, and daily lesson plans. We then address what it means to align goals and objectives with the concept of literacy. The remainder of the chapter explores strategies for creating goals and objectives for FL learning consistent with the multiliteracies approach as well as the question of how instruction can be coherently linked to assessment.

Rethinking the teaching and assessment of grammar and vocabulary from a multiliteracies perspective is the focus of Chapter 3. "Reconceptualizing Grammar and Vocabulary as Meaning-Making Resources" presents strategies for teaching and assessing FL grammar and vocabulary focused on the notion of meaning design. We thus reconsider the role of grammar and vocabulary in lower-level language courses by moving beyond a mastery-oriented view to a meaning-oriented view in which grammar and vocabulary are two among the multiple linguistic, cultural, and social resources that learners' draw on to understand and create texts. After recycling key concepts from Chapter 1, we demonstrate how the four pedagogical acts, with an emphasis on overt instruction, can facilitate the acquisition of new grammar and vocabulary when such activities are grounded in FL texts.

Chapter 4, "Scaffolding Oral Language Use in the Classroom," focuses on rethinking the role of speaking in classroom learning and assessment. We begin by examining concepts and empirical research related to classroom discourse, such as input and interaction, the contribution of accuracy, fluency, and complexity to oral competencies, classroom discourse patterns and student participation structures, and differences between one-way (e.g., presentational) versus two-way (e.g., interpersonal) oral language use. We further discuss the differing objectives for oral language use as learners carry out activities centered on each of the four pedagogical acts as well as how reading and writing can serve as tools for maximizing oral participation in classroom learning and assessment. We conclude with examples of how the multiliteracies framework can overcome problems associated with typical classroom discourse patterns through implementation of learning activities centered on textual content.

Rethinking the role of reading in FL instruction is the subject of Chapter 5, "Teaching Reading as Constructing Meaning From Texts." First, we overview the treatment of FL reading in previous research, focusing on concepts related to reading ability and cognitive processing models that have informed CLT-based approaches to reading. We then introduce concepts relevant to an integrated, multiliteracies-oriented approach, such as the sociocultural dimensions of reading and reading as meaning design. We then reconsider goals of reading instruction and assessment within a multiliteracies framework to help organize activities based on the four pedagogical acts. We follow with an overview of existing literacy-based approaches to teaching and assessing textual interpretation and present a model for designing text-based lesson plans and assessments.

Chapter 6, "Teaching Writing as Designing Meaning Through Texts," explores how the purposes and goals of FL writing instruction can be aligned to reflect the multiliteracies framework. We review the treatment of FL writing in previous research and explore how, in a multiliteracies approach, writing, like reading, is understood as an act of meaning design with linguistic, cognitive, and sociocultural dimensions. In addition, we outline how writing instruction can be organized in a manner consistent with the multiliteracies framework, highlighting several previous models and proposing an instructional sequence for writing-focused activities and assessments based on the four pedagogical acts. Throughout the chapter we underscore the interconnectedness and complementarity of writing and reading, consistent with a multimodal perspective of texts and communication.

In Chapter 7, "Teaching Video-Mediated Listening as Constructing Meaning From Texts," we broaden the concept of listening to encompass listening and viewing oral and visual messages to build meaning through interaction with texts. As with previous chapters, we first examine key concepts related to FL listening and viewing, including differences between oral, visual, and written discourse, the nature of audio- and videotexts, and text authenticity. We then focus on videotexts and reconsider the goals of FL viewing instruction in a multiliteracies framework. We conclude by examining existing literacy-based models of listening–viewing instruction and propose a template for teaching and assessing interpretation of videotexts.

Chapter 8, "Teaching New Literacies: Constructing Meaning in Web 2.0 and Beyond," reconsiders the role technology plays in FL instruction and assessment and addresses the development of FL digitally mediated literacies. We further highlight the potential of such technologies to provide learners with opportunities to participate in the wider world of computer-mediated FL use and to analyze shifting social practices and emerging literacies associated with digitally mediated texts. After overviewing widely used Web 2.0 tools (e.g., blogs, wikis) and games for FL learning and the opportunities they provide learners for new literacies development, we examine concepts related to technology, such as digitality, mindset, and affinity spaces. We conclude this chapter by considering literacy-based models of teaching and assessing FL digitally mediated texts and propose a template for designing and implementing lesson plans centered on the development of new literacies.

We conclude with a brief Afterword in which we revisit the goals and key themes of the book and consider them within the broader context of the undergraduate FL curriculum. We furthermore consider applications of the multiliteracies framework beyond the pages of this book and suggest some final thoughts for novice teachers embarking on careers as teacher–scholars.

To facilitate interaction with the content of these chapters, the format of each one is consistent, with the exception of Chapter 1 and the Afterword. Each chapter begins with an overview that serves to introduce the topic and provide an outline of its contents. Next, a "Conceptual Background" section summarizes essential research and outlines key concepts, whereas the section entitled "Pedagogical Applications" puts theoretical and conceptual knowledge into practice and provides instructional models and examples. The "Final Considerations" section summarizes the main points of a chapter before readers move on to the two application activities in "Transforming Knowledge"; one activity is a reflective journaling topic and the other a research topic. Finally, "Key Resources" and "For Further Reading" identify important references related to the topic of each chapter; the former provides annotations of the most important scholarship on the topic, the latter does not. Each chapter additionally includes several Learning Activities intended to encourage you to engage with and think critically about the chapter's content.

5. FINAL CONSIDERATIONS

Throughout this Introduction, we have made a case for literacy as a response to recent calls for change in collegiate FL programs and have argued that a literacy orientation provides the foundation on which to build broad and coherent curricula, instructional approaches, and assessment practices. A literacy orientation expands our understanding of communication beyond functional oral language use in generic contexts to include linguistic, cognitive, and sociocultural dimensions and to underscore the importance of texts for developing language modalities through exploration of literary–cultural content. As you see from the chapter summaries, this book serves as a tool to help you rethink what is taught and assessed in FL courses and how it is taught and assessed. Throughout, we challenge you to reconsider your beliefs and assumptions related to FL teaching and learning and to frame traditional concepts within a literacy orientation. Moreover, we ask you to engage in multiple application activities in which you interpret the content you have read, collaborate with your peers to deepen understandings, solve problems related to classroom instruction and assessment, and reflect on your current instructional beliefs and practices as well as on your own learning. We hope that once you have read this book, you will have a transformed view of FL teaching and learning, one that you carry with you throughout your career and that helps you succeed within reconfigured undergraduate FL programs of the twenty-first century.

For Further Reading

Canale, M., & Swain, M. (1980). Theoretical bases of communicative approaches to foreign language teaching and testing. *Applied Linguistics, 1*, 1–47.

Gee, J. P. (2012). *Social linguistics and literacies: Ideology in discourses* (4th ed.). New York, NY: Routledge.

Kern, R. G. (2003). Literacy as a new organizing principle for foreign language education. In P. C. Patrikis (Ed.), *Reading between the lines: Perspectives on foreign language literacy* (pp. 40–59). New Haven, CT: Yale University Press.

Littlewood, W. (2011). Communicative language teaching: An expanding concept for a changing world. In E. Hinkel (Ed.), *Handbook of research in second language teaching and learning* (Vol. II, pp. 541–557). New York, NY: Routledge.

OpenLearn. (2010). *Language and literacy in a changing world*. Retrieved from http://labspace.open.ac.uk/course/view.php?id=7134

Spada, N. (2007). Communicative language teaching: Current status and future prospects. In J. Cummins & C. Davis (Eds.), *International handbook of English language teaching* (pp. 271–288). New York, NY: Springer.

CHAPTER 1

Understanding the Multiliteracies Framework

In the Introduction, we challenged you to rethink your ideas about foreign language (FL) teaching and learning by proposing a literacy-based approach as an alternative to communicative language teaching (CLT) and suggesting that literacy serve as an overarching concept to frame FL curriculum, instruction, and assessment. Our conceptualization of literacy includes the following key components: an understanding of the relationships among various oral, written, and visual forms and how these forms contribute to textual meaning; the ability to construct meaning through the processes of creating and transforming knowledge; and a recognition of the dynamic nature of language and the socially and culturally embedded resources used in literacy-based practices. As a response to the calls for curricular and pedagogical change we laid out in the Introduction (e.g., Byrnes, 2001; Maxim, 2009; MLA, 2007; Swaffar & Arens, 2005), this alternative conceptualization of FL teaching and learning has the potential to increase the intellectual viability of FL study, merge the language and content sides of the curriculum, develop language competencies holistically, and prioritize learners' interaction with target language texts.

At this point, however, how the concept of literacy can be used to organize curriculum, instruction, and assessment may still be quite abstract to you. Similarly, how we might move from a pedagogy that prioritizes functional, oral language use to one that prioritizes meaning construction through interaction with target language texts may also be hard to grasp. The purpose of this chapter, therefore, is to develop the theoretical and pedagogical framework that underlies a literacy-based approach and to lay the foundation for practical applications of this framework in subsequent chapters. Our focus here is on the *multiliteracies framework*, also called a *pedagogy of multiliteracies* (Cope & Kalantzis, 2009; Kern, 2000; New London Group, 1996), which is a "socially responsive pedagogy that helps us understand how to connect a sociocultural perspective of learning to classroom teaching" (Hall, 2001, p. 51). This pedagogical approach "emphasize[s] interdependence among speaking, listening, reading, and writing skills and focus[es] students' attention on the interactions between linguistic form, situational context, and communicative and expressive functions" (Kern, 2003, p. 51). As such, multiliteracies pedagogy not only reflects the definition of literacy we have developed thus far, but unifies, rather than separates, the study of language and the study of literary–cultural content.

The chapter begins by exploring the act of meaning design, which forms the backbone of the multiliteracies framework. We then examine the what (i.e., the content) and the how of multiliteracies pedagogy—Available Designs, texts, and learning processes based on Kern's (2000) principles of literacy—and introduce four pedagogical acts that allow instructors to apply the what and the how. By the end of this chapter, you will have a working knowledge of the multiliteracies framework that you will further develop as you apply it to various classroom practices in subsequent chapters. Before delving into the theoretical framework of multiliteracies pedagogy, complete Learning Activity 1.1, which asks you to reflect on your beliefs and experiences related to classroom teaching and learning.

LEARNING ACTIVITY 1.1

Identifying Beliefs and Experiences Related to Classroom Teaching and Learning

Part 1. Take a moment to reflect on the following three questions. Summarize your responses in the first column of the table.

1. *What* should the content of introductory language courses be? What should students learn (e.g., grammatical forms, informational texts, cultural facts, literature, survival skills)?
2. *How* should learners engage with that content? What learning processes or cognitive acts (e.g., memorizing information, predicting, interpreting information, understanding form–meaning relationships, repeating) should learners carry out in classroom activities and assessments to engage with course content, with the teacher, and with other learners?
3. How do you *apply* the what and the how? What in-class and out-of-class activities should you implement to help students learn the content and engage in the learning processes you identified in your answer to the previous question (e.g., mechanical drills, creative writing, role playing, textual analysis, choral repetition)?

Part 2. As you read this chapter, note down what you understand about the what, the how, and their application according to the multiliteracies framework. Add this information to the second column of the table. You will be asked to compare the information in these two columns in your reflective journal entry, found in the "Transforming Knowledge" section at the end of this chapter.

		My Beliefs and Experiences	The Multiliteracies Framework
1	The *what*		
2	The *how*		
3	*Applying* the what and the how		

1. MEANING DESIGN: INTERPRETING AND TRANSFORMING TEXTS

Although one of the goals of this chapter is to make ideas related to literacy more concrete, we begin with a concept that some may find abstract: meaning design. Meaning design underlies every aspect of multiliteracies pedagogy and reflects many of the ideas you read about in the Introduction. Meaning design is related to the linguistic, cognitive, and sociocultural dimensions of literacy; it is compatible with the seven principles of literacy; and it encourages a multimodal view of language development and use.

1.1 What Is Meaning Design?

Within the multiliteracies framework, learning is viewed as a process of discovery. *Meaning design* reflects this view of learning because it is a dynamic process of discovering form–meaning connections through the acts of interpreting and creating written, oral, visual, audiovisual, and digital texts. To establish such form–meaning connections, we must attend to the written, verbal, and visual forms of a text, the text's structure and organization, and our own cultural knowledge and experiences. Because establishing form–meaning connections depends on both the content of a text and how learners interact with it, we can say that design has a dual function: It may refer to the process of creating or interpreting a text or to a particular product—that is, the text itself and its configuration of structures (Kern, 2000).

Meaning design involves three elements: Available Designs, Designing, and the Redesigned (Cope & Kalantzis, 2009; New London Group, 1996).[1] *Available Designs*, which we discuss in detail in the next section, involve the linguistic, cultural, and social resources that a learner draws on in understanding and creating texts. Examples of Available Designs include knowledge of vocabulary and grammar, expectations related to the organization of information in different text types, or personal experiences related to a particular topic.

[1] In scholarship on the multiliteracies framework, the terms Available Designs, Designing, and the Redesigned are consistently capitalized, and we follow this convention throughout the book.

To interpret or create a text, learners engage in *Designing*, "the act of doing something with Available Designs of meaning, be that communicating with others (such as writing, speaking, or making pictures) or representing the world to oneself or others' representations of it (such as reading, listening, or viewing)" (Cope & Kalantzis, 2009, p. 177). Designing is a process of accessing, applying, and recycling Available Designs in fresh ways to create meaning from texts. It always results in something new called the *Redesigned*, understood as a transformed representation of Available Designs. The product resulting from Designing might be a new text, image, or idea that can become a resource in another person's repertoire of Available Designs.

The concept of *transformation* underlies the theory of learning that frames multiliteracies pedagogy and is the main goal of meaning design. Cope and Kalantzis link transformation to meaning design as follows:

> In a pedagogy of multiliteracies, all forms of representation, including language, should be regarded as dynamic processes of transformation rather than processes of reproduction. That is, meaning makers are not simply replicators of representational conventions. Their meaning-making resources may be found in representational objects, patterned in familiar and thus recognizable ways. However, these objects are reworked. Meaning makers do not simply use what they have been given: they are fully makers and remakers of signs and transformers of meaning. (2009, p. 175)

As this quotation illustrates, transformation is not rote, mechanical, or repetitive; it is instead creative, open ended, and evolving. Designing meaning through transformation furthermore involves negotiating discourse differences (e.g., register, style, mode) by accessing knowledge about language use, cultural content, and conventions, and engaging in the learning processes of interpretation, collaboration, problem solving, and reflection and self-reflection (Kern, 2000).

This perspective on why learners interact with texts—that is, to design meaning—and what this kind of interaction entails is quite different from communicatively oriented perspectives on working with texts. In CLT, texts have a functional purpose: They are used primarily to practice language forms en route to developing functional competence and secondarily to synthesize previously learned rules of grammar and vocabulary. Moreover, the functional texts used for language practice in CLT textbooks (e.g., personal ads, menus, travel brochures) are often an add-on at the close of a lesson, chapter, or unit and are thus not always fully integrated with other (i.e., linguistic) content students are learning. As a result, a resource such as grammar is simply a set of morphosyntactic rules learned on their own and practiced through oral and written texts. Reading and writing, then, are acts of replication wherein learners identify and imitate the grammatical forms they have learned without deep engagement with and analysis of cultural content. Lacking in this perspective are the acts of transformation and interpretation and thus an awareness of sociocultural and contextual aspects of grammar use. Alternatively, in the multiliteracies framework, grammar is one of several Available Designs learned (or discovered) through texts; it includes the morphosyntactic structure of language as well as other linguistic and schematic resources. In interpreting and transforming meaning from oral, written, visual, audiovisual, or digital texts, learners discover established grammatical patterns, but they also learn that these patterns and the meanings associated with them are "open-ended and shifting" (Cope & Kalantzis, 2009, p. 176) based on their use in a particular sociocultural context.

The implications of the meaning design perspective for language learning are significant. Because we already possess a myriad of designs in our first language, FL learning includes making students aware of existing Available Designs and helping them apply these designs to interpret and create FL texts. Moreover, FL learning involves moving from the known to the unknown, or from our existing Available Designs to new, as yet undiscovered designs. If we fail to make meaning design a priority in FL instruction and assessment, language learning cannot take place effectively. Indeed, "language learning both promotes and depends on a learners' ability to design meaning" (Kern, 2000, p. 60). Another important implication of the design perspective is that it allows us to think about language learning holistically. Instead of acting as a set of distinct skills to be mastered, linguistic modalities such as reading, writing, listening, or speaking overlap and complement one another. As such, meaning design encourages engagement in multimodal communication, wherein literacy is not just about reading and writing, but is also oral, aural, visual, spatial, tactile, and gestural.

In sum, five key features of meaning design emerge from our discussion:

1. Design is the dynamic process of discovering meaning through textual interpretation and creation;
2. Design may refer to both a process (the act of creating or interpreting a text) and a product (a text and the forms, organization, and content that characterize it);
3. Design encompasses the linguistic and schematic resources that contribute to a text's meaning;
4. Design involves attention to our social and cultural knowledge and experiences; and
5. Design engages learners in the processes of interpretation, collaboration, problem solving, and reflection.

We illustrate these how these features are put into practice in the next section.

1.2 A Concrete Example: Cooking and Food

To make the abstract concept of meaning design more concrete, consider the example of Sarah, a home cook who knows how to make a fried egg but who has never made an omelet. Sarah brings a number of resources (or Available Designs) to the task of making an omelet. For example, she has experience cooking with eggs and eating omelets, as well as experience reading and following a recipe. She also has a number of kitchen utensils, such as a good sauté pan, a whisk, and a spatula. She has watched Ina Garten of *Barefoot Contessa* make an omelet on television, which further adds to her background knowledge. Sarah puts these resources to use through the acts of interpretation and transformation as she makes her first omelet. Interpretation might involve reading a recipe in a cookbook and thinking about how it is similar to or different from the recipe she saw Ina Garten implement on television. It might also involve tasting ingredients as she goes through the process of preparing the omelet to better understand how and why it is prepared the way it is. Transformation might involve adding fresh herbs to the omelet, even if the recipe does not call for them, or substituting water for the milk in the recipe because her husband is lactose intolerant. Sarah further engages in learning processes such as reflection when she thinks about how the recipe might be improved, or problem solving when she finds that the omelet does not set properly the first time around. All of Sarah's decisions are grounded in the recipe she has selected, her experiences as a home cook, her knowledge of various techniques, tools, and ingredients, and the particular context of her home life. As Sarah cooks, which involves using available resources to interpret and transform her omelet recipe, she is engaging in the process of Designing; the product is a retooled version of the omelet, or the Redesigned, which we might call "Sarah's omelet."

This perspective on the process of cooking and the product that results from it is different from a functional perspective. Indeed, learning to prepare a new dish is not a mechanical act of following directions in a recipe; although the recipe itself is crucial to Sarah's success, following its directions further involves reflection about and interpretation of them based on Sarah's particular set of resources and the sociocultural context in which she operates. Moreover, Sarah's ability to engage in the process of meaning design is what drives her learning with respect to cooking: If Sarah did not interpret and transform recipes, she would not learn how to make new things or to perfect the ones she has already prepared. The act of meaning design also provides opportunities for Sarah to become aware of the resources at her disposal and to acquire new resources through experimenting with different recipes or kitchen tools or through watching other cooking shows on television. Finally, engaging in design allows Sarah to see cooking as more than just a list of ingredients in a recipe; it is also visual, tactile, and olfactory, thus making cooking a multimodal act.

This practical example of meaning design is consistent with the New London Group's original conception of this idea:

> The notion of design connects powerfully to the sort of creative intelligence the best practitioners need in order to be able, continually, to redesign their activities in the very act of practice. It connects well to the idea that learning and productivity are the results of the designs (the structures) of complex systems of people, environments, technology, beliefs, and texts. (1996, p. 73)

As a final step toward solidifying your understanding of meaning design and the related concepts of Available Designs, Designing, the Redesigned, and transformation, complete Learning Activity 1.2.

LEARNING ACTIVITY 1.2

Explaining Meaning Design

Choose a second concrete example (e.g., writing a thank you note, cleaning the house, driving to work) and explain to a classmate (or in a blog post) how it illustrates the act of meaning design. Be sure that your explanation addresses each of the main characteristics of meaning design summarized in the five-item list above. As you share your example, your classmate should point out ideas that are unclear or lacking detail, so that together you can fill in the gaps.

2. ENGAGING LEARNERS IN MEANING DESIGN: APPLYING THE WHAT AND THE HOW OF MULTILITERACIES PEDAGOGY

Three intertwined components comprise the framework through which we encourage learners to design meaning from target language texts: (1) the *what* of multiliteracies pedagogy; (2) the *how* of multiliteracies pedagogy; and (3) the *application* of the what and the how. This framework is represented graphically in Figure 1.1.

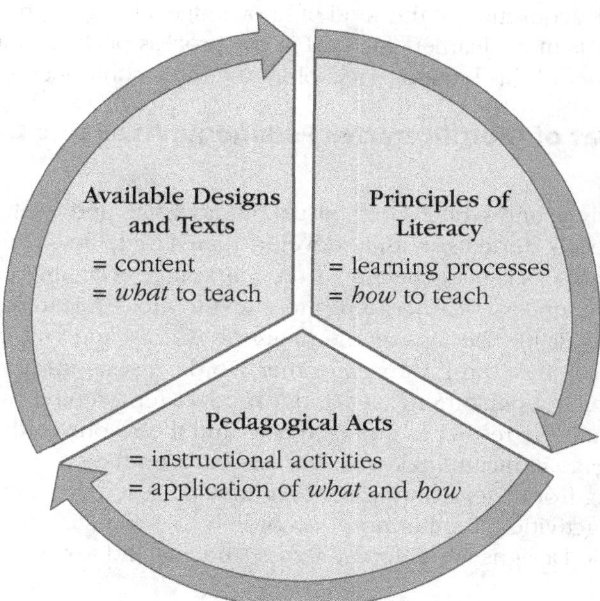

FIGURE 1.1 Components of Multiliteracies Pedagogy

You have already learned the basics of the what and the how in the previous section of this chapter and in the Introduction. The what includes Available Designs, which are the content we teach through the medium of target language texts. As we saw earlier, Available Designs are linguistic, cultural, and social resources that a learner draws on in understanding and creating texts, and as we saw in the Introduction, texts are understood broadly to include oral, written, visual, audiovisual, and digital documents that convey meaning. The what of multiliteracies pedagogy also reflects three of Kern's (2000) seven principles of literacy: language use, cultural knowledge, and conventions. The learning processes that are the remaining four principles of literacy—interpretation, collaboration, problem solving, and reflection/self-reflection—comprise the how of multiliteracies pedagogy. In addition to these familiar concepts, this framework includes several new concepts: four pedagogical acts—situated practice, overt instruction, critical framing, and transformed practice—that allow us to apply the what and the how.

This three-part framework helps students learn what they need to know as their FL literacy develops. Specifically, they need to know how conventions and acts of communication in the FL are similar to or different from the language(s) and culture(s) they already know; they need to know new rules of spelling, punctuation, sound–spelling correspondences, and the like; they need to know new conventions governing written, oral, and visual genres; and they need to know new social practices. In sum, FL learners need to know how to notice form–meaning relationships in texts and how these relationships reflect conventions of language use within certain sociocultural contexts (Kern, 2000). The three components of multiliteracies pedagogy, which you will apply throughout this book, facilitate acquisition of this kind of knowledge, engage learners in meaning design, and thus move learners forward in the process of developing FL literacy. In the remainder of this section, we explore the three components in detail.

2.1 The What of Multiliteracies Pedagogy: Available Designs and Texts

Available Designs and written, oral, visual, audiovisual, and digital texts are the content we teach students as they develop their FL literacy. We have already defined Available Designs generally as the linguistic, social, and cultural knowledge and experiences a learner brings to a text to create meaning. We can also think about Available Designs as the linguistic, social, and cultural knowledge and experiences that form a text. In other words, just as meaning design is a process in which a person engages and a product represented by a text, Available Designs are the resources a person uses and the resources that characterize a text. To engage in meaning design, learners draw on their existing resources to make meaning from a text, and instructors draw on resources in a text to design instructional activities. Furthermore, according to Kalantzis and Cope (n. d.), these Available Designs are different across students and texts:

> Every student brings to the class a repertoire of 'available designs' of meaning across a number of modes—the things they have read, heard, and seen as a part of their lifeworld and previous educational

> experiences. From learner to learner, no two experiences of 'available designs' can ever be quite the same. These may be supplemented by new designs offered by the teacher—different kinds of written, oral, visual, gestural and other texts. ("Differentiated literacies instruction 1," para. 2)

Available Designs may be linguistic, schematic, visual, audio, gestural, or spatial. We begin by discussing linguistic and schematic resources, as they are characteristic of all text types, be they written, oral, visual, audiovisual, or digital. Linguistic resources are associated with parts of a language and how those parts are put together; they constitute the tool kit necessary to form words, sentences, and paragraphs. Examples of linguistic Available Designs are punctuation, sound–spelling correspondences, word formation patterns, and agreement rules. Schematic resources are associated with how textual meaning is organized and what knowledge is required to process the meaning in texts. Examples of schematic Available Designs include lived experiences, scholarly knowledge, and the ability to recognize different genres. Kern (2000) represents these sets of Available Designs on a continuum, with linguistic resources on one end, and schematic resources on the other. This continuum idea, represented visually in Figure 1.2, helps to illustrate that linguistic and schematic resources can overlap. For instance, the linguistic resources of coherence and cohesion devices also contribute to textual organization, just as the schematic resource of genre is characterized by specific language features.

Some of the concepts listed in Figure 1.2, such as vocabulary or grammar, may already be clear to you, whereas others, such as content schemata or coherence devices, may be less so. You may also notice that the Available Designs listed here overlap with some of the principles of literacy you learned about in the Introduction; namely, language use, conventions, and cultural knowledge, also understood as the basic elements of multiliteracies instruction. To create clear connections with what you already know and what is new to you in this

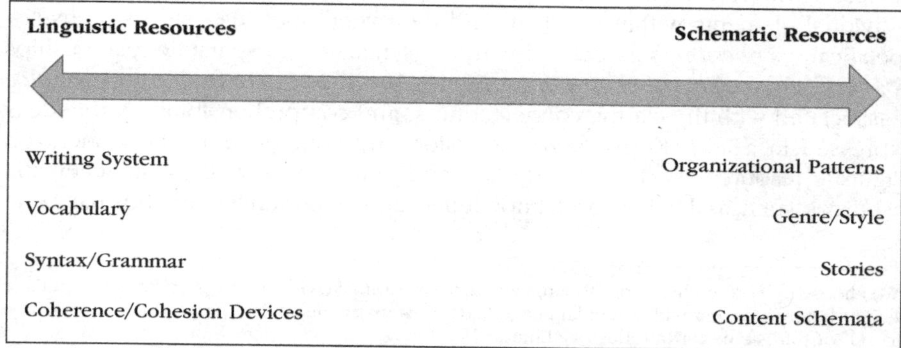

FIGURE 1.2 Continuum of Available Designs (adapted from Kern, 2000, p. 67)

chapter, we frame our discussion of linguistic and schematic resources within these three principles of literacy. We furthermore provide concrete examples of these resources using the September 30, 2007 cover of *Time* magazine. To locate this text online, google the keywords "time magazine cover national service 2007."[2]

In relation to language use, Kern (2000) argues that "literacy is not just about writing systems, nor just about lexical and grammatical knowledge; it requires knowledge of how language is used in spoken and written contexts to create discourse" (p. 17). Language use, therefore, is always contextualized, involves linguistic and sociocultural knowledge, and occurs in the FL classroom through encounters with texts. This view of language use, which includes the linguistic Available Designs listed above, is quite different from a CLT-oriented view of language use. Whereas the former focuses on the interpretation and creation of meaning by establishing form–meaning connections in texts, the latter focuses on the comprehension and production of accurate forms with texts serving as a vehicle for language practice.

The multiliteracies view of language use becomes clearer as we examine the *Time* magazine cover. For example, because this is journalistic language, features of the *writing system* include the use of capital letters and larger bold font for headlines and smaller font without capital letters for subheadings; both types of headings also lack end punctuation. These writing conventions give learners clues as to the genre of the text and the type and style of content they might find behind the cover. Additionally, the *syntax* or *grammar* of these headlines is different from that of more conventional prose. For instance, the headline "The Case for National Service" lacks a verb. Again, students can make predictions about the genre of the text based on this syntactic feature; moreover, they can compare this feature to conventional prose and speculate about why this grammatical choice was made for a magazine cover. The magazine cover is also characterized by interesting *vocabulary* that requires students to draw on the known and to explore the new. For example, the name of the magazine, *Time*, has a dual meaning: Learners may already be familiar with the use of this word to ask the time of day, but unfamiliar with its use to talk about issues that are timely, in the sense of new or of the moment. Finally, coherence and cohesion devices contribute to the connectedness and comprehensibility of a text, the individual elements within that text, and the overall message the text conveys. Specifically, *cohesion* is associated with the syntactic and semantic relationships in a text, such as use of pronouns, transition words, or conjunctions. *Coherence* is associated with the clarity, connectedness, and comprehensibility of the ideas expressed in a text (Kern, 2000). Cohesion and coherence are dependent on linguistic resources such as vocabulary and grammar as well as on schematic resources such as background knowledge and experiences. In the magazine

---

[2] We choose to work with an English-language text here to make clear concepts related to Available Designs before working with target language texts. This magazine cover is appropriate for use in a second- or third-semester introductory English as a foreign language course on a unit covering the theme of society and civic engagement.

cover example, one might argue that the text is incoherent because the various headlines provided are not connected to one another; however, we can also see that portions of the text are coherent because any given headline and its subheading are semantically linked. For instance, in the headline related to volunteering, the use of words like *service*, *help*, and *action* clearly connect ideas expressed in the main and subheadings. In addition, the use of the pronoun *their* acts as a cohesion device referring to *Americans*. The imperative phrase at the end of the subheading links to this pronoun as well, suggesting that it is these Americans who will be putting the proposed plan into action.

The conventions principle is a perfect illustration of the linguistic–schematic continuum represented in Figure 1.2. Conventions are viewed as culturally situated, shaping how people interpret and create textual meaning, and evolving over time. Thus, conventions include the linguistic resources of writing system, grammar, vocabulary, and coherence and cohesion devices, but they also include schematic resources related to a broad range of textual genres (e.g., editorials, magazine covers, television commercials, poetry), their organizational patterns, and their particular ways of using language. According to Kern (2000), awareness of conventions and the genres they typify is essential because learners can then see relationships between new patterns of discourse and those they have already encountered and they can become "aware of the characteristically patterned ways that people in the community use language to fulfill particular communicative purposes in recurring situations" (p. 183). This understanding of conventions differs significantly from CLT, where the instructional focus is primarily on acquisition of linguistic conventions to carry out specific functions such as narrating in the past or asking for directions. Absent from this viewpoint are the schematic resources necessary to understand various genres and their socially situated nature (Allen & Paesani, 2010).

We have already identified conventions evident in the magazine cover in our discussion of language use. Specifically, the use of capitalization, the lack of punctuation (both features of the writing system), and the absence of verbs (a feature of the syntax) in headlines are conventions specific to journalistic prose. The schematic resource of *organizational patterns* also falls within the category of conventions. Organizational patterns have to do with how ideas are represented in a text and how these ideas are organized through use of vocabulary and grammar. In the magazine cover, for example, ideas are organized in a headline/subheading format wherein the main idea is expressed in the headline and a detail related to that main idea is expressed in the subheading. Taken together, these linguistic and schematic features characterize the genre of magazine writing. *Genre*, a schematic resource, is "an oral or written rhetorical practice that structures culturally embedded communicative situations in a highly predictable pattern, thereby creating horizons of expectations for its community of users" (Swaffar & Arens, 2005, p. 99). Some genres, such as personal ads, poetry, or movie previews, may be more accessible to lower-level learners than other genres such as theater, news broadcasts, or editorials. However, exposing learners to a range of text types expands their repertoire of Available Designs and furthers development of their FL literacy. Regardless of the genre, learners approaching a particular text have expectations about features that genre possesses, as the quotation above suggests. An American familiar with *Time*, for instance, will expect other news magazine covers to look similar to the one presented in this chapter and will further expect the contents of that news magazine to follow certain patterns. When learners encounter this genre in a target language text, there may be mismatches between their existing Available Designs related to the genre in their first language (L1) and the Available Designs that characterize the genre in the FL. When creating learning activities for such texts, instructors therefore need to help learners recognize conventions they already know and navigate the new conventions of the FL text. Awareness of conventions therefore helps learners communicate more effectively; indeed, as Kern suggests, without knowledge of context-specific conventions, learners "may seem or feel communicatively inept" (2000, p. 183).

Cultural knowledge entails the beliefs, practices, perspectives, values, and products that characterize a cultural group or system. Misunderstanding often occurs when there is a mismatch between the cultural knowledge a learner possesses and the beliefs, practices, perspectives, values, and products that are part of the target culture (Kern, 2000). Although cultural knowledge can be linguistic (e.g., understanding when to use formal versus informal *you*), it is often understood as a learner's background knowledge, or content schemata, as well as the stories associated with that knowledge. *Content schemata* "have to do with topical knowledge, familiarity with real world events, and cultural notions" (Kern, 2000, p. 83). They are the organized networks of knowledge we possess based on our lived experiences (e.g., our upbringing, our interactions with friends and strangers, our successes and failures) and our formal instruction (e.g., school, on-the-job training, apprenticeships). Content schemata and the related framework of schema theory (Bartlett, 1932; Carrell & Eisterhold, 1983; Rumelhart, 1981) may already be familiar to you; these concepts are also associated with CLT-based pedagogy and have informed process-oriented approaches to reading, for instance (see Chapter 5 for details). Whereas content schemata are abstract representations of knowledge in the brain, *stories* are narratives representing "the overt expression of schematic knowledge" (Kern, 2000, p. 99). We have all grown up hearing stories and those stories have helped us understand the world. For instance, the children's story *The Ugly Duckling* teaches us not to judge a book by its cover, and a news story of a dog that can sniff out cancer tells us that humans and animals can help one another. Moreover, the knowledge gained from these stories (e.g., ugly ducklings transform into beautiful swans) becomes part of our content schemata. In the *Time* magazine cover we have already discussed, various aspects of learners' cultural knowledge may come into play as they try to gain an understanding of the text. For instance, in relation to the main headline, some learners may have had experience volunteering; others may think the word *service* is related to waiting on tables in a restaurant or to serving time in the military. Likewise, some readers might be aware that *Time* has a particular political viewpoint that differs from that of other weekly news magazines such as *Newsweek* or *The New Yorker*, whereas other readers may not posses this knowledge. It is up to the instructor to find ways to tap into this background knowledge, to help learners see where there may be mismatches between their experiences and characteristics of the target culture, and to identify the kinds of cultural knowledge learners must have to interpret the text effectively.

To exemplify your understanding of linguistic and schematic Available Designs before moving on to explore visual, audio, gestural, and spatial resources, take a moment to complete Part 1 of Learning Activity 1.3. This activity asks you to identify the linguistic and schematic resources in another English-language text. Later, you will come back to this activity to identify the visual, audio, gestural, or spatial resources in the text you choose.

LEARNING ACTIVITY 1.3

Identifying Available Designs in Texts

Go to the YouTube channel of the Corporation for National and Community Service or search YouTube using the terms *corporation for national and community service.* Select one of the videos related to service and volunteering to watch for this activity.

Part 1. Make a list of the linguistic and schematic Available Designs that characterize the videotext, using the discussion above and the list of resources in Figure 1.2 as a guide. Use the discussion of the *Time* magazine cover as a model and keep in mind that the videotext you choose may not have examples of all of the types of Available Designs listed in Figure 1.2.

Part 2. Read the rest of this Section 2.1 on the what of multiliteracies pedagogy, then watch the video a second time and list any visual, audio, gestural, or spatial resources that characterize the videotext.

Part 3. Which of these Available Designs do you think might be part of a beginning- or intermediate-level English learner's previous knowledge? Which of these Available Designs might you want to highlight in instructional activities?

Given that texts are often multimodal in nature and thus are characterized by more than written words, we must also attend to the visual, audio, gestural, and spatial Available Designs that learners may encounter. These resources are "structured set[s] of conventions" (New London Group, 1996, p. 74) organized and used in certain ways in different sociocultural contexts. By their definition, then, visual, audio, gestural, and spatial Available Designs overlap with the literacy principles of conventions and cultural knowledge, just as linguistic and schematic Available Designs do. For instance, the ability to interpret *gestural resources* such as the thumbs-up gesture is culturally dependent, and the meaning of this gesture can vary across contexts. In the United States, the thumbs-up gesture indicates a positive reaction to something; however, in some cultures, it is used to indicate the number one when counting, whereas in others, it means you are telling someone to go away. Likewise, gestures such as the handshake are conventions that may be used differently in different cultures. In some contexts it may be inappropriate for women to shake hands; in others, a soft or firm handshake may mean different things. Moreover, in some cultures the handshake convention has evolved over time. In the United States, for example, men and women did not shake hands to greet one another until relatively recently. *Visual resources* also reflect culturally situated conventions and can include things like colors, photos, drawings, camera effects (e.g., close up, panning), or shapes. It is easy to imagine that in a television news broadcast, for instance, camera effects or background images may be different from one culture to another. Likewise, foreign films often possess a set of visual characteristics and camera effects (i.e., conventions) that set them apart across cultures: The French *nouvelle vague* is known for naturalistic cinematic techniques and jump cuts, whereas German expressionist film is characterized by distorted shapes and heavy shadowing. Similarly, the way we interpret *audio resources* such as music is dependent on our cultural knowledge and background experiences. The familiar sounds of traditional classical music may appeal to American sensibilities, whereas the sparse rhythms of traditional Japanese folk music may not. Certain audio resources also overlap with the literacy principle of language use: Each language is characterized by a specific set of sounds, and those sounds are organized in unique ways to create words and phrases. Finally, *spatial resources* have to do with things like page layout, proximity and size of objects, and so on. In a film, for instance, one may be struck by the size of buildings in another culture or by notions of personal space that may be different from one's own. These Available Designs overlap with conventions and cultural knowledge because the way in which spatial resources are organized and interpreted is socioculturally constrained. All of these Available Designs play a role in a learner's ability to understand information present in target language texts and his or her expectations about how that information is organized. Furthermore, instructors can foreground such Available Designs to help learners understand why their expectations related to visual, audio, gestural, or spatial resources are or are not borne out in the texts with which they interact.

In addition to the linguistic and schematic resources we already identified, several visual, gestural, and spatial features characterize the *Time* magazine cover we have been analyzing. Visually, the color scheme is striking. Each section of the cover—the three headlines at the top and the main story on the remainder of the page—has a different background color, and the entire cover is banded in red. Moreover, the text includes both photos and drawings. To predict the content of the stories featured in the headlines, learners might try to draw connections between the use of photos versus drawings based on what they know about how each is typically used in magazines or based on the meaning of the headline with which these images are associated. The feature story headline is accompanied by a drawing depicting a woman gesturing with her fist. Although this gesture is meant to indicate strength, and particularly the strength of women in the workforce (indeed, this drawing is a play on the well-known Rosie the Riveter poster from the World War II era), some learners might interpret this fist differently. Finally, the layout of the magazine cover, its spatial Available Designs, can help students further understand how information is organized and what it might mean. The cover is organized into a series of boxes, each with a different background color; this layout feature sets the headlines apart and signals that each is different from the other. In addition, one headline and its associated image is in a much larger box, suggesting that this is a feature story that may be more significant than the others. If learners do not already possess these Available Designs and cannot make these kinds of predictions based on the visual, gestural, and spatial features of the text, instructional activities can guide learners to these conclusions. Taken together, these resources, combined with the linguistic and schematic resources discussed above, comprise the *Time* magazine text and the content with which learners interact to make meaning.

To conclude this discussion of the what of multiliteracies pedagogy, return to Learning Activity 1.3 to identify the visual, audio, gestural, or spatial resources of the videotext you chose (Part 2) and to reflect on the role of these Available Designs in learners' knowledge base and in potential instructional activities (Part 3).

2.2 The How of Multiliteracies Pedagogy: Learning Processes

In the previous section, we discussed the literacy principles of language use, conventions, and cultural knowledge, their relationship to Available Designs, and their contribution to the textual content we teach our students. The remaining four principles of literacy—interpretation, collaboration, problem solving, and reflection/self-reflection—form the *how* of multiliteracies pedagogy. These are the learning processes in which students engage when carrying out instructional activities. In the Introduction, we provided an overview of these four literacy principles as we built our definition of the concept of literacy. In this section, we revisit and expand upon these concepts, focusing on the relationship between literacy-based and CLT-oriented learning processes. We exemplify each learning process through reference to a lesson plan developed for the *Time* magazine cover (to find this text online, google the keywords "time magazine cover national service 2007"). The complete lesson plan, intended for use in a second- or third-semester English as a foreign language class, can be found in the Appendix to this chapter.

Interpretation involves moving beyond literal, surface-level comprehension of textual meaning to a deeper understanding of the cultural perspectives, personal opinions, and points of view embedded in texts. Interpretation involves inferencing, "a thinking process that involves reasoning a step beyond the text, using generalization, synthesis and/or explanation" (Hammadou, 2002, p. 219). Interpretation also entails the ability to bring one's background knowledge and ideas to a text. From a multiliteracies perspective, then, when a learner interacts with a text, he or she interprets a writer's or a speaker's view of the world from his or her world view (Kern, 2000, 2003). To illustrate, in the

Time magazine lesson plan, students engage in textual interpretation when they answer critical focus questions (Activity 7) regarding service activities and how those activities might differ across cultures.

This perspective is quite different from that of CLT, in which textual interaction often involves surface-level comprehension of information and in which reading, writing, speaking, listening, and viewing are acts intended to help learners practice target language forms. Indeed, Kern (2000), expanding upon Widdowson's (1978) work, suggested that this is a contrast of *usage* versus *use*. That is, whereas CLT focuses on language usage, or the development of language skills through comprehension and production of accurate forms, a pedagogy of multiliteracies focuses on language use, or the interpretation and creation of meaning through texts and the language forms used to express that meaning.

Collaboration involves interactions between a writer and his or her audience, a reader and the text he or she is interpreting, or students and instructors participating in a classroom community. Collaboration therefore entails collective social engagement with textual content (Hall, 2001; Kern, 2000). Although CLT-oriented activities include pair, group, and teacher-led interactions, the focus is more on individual oral self-expression than on collective social engagement with texts. The purpose of collaboration in CLT is typically to practice language forms through the exchange of information about oneself, often implemented within an instructor-created context in which students play roles, rather than within a socioculturally appropriate context grounded in texts. Moreover, the development of reading and writing competence is often solitary, taking place outside of the classroom. In contrast, in multiliteracies pedagogy collaboration is a socially situated act that takes place through interaction with texts and with others within a classroom community. As such, collaboration allows students to construct meaning jointly as they give and receive assistance in textual creation and interpretation (Allen & Paesani, 2010; Kern, 2003). Activity 3 of the sample lesson plan, in which students interact with the text and with one another to categorize information related to the magazine cover's headlines, is an example of multiliteracies-oriented collaboration. Learners must construct meaning jointly by reaching a consensus on how information is categorized, what word from the text justifies their choice, and how the associated image further supports their answers.

The final two learning processes, problem solving and reflection, do not figure prominently in pedagogical practice in the current version of CLT. In the multiliteracies framework, *problem solving* is text centered: It is related to language use in texts and how language forms are linked to meaning. As Kern stated, making meaning from texts entails "figuring out relationships between words, between larger units of meaning, and between texts and real or imagined worlds" (2003, p. 49). Learners thus solve problems related to form–meaning connections to facilitate textual interpretation. In the sample lesson plan, students engage in problem solving in Activity 4 when they first identify patterns regarding the grammar of the headlines and then analyze why headlines have these syntactic features. This activity helps students see connections between the way language is used and the kind of meaning it expresses and thus deepens students' interpretation of the magazine cover. Given that the main goals of textual interaction in current CLT are to gain surface-level comprehension of facts and to practice language forms, problem solving with the purpose of understanding how forms contribute to meaning and aid in textual interpretation is absent from this approach.

Reflection and *self-reflection*, also not prominent in current CLT, involve learners thinking "about language and its relations to the world and themselves" (Kern, 2003, p. 49). This reflective component has a number of cognitive benefits for learners. First, reflection contributes to development of a metalanguage that helps learners talk about language forms, textual conventions, and their experiences with texts. Furthermore, this learning process can contribute to strategy development as learners reflect on which strategies are and are not useful for them as they create and interpret textual meaning. Finally, reflecting on how textual content and the language used to express that content relates to them personally and to the larger world enhances learners' critical thinking skills. The learning process of reflection is present in several parts of the sample lesson plan. For instance, in Activity 1, students reflect on issues that might be important to Americans based on their understandings of American culture. Likewise, in Activity 6, students reflect on what the image on the magazine cover means to them and how the words they associate with the image relate to the topic of national service.

The learning processes summarized here form the how of multiliteracies pedagogy. The next step in understanding the framework that engages learners in meaning design through textual interaction is to apply the what and the how of multiliteracies pedagogy. It is this application, achieved through four pedagogical acts, to which we now turn.

2.3 Applying the What and the How of Multiliteracies Pedagogy: Four Pedagogical Acts

The pedagogical acts of situated practice, overt instruction, critical framing, and transformed practice provide the structure to organize multiliteracies instruction, engage learners in meaning design, and apply the what and the how of the multiliteracies framework discussed in this chapter. These pedagogical acts therefore serve as tools that help instructors teach in a way that facilitates students' access to the language, conventions, cultural content, and other Available Designs in texts and also engages them in the learning processes of interpretation, collaboration, problem solving, and reflection. We describe each of these pedagogical acts in this section, providing examples from the lesson plan (see Appendix) organized around a *Time* magazine cover. Keep in mind that you will build your conceptual understanding of the four pedagogical acts as you read the remaining chapters of this book and evaluate additional sample lesson plans and activities.

Situated practice, or experiencing, is defined as spontaneous, immersive, experiential learning that does not involve conscious reflection (Cope & Kalantzis, 2009; New London Group, 1996). Through situated practice, learners use the target language to participate in authentic activities related to texts from the beginning of language instruction. Contrary to traditional approaches to FL instruction, this participation leads to competence, rather than competence leading to participation in authentic activities. The role of the instructor is to model the kinds of activities in which students are expected to participate and to guide students through the learning process such that they eventually participate in these activities on their own (Hall, 2001). Cope and Kalantzis (2009) distinguish two types of situated practice activities: *experiencing the known* and *experiencing the new*. The former "involves reflecting on our own experiences, interests, perspectives, familiar forms of expression and ways of representing the world in one's own understanding" (p. 18), whereas the latter "entails observing or reading the unfamiliar, immersion in new situations and texts, reading new texts or collecting new data" (p. 18).

Examples of situated practice activities are provided in the sample lesson plan in the Appendix. For instance, Activity 6 illustrates a situated practice activity in which students experience the known. They must examine an image from the magazine cover and interpret it based upon their worldview, their existing linguistic Available Designs, and their understanding of what national service entails in their respective cultures. In Activity 2, students experience the new by immersing themselves in the text for the first time: They engage with the language and images of the text and match headlines and words with topic categories.

Overt instruction activities are the site for explicit learning related to language use and conventions. Also understood as conceptualizing, overt instruction includes interventions from the instructor that focus learners on developing the knowledge needed to participate in communication activities (Cope & Kalantzis, 2009; New London Group, 1996). These activities involve systematic practice of language forms and conventions found in texts and allow learners "to mindfully abstract, reflect on, and practice the use of" that knowledge (Hall, 2001, pp. 52–53). As a result, students are able to recognize form–meaning connections in texts, learn how texts are organized, and see how ideas are presented.

The sample lesson plan includes overt instruction activities (Activities 4 and 5) in which students must identify the features of the language that typify headlines, which often include the absence of verbs, distinctive use of capitalization, and unexpected punctuation. Students are furthermore asked to reflect on why the language of headlines is this way, and how reformulating headlines as declarative sentences might affect their meaning. As such, students learn what language forms and conventions are necessary to communicate in the headline genre and, furthermore, how these forms and conventions are connected to textual meaning.

Learners relate meaning to social contexts and purposes in *critical framing* activities. Also understood as analyzing, critical framing encourages learners to analyze and question the meaning, importance, and consequences of what they learn. These kinds of activities can add to students' cultural knowledge in preparation for interacting with textual content or allow students to gain distance from what they have already learned after interacting with textual content. Critical framing further helps learners constructively critique and evaluate their knowledge and account for its sociocultural significance (Cope & Kalantzis, 2009; New London Group, 1996). These kinds of activities provide opportunities to make cross-cultural comparisons, to raise questions about one's own culture, and to develop understandings of how one's perspective is similar to or different from the perspectives embedded in texts (Hall, 2001). Cope and Kalantzis thus distinguish between two types of critical framing activities. On the one hand, *analyzing functionally* "includes processes of reasoning, drawing inferential and deductive conclusions, establishing functional relations such as between cause and effect and analysing logical and textual connections." *Analyzing critically*, on the other hand, "involves evaluation of your own and other people's perspectives, interests and motives" (2009, p. 18).

The *Time* magazine lesson plan includes two critical framing activities requiring students to analyze functionally and critically. Activity 1 asks students to critically reflect on the nature of news magazines and make connections between their understandings of American culture and news magazine topics that might appeal to this culture. Activity 7 also asks students to make connections between the content of the magazine cover and American culture and, further, to evaluate that content within the context of their respective culture(s). In both activities, learners must make links between language, images, and content to help them analyze connections and evaluate their own and others' perspectives.

In *transformed practice* activities, learners apply the understandings, knowledge, and skills gained through textual interaction and use them to produce language in new and creative ways (Cope & Kalantzis, 2009; New London Group, 1996). According to Hall (2001), these transformation and application activities provide learners the opportunity to use their understandings, knowledge, and skills in various ways, thereby personalizing their learning experiences and helping them realize their goals. Transformed practice activities can take the form of *applying appropriately* or *applying creatively*. The former involves "the application of knowledge and understandings to the complex diversity of real world situations and testing their validity" (Cope & Kalantzis, 2009, p. 18) and thus includes activities such as writing research papers or participating in debates. The latter entails "making an intervention in the world which is truly innovative and creative and which brings to bear the learner's interests, experiences and aspirations" (Cope & Kalantzis, 2009, p. 19) and includes activities such as inventing story continuations or writing reading journals.

The transformed practice activity that concludes the sample lesson plan (Activity 8) is an example of applying creatively. Learners must create a personal action plan in which they propose a plan for engaging in national service. This activity helps learners predict the content of what they will read inside the magazine by applying what they learned through reading the headline on the cover. It furthermore encourages them to reformulate what they have learned in the activities leading up to the activity by writing a definition of national service.

Before moving on to discuss additional details related to the application of the what and how of the multiliteracies framework, complete Learning Activity 1.4. This activity will help develop your understanding of the four pedagogical acts and prepare you to interact with these tools in subsequent chapters of the book.

LEARNING ACTIVITY 1.4

Categorizing Instructional Activities

Follow the steps below to categorize additional examples of activities representing the pedagogical acts of situated practice, overt instruction, critical framing, and transformed practice.

Part 1. List four or five key words that best describe each pedagogical act: situated practice, overt instruction, critical framing, and transformed practice.

Part 2. Decide whether each of the activities described below is an example of situated practice, overt instruction, critical framing, transformed practice, or a combination of more than one pedagogical act. Use your key words to help justify your choices.

Activity	Situated Practice	Overt Instruction	Critical Framing	Transformed Practice
Connecting with text chart: students write personal connections they find in a text they are reading/viewing/listening to				
Extra words: students and instructor determine which words are less essential to a text and discuss how textual meaning changes if these words are eliminated				
Information / idea / semantic mapping: students represent textual events, facts, or ideas in a table, diagram, semantic web, or illustration				
Instructional conversations: teacher-managed discussions that help students understand and communicate about concepts and language features central to their learning				

Activity	**Situated Practice**	**Overt Instruction**	**Critical Framing**	**Transformed Practice**
Jigsaw: students become experts about one aspect of a topic and share this information with others to construct a complete picture of the topic				
Multiple interpretations: students examine their understanding of a text and consider all possible interpretations				
Personal action plan: students turn an idea into action by identifying a goal, steps toward achieving it, resources needed, and performance measures				
Reader's theater: students identify the parts or characters in a text, then color code sentences and phrases according to these parts or characters and perform the scripted text				
Reading journals: learners summarize and reflect on a text they have read				
Revising and editing: students learn to revise and edit the style, organization, and grammar of their written work				
Story retelling: students tell a story from a different perspective (e.g., character, time frame)				
Text annotations: students mark up a text as they read to focus on language features				

Part 3. Look up each of the activities listed above in the index to this book. Read the description of the activity on the page(s) listed and verify whether your choices were correct.

The pedagogical acts of situated practice, overt instruction, critical framing, and transformed practice are neither hierarchical nor sequential; they are sometimes overlapping parts of a complete pedagogy that may be implemented in whatever order best meets students' literacy needs. For instance, in the sample lesson plan in the Appendix, you may have been struck by the fact that instruction begins with critical framing rather than with situated practice, as you might have expected. Activity 1 is an appropriate way to begin the lesson because it taps into students' Available Designs related to U.S. culture and news magazines and prepares them for the subsequent pedagogical acts in the lesson. Likewise, Activities 4 and 5, which represent overt instruction, are followed by a second situated practice activity rather than critical framing, as you might have expected. This progression is logical given that Activity 6 immerses learners in examination of the magazine cover's main image before asking them to focus on the associated headline in critical focus questions in Activity 7, that is, it moves students from concrete to more abstract thinking.

You may have also noticed that this lesson plan includes more than one activity representing each pedagogical act. Again, these choices were made to adequately prepare students to interact with the content of the magazine cover, to encourage them to make form–meaning connections, to understand the sociocultural perspectives represented in the magazine cover, and to use their knowledge to engage in transformative language use. This sequencing best engages students in meaning design to meet the objectives of this particular text and lesson within the context of a particular course.

Finally, the sample lesson plan includes one activity labeled as overt instruction and transformed practice. Indeed, this example shows that pedagogical acts are sometimes overlapping and that activities can have features of one or more pedagogical act. In Activity 5, students are establishing form–meaning connections in the text through explicit learning about grammar and conventions; however, they are also transforming the text by applying their knowledge of grammar and conventions and using that knowledge to create something new. You will find as you read the remaining chapters of this book that some activities are labeled as one pedagogical act in one instance and as a different pedagogical act in another instance. Indeed, the pedagogical act that an activity targets may vary depending on the objectives of the lesson plan or course. For example, in Chapter 5 we suggest that reading journals can be an example of situated practice or critical framing. As a situated practice activity, learners immerse themselves in a text by providing a summary, their response to the text, and some reflection regarding the process of reading the text. This activity is illustrative of critical framing when learners are further asked to situate the text within their own sociocultural context to highlight similarities or differences compared to the sociocultural context of the text. We can further imagine reading journals fitting within transformed practice if learners are asked to imagine what would have happened in a text if, for instance, a character had made a different decision, if the sociocultural context had been different, or if the story were to take place in the future.

As a final point, it is important to note that in traditional FL programs, situated practice, overt instruction, critical framing, and transformed practice do not always have equal emphases in all parts of the curriculum. Typically, situated practice and overt instruction activities are prevalent in CLT-oriented introductory and intermediate language courses, whereas critical framing and transformed practice activities (in the form of analytical/research papers) are privileged in advanced-level literature and culture courses. When introductory and intermediate courses do include critical framing and transformed practice, they are incorporated into the curriculum less systematically than situated practice and overt instruction. Likewise, when situated practice and overt instruction activities form part of the advanced curriculum, it is most often in language-oriented courses such as advanced grammar, composition, phonetics, or conversation; these kinds of activities are typically not systematically integrated into advanced literature or culture courses (Allen & Paesani, 2010). Furthermore, advanced language-oriented courses often lack a focus on critical framing or transformed practice, particularly when texts do not form an integral part of the course. One reason for this bifurcation is the assumption that the limited linguistic abilities of lower-level students prevents them from being able to engage in critical thinking, reflection, or interpretation, or to explore sociocultural perspectives using the FL (Meyer, 2009; Walther, 2007). This assumption further supposes that learners cannot interact with authentic FL texts at this level. Indeed, the focus of introductory and intermediate courses tends to be more on explicit instruction of language forms separate from content. Yet the multiliteracies framework presented here and expanded upon in subsequent chapters facilitates development of grammatical and lexical knowledge as resources for meaning making put into practice through contextualized language use within the context of FL texts. Because this pedagogy places texts at the center of the curriculum from the very start of language study, even introductory learners can engage in the kinds of critical framing and transformed practice activities to which they are typically not exposed at this level.

3. FINAL CONSIDERATIONS

In this chapter, we built upon your conceptual knowledge related to literacy, the principles of literacy, and its sociocultural, linguistic, and cognitive dimensions, and introduced the theoretical and pedagogical framework that allows us to translate the concept of literacy into classroom practice: the multiliteracies framework. The goal of this framework is to engage learners in the act of meaning design, the dynamic process of discovering form–meaning connections through the acts of interpreting and creating written, oral, visual, audiovisual, and digital texts. To understand how meaning design can take place in FL classrooms, we discussed three interrelated aspects of our framework: the what of multiliteracies pedagogy, or the content of instruction; the how of multiliteracies pedagogy, or the learning processes in which students engage; and the application of the what and how of multiliteracies pedagogy, or the pedagogical acts that help organize instructional activities. The concepts discussed herein not only build upon what you learned in the Introduction, they form the theoretical and pedagogical grounding for subsequent chapters in this book. Indeed, as you will see, with the exception of Chapter 2, each of the remaining chapters of this book reconsiders various aspects of lower-level language instruction (grammar and vocabulary, oral participation, reading, writing, listening and viewing, technology) within the context of the multiliteracies framework and presents instructional sequences that engage learners with texts through activities representing the four pedagogical acts.

A reconsideration of FL teaching and learning cannot take place without advance planning, and the first step in such planning is establishing goals and objectives. Course, unit, and daily goals and objectives are a guide for teachers and learners, as well as a base from which to select appropriate texts and design appropriate instructional interventions and assessments. According to Hall (2001), the ability to articulate clear goals and objectives forms part of an instructor's pedagogical knowledge, along with knowing how to plan lessons and design assessments that meet particular goals and objectives. As a final thought for this chapter, consider how the concepts and their applications that you have learned about in this chapter have contributed to your pedagogical knowledge. Which new concepts and applications have contributed the most to your pedagogical knowledge? Which are still unclear to you? Which do you disagree with? How does this reconfigured version of your pedagogical knowledge relate to your instructional goals and objectives? How do you hope Chapter 2 will further contribute to this knowledge base? To help organize these thoughts, complete the final learning activity for this chapter.

LEARNING ACTIVITY 1.5

A Concept Map of the Multiliteracies Framework

Create a concept map that illustrates how key components of the multiliteracies framework fit together (google the phrase "concept map" to get an idea of what a map looks like and how it is constructed). Your map should include at least the following main concepts: literacy, meaning design, Available Designs, learning processes, and pedagogical acts. You should begin by mapping how these main concepts fit together and then continue by expanding this map with any other concepts or ideas presented in this chapter and in the Introduction (e.g., transformation, sociocultural dimension, overt instruction). The goal of this activity is to illustrate in as much detail as possible your current understanding of the multiliteracies framework and how the various components of that framework fit together. Hold on to this concept map—you will revisit it in subsequent chapters of this book.

4. TRANSFORMING KNOWLEDGE

4.1 Reflective Journal Entry

Go back to Learning Activity 1.1 at the beginning of the chapter and review the beliefs you identified related to the what and the how of FL teaching and learning and how you apply these in the classroom. Have your beliefs changed after reading this chapter? How have the concepts you have read about here influenced the way you think about classroom teaching and learning? Do any of these concepts support or refute the beliefs you identified in this initial activity? Would you complete Learning Activity 1.1 differently based on what you now know about the multiliteracies framework?

4.2 Researching the Multiliteracies Framework

To fill in the gaps related to your knowledge about the multiliteracies framework, complete the K–W–L chart that follows. First, list what you know or understand about the multiliteracies framework in the first row of the table. Next, identify what you want to know or questions you still have about the framework and write them in the second row. Finally, research answers to your questions by reading the article and chapter listed in the "Key Resources" section of this chapter. Complete the third row of the table with the additional information you learned about the multiliteracies framework through this research. Were all of your questions answered? If not, research additional publications (in the "For Further Reading" section of this chapter, in the bibliography to this book, or elsewhere) where you might find the answers you need.

What I *know*	
What I *want to know*	
What I *learned*	

Key Resources

Kern, R. (2000). *Literacy and language teaching*. Oxford, England: Oxford University Press.

Chapter 3, "Available Designs in Literacy," presents an overview of the linguistic and schematic resources that characterize texts and that learners use to interpret and produce texts. Kern discusses a number of these resources (writing systems, vocabulary, syntax, cohesion and coherence, formal schemata, rhetorical organization patterns, genres, style, and stories) in detail, with English-language examples to illustrate their meaning. These resources are distinct yet overlapping, and make it possible to make meaning from oral and written texts and engage in communicative acts. Kern underscores the idea that in more traditionally-oriented FL classrooms, only certain Available Designs—grammar, vocabulary, sounds, writing systems—are addressed, but that to be truly literate users of a FL, schematic Available Designs must also be privileged so that learners may engage with language in coherent, contextualized, and discourse-appropriate ways.

New London Group. (1996). A pedagogy of multiliteracies: Designing social futures. *Harvard Educational Review, 66*(1), 60–92.

In this article, the New London Group presents the theoretical foundation for their approach to literacy teaching, which they call a pedagogy of multiliteracies. After contextualizing their discussion within the changing social climate and the cultural and linguistic diversity of the worlds in which we live, the authors present key concepts of their approach: design of meaning, Available Designs, Designing, the Redesigned, and the four pedagogical acts of situated practice, overt instruction, critical framing, and transformed practice. The authors argue that multiliteracies pedagogy develops students' literacy by creating access to the diverse uses of language in different sociocultural contexts and by fostering the critical engagement with language necessary for future success.

For Further Reading

Allen, H. W., & Paesani, K. (2010). Exploring the feasibility of a pedagogy of multiliteracies in introductory foreign language courses. *L2 Journal, 2*(1), 119–142.

Cope, C., & Kalantzis, M. (2009). 'Multiliteracies': New literacies, new learning. *Pedagogies, 4*(3), 164–195.

Kalantzis, M., & Cope, C. (n. d.). *New learning: Transformational designs for pedagogy and assessment.* Retrieved from http://newlearningonline.com/

Kress, G. (2000). Design and transformation: New theories of meaning. In B. Cope & M. Kalantzis (Eds.), *Multiliteracies: Literacy learning and the design of social futures* (pp. 153–161). New York, NY: Routledge.

APPENDIX

Sample Lesson Plan: Time Magazine Cover

1. Critical Framing: *Predicting*

Students are told they will read the cover of an American news magazine called *Time.* Students then predict what the cover might look like and what topics might be presented based on what they understand about U.S. culture: What news-related topics are important to Americans? How would these topics be represented on the cover of a news magazine? What kinds of Americans might read a news magazine?

2. Situated Practice: *Categorizing Information*

Working in small groups, students scan the magazine cover and categorize each of the four headlines/stories according to the topics below. Groups must include one word from each headline to justify their choice and add a second word that tells how the associated image informed their choice.

1. Volunteering
2. Politics
3. Beauty
4. Entertainment

3. Situated Practice: *Verifying Predictions*

As a follow up, students indicate if the topics on the magazine cover are similar to those they identified in the predicting activity and whether the appearance of the magazine cover is as they had predicted.

4. Overt Instruction: *Pattern Analysis* (Hall, 2001)

Students are told that "Why Iowa ♥ John Edwards," "To Gray or not to Gray: A Hair-Raising Question," and "The Case for National Service" are all headlines. They then identify the language features each of the headlines has in common (e.g., lack of verbs, use of capitalization) and speculate about why headlines usually have these features.

5. Overt Instruction / Transformed Practice: *Sentence Reformulation*

Students rewrite each headline as a declarative sentence, with the conventional subject–verb–object structure. As a follow up, they are asked whether this transformation changes the meaning of each headline.

6. Situated Practice: *Matching Images and Ideas*

Students next examine the image associated with the national service headline and answer the following questions with a partner: What does this image represent for you? Write down five words you associate with this image. How do these words relate to doing service or volunteer activities? Why is volunteering represented by this image?

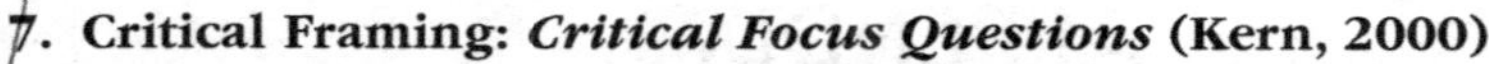

7. Critical Framing: *Critical Focus Questions* (Kern, 2000)

Students are reminded that the headline related to national service states that Americans want to help their community, their country, and their world. In a teacher-led activity, they discuss the following questions: What are the differences among these three things? What are some activities Americans might do to achieve this goal? What service activities are common in your culture? How are these activities similar to or different from service activities in the United States?

8. Transformed Practice: *Personal Action Plan* (Kalantzis & Cope, 2012)

According to the headline, the article on national service will propose a plan for putting the desire to serve into action. In groups of three, students first define what national service means for them and then write their own action plan for carrying out national service, using the information gathered in previous activities to help guide them. The action plan should include a definition, at least three steps, and an image that expresses their ideas visually.

NOTE: To access the text for this lesson plan online, google the keywords "time magazine cover national service 2007."

CHAPTER 2

Reconsidering Goals, Objectives, and Assessment From a Multiliteracies Perspective

Thus far in this book you have explored the theoretical underpinnings of the concept of literacy in the Introduction and the pedagogical framework for multiliteracies instruction in Chapter 1. You now possess a basic understanding of the focus of foreign language (FL) instruction in a multiliteracies approach—text-based literacy events and meaning design—and how such a focus can be organized to structure student learning using the four pedagogical acts. As explained in the Introduction, carrying out FL instruction consistent with the multiliteracies approach entails goals, objectives, instructional techniques, and assessments that differ from those used in lower-level FL courses grounded in communicative language teaching (CLT) and, by extension, those that typically dominate commercially produced textbook materials. In addition, given the frequently disparate goals of lower-level language courses versus advanced literature and culture courses, the multiliteracies approach can close the pedagogical gap between them and create a more coherent curriculum.

This chapter builds on the foundation we have laid thus far and expands on the practical applications of multiliteracies instruction. Specifically, we explore (1) how goals and objectives can be articulated in a manner consistent with this framework, and (2) how assessment practices relate to classroom teaching and learning to function within this framework. This chapter also serves as the basis for further discussions of instruction and assessment in subsequent chapters related to areas such as the teaching of Available Designs (e.g., grammar, vocabulary, background knowledge, conventions) and language modalities (e.g., reading, writing, speaking, listening, viewing).

The chapter begins by explaining why goals and objectives are a critical part of FL instruction even though explicit attention to them may be minimized during one's early teaching experiences. In addition, the difference between a goal and an objective is described, along with how they relate to various components of the collegiate FL curriculum. Next, we explore relationships among goals and objectives, instruction, and assessment, and we define different types of assessments and their purposes. The remainder of the chapter explores strategies for creating goals and objectives for FL learning consistent with the multiliteracies approach as well as the question of how instruction can be coherently linked to assessment. By the end of this chapter, you will have experience in writing goals and objectives for student learning from a multiliteracies perspective, and you will see how assessment can be used to measure student learning en route to developing FL literacy.

1. CONCEPTUAL BACKGROUND

To begin our discussion of the role of goals and objectives in FL teaching and learning, we start with what may seem like an unlikely comparison: travel. Imagine two types of travelers: The first one is spontaneous, touring through Europe on a multi-country rail pass that does not require the traveler to make strategic choices as to where he or she ends up each day or what the final destination may be. This way of traveling affords much flexibility as to what is done and seen during the journey, since there are no constraints and plans can be changed depending on the tourist's mood, energy level, and other conditions. The second traveler, however, operates differently, traveling through Europe in a GPS-equipped car with a set end destination in mind as well as definitive plans for what he or she visits daily and what progress has been made toward the end destination. The advantages of this style of travel are that the tourist has planned the trip in advance and can focus his or her energies on the pleasures of the journey itself rather than on making decisions each day.

In many ways, the spontaneous rail-pass traveler and the deliberate GPS-reliant traveler are an apt comparison for the teacher who delivers instruction without explicit goals and objectives in mind versus the teacher whose instruction is informed by explicit goals and objectives. In fact, many FL teachers, particularly those new to the classroom, find themselves operating much like the spontaneous traveler—making instructional decisions on a day-to-day basis and looking ahead only to the content to be covered in the immediate future—rather than having a more long-term perspective on what needs to be taught by the end of the course and a specific idea of what will be accomplished during each lesson and unit leading to that point. Why is this the case? First, novice FL teachers typically are not responsible for setting the curriculum for their courses. In many introductory and intermediate collegiate FL courses, a language program director is the person charged with that task, including writing course syllabi and setting course goals and objectives. Second, lower-level FL courses normally are shaped by commercial textbooks, which have been called "the bedrock of syllabus design and lesson planning" (Kramsch, 1988, p. 63). Thus, the textbook itself typically dictates the themes, linguistic functions, vocabulary, and grammatical content covered in a course, as well as the order in which they are taught. In addition, textbooks often feature unit-level objectives, either in the table of contents or on the first page of each chapter. For these reasons, new teachers may not initially see the necessity for individual reflection on overarching goals and objectives, given that their program and textbook appear to provide structure and direction for what should be taught and learned.

We contend, however, that just as careful advance planning with a GPS device maximizes the deliberate traveler's enjoyment of the journey, a clear vision of goals and objectives and how they relate to one's language program, course, units within a course, and lessons within a unit maximizes the effectiveness of FL teaching and student learning outcomes. That is to say, an explicit understanding of goals and objectives contributes to instructors possessing a coherent view both of how parts of the language program relate to the whole (i.e., the relationship of the course to the larger curriculum) and of how classroom instruction and assessment should be carried out to target lesson, unit, and course goals and objectives. Moreover, for students, goals and objectives serve as a road map that indicates what elements of FL study are viewed as important by their program and teacher. Thus, making goals and objectives explicit is an indirect means of communicating your beliefs about FL teaching and learning and of making your approach to FL teaching tangible for your students. Finally, from a programmatic perspective, as Byrnes, Maxim, and Norris (2010) have pointed out, creating statements of "valued and realistic learning outcomes for each of the stages of the undergraduate curriculum" is necessary for collegiate FL departments to "implement appropriate, articulated educational action for the entire program in terms of curriculum building, pedagogical approaches, and assessment practices" (p. 4). Therefore, determining goals and objectives for lower-level courses contributes to the overall coherence of the undergraduate FL curriculum. Before moving on to a detailed discussion of the role of goals, objectives, and assessment in multiliteracies instruction, complete Learning Activity2.1

LEARNING ACTIVITY 2.1

Reflecting on Beliefs and Experiences Related to Instructional Goals and Objectives and FL Learning

Take a moment to reflect on the following two questions and jot down your responses to them based on your beliefs and experiences as both a FL learner and instructor.

1. Think back to your experiences as a FL learner. Was the way in which instruction was organized more similar to the spontaneous rail-pass traveler (i.e., you were not aware of explicit instructional goals and objectives) or to the deliberate GPS-reliant traveler (i.e., instructional goals and objectives were clear to you)? How did you experience this as a learner? Explain your response and cite specific examples of learning and instruction.
2. Now think about your beliefs and experiences as a FL instructor. Are you more apt to resemble the spontaneous rail-pass traveler or the deliberate

GPS-reliant traveler in terms of how you might approach establishing goals and objectives? What advantages and disadvantages do you see to your approach?

1.1 Defining and Articulating Instructional Goals and Objectives

The first step to a clear vision of the role of goals and objectives in one's teaching is to understand the difference between the two, a distinction that may not be readily apparent given that the terms are often used interchangeably in non-pedagogical contexts (e.g., *My number one goal / objective for our trip to Mexico was to relax!*). *Goals*, which serve as organizational principles for FL programs or courses, are general statements of educational direction or intended outcomes, often articulated in broad terms. *Objectives*, sometimes referred to as learning outcomes, relate to a course, a unit within a course, or a lesson within a unit; they are specific statements about how goals will be achieved and what students will be able to do as a result of instruction (Graves, 1999; Hall, 2001; Shrum & Glisan, 2010). Thus, goals and objectives are in a hierarchical relationship to one another, such that several specific objectives may contribute to one broader goal. According to Graves (1999), one way to think about the goal–objective relationship is analogous to a journey: "The destination is the goal; the journey is the course. The objectives are the different points you pass through on the journey to the destination" (p. 76). An example of a course-level goal for students in an introductory-level FL course is to demonstrate awareness of practices associated with the target culture that relate to course themes. Related unit-level objectives for a chapter on everyday life might include (1) being able to describe in speech or writing how members of the target culture spend their free time (e.g., a brief recorded message or short email) with sufficient comprehensibility to be understood by a native speaker accustomed to communicating with non-native speakers; and (2) being able to compare in speech or writing eating habits of people in their culture versus the target culture (e.g., a short conversation or short letter) with sufficient comprehensibility to be understood by a native speaker accustomed to communicating with non-native speakers.

How goals and objectives are formulated is an important consideration. Notice that in the example above, the goal is broad, but not vague. The alternative "Students will learn about culture" is an example of a vaguely worded goal. Clarity in writing statements about student learning is essential because the clearer these statements are, the easier it is to plan classroom activities and the more likely students will understand and meet instructors' expectations (Hall, 2001). Also note that the sample objectives provided in this section contain three key elements:

1. a description of the actions or behaviors showing the skills or knowledge to be learned (e.g., being able to describe how members of the target culture spend their free time);
2. the conditions of performance (e.g., in speech or in writing); and

3. the degree of expected performance (e.g. largely comprehensible to a sympathetic native or near-native speaker). (Hall, 2001)

Further, each sample objective is defined in terms of observable student behavior; the objectives do not state that students will understand or appreciate cultural practices, but that they will describe and compare cultural practices using the FL. Indeed, well-designed objectives should be articulated using action words such as *classify, compare, contrast, create, critique, define, design, describe, evaluate, explain, give examples, identify, list, name, recognize,* and *summarize*.

The same principles for writing instructional objectives at the course level apply to the unit (i.e., chapter or module within a course) and lesson levels: Objectives should still contain the three elements described earlier, focus on observable student behaviors, and use action words to describe the behaviors. What distinguishes unit- and lesson-level objectives from course-level ones is the degree of specificity, with objectives at the unit level being more specific than those at the course level, and with lesson-level objectives being even more specific than unit-level objectives. For example, in relation to a course-level goal for students to be able to use the FL effectively in written presentational communication (i.e., presenting information, concepts, and ideas to listeners or readers) in a unit on family, a lesson-level objective might be written as follows: Students will be able to demonstrate the relationships of the members of their immediate family to themselves in a graphic organizer (e.g., family tree) using simple vocabulary. As a second example, in relation to a course-level goal for students to develop awareness of how the FL functions with a focus on knowledge critical for speaking and writing in the present time in relation to course themes, a lesson-level objective in a unit on housing might be written as follows: Students will be able to use various prepositions of location to compare their bedroom in their parents' home to their bedroom where they live at the university in a short email to a friend. Characteristics of instructional goals and objectives at the course, unit, and lesson level are summarized in Table 2.1.

As we discuss in the next section, establishing lesson-level objectives should precede selecting content for the actual lesson or deciding what types of instructional activities will be used to structure classroom learning. Now complete Learning Activity 2.2, which will give you an opportunity to practice writing instructional objectives at the lesson level.

LEARNING ACTIVITY 2.2

Articulating Instructional Objectives for FL Learning

Based on the definitions and examples of instructional goals and objectives provided in this section, write one unit-level objective and one lesson-level objective for each of the three introductory-level FL course goals listed below. While writing your objectives, remember to include Hall's (2001) three required elements and to use action words that define objectives in terms of observable student behaviors. Select one of the following themes for which you will write the objectives: university life, food, or travel. Refer to an introductory-level FL textbook for this activity, using a chapter related to the theme that you have chosen as a starting point for writing unit-level objectives and locating potential ideas for lesson content.

> **Course Goal 1:** Students will be able to use the FL effectively in oral interpersonal communication about course themes.
>
> **Course Goal 2:** Students will be able to use the FL appropriately in presentational communication to produce texts of various genres that relate to course themes.
>
> **Course Goal 3:** Students will be able to participate in interpretive communicative activities in the FL, including understanding the main idea and some details of audio and videotexts of various genres that relate to course themes.

Next, compare and discuss the objectives you have written for each goal with those of a classmate, offering feedback to him or her on how each one has been formulated. If possible, work with someone who has chosen the same theme as you. Make changes to your objectives based on the feedback that your classmate provides.

TABLE 2.1 Characteristics of Instructional Goals and Objectives

Program- and Course-Level Goals	Course-Level Objectives	Unit-Level Objectives	Lesson-Level Objectives
Hierarchically superior to instructional objectives, written before objectives	Facilitate meeting program or course goals; more than one objective can contribute to a course goal; written before unit- and lesson-level objectives	Facilitate meeting course-level objectives and goals; should be established prior to writing lesson-level objectives	Facilitate meeting unit- and course-level objectives and course-level goals; should be established prior to selecting lesson content
General statements of educational direction or intended outcomes articulated in broad terms	Specific statements about how goals will be achieved and what students will be able to do as a result of instruction ❑ Contain (1) a description of the actions or behaviors showing the knowledge or skills to be learned, (2) the conditions of performance, and (3) the degree of expected performance ❑ Defined in terms of observable student behavior ❑ Expressed in a way that maximizes clarity ❑ Often expressed as "Students will be able to . . ." + action words (e.g., *compare, critique, define, describe, evaluate, explain, list, recognize, summarize*)		

1.2 Conceptualizing the Relationship Among Goals and Objectives, Instruction, and Assessment

As previously stated, a parallel can be seen between instructional goals and the destination of a journey, between a course and related pedagogical practices and the journey itself, and between instructional objectives and different points along that journey. But where does assessment fit into this scheme? And how does assessment relate to goals, objectives, and instruction? Returning to the idea of the deliberate GPS-reliant traveler, we can see an analogy between the use of the GPS device and assessment because both involve a process of collecting data. In the case of the GPS, data include information such as current location and distance remaining toward a specific destination and, in the case of *assessment*, the process entails gathering information on student learning and performance. Processes that are related (but not synonymous) with assessment include *evaluation*, or assigning a value, interpreting, and judging the results of assessment; and *grading*, or reporting the results of assessment to the learner with a letter, numeric, or percentage grade. According to Kern (2000), these processes are significant in terms of what they communicate about a FL course: "What is evaluated reflects the *de facto* curriculum, and how it is evaluated reflects the *de facto* philosophy of learning and teaching, regardless of what the teacher or course description says" (p. 267). As a result, assessment practices that focus on discrete points of grammar on a written examination, for instance, reinforce the notion for students that the goal of the course and the curriculum is acquisition of grammar, even if classroom teaching practices or course goals and objectives reflect a CLT or multiliteracies approach.

The notion of *backward design* (Wiggins & McTighe, 2011) captures the relationship among goals and objectives, assessment, and instruction, and it conceptualizes the order in which each of those elements should be planned to maximize student learning. Just based on the wording—backward design—you may already intuit that this involves doing things in a different order from the traditional path: planning day-to-day instruction and selecting course content prior to setting goals and objectives and making decisions about assessment. The three chronological stages of backward design are (1) identifying desired results through the establishment of instructional goals and objectives; (2) determining assessment evidence to decide if the desired results identified in Stage 1 have been achieved; and (3) planning learning experiences and instruction. Thus, the learning sought (i.e., goals and objectives) is clarified prior to thinking about assessment evidence; finally, the means (i.e., type of learning opportunity, structures for learner participation, materials and other resources) to the end are designed (Hall, 2001; Wiggins & McTighe, 2011).

What are the advantages of planning curricula based on the notion of backward design? According to Wiggins and McTighe (2011), this process helps avoid the problem of treating the textbook as the curriculum rather than as a resource, and of creating isolated classroom activities with no clear purpose in relation to goals and objectives. In fact, both of these challenges are common in collegiate FL courses, in particular in lower-level language courses. Given the likelihood that you are using a textbook based on CLT, which remains the predominant approach in commercial introductory- and intermediate-level FL pedagogical materials, backward design may serve as a useful way to weave together instructional priorities and textbook resources for teaching and learning in line with the multiliteracies approach.

1.3 Identifying Types of Assessment and Their Uses

In the previous section, we recommended setting instructional goals and objectives using a backward design model as the first of a three-stage process that culminates in planning day-to-day instruction. Although the third stage, everyday instructional planning, may be familiar, the second stage, determining assessment evidence to decide if goals and objectives have been achieved, may not be familiar. Like establishing goals and objectives, assessing student learning may be largely determined at the program level because many introductory- and intermediate-level FL courses are multi-section, and common assessment tools are often used across sections of the same course. Nonetheless, it is important to possess a general understanding of the various types of assessment, the forms they may take, and the rationale for their use. In addition, it is likely—whether you are aware of it or not—that you are already making decisions about informal assessment in your classroom, and it is probable that in the future you will have greater autonomy and need to know how to design assessments for courses that you teach that fit with your instructional approach, goals, and objectives. Beyond the individual course level, assessment can also contribute to shaping curricular development and instructional improvement, as well as to greater specificity in identifying student learning outcomes (Byrnes, Maxim, & Norris, 2010).

Reflection on the varied types and uses of assessment is a critical element of designing FL courses and curricula. As Shrum and Glisan (2010) explained, today's view of assessment involves more than administering tests and assigning grades; instead, it may entail one or more of the following: "understanding the language learning process, determining the difficulties students may experience and misconceptions that they may have, and documenting students' language development over time" (p. 395). Thus, rather than being limited to evaluating learner achievement, assessment is now used to provide feedback on learning and improve learner performance. One way to think about the various types of assessment is according to their purposes, which can be characterized as diagnostic, formative, or summative. These are defined as follows:

1. *Diagnostic assessment* occurs before instruction to identify students' strengths and weaknesses or to place them at an appropriate instructional level (e.g., entrance exam, placement exam, standardized test);
2. *Formative assessment* occurs during instruction to help teachers identify areas of learner difficulty so instruction and assessment can be adjusted as necessary and learning and performance can be improved (e.g., concept map to illustrate students' understanding of a topic, audio journal entry to summarize students' reaction to a text);

3. *Summative assessment* occurs after an instructional sequence such as a chapter in a textbook or at the end of a course to determine the extent to which learners have met instructional goals and objectives or mastered content (e.g., written midterm examination, end-of-semester project).

The assessment plan for a FL course usually involves both formative and summative statements.

Determining which forms of assessment to include depends on one's instructional goals and objectives and the relative importance of the various language modalities and content focus. For example, a course with a strong emphasis on oral communication might place heavier weight on formative assessments, such as in-class participation, and less emphasis on summative assessments, such as formal essays. Similarly, a course might feature both traditional and alternative assessments, a distinction related to the nature of these assessment tools. *Traditional assessment* usually involves discrete-point criterion-referenced tests to evaluate student knowledge of the FL, whereas *alternative assessment* entails performance-based activities used within the context of instruction to show what students can do with language (Hall, 2001;NCLRC, 2013). Whereas a traditional assessment such as a written vocabulary quiz focuses on the products of learning, alternative assessments like teacher observations and student demonstrations center on both the processes and products of learning (Hall, 2001).

Among various forms of alternative assessment, *portfolios,* which involve a systematic, longitudinal collection of work from multiple sources that represents a student's development and achievements, have become a favored practice in U.S. FL education in recent years (NCLRC, 2013). Distinguishing portfolios from more traditional forms of assessment is that students participate in both the selection of content and reflection on the process of learning and the evidence of learning in their portfolio. Examples of items that might be included in a portfolio include lists of student goals and other self-assessment records, digitally recorded oral speech samples, journal entries, drafts of written portfolio artifacts, analyses of cultural products, practices, and perspectives, and teacher feedback (Shrum & Glisan, 2010). The advantages of this form of alternative assessment have been confirmed by recent research on student goal setting and achievement using portfolios (LinguaFolio), which revealed a positive relationship between FL reading, writing, and speaking outcomes and creating goals, action plans, and reflections (Moeller, Theiler, & Wu, 2012). However, as Kern (2000) noted, portfolio assessment requires more than adding a new tool to established practices for assessment and evaluation; rather, it involves significant shifts in teachers' and students' roles and how work is prepared and evaluated. Therefore, it should be understood that implementing portfolio assessment effectively is a recursive process that takes time to realize.

Finally, it is also useful to keep in mind that a certain fluidity exists when labeling assessments, and that whether a particular assessment tool serves a formative or summative function may vary according to course goals and objectives. Poehner (2007) explained it as follows:

> The summative-formative distinction pertains to the reasons for conducting the assessment rather than the instruments or tasks employed . . . . Traditional assessments, including multiple-choice exams and open-response essays, as well as so-called alternative assessments, such as portfolios, projects, and presentations, can all serve a summative or formative function depending on how their results are used. (pp. 323–324)

Now that you have been introduced to the various types of assessments and examples of each, complete Learning Activity 2.3, which focuses on brainstorming elements of an assessment plan, before moving on to pedagogical applications of the concepts discussed thus far in the chapter.

LEARNING ACTIVITY 2.3

Using Backward Design to Choose Assessments That Fit Course Goals and Objectives

After rereading the course goals and related instructional objectives that you wrote and revised in Learning Activity 2.2, now plan what assessments can be used to determine if those goals and objectives have been achieved. Be sure to include more than one type of assessment (formative, summative, traditional, alternative). In addition to making a list of the assessments, write a brief rationale statement for the use of each (e.g., To determine if Goal 1, Objective 2 has been reached, Assessment A will be implemented because. . .). As you did in Learning Activity 2.2, share and compare your assessment components with a classmate, offering feedback on your partner's ideas and noting his or her ideas about your own assessment plan.

2. PEDAGOGICAL APPLICATIONS

Up to this point in the chapter, you have been introduced to the definitions of instructional goals and objectives, types of assessment, and backward design, a means of bringing coherence to FL teaching and learning and assessment of learning outcomes. We now turn to the issue of how these elements can be aligned in a manner consistent with the multiliteracies framework. Related questions include the following: (1) What should instructional goals and objectives focus on to facilitate literacy development? (2) How might instructors move beyond a focus on functional communication toward a broader view of language competencies when writing instructional goals and objectives, particularly in lower-level FL courses? (3) What role do FL texts play in the articulation of instructional goals and objectives from a multiliteracies perspective, particularly in lower-level courses? and (4) How does assessment facilitate students' literacy development? Before we discuss answers to these questions, complete Learning Activity 2.4

LEARNING ACTIVITY 2.4

Mapping Relationships Between Multiliteracies Concepts and Instructional Goals and Objectives and Assessment

Part 1. The Introduction and Chapter 1 introduced you to a number of key concepts for multiliteracies instruction, both in terms of its theoretical underpinnings and its implementation in the classroom. Reflect on each of the multiliteracies concepts listed on the left-hand side of the table and decide which one(s) relate(s) to the focus of the four questions listed above, briefly explaining their relationship. Fill in only those boxes where you do see a relationship—leave the remainder of the boxes empty. You may want to revisit definitions of the five multiliteracies concepts by re-reading relevant sections of the Introduction and Chapter 1 before proceeding.

	Defining the Focus of Goals and Objectives	**Moving Beyond Functional Communication and Articulating the Role of Textual Learning**	**Identifying the Role of Assessment**
Dimensions of literacy			
Principles of literacy			
Meaning design			
Available Designs			
Pedagogical acts			

Part 2. Read the remainder of this chapter (i.e., until you reach the "Final Considerations" section) and then return to this activity, revising your answers in the table based on what you have read and how it has changed your understandings of the concepts in the table.

2.1 Defining the Focus of Goals and Objectives for Literacy Development

Although you have been introduced to how one goes about writing instructional goals and objectives for FL learning, the question still remains as to what the content of such statements should be in a program that prioritizes development of students' FL literacy. Indeed, designing goals and objectives in a way that reflects the theoretical underpinnings of the multiliteracies framework can be challenging, especially for novice teachers still in the midst of gaining a basic understanding of our expanded notion of literacy and of theoretical and pedagogical concepts such as those in the table in Learning Activity 2.4.

An additional challenge is that learning outcome statements in FL textbook materials often reflect the concepts and objectives of CLT and emphasize the development of functional abilities to communicate personal opinions and everyday needs. An example of this tendency can be seen on the opening page of an introductory-level French textbook chapter about everyday life and leisure activities, whose objectives read as follows: "You will talk about the weather, your recreational activities, and your routine. You will also learn to describe your abilities and express plans and wishes" (Terrell, Rogers, Kerr, & Spielmann, 2009, p. 73). This example reveals a heavy emphasis on oral interpersonal communication with no mention of interpretive (i.e., understanding written and spoken language in relation to course themes) or presentational (i.e., creation of written and spoken language in relation to course themes) communicative objectives. A perusal of the chapter reveals a focus on presenting and practicing linguistic functions for communicating about everyday life and leisure activities, accompanied by related lexical and grammatical elements (e.g., sports and leisure vocabulary, verbs for describing everyday activities and one's routine). Although the chapter does incorporate several short texts (a poem and three author-created texts about French culture), the texts do not serve interpretive purposes or act as the starting point for exploring how chapter themes are instantiated in the French-speaking world. Rather, the texts provide contextualized examples of targeted forms and linguistic functions and serve as a means of practicing the skill of reading, albeit reading of highly controlled passages. Thus, their use supports the assumption that understanding a text's language must come before understanding its meaning (Swaffar & Arens, 2005). Writing plays a minor role in the chapter, with the exception of a final activity that asks students to complete a letter to a French student who will attend their university, giving him or her advice on what clothes to pack, taking into account the climate, seasons, and typical university activities.

How might a focus on literacy as a curricular and course goal reorient the learning outcomes and content of the chapter described above? Kern (2004) explained it this way:

> An overarching goal of literacy can provide a unifying focus by drawing students' attention to the interactions among form, context, and function in all their uses of language—whether they are speaking, listening, reading, or writing . . . a focus on literacy removes the artificial separation of skills and content. (p. 7)

Regardless of the curricular level or course focus, Kern (2004) identified several common goals for a literacy-based curriculum: (1) preparing learners to interpret multiple forms of FL use in multiple contexts; (2) fostering communicative ability in the FL while also emphasizing the development of the ability to analyze, interpret, and transform discourse; (3) integrating communicative approaches to FL teaching with more analytic, text-based approaches; (4) incorporating a range of texts that broadly represent the signifying practices of a society; (5) paying attention to the relationships among particular textual genres, their purposes, and conventions of reading and writing in specific contexts; (6) problematizing discourse and providing learners with guidance in the thinking that goes into reading, writing, and speaking appropriately in specific contexts; (7) focusing on linguistic, cognitive, and social dimensions of language use in an integrated way; and (8) encouraging students to take an active, critical stance to the discourse conventions that we teach them.

A logical starting point for using these overarching literacy-oriented goals to determine curricular and course goals and objectives is to reflect on the nature of literacy as a linguistic, cognitive, and sociocultural concept. As Kern (2000) pointed out, individually, any one of the three dimensions gives just a partial view of literacy, whereas, taken together, the three dimensions complement one other and elucidate literacy's multidimensional character.

Traditionally, instructional goals (and, in particular, those of lower-level collegiate FL courses) have aligned most closely with the linguistic dimension of literacy, given the preoccupation with the acquisition of morphological, lexical, and syntactic features of the FL. Limiting instructional goals to linguistic elements deprives students of the opportunity to experience language in its range of uses and to deepen their understanding of the connections between language and culture (Kern, 2000). As you learned in the Introduction to this book, in the multiliteracies framework an expanded vision of the linguistic dimension of literacy includes the traditional focus of FL instruction, but also goes beyond it to include relationships between oral and written language and across different genres, language varieties, and styles. The cognitive dimension of literacy, or the mental strategies and processes that influence how learners construct meaning from texts, is the second element to be explicitly incorporated into instructional goals. Targeting this dimension means embracing a view of language learning not as mere decoding and encoding of information, but as engaging in a complex meaning-making process that, for language learners, requires more than knowledge of the code (i.e., grammar and vocabulary). Rather, it also involves having students learn strategies related to interacting with texts, including raising their awareness of the culturally situated nature of meaning making with texts, and facilitating goal setting, planning, and revision as they move from comprehension to production of texts. Finally, instructional goals should target the sociocultural dimension of literacy, or the conventions for creating and interacting with texts that are considered appropriate by a given discourse community. In other words, learners must be taught to navigate and evaluate cultural perspectives and communicative norms associated with the literacy practices of the FL discourse community (Kern, 2000).

After determining the focus of curricular or course goals, the next step in designing student learning outcomes is consideration of instructional objectives. Grounding objectives in the multiliteracies framework requires turning to the seven principles of literacy and the concept of meaning design, which "provide [guidance] in identifying what and how to teach, in order to support a general goal of reflective communication" (Kern, 2002, p. 22). (Reflective communication is informed by an awareness of the situated nature of language use.) Furthermore, the literacy principles of language use, conventions, and cultural knowledge, which form part of the Available Designs or resources students learn when interacting with FL texts, are taught in conjunction with the principles of interpretation, collaboration, problem-solving, and reflection, which are the learning processes in which students engage (Kern, 2000). By embracing these notions, instructional objectives shift from an emphasis on functional communication and the acquisition of language forms, "to the development of learners' ability to interpret and critically evaluate language use in a variety of spoken and written contexts" (Kern, 2000, pp. 304–305). The question still remains, however, as to how instructional objectives for FL learning can be written to incorporate the seven principles of literacy and meaning design and also avoid falling back into a functional skills orientation.

2.2 Moving Beyond Functional Communication and Articulating the Role of Textual Learning in Writing Goals and Objectives

Orienting one's instructional goals and objectives to carry out multiliteracies instruction involves an expanded view of literacy and, by extension, of communication, language use, and textual learning. Thus, it is necessary to re-envision the way that we as teachers articulate learning outcome statements to reflect the multi-dimensional nature of literacy, the seven principles of literacy, and the act of meaning design. As such, two specific elements of instruction that can be particularly challenging to re-envision are the roles of communicative language use and textual learning.

One preoccupation of multiliteracies instruction is reconciling the separation of teaching language as a means of communication from the teaching textual analysis, as typically seen in lower-level language courses versus advanced content-focused courses (Kern, 2000). In language courses, the consequences of this bifurcation may de-motivate students and limit their learning if the course is devoid of intellectually challenging content. Instead, aiming to reconcile this separation that impacts both ends of the curriculum, Kern argued for synthesizing these goals by "enveloping the 'textual' within a larger framework of the 'communicative'" (p. 5).

So how might we go about operationalizing this somewhat abstract idea of weaving together the communicative and the textual in writing instructional goals and objectives? To begin, doing so requires a reconceptualization of the CLT "four skills" orientation (speaking, listening, reading, and writing), given that this orientation leads to articulating goals and objectives related to discrete knowledge and behaviors rather than the interrelated language abilities (Kern, 2000). Instead, we foreground an integrative notion of communication in which linguistic modalities overlap and take on new dimensions. For example, reading and writing play roles not as mere support skills, but rather as cognitive and social processes that function as "a crucial hub where language, culture, and thought converge" (Kern, 2003, p. 48). Consequently, reading and writing facilitate students engaging in real literacy events through acts of text-focused meaning design. In other words, rather than function as ends in and of themselves, reading and writing now serve as means to other literacy-oriented ends.

As you learned in the Introduction, the National Standards for FL Learning offer a curricular vision that shares similarities and differences with the multiliteracies framework. One area of similarity is relevant to our focus on writing instructional goals and objectives. Arens (2008) offers the following explanation:

> The Standards emerge as a heuristic for interactions among the many aspects of the post-secondary curriculum, because they point the way to advanced literacies, beyond conversational language and past the marginalization of everyday culture often instantiated in traditional literary studies. Most specifically, the Standards outline how to join literary, cultural, and language studies and overcome the language/literature split . . . by stressing content-based instruction to be assessed for both content and language. (p. 35)

Beyond this shared view of the interwoven nature of language and content, the Standards' goal areas include a conceptualization of communication consistent with multiliteracies instruction:

> The Communication standard highlights language but does so by placing individual communication within the media, pragmatic, and sociocultural norms of a culture. It focuses not just on how to make messages in words but also how to send them, who they can be sent to or received from, and what status obtains for them. (Arens, 2010, p. 323)

In other words, communication is defined not only in terms of its linguistic dimension, but also in terms of its sociocultural dimension, including the literacy-oriented principles of language use, conventions, and cultural knowledge. In addition, within the Communication standard, language use is envisioned in a way that "explicitly move[s] us away from an orientation toward the four skills of listening, reading, speaking, writing . . . toward a focus on *interpersonal, interpretive,* and *presentational* modes—these latter two modes being clearly issues of literacy" (Kern, 2004, p. 8). Like Kern, Arens (2008) also named interpretive and presentational modes of communication as "critical to advanced problems of language literacy," citing examples such as register, complex language use, and politeness (p. 38).

Thus, the Standards provide concepts to articulate areas of student learning not based on linguistic skills but on specific, contextualized uses of language. Most clearly associated with multiliteracies instruction, interpretative communication is consistent with an interwoven notion of language use and textual content broadly conceived as well as the literacy-based learning processes of interpretation, collaboration, problem solving, and reflection. As Kern (2008) explained, the goal is not for students to arrive at normative, native-like interpretations, but to explore multiple meanings and understand the situated nature of their interpretations based on their attitudes, beliefs, and experiences.

In addition, presentational communication and the related notion of sharing information and ideas with an audience of listeners or readers reflect the design metaphor and the view of communication involving writer–reader and speaker–listener relationships. It is perhaps interpersonal communication and its emphasis in the Standards on the expression of feelings, emotions, and opinions that requires the most reinterpretation for multiliteracies instruction. Instead of focusing on students expressing their personal opinions about themes that may or may not be anchored in texts (e.g., explaining what you like to do for fun on the weekend), the multiliteracies framework shifts toward students' personal readings of texts based not only on feelings and opinions, but also on interpretive constraints associated with specific types of texts (Kern, 2000, 2008). As an example, in an introductory-level FL course, rather than designing a lesson limited to a functionally oriented objective of students describing preferences for weekend activities, the lesson might involve activities that build toward interpretive communication and identifying similarities and differences between their own preferences for weekend activities and those of members of the FL culture based on published survey results. This re-imagined notion of interpersonal communication is consistent with the learning processes of interpretation, collaboration, problem solving, and reflection.

In addition to redefining the role of communicative language use and its relation to instructional goals and objectives, the multiliteracies framework demands a different conceptualization of the role of textual learning in comparison to pedagogical approaches such as CLT. Texts no longer serve as springboards for practice of vocabulary and grammar or appear periodically (e.g., at the end of a textbook chapter) as a means of conveying cultural facts. Instead, they function as a vehicle for communicative language use and cultural inquiry as students analyze, interpret, and transform discourse and relate the world of the FL culture to their experience and thinking (Kern, 2000). These ideas may already be apparent to you in light of the discussion of the various modes of communication described in this section and the relation of each mode to textual learning. What may be less obvious to you, however, are the consequences of integrating this vision of textual learning into instructional goals and objectives. If, as Kern (2000) argued, texts are more than something to talk about, how should they be mapped onto student learning outcomes? What principles should be used to guide text selection?

Swaffar and Arens (2005) offered a succinct explanation of the role of textual learning in students' literacy development: "Students need to see the patterns of messages within cultural contexts of communication, textuality, and negotiation, to manage them and their implications in various situations" (pp. 40–41). But what sorts textual messages should be taught and on what basis? According to Byrnes, Maxim, and Norris (2010), text choice should be "first and foremost educational choices about what students can and should learn at a particular stage of the curriculum" rather than "motivated by a claimed responsiveness to student interest" (p. 59). Taken at face value, this statement seems counter-intuitive, insomuch that when attempting to map textual content onto a curriculum primarily focused on language development, teachers often turn first to texts that are relevant to students' cultures and identities based on their thematic content and perceived accessibility (e.g., contemporary music, videotexts, advertisements). However, as Arens (2010) explained, "the use of non-literary texts relevant to our students' interests and lives may exacerbate the famous gap between lower and upper divisions by taking one kind of culture for the lower division and another for the majors" (p. 321). This is not to say that non-literary texts should not play an important role in language courses; rather, that textual choice should not be guided primarily by considerations of thematic relevance to students' lives.

Instead, instructional goals and objectives should target the teaching of specific textual genres relevant to the FL and its discourse communities. Once again, by foregrounding the concept of genre, described in Chapter 1 as structuring culturally embedded communicative situations in a highly predictable pattern, the notion of integrating language use and content emerges since genres exist at the intersection of linguistic expression and social convention (Swaffar & Arens, 2005). Put differently, "genres perfor[m] acts of culture" (Arens, 2008, p. 45). Genre-focused textual learning sensitizes students to the logics (or obligatory and optional textual moves) associated with specific text types and how those logics impact meaning, a topic to be explored in greater detail in Chapters 5 and 6 in relation to the modalities of reading and writing.

A logic for guiding text choice in multiliteracies instruction that can be useful for articulating student learning outcomes is the notion of primary versus secondary discourses, or socially situated ways of using language and signs (Gee, 2011). Whereas *primary discourses* are often familial and private, involving meaning making in the home and with peers, *secondary discourses* are public and often formal, entailing language use in groups and institutions such as school, work, or religious entities. Byrnes, Crane, Maxim, and Sprang (2006) described the roles primary and secondary discourses play in a multiliteracies-oriented introductory-level FL curriculum:

> The majority of texts that represent Level I belong to the sphere of primary discourses characterized by informal communication between intimates on topics of common knowledge like personal information, food, housing, and travel. The most prominent and frequent genres on this level are casual conversations, picture stories involving narration about aspects of personal life, cartoons, and personal narratives. Nevertheless, already at this level, students are familiarized with genres that stand at the middle of the continuum of primary to secondary discourses and are introduced to secondary genres used in the discourses of public life such as ads for housing and travel found in newspapers, various service encounters, newspaper feature articles, and statistics on health care. (p. 93)

Notable in this description is that although text themes and types mesh well with students' lives and interests, this is not the basis for their choice. Rather, a principled selection is made based on a larger progression from texts reflecting primary discourses in lower-level language courses to texts reflecting secondary discourses in advanced-level courses. By identifying which genres will be used as models or topical bases for speaking and writing tasks in instructional units within a curricular level, unit- and lesson-level objectives (e.g., for interpretive communication) can be clarified and potentially used as a mechanism to bring about coherence across various sections of the same course.

At this point, before moving on to a discussion of assessment in multiliteracies instruction, it may be helpful to synthesize the ideas explained in this section regarding the articulation of instructional goals and objectives with a concrete illustration. To do so, recall the example of an introductory-level FL unit on everyday life and leisure activities, whose stated objectives included (1) talking about the weather, recreational activities, and personal routines; and (2) describing abilities and expressing plans and wishes. To better orient these objectives for multiliteracies instruction, concepts including the principles of literacy, meaning design, the modes of communication, and genre could be incorporated. A revised and expanded version of those objectives might read as follows: Students will (1) describe their daily activities and routines and compare them to those of people their age from the FL culture; (2) understand and produce short personal narratives about their plans and wishes for everyday life; and (3) present information to peers regarding weather and recreational activities in locales where the FL is used. To realize these objectives, students could analyze linguistic, schematic, audio, visual, and gestural Available Designs found in several textual genres (e.g., blog posting, personal ad, video weather report, survey) and interpret, collaborate, problem-solve, and reflect on the texts used. Meaning design would be emphasized as students move from analyzing language use and content in texts to creating their own texts. Do note that a certain degree of overlap exists in the functionally based objectives and the multiliteracies-oriented ones. However, the revised objectives are grounded in the three modes of communication, can be realized only through analysis of FL texts, and weave together communicative language use and textual learning in a way that the functionally based objectives do not.

Before moving on to consider assessment within the multiliteracies framework, complete Learning Activity 2.5, which gives you an opportunity to apply what you have learned about writing instructional goals and objectives focused on literacy development.

LEARNING ACTIVITY 2.5

Redesigning Instructional Goals and Objectives for Multiliteracies Instruction

Rewrite the following goals and objectives to reflect the premises of the multiliteracies framework. Incorporate concepts such as the dimensions and principles of literacy, meaning design, the modes of communication (interpersonal, interpretive, presentational), and genre into your revised statements. In addition, think about the role that communication and textual learning will play in the goal and objective statements. This activity may entail combining or reorganizing some of the objectives listed below. Note: Your objective statements need only contain a description of the behaviors demonstrating the knowledge or skills to be learned.

	Original Statements
Course Goals	By the end of this introductory-level language course, students will acquire basic skills in listening, speaking, reading, and writing and develop a basic awareness of the cultures being studied.
Course Objective 1: Speaking	A. Students will acquire the basics of pronunciation, vocabulary, and grammatical structures necessary for the expression of introductory needs and basic courtesy formula. B. Students will produce vocabulary relevant to the student's own environment and interests and to the culture(s) being studied.
Course Objective 2: Listening	A. Students will acquire vocabulary sufficient to comprehend basic information and expressions relevant to introductory needs and basic courtesy formula. B. Students will comprehend spoken language in situations where the context aids understanding.
Course Objective 3: Writing	A. Students will write meaningful sentences that include idiomatic expressions and reproduce memorized material in a meaningful way. B. Students will supply basic information (biographical, travel, etc.). C. Students will write short compositions.
Course Objective 4: Reading	A. Students will develop basic strategies and skills for reading non-technical texts of moderate difficulty. B. Students will work with a variety of reading materials.
Course Objective 5: Culture	A. Students will begin to be aware of cultural similarities and differences, cultural practices, and the relationship between language and cultural identity. B. Students will acquire some knowledge of the geography of the country/countries being studied. C. Students will be exposed to cultural realia.

2.3 Understanding the Role of Assessment in Multiliteracies Instruction

Although familiarity with the types and uses of assessments and the relation of assessment to instruction and learning outcomes is a useful starting point, a key question remains: Namely, what is the role of assessment in multiliteracies instruction? Once more, you will find that aligning instructional practices, in this case assessment, with the multiliteracies framework involves a shift in thinking from traditional approaches, which typically focus on summative tests and mastery of discrete forms or skills. Kern (2000) explained that although the goal of assessment in multiliteracies instruction entails familiar foci, such as knowledge of grammar and vocabulary and the ability to use the FL to fulfill specific communicative functions, it also goes far beyond those components. Assessment in a multiliteracies framework involves evaluating how learners interpret and produce meaning, understanding how learners analyze texts and the knowledge they gain from that analysis, and encouraging learners to reflect on form-meaning relationships, communicative intent, and links between language and culture. According to Kern (2000), this view of assessment boils down to measuring students' ability to think critically and creatively through language use. Evident in this conceptualization of assessment is the inclusion of the three dimensions of literacy—linguistic, sociocultural, and cognitive elements—and the idea that assessment practices, like instructional practices and goal setting, target the integration of language use and textual content to facilitate the design of meaning.

The following principles should be heeded when designing a literacy-based assessment and evaluation plan for a FL course or curriculum: Assessment should be (1) based on a broad view of language and literacy, (2) multi-dimensional in nature, and (3) interwoven with teaching and learning (Kern, 2000). Regarding the first principle, assessment practices have traditionally lagged behind instruction such that even when teaching goals and classroom activities have centered on expanded notions of communicative abilities, assessment has been carried out with narrowly conceived tools that do not always align with instruction and targeted learning outcomes. Street (1997) argued that this should not be the case in multiliteracies instruction:

> Assessment that reduce[s] literacy to a few simple and mechanistic skills fail[s] to do justice to the richness and complexity of actual literacy practices . . . We need curricula and assessment that are themselves rich and complex and based upon research into actual literacy practices. (p. 84)

In other words, assessment cannot be a one-shot venture in which students' literacy development is evaluated narrowly based on a single instance of comprehension or production; instead, students should have multiple opportunities to design meaning in the FL and demonstrate control of new Available Designs introduced through instruction. In addition, assessment should mirror "actual literacy practices" (Street, 1997, p. 84), so it should be meaningful and contextualized, reflecting language use in discourse communities.

In relation to the second principle, the need for a multidimensional notion of assessment, instructors should use a variety of language and literacy activities rather than rely solely on tests (Kern, 2000). In so doing, we gain multiple perspectives on our students' performance, including tools that target new understandings of multiple textual genres and involve both individual and joint performance through interpretation, collaboration, problem solving, and reflection. In practice, this may entail formative assessments such as written journals, concept maps, or self-assessment of oral participation alongside summative assessments like written quizzes or small-group writing or performance projects. It is important to note that the multiliteracies framework does not involve doing away entirely with traditional assessment tools like form-focused mechanical practice activities or exams; rather, they play a smaller role in the overall assessment plan (i.e., they are weighted more lightly than work such as projects or portfolios) and are used for formative purposes (Kern, 2000).

In addition, the third principle for multiliteracies-focused assessment urges that it not be divorced from teaching and learning. This notion is consistent with a larger trend in the FL profession during the past two decades that takes the concept of *washback* (i.e., that good tests will promote good instructional practices) a step further to seek a more intimate relation between instruction and assessment (Bachman, 2000). The multiliteracies framework is particularly well suited for carrying out such pedagogically oriented assessment for at least two reasons. First, the concept of meaning design, which forms the backbone of multiliteracies instruction, and the related notion of the Redesigned are consistent with the idea of the pedagogy–assessment relationship involving a process of creating and interpreting textual meaning and products. Second, the pedagogy at the heart of the multiliteracies framework (i.e., the four pedagogical acts of situated practice, overt instruction, critical framing, and transformed practice) includes multiple opportunities for use of varied assessment tools within the context of instruction, namely in relation to transformed practice activities. As described by the New London Group (1996), transformed practice can be understood as a return to situated practice with the following purpose:

> [To help learners] show that they can implement understandings acquired through Overt Instruction and Critical Framing in practices that help them simultaneously to apply and revise what they have learned. In Transformed Practice we are offered a place for situated, contextualized assessment of learners and the learning processes devised for them. (p. 87)

Examples of how the four pedagogical acts can be used to structure assessment can help to clarify these concepts. Returning to the illustration of an introductory-level FL unit on everyday life and leisure activities, whose revised objectives include students (1) describing their daily activities and routines and comparing them to those of people their age from the FL culture; (2) understanding and producing short personal narratives about their plans and wishes for everyday life; and (3) presenting information to peers regarding weather and recreational activities in locales where the FL is used, we now add a plan for both formative and summative assessment. Formative assessment components include the following:

- Situated practice. In relation to Objectives 1–3, students complete matrices to check comprehension of texts related to unit themes; in addition, in relation to Objectives 1 and 2, students write brief journaling assignments that expand on text-based activities; finally, students participate in self-assessment of oral participation in class using a rubric as well as written reflection in their native language;
- Overt instruction. For lexical items and grammatical points related to Objectives 1–3, students complete online machine-scorable workbook

assignments to verify comprehension of new structures; in addition, for text-based pre-reading activities, students prepare graphic organizers to activate schemata and vocabulary related to text themes;

- Critical framing. In relation to Objectives 1 and 2, students reflect on similarities and differences between practices and perspectives in their own culture versus the FL culture as viewed in texts introduced in class; these written reflections are part of journaling activities but, unlike the situated practice part of these assignments, they are written in the student's first language;
- Transformed practice. In relation to Objectives 1 and 2, students present either personal information or ideas about a classmate in short writing assignments and digital recordings modeled on written and videotexts analyzed in class.

In addition to these formative assessment tools, two summative assessments are used, which are described in Table 2.2.

TABLE 2.2 Sample Summative Assessment for an Elementary-Level FL Course

Summative Assessment Format	Activity
Oral Assessment	*Situated practice / Transformed practice:* Students work in pairs to describe a detailed travel itinerary for an ideal vacation (weather, activities, daily routine, and plans) in one location where the FL is used; classmates listen and ask questions, eventually voting on the location they judge most interesting to visit.
Written Assessment	*Critical framing:* Students respond to pre-listening questions in English about daily life in their culture versus the FL culture. *Situated practiced / Critical framing:* Students watch and respond to comprehension questions on a videotext of brief interviews on the street wherein three speakers of the FL describe everyday life and recreational activities in their culture; an expansion question asks students to compare their own daily routine to one of the individuals in the videotext in a short paragraph using the FL. *Situated practice:* Students read two travel guide excerpts and complete comprehension activities related to both the textual genre and the content of the texts. *Transformed practice / Overt instruction:* Students select a travel destination among those introduced in the travel guide excerpts and write an e-mail message wherein they ask a friend to join them on a vacation there, including detailed description of weather, activities, and plans. Before writing their e-mail message, as a pre-writing activity, students brainstorm useful vocabulary and action verbs and present those lexico–grammatical structures in a graphic organizer.

In summary, this plan reflects each principle of literacy-oriented assessment. In its scope, it represents a broad vision of language and literacy and a multidimensional view of evaluating students' comprehension and use of the FL. Traditional and alternative assessment tools are used, and assessment is conducted both in class and at home and includes individual and collaborative activities. Traditional tools for assessment find new roles; for example, mechanical language practice is relegated to a minor role outside class whereas the written examination is redefined using the four pedagogical acts. Finally, a common thread running throughout the assessment plan is the central role of texts in weaving together instructional and assessment activities; in fact, they are often one in the same. To further solidify your understanding of the relationships among assessment, text-based learning, and instructional goals and objectives from a multiliteracies perspective, complete Part 2 of Learning Activity 2.4.

3. FINAL CONSIDERATIONS

In this chapter, we have defined instructional goals and objectives and their relevance for FL teaching and learning, described various types and purposes for assessment, and established the relationship among student learning outcomes (i.e., goals and objectives), assessment, and instruction as posited in the notion of backward design. In addition, we presented arguments that speak to the importance of establishing carefully articulated goals and objectives for FL instruction and of crafting an appropriate assessment plan that is well aligned with learning outcomes for teachers and students, and determined in light of larger curricular considerations.

The second half of this chapter delved into the challenging question of how instructional goals and objectives and assessment practices are instantiated in the multiliteracies framework. Building on knowledge about literacy development to which you were introduced in the Introduction and Chapter 1, we established the relevance of several literacy-oriented concepts (dimensions of literacy, principles of literacy, meaning design, modes of communication, textual genres) for writing student learning outcome statements and aligning assessment and instructional practices. Based on a number of illustrations and your participation in Learning Activities in this chapter, you should now be more familiar with differences between CLT-oriented and multiliteracies-based instruction and assessment and the shift in pedagogical thinking that is necessary to put the multiliteracies framework into practice.

The treatment of instructional goals and objectives and, to a greater extent, assessment offered in this chapter is only an introduction to these critical elements. Subsequent chapters will solidify and expand your understanding of how these components function in the context of different areas of instruction—the Available Designs of grammar and vocabulary (Chapter 3), oral language use (Chapter 4), meaning design centered on the modalities of reading, writing, and listening/viewing (Chapters 5 through 7), and development of new literacies through Web 2.0 tools (Chapter 8). It is our intention to foreground the discussion of instructional goals and objectives and assessment practices to underscore their importance and potential contribution for maximizing students' literacy development.

4. TRANSFORMING KNOWLEDGE

4.1 Reflective Journal Entry

After reading the current chapter and completing the related Learning Activities, you most likely have a different understanding of the multiliteracies framework and its relevance for FL teaching and learning than you did previously. Return now to Learning Activity 1.5 in Chapter 1, in which you completed a concept map that illustrated how key components of the multiliteracies framework fit together. How have your understandings of the relationships among the concepts in your map changed? Are there any new concepts that you wish to incorporate, particularly in relation to instructional goals and objectives and assessment practices? The goal of this activity is for you to revise your concept map to reflect the evolution of what you know about multiliteracies instruction.

4.2 Researching the Role of Goals, Objectives, and Assessment in Text-Based FL Learning

As you have learned to this point, FL texts play a critical role in both multiliteracies instruction and assessment practices. In his 2008 article entitled "Making connections through texts in language teaching," Kern argued for the importance of textual analysis for both meaning design and making connections between language and culture as well as with other disciplines. Included in the appendix of the article (pp. 380–386) are sample projects that illustrate how text-based activities can be integrated with course themes such as media, colonialism, cultural transmission, and crime. First, read Kern's article (see References for publication information), including the Appendix. Next, select one of the following projects from the Appendix—1, 2, 3, or 5—and review its goals and procedures. Next, reflect on the following questions in relation to the project:

1. What types of unit-level objectives would align with this project?
2. Which multiliteracies concepts and instructional practices do you see embodied in the project? Explain how these concepts are put into practice.
3. How well would this project fit into the curriculum of the FL course that you are teaching and what revisions to the project would you make if you were to include it in your course (and why)?

Finally, based on your responses to these questions, prepare a report in which you (1) describe how this project instantiates multiliteracies instruction and assessment practices, and (2) critique the suitability of the project for your educational context.

Key Resources

Department of German. (2011). Curriculum. *Georgetown University*. Retrieved from http://german.georgetown.edu/undergraduate/curriculum/

This web site contains links to the Georgetown University undergraduate German program's ongoing curricular renewal project, which is literacy and genre oriented and task based. The site includes curricular goals, level-specific objectives, assessment practices, and course syllabi.

Hall, J. K. (2001). *Methods for teaching foreign languages: Creating a community of learners in the classroom*. Upper Saddle River, NJ: Prentice Hall.

Chapter 5, "Planning Instruction and Assessment," contains a discussion of instructional planning at the course, unit, and lesson level and an explanation of the role of goals and objectives in FL teaching and learning. An overview of assessment is presented, including dimensions of assessment, traditional and alternative assessment tools, and principles for designing effective assessment tools. The pedagogical approaches foregrounded in this chapter are both Standards and literacy based.

Kern, R. (2000). *Literacy and language teaching*. Oxford, England: Oxford University Press.

Chapter 9, "Evaluating Learners' Performance," presents an overview of principles for assessment and evaluation practices in literacy-based FL teaching. Discussion includes issues of validity and reliability in assessment, a model for assessment and evaluation of reading and writing, and examples of scoring rubrics.

For Further Reading

Byrnes, H., Maxim, H. H., & Norris, J. (2010). Realizing advanced foreign language writing development in collegiate education: Curricular design, pedagogy, assessment. *Modern Language Journal*, 94, Supplement, 1–221.

Kern, R. (2004). Literacy and advanced foreign language learning: Rethinking the curriculum. In H. Byrnes & H. H. Maxim (Eds.), *Advanced foreign language learning: A challenge to college programs* (pp. 2–18). Boston, MA: Heinle.

CHAPTER 3

Reconceptualizing Grammar and Vocabulary as Meaning-Making Resources

For many foreign language (FL) instructors, grammar and vocabulary are the most important parts of language learning; they form the foundation for acquiring all other aspects of the language, including pronunciation, oral expression, reading and listening comprehension, and writing. Grammar and vocabulary are certainly important building blocks for developing not only linguistic accuracy, but also overall fluency, both of which contribute to learners' ability to understand and use language orally and in writing. Indeed, second language acquisition (SLA) research confirms that lexical and grammatical knowledge is crucial to development of FL proficiency and persistence in FL study (e.g., Broady, 2008; Nation, 2001; Spada, 2011; Zhang, 2012).

Yet despite—or perhaps because of—their importance, many FL instructors find teaching grammar and vocabulary effectively to be the most challenging part of their job. For some teachers, who may themselves have learned language forms through memorization of rules or word lists, it is difficult to think about how to teach grammar and vocabulary in ways that focus simultaneously on form and meaning. Moreover, it may be hard to imagine that students can interact with FL texts before they have mastered an adequate number of a language's formal features. In fact, you may already be asking yourself, after learning about the multiliteracies approach in the Introduction and in Chapter 1, how grammar and vocabulary instruction can possibly take place within a text-based lower-level FL curriculum. Such concerns often arise from exposure to or reliance on traditional, grammar-based approaches to language teaching, grounded in methods such as grammar–translation and audiolingualism, and have lived on in the current, or weak, version of communicative language teaching (CLT). Indeed, in rule-driven FL textbooks and teaching approaches, grammar and vocabulary are often presented in neutral dialogues created by textbook authors; grammar and vocabulary are developed separately from other skills, such as reading or writing; learning language forms is linked to formal accuracy; and vocabulary is memorized in lists before being put to active use (Swaffar & Arens, 2005).

This traditional view of teaching and learning language forms reflects the beliefs of many FL students and instructors and shapes the way grammar and vocabulary are taught. For example, Schulz (1998, 2001) reported that U.S. and Colombian university students believe that grammar learning is essential to mastery, expect to be corrected by their teachers, and think about grammar rules when using the language in communicative activities. She also found that instructors believe grammar learning is important, although slightly less so than students. Jean and Simard's (2011) survey of Quebecois high school students and teachers yielded similar results. They furthermore found that both groups see grammar as a necessary evil—they do not like learning or teaching grammar but acknowledge its importance. Likewise, Simon and Taverniers (2011) reported that advanced Dutch speaking learners of English consider vocabulary learning to be highly important because vocabulary errors can easily cause breakdowns in communication.

We agree that grammar and vocabulary play a crucial role in FL learning and recognize the importance of meeting students' expectations related to instruction. Yet we believe that these aims can be met by focusing simultaneously on language forms and culturally authentic textual content. Indeed, studies investigating students' perceptions of contextualized grammar and vocabulary learning suggest that this is feasible (Bournot-Trites & Séror, 2003; Manley & Calk, 1997; McQuillan, 1994). This research reports that students recognize the contribution of textual interaction to learning language forms and perceive grammar and vocabulary instruction as beneficial to increased linguistic accuracy as well as writing competence. Additionally, this research suggests the need for an integrated instructional approach to grammar and vocabulary teaching grounded within FL texts.

The purpose of this chapter is, therefore, to reconsider the role of grammar and vocabulary in lower-level language courses by moving beyond a mastery-oriented view to a meaning-oriented view in which grammar and vocabulary are two among the multiple linguistic, cultural, and social resources that learners draw on to understand and create texts. In the "Conceptual Background" section, we present key concepts related to grammar and vocabulary, review relevant SLA research, including identification of issues common to grammar and vocabulary teaching and learning, and then consider the role of language forms within the multiliteracies framework. In the "Pedagogical Applications" section, we first review how language forms are typically presented in commercially available textbooks and identify shortcomings of these materials; we then turn to an overview of text-based approaches to teaching and assessing grammar and vocabulary. Finally, we present a template for designing instruction of language forms following the multiliteracies framework and walk through a sample lesson plan and assessments based on this model. By the end of this chapter, you will have a different perspective on the role of texts in teaching grammar and vocabulary and learn how the multiliteracies approach can meet students' and instructors' needs for explicit instruction of FL forms while simultaneously focusing on culturally authentic content. To prepare to interact with the content of this chapter, complete Learning Activity 3.1.

LEARNING ACTIVITY 3.1

Finish the Thought

To activate your background knowledge and reflect on your beliefs about grammar and vocabulary learning, complete the following sentences based on your FL learning experiences.

1. When I was a beginning language learner, my instructors taught grammar and vocabulary by . . .
2. The most effective techniques my instructors used in teaching FL grammar and vocabulary were . . . because . . .
3. The least effective techniques my instructors used in teaching FL grammar and vocabulary were . . . because . . .
4. When I was a beginning language learner, the strategies I used to learn grammar and vocabulary were . . .
5. The most effective strategy I remember using to learn FL grammar and vocabulary was . . . because . . .
6. The least effective strategy I remember using to learn FL grammar and vocabulary was . . . because . . .

Finally, reflect on the following questions: Taken as a whole, what do your statements say about how you view the teaching and learning of language forms? What is the best way to teach and learn grammar and vocabulary? Do your experiences and beliefs reflect the traditional approach to grammar teaching and learning mentioned above? Do your experiences and beliefs reflect any of the literacy-based concepts you have learned up to this point?

1. CONCEPTUAL BACKGROUND

This section provides an overview of SLA research on grammar and vocabulary. We begin by considering key concepts and definitions related to grammar and vocabulary and then focus on the effects of implicit and explicit instruction on the acquisition of language forms. With this background established, we then explore various perspectives on explicit grammar and vocabulary instruction, including teaching forms in isolation or in a meaningful context, deductive and inductive approaches, and the role of output. This research review provides a foundation for considering form-focused instruction in the multiliteracies framework and the role of grammar and vocabulary in the interpretation and creation of FL texts.

1.1 Defining Grammar and Vocabulary

Grammar and vocabulary are crucial components of any FL curriculum, and they are essential to fluent and accurate expression in a FL. It is therefore important to understand what grammar and vocabulary are and what knowledge of these language features entails. Traditionally, *grammar* has been defined prescriptively as "what one should and should not say in order to speak and write a language 'correctly'" (Katz & Blyth, 2007, p. 264). This definition implies that grammar learning involves memorization of rules and a focus on accurate production of forms. *Vocabulary* has been similarly defined in terms of accuracy, with the focus on retention or memorization of words in isolation without any connection to their use in context. Yet with new discoveries regarding the acquisition of formal language features, prescriptive definitions of grammar and vocabulary are no longer adequate. For example, Broady (2008) stated that "'vocabulary knowledge' is no longer assumed to be simple retention of words or recognition of their meaning, or somehow divorced from other language knowledge or processes" (p. 264), and the same can be said for grammar.

In SLA research, less prescriptively oriented concepts include explicit and implicit knowledge of language forms and the multidimensional nature of word knowledge. *Explicit knowledge* is an understanding of language forms that students can consciously learn and then explain to others. In contrast, *implicit knowledge* is unconscious, used in spontaneous conversation, and not easily explained (Spada & Tomita, 2010). The contrast between explicit and implicit knowledge becomes clear if we consider how native speakers know their language. As a native speaker of English, for instance, you may have implicit knowledge that allows you to use with ease subordinate clauses headed by a preposition (e.g., *Here's the book to which I was referring.*), but you may not have the explicit knowledge that allows you to explain what a subordinate clause is, why the preposition comes before the relative pronoun, or why there is even a preposition in the sentence at all.

Related to explicit and implicit knowledge are productive and receptive understandings of language forms. When learners have *productive knowledge,* they can actively use a given language form orally or in writing; when they have *receptive knowledge,* they are able to understand the structure and meaning of a given language form without necessarily being able to produce it. Often learners understand language forms implicitly without being able to articulate that understanding explicitly. Likewise, receptive knowledge of language forms is often more easily acquired than productive knowledge (Sonbul & Schmitt, 2010).

Because FL learning usually involves classroom instruction, we tend to focus more on explicit knowledge because it is easier to teach and assess. When we define grammar and vocabulary prescriptively, we place primary importance on explicit knowledge and the ability to understand and explain language rules. Alternatively, if we consider grammar and vocabulary within the context of other language knowledge and processes, we move away from a purely prescriptive understanding of language forms and emphasize both implicit and explicit learning.

Just as prescriptively oriented definitions of grammar focus on rule memorization, similar definitions of vocabulary focus on word memorization. Such definitions suggest there is a one-to-one correspondence between a word and its meaning, and that vocabulary knowledge entails understanding this correspondence as well as the correct spelling of the word in question. Yet word knowledge is more complex than the prescriptive definition suggests. According to Nation (2001), vocabulary knowledge is multidimensional: It involves understanding a word's form (spelling, pronunciation, morphology), its meaning or meanings (literal, figurative, implied), and its use (grammatical function, frequency, formality, etc.). These aspects of word knowledge, which combine productive and receptive understanding, "are interrelated, and are holistically connected" (Schmitt, 2010, p. 18). A multidimensional knowledge of words also includes understanding fixed expressions, phrases, and relationships between words (Lewis, 1993; McCarthy, 1984). For example, when considered in isolation, the word *jerk* is ambiguous: It could be a verb or a noun, and it has multiple meanings. When used as a verb, *jerk* can refer to a short, quick pulling motion as in *He jerked the lawn mower to get it started.* Yet in the phrase *He really jerked me around,* the verb takes on a figurative meaning related to treating someone badly by being underhanded. Likewise, when used as a noun, *jerk* can have two meanings: It can refer to a short, sharp, sudden movement, as in *The lawn mower started with a jerk,* and it can also refer to an obnoxious person, as in *He has a reputation for being a real jerk.* To further your understanding of the concept of multidimensional word knowledge, complete Learning Activity 3.2.

LEARNING ACTIVITY 3.2

Reflecting on Multidimensional Word Knowledge

Look at the descriptions of women's and men's clothing in the tables below. Underline vocabulary words in the descriptions that are similar to those presented in a typical introductory FL textbook chapter focused on clothing. Circle words that are different from those presented in a typical introductory FL textbook.

Long Tankdress	The Jessie Sandal	Silk Peplum Top
The comfort of your favorite tank extended into a slouchy, knee-slit maxidress? Yes, please.	A modern take on the traditional leather gladiator, without the hassle of any buckles or ties—easy on, easy go.	Wear this peplum-style top with jeans, under a blazer, or with a cardigan (basically, anything) to add a bit of easy femininity.

Source: www.madewell.com.

Cotton Polo	Ludlow Club Sportcoat	Broken-In Chino
Knit in the same cotton as our tees, this polo is the best way to get away with wearing a T-shirt to "collar-required" places.	Crafted in world-class Italian wool, our navy blazer is cut in our trim Ludlow fit and has traditional details like brass anchor buttons and a patch pocket for a vintage feel.	A little worn and a little faded, they're made from heavily washed cotton twill to give them a vintage look with the timeworn characteristics of a well-aged pair of jeans.

Source: www.jcrew.com

How are clothing-related vocabulary words usually presented in an introductory FL textbook? Are those presentations different from what you see in the descriptions above? Would knowledge of typical textbook clothing vocabulary prepare learners to read descriptions such as those in the table? How does the context of the descriptions help you understand what the clothing items are like? Are there meanings or relationships between words that become clear because of the context? Are there words that would mean something different if they were not used in the context of these clothing descriptions?

Although this discussion of the definitions of grammar and vocabulary is by no means exhaustive, it should give you an idea of the complexities of these linguistic resources and why an exclusive focus on learning prescriptive rules and word lists falls short. To provide empirical support for this idea, we turn now to SLA research related to how grammar and vocabulary are best learned in light of these definitions, focusing in particular on investigations into implicit and explicit instructional approaches and their effects on FL learning.

1.2 The Case for Teaching Language Forms: Implicit Versus Explicit Instruction

As we stated at the start of this chapter, many instructors believe that grammar and vocabulary are the most important aspects of language to teach FL learners, and the teaching of language forms has a long and important history. Prior to the development of communicative approaches, language teaching meant teaching grammar, and grammar teaching meant teaching rules. This focus was evident in the grammar–translation method, which included rule explanation, memorization, and translation from the FL into the first language and vice versa; and the audiolingual method, which included habit formation through drilling, memorization of structural patterns, and repetition of language forms. Both methods were synthetic in that they focused on parts of the language in isolation; neither was concerned with developing learners' ability to communicate independently in the language (Nassaji & Fotos, 2011). Indeed, these methods were ultimately considered insufficient because they did not meet learners' communicative needs. Moreover, with developments in SLA research came the understanding that language is not acquired in a discrete, linear fashion. Instead, the acquisition of a second language is a developmental process that follows systematic patterns and sequences (e.g., Ellis, 2002; Long & Crookes, 1992; Long & Robinson, 1998).

The advent of CLT meant a shift away from an exclusive focus on language forms toward meaning-based communication. Informed by the concept of communicative competence as well as Krashen's (1981, 1985) work suggesting that FLs are acquired implicitly and unconsciously through exposure to large amounts of comprehensible input, proponents of the strong version of CLT argued that language was learned implicitly through communication with no explicit attention to forms. Nonetheless, empirical evidence suggests that even immersion environments, with their rich opportunities for implicit learning, are not sufficient for learners to acquire many linguistic features fully (e.g., Harley & Swain, 1984; Lapkin, Hart, & Swain, 1991; Swain, 1985).

SLA research shows us that approaches to teaching language forms focused exclusively on grammar or exclusively on communication are both inadequate. So where does this leave us? Published reviews of studies related to implicit and explicit teaching and learning support the idea that some classroom instruction related to language forms is indeed necessary and, furthermore, that this instruction should take place within a meaningful context (Broady, 2008; Nation, 2011; Norris & Ortega, 2001; Spada & Tomita, 2010). With respect to grammar, explicit instruction results in linguistic gains that are sustained over time (Norris & Ortega, 2001; Spada & Tomita, 2010) and "there is increasing evidence that instruction, including explicit FFI [form-focused instruction], can positively contribute to unanalyzed spontaneous production, its benefits not being restricted to controlled/analyzed L2 knowledge" (Spada, 2011, p. 233). With respect to vocabulary, repetition (e.g., seeing and using a word multiple times) in combination with instruction seems to play an important role in acquiring vocabulary, and some studies show that learners engage in deeper processing of vocabulary when they make a range of connections with previous knowledge and use new words in meaningful ways (Broady, 2008, p. 261). Finally, and important for considering the role of grammar and vocabulary from a multiliteracies perspective, the research suggests that explicit instruction grounded in a meaningful context is more effective than explicit instruction of forms in isolation (e.g., Doughty & Williams, 1998; Laufer & Girsai, 2008; Spada & Lightbown, 2008). It is to a discussion of research on explicit meaning-focused instruction of forms that we now turn.

1.3 Form-Focused Instruction = Meaning-Focused Instruction

For a number of years, researchers and practitioners have underscored the need to teach grammar and vocabulary within a communicative context. The merging of form and meaning in classroom contexts is referred to as focus on form (FonF), form-focused instruction, or integrated form-focused instruction. *Form-focused instruction* differs from traditional grammar activities and from explicit instruction of forms in isolation because it "entails a prerequisite engagement in meaning before attention to linguistic features can be expected to be effective . . . the learner's attention is drawn precisely to a linguistic feature as necessitated by a communicative demand" (Doughty & Williams, 1998, p. 3). Form-focused instruction can be either *incidental,* by drawing learners' attention to a form as it arises in communication (Long, 1991), or *planned,* by drawing learners' attention to pre-selected forms within a meaningful context (Doughty & Williams, 1998; Ellis, 2001). SLA research related to planned form-focused instruction provides evidence of its effectiveness for both grammar and vocabulary development. Several strands of research exist, and we briefly review three of them before considering the role of explicit, meaning-based instruction of language forms from a multiliteracies perspective.

One type of planned focus on form is the inductive presentation of grammar. *Inductive approaches* focus on meaning first, then on form: Grammar is usually presented in a meaningful context intended to highlight the targeted form and draw students' attention to linguistic patterns. In contrast, *deductive approaches* to grammar instruction involve direct teacher explanation of rules followed by related examples and mechanical exercises. Although both approaches have supporters and detractors, several research studies point to the effectiveness of inductive over deductive presentation of grammar. Much of this research investigates the effect of guided induction, in which learners see a language form in context and then, through leading questions and interactions with the instructor, hypothesize, reflect, and collaborate to discover grammatical patterns and explanations themselves. At introductory levels, FL learners who were exposed to grammatical forms through guided induction outperformed those who learned forms deductively on short-term and long-term written tests (Herron & Tomasello, 1992; Haight, Herron, & Cole, 2007). In a similar study at the advanced level, both groups of learners performed similarly on short-term tests, but the guided induction group outperformed the deductive group on long-term tests (Dotson, 2010). Finally, in a study investigating the effects of content-enhanced instruction and focus on form on the acquisition of grammar, vocabulary, and content knowledge, Grim (2008) found that beginning FL students who were encouraged to notice targeted forms in a meaningful context performed better on grammar and vocabulary tests than those who did not. The results of these studies suggest that a pedagogical framework consistent with the inductive approach is important for learners' acquisition of language forms.

A second strand of SLA research on planned form-focused instruction explores the relationship between reading comprehension and knowledge of language forms. In general, this research shows that grammatical and lexical knowledge correlate strongly with reading comprehension and, moreover, that a combination of instructional activities that focus on both implicit and explicit learning through reading are most effective for increasing grammar and vocabulary knowledge (e.g., Zhang, 2012). For instance, Sonbul and Schmitt (2010) found that a combination of implicit and explicit learning was effective for reading comprehension. In their study, learners were subjected to a "read only" condition—silent reading with no explicit instruction—or a "read plus" condition—silent reading in conjunction with explicit explanation of vocabulary words. Although both groups showed gains in vocabulary learning, learners in the read only condition showed very little gain in knowledge related to recall of word meaning and form, whereas learners in the read plus condition showed higher vocabulary gains in the ability to recall word form and meaning and to recognize word meaning. Likewise, Ellis (2006), investigating the grammatical knowledge of collegiate learners of English as a second language (ESL), found that both implicit and explicit knowledge of grammar were related to overall language proficiency, with explicit knowledge correlating more strongly with proficiency in reading and writing than implicit knowledge. These results not only underscore the important relationship between reading and implicit and explicit knowledge of language forms, but also suggest that explicit attention to grammar and vocabulary while interacting with texts is essential for such learning.

Finally, SLA research related to form–meaning instruction highlights the importance of production tasks for the acquisition of language forms. Overall, studies in this area show that learners who perform production tasks have greater vocabulary gains than those who do not (Atay & Kurt, 2006; Huang, Eslami, & Willson, 2012). Moreover, learners who read in a variety of textual genres (expository, narrative) and complete a variety of output tasks (fill-in-the-blank, sentence completion, composition writing) tend to have higher gains in vocabulary learning than those who do not (Huang, Eslami, & Willson, 2012). Regarding the importance of production tasks on grammar learning, Reinders (2009) investigated the correct use of negative adverbs among adult ESL learners in three types of production tasks: dictation, individual written story retelling, and collaborative written story retelling. He found that all three tasks had an effect on the correct use and acquisition of targeted grammatical forms. Taken together, this research suggests that in addition to elaborating form–meaning connections while reading, instruction should include post-reading production activities to increase grammar and vocabulary gains.

The SLA research summarized here may be a lot for you to digest, but our hope is that you now possess a general understanding of the importance of form-focused instruction and how it informs grammar and vocabulary teaching. To summarize, this research supports the idea that language forms taught in a meaningful context are more easily and effectively learned than language forms taught in isolation. Moreover, grammar and vocabulary can be taught meaningfully and effectively at multiple points in the reading (or listening or viewing) process: when introducing new forms through an inductive approach, when carrying out reading tasks, or when completing post-reading production tasks. These conclusions confirm that language forms "should never be taught as an end in [themselves] but always with reference to meaning, social factors, or discourse—or a combination of these factors" (Celce-Murcia, 1991, pp. 466–467). The research on form-focused instruction is, therefore, incompatible with the grammar-based approaches described earlier. Instead, the research points to the value of a literacy-oriented approach to grammar and vocabulary instruction grounded in texts. Learning Activity 3.3 will help prepare you to read about the role of language forms in the multiliteracies framework.

LEARNING ACTIVITY 3.3

Redefining Grammar and Vocabulary

Part 1. To refresh your memory about grammar, vocabulary, and the multiliteracies framework and to help you predict the content of the next section of the chapter, begin by completing activities 1–3.

1. Revisit the traditional definitions of grammar and vocabulary presented at the start of the "Conceptual Background" section and list key words you associate with these definitions.

2. How do you think grammar and vocabulary will be defined from a multiliteracies perspective? Brainstorm a second set of key words related to this definition.
3. Look at the list of multiliteracies-based concepts you read about in Chapter 1 provided below. Circle the concepts you think will be relevant to the definition of grammar and vocabulary developed in the next part of the "Conceptual Background" section.

   Literacy / Dimensions of literacy / Meaning design / Linguistic Available Designs / Schematic Available Designs / Language use / Conventions / Cultural knowledge / Interpretation / Collaboration / Problem solving / Reflection / Situated practice / Overt instruction / Critical framing / Transformed practice

Part 2. After you read Section 1.4 of the "Conceptual Background" section, revisit your answers to activities 1–3. Were your ideas about how grammar and vocabulary are defined from a multiliteracies perspective correct? Do you need to add to or delete from the list of key words you brainstormed in activity 2? Should you delete or add to any of the concepts you circled in activity 3?

1.4 Grammar, Vocabulary, and the Multiliteracies Framework

The prescriptive definition of grammar and vocabulary provided at the beginning of the "Conceptual Background" section suggests that language forms are learned through memorization of rules and word lists, that individual words and rules are learned in isolation without considering their relationship to other parts of language, and that knowledge of forms must precede textual interpretation or creation. As you probably already predicted in Learning Activity 3.3, this prescriptive definition is inconsistent with the multiliteracies framework. From a multiliteracies perspective, learning entails discovering form–meaning relationships in texts and how these relationships reflect conventions of language use within certain sociocultural contexts (Kern, 2000). Grammar and vocabulary are two linguistic Available Designs, or the linguistic, social, and cultural resources that influence meaning making. These resources help learners engage in the act of meaning design, which is a dynamic process of discovering form–meaning connections through interpreting and creating written, oral, visual, audiovisual, and digital texts. What distinguishes this perspective from others, such as grammar-based approaches or the current version of CLT, is that language forms are conceptualized as "tool[s] or resource[s] to be used in the comprehension and creation of oral and written discourse rather than something to be learned as an end in itself" (Celce-Murcia, 1991, p. 466). Knowledge of grammar thus entails understanding not only rules, but also relationships between parts of sentences or discourse and how structures signal these relationships. Likewise, knowledge of vocabulary goes beyond definitions of isolated words provided in a dictionary or textbook glossary to encompass an understanding of how words function in context and the culturally situated meanings with which they are associated.

Relationships between parts of sentences and discourse are clearly expressed in the following example, presented earlier in this chapter: *Here's the book to which I was referring*. Not only does the subordinate clause signal a relationship to the noun in the main clause, the use of the article *the* in the main clause indicates a relationship to something previously mentioned in the discourse, namely *the book*. Taken out of context, these relationships are harder to see, but in a conversation, they are obvious. Imagine that you and your professor have a conversation after class about something you did not understand and your professor suggests that you consult a certain book to help clarify things. The next day, you go to see your professor during office hours, and upon seeing you, he or she says "Oh, John, here's the book to which I was referring yesterday," and he or she elaborates by indicating where in the book you might find the answer to your question.

As an example of the contextualized nature of vocabulary, consider the concept of dinner. This concept is tied to the time of day at which people typically eat, the duration of the meal, where the meal takes place, how the meal is presented, and what one eats; each of these notions varies across and within cultures. For instance, in the United States dinner is the main meal of the day, and while a common time to eat dinner during the week is 6:00 pm, on holidays or Sundays, dinner might take place in the early afternoon. In France, dinner is sometimes a lighter meal than lunch, which for many is the main meal of the day, and it is commonly served at 8:00 pm or later. In the United States the evening meal tends to be rather brief and most parts of the meal are served at once; in France the evening meal can last more than an hour and parts of the meal may be presented sequentially in courses. In the United States dinner is sometimes eaten in front of the TV or at a kitchen island; in France dinner is most often eaten at the dining table. Finally, an American dinner often consists of a main dish, a vegetable, and a starch; in France, dinner usually includes a main dish, salad, bread, and cheese. These general statements about dinner in the United States and France underscore that dinner is more than just a word; it is a culturally embedded concept with multiple meanings that vary from country to country, family to family. These meanings are revealed only when one is familiar with the specific sociocultural context in which the concept is used and understood.

Grammar and vocabulary conceptualized in this way fall under the literacy principle of language use, which is always contextualized, involves linguistic and sociocultural knowledge, and occurs in the FL classroom through encounters with texts. Language use also includes the linguistic Available Designs of writing and phonetic systems, coherence, and cohesion; grammar and vocabulary are linked to each of these. For instance, in the *Time* magazine cover depicted in Chapter 1, we saw that the text's coherence was dependent on relationships between words in a headline and its subheading, and its cohesion was dependent on relationships between the pronoun *their* and other grammatical and lexical features of the text. Grammar and vocabulary are also linked to the literacy principle of conventions and are thus crucial to understanding textual organization and the features of various genres. For instance, returning to the magazine cover example in Chapter 1, the absence of verbs in headlines is an important convention in journalistic prose. By adopting this broader conceptualization of language forms, it is easy to understand that reading, writing, viewing, and listening to whole texts allows learners to see how grammar and vocabulary function in context to express linguistic relationships and contribute to the overall structure of a particular genre. Moreover, as these examples show, grammar and vocabulary are not isolated linguistic features, but rather interact with one another in complex ways.

In addition to being linked to the literacy principles of language use and conventions, the Available Designs of grammar and vocabulary also play a role within the linguistic, cognitive, and sociocultural dimensions of literacy. As you read in the Introduction, the linguistic dimension of literacy includes knowledge related to syntactic, morphological, and lexical features and knowledge about how these features can be combined to create sentences and units of discourse (Kern, 2000). This dimension is clearly tied to the literacy-based principles of language use and conventions and thus to grammar and vocabulary. The cognitive dimension of literacy involves the ability to use strategies to establish connections between pieces of information and to interpret and create texts (Kucer, 2009). For example, inductive approaches to teaching linguistic forms engage learners in hypothesizing about and evaluating grammatical and lexical patterns found in contextualized language samples. This process connects with the cognitive dimension of literacy as learners use meaning-making resources to create new knowledge. Finally, grammar and vocabulary are relevant for the sociocultural dimension of literacy because their meaning and use are socially constructed and are culturally dependent (Kucer, 2009), as was evident in the dinner example provided earlier.

An important implication of a multiliteracies perspective on grammar and vocabulary is that the focus of instruction shifts from one of mastery to one of meaningful language use. These Available Designs are discovered within the context of texts, are incorporated into learners' existing knowledge, and are transformed to make meaning in new ways. As such, grammar and vocabulary help learners engage in the act of meaning design. Empirical evidence shows that such text-based practices do not impede grammatical and lexical development and instead help further it. For instance, Maxim (2002, 2006), who studied a comparison group in which class time was spent carrying out communicative language practice and a treatment group in which half of class time was spent reading a full-length romance novel and the other half was spent completing communicative language practice, found that students in the treatment group fared just as well on language-focused exams as those in the comparison group. Herron and Seay (1991) found similar results in their study of the effects of authentic audio texts on listening comprehension. There were no significant differences in grammar and vocabulary quiz scores between students who spent approximately half class time listening to authentic audio segments and the other half completing communicative language practice and students who spent the entire class time completing communicative language practice activities. Taken together, this research, along with the SLA research reviewed earlier, sends the clear message that devoting class time to work with authentic texts does not compromise acquisition of language forms but rather can contribute to learners' ability to understand and use them correctly. In the next section, we discuss strategies for teaching grammar and vocabulary through texts using multiliteracies pedagogy. Before you read on, however, go back and complete Part 2 of Learning Activity 3.3.

2. PEDAGOGICAL APPLICATIONS

Although we have made the case for teaching grammar and vocabulary in meaningful contexts, you may still have questions about how to teach and assess language forms using multiliteracies pedagogy while still ensuring that students are able to use these forms accurately. One obstacle to adopting a contextualized approach to grammar and vocabulary teaching and assessment may be your textbook. In fact, you may have already noticed a mismatch between the way language forms are presented in your textbook and the way we have been talking about them in this chapter. To better prepare you to teach and assess grammar and vocabulary using multiliteracies pedagogy, we first consider how these Available Designs are commonly presented in introductory FL textbooks and the types of practice activities these books provide.

2.1 Presenting and Practicing Language Forms: Moving Beyond the Limitations of Introductory Textbooks

A quick perusal of your introductory FL textbook may reveal that grammar and vocabulary are presented in author-created dialogues or paragraphs followed by lists of words or rule explanations and sequenced practice that moves from several mechanical (i.e., form-focused) activities to one or two communicative (i.e., meaning-focused) activities. If this is an apt description of your textbook, you are not alone. In a survey of introductory French textbooks, Askildon (2008) found that they lacked balance between focus on meaning and focus on form, the language used to present forms was not authentic, textbooks were organized around grammatical content, and many practice activities were mechanical in nature. These findings echo a similar study by Aski (2003), who concluded that grammar activities in introductory Italian textbooks include pattern, or mechanical, practice and that these activities tend to be more frequent than those designed for communicative practice of forms. Likewise, in a study of instructor reactions to introductory French and Italian textbooks (Allen, 2008), participants reported a number of drawbacks in addition to the "rule followed by practice" format, including "a lack of usable oral student-to-student activities, relevant topics, and limited cultural content" (p. 21). Finally, in a survey of ESL textbooks to determine what aspects of vocabulary knowledge are targeted in activities, Brown (2010) found that across nine textbooks, the focus was consistently on practicing the spoken form of a word, one-to-one correspondences between a word's form and its meaning, and the grammatical functions of words. Missing from activities to practice vocabulary were word parts, conceptual understandings of words, collocations, and constraints on word use, among others. These traits of introductory textbooks reflect the prescriptive view discussed earlier that learning vocabulary means learning definitions and that learning grammar means learning rules.

Yet this view of language forms in textbooks does not reflect the SLA findings you learned about in the "Conceptual Background" section, particularly the idea that meaning-focused teaching of forms is more effective than isolated teaching of forms. Furthermore, the approaches taken by many textbooks suggest that mechanical practice of structural patterns is effective for acquisition of grammar and vocabulary. However, research in this area shows that the opposite is true (e.g., VanPatten, 2002; Wong & VanPatten, 2003). One consequence of presenting language forms in an artificial context and prioritizing mechanical practice activities is that "the learner is called upon to repeat structures and lexicon in ways that either strike the native speaker as unnatural, or create implicatures unintended by the [textbook] authors" (McCarthy, 1984, pp. 13–14). To further explore how language forms are treated in introductory textbooks and how this treatment is disconnected from SLA research, complete the first part of Learning Activity 3.4.

LEARNING ACTIVITY 3.4

Analyzing Grammar Activities

This Learning Activity is comprised of two parts and may take more time than some of the other activities you have completed up to this point as it involves reading and analyzing a grammar lesson plan and watching a related video. Complete Part 1 now and then come back to Part 2 after you have read the remainder of Section 2.1.

Part 1. The link below will take you to Lesson 1 of the Grammar module of *Foreign Language Teaching Methods*, an online resource at the University of Texas at Austin (Salaberry, 2010). You will use the downloadable lesson plans and related video within the module to complete activities 1–3.

www.coerll.utexas.edu/methods/modules/grammar/01/oralorwritten.php.

1. Download the two grammar lessons in the textbox entitled "Analyze Two Grammar Lessons" and describe each of them according to the SLA and pedagogical concepts listed in the table below. Check *Yes* if the lesson reflects the concept and *No* if it does not.

	Lesson Plan 1		**Lesson Plan 2**	
	Yes	No	Yes	No
Deductive				
Inductive				
Isolated				
Meaning-Focused				

(continued)

	Lesson Plan 1		Lesson Plan 2	
Mechanical (pattern) practice				
Communicative (meaningful) practice				
Inauthentic language				
Authentic language				
Inauthentic cultural content				
Authentic cultural content				

2. Does one lesson have a more prescriptively oriented view of language forms than the other? Does one have a more meaning-focused view? Which of the lesson plans is more reflective of introductory FL textbooks as described above? Which is more representative of the textbook you currently use?
3. Watch the video entitled "A discussion about the lesson plans" and answer the following questions, also provided in the module: What specific features of these lesson plans do [the people in the video] identify in detail? Do you agree with their analysis?

Part 2. Read the remainder of Section 2.1, entitled "Presenting and Practicing Language Forms: Moving Beyond the Limitations of Introductory Textbooks." To review your understanding of multiliteracies pedagogy, look at the two lesson plans you downloaded for Part 1 and determine which of the four pedagogical acts, if any, are represented in each one. Use the table to organize your analysis and then compare your answers with a classmate.

	Situated Practice	Overt Instruction	Critical Framing	Transformed Practice	N/A
Lesson 1					
paso 1					
paso 2					
paso 3					
paso 4					
Lesson 2					
paso 1					
paso 2					
paso 3					
paso 4					

The video excerpt in Learning Activity 3.4, "A discussion about the lesson plans," showed that the methods course students perceived the first lesson as more focused on the mechanics of grammar and less reflective of authentic language use, and the second lesson as more focused on meaning and more reflective of authentic language use. These perceptions are consistent with research on instructor and student perceptions of introductory FL textbooks. For instance, Askildon (2008) found that instructors perceived the heavy reliance on rule explanation followed by mechanical practice as a hindrance to students in acquiring grammatical forms. Likewise, some of the teachers Allen (2008) surveyed felt that "the textbook helped students learn *about* grammar, but this knowledge did not mean the forms were integrated into the students' FL" (pp. 14–15, emphasis in the original). Interestingly, students and instructors do not always perceive the treatment of forms in introductory textbooks similarly. Askildon found that although both groups were satisfied with the quantity of grammar in textbooks, they did not prioritize grammar in the same way: "Teachers do not place grammar at the center of teaching French. Students, on the other hand, demand more focus on form" (p. 219), that is, more explicit instruction of grammatical information.[1]

The seemingly conflicting goals that teachers want more meaningful treatment of language forms whereas students want more explicit focus on form can be reconciled with a multiliteracies-oriented approach to grammar and vocabulary instruction and assessment. Learning these Available Designs through textual interpretation and creation facilitates a balance between meaning and form while still allowing for explicit, inductive instruction of grammar and vocabulary. Moreover, this approach allows students to integrate grammatical and lexical knowledge into their ability to use the language, not just to learn about it, such that these two types of knowledge are complementary. Overt instruction activities, which represent one of the four pedagogical acts of multiliteracies pedagogy, are particularly well suited for bringing together form and meaning through interaction with FL texts because they include instructor interventions that focus learners' attention on conceptualizing and developing the linguistic knowledge needed to participate in communication activities. The remaining pedagogical acts of situated practice, critical framing, and transformed practice also afford opportunities to combine knowledge about form and meaning and to apply this knowledge to authentic cultural content. Recall that situated practice activities allow learners to experience a text through spontaneous, immersive, and experiential learning; critical framing activities encourage learners to analyze and question the meaning, importance, and consequences of what they learn; and transformed practice activities provide learners with opportunities to apply the understandings, knowledge, and skills gained through textual interaction and use them to produce language in new and creative ways.

---

[1]In SLA research, there is a distinction made between *focus on form* and *focus on formS*, the former referring to grammar use in communicative contexts, the latter to explicit instruction of grammatical forms (Long, 1991). Although we argue in favor of grammar instruction that reflects a focus on form, Askildon's data suggest that students prefer instructional approaches that reflect a focus on formS.

In the following subsections, we consider how to organize multiliteracies-oriented instructional activities and assessments that engage learners in meaning design (i.e., discovering form–meaning connections through interpreting and creating texts) by focusing on grammar and vocabulary use in texts. To do so, we draw on text-based models from pedagogical research to propose a template for creating form-focused lessons, followed by a sample lesson plan that illustrates its use. We further suggest literacy-based formative and summative assessments that complement the lesson by evaluating students' ability to understand and use the linguistic Available Designs of grammar and vocabulary. To prepare to read this next part of the chapter, go back and complete Part 2 of Learning Activity 3.4.

2.2 Text-Based Models of Form-Focused Instruction and Assessment

Teaching language forms through texts allows us to define "student command of a language's formal features as a function of successful comprehension and communication of learning, not as forms in isolation" (Swaffar & Arens, 2005, p. 30) and furthermore provides an authentic cultural context in which to embed form-focused instruction and assessment. Swaffar and Arens proposed that such text-based learning of language forms should be organized around instructional sequences that include a model for correct usage within a text, reproduction of the targeted form in a communicative context, language use that focuses on textual meaning, discourse-based communication, and the exchange of information. Similarly, Nation (2008) suggested that vocabulary teaching include meaning-focused input and output, deliberate vocabulary teaching through texts, and a focus on vocabulary accuracy and fluency. These suggestions are consistent with SLA-related concepts such as implicit and explicit learning, explicit instruction, inductive presentation of forms, and creative production, as well as with multiliteracies-based concepts such as meaning design, interpretation, transformation, language use, and linguistic, cognitive, and sociocultural dimensions of literacy. In this section, we outline three approaches to grammar and vocabulary instruction that reflect these concepts. First, we present Paesani's (2005) model for teaching grammar inductively through literary texts. Second, is Adair-Hauck and Donato's (2010) PACE model, a dialogic approach to teaching grammatical forms through story telling. We conclude by outlining the model of vocabulary teaching in *Français interactif,* an online introductory French program (Kelton, Guilloteau, & Blyth, 2004) framed by concepts from the lexical approach (Lewis, 1993, 1997a, 1997b) and processing instruction (Lee & VanPatten, 2003).

Grounded in inductive teaching strategies and process-oriented (see Chapter 5 for details) approaches to reading, Paesani (2005) presents a model of grammar instruction in which a literary text (e.g., poem, short story, excerpt from a novel) forms the basis for the presentation of targeted grammatical forms, reading comprehension, grammar practice, and creative production activities. The three-stage model is exemplified with a French-language poem and targets relative pronouns. The instructional sequence begins with several pre-reading activities to prepare learners to interact with textual content. First, students brainstorm vocabulary associated with the poem's title; next, students predict the poem's story line based on a list of instructor-provided vocabulary words from the text; last, students link ideas about the new text to similar texts (e.g., film, literature, television, music) with which they are already familiar. During the while-reading phase, activities move students from global to detailed text comprehension and include a focus on the content and form of the text. It is here that learners' attention is drawn to the targeted grammar, and they are encouraged to form and test hypotheses regarding its use in the context of the text. Paesani suggests several activities for the while-reading phase, including determining the poem's chronology, formulating personal interpretations of the text, identifying language patterns, and constructing grammatical rules. Once students understand the meaning of the text and how the targeted grammar functions within it, the instructional sequence moves into the post-reading phase. The first part of this phase includes patterned practice of the targeted grammar, such as sentence rewriting and sentence completion. Next, learners critique the content of the poem by interpreting the role of the narrator or identifying themes in the text. The post-reading phase concludes with creative production, during which students imitate the genre of the text they have read by writing their own poem using the targeted grammar. Paesani's inductive and process-oriented approach allows learners to focus on meaning before form and to develop reading and writing competence. Moreover, using a literary text not only serves as authentic cultural content, but also as a tool to teach and practice grammatical forms meaningfully.

The creative writing activity that concludes the post-reading phase serves as a summative assessment for the entire lesson. Paesani suggests that instructors incorporate peer editing and revision activities into this task and that students present their work to the class during a writing roundtable or publish their work in a class blog or portfolio. This model also provides opportunities for formative assessment throughout the reading process, as exemplified by the tasks in the instructional sequence. For instance, determining the chronology of the events of the text allows instructors to gauge students' progress related to global comprehension of the text; identifying structural patterns and explaining how they work within the context of the text allows instructors to evaluate learners' problem-solving skills as they work to link form and meaning.

Adair-Hauck and Donato's (2010) PACE model builds on inductive approaches to grammar instruction using a dialogic approach in which learners are guided to consciously reflect on the meaning of language forms in context, to link form and meaning, and to problem solve in collaboration with the instructor and their fellow students. Authentic cultural stories, as represented in folktales, legends, songs, cartoons, real-life activities, and the like, form the basis for all activities within the model. The stories and activities highlight aspects of a grammatical form that are essential to understanding and communicating about the story's content. As its acronym suggests, the PACE model comprises four phases: Presentation, Attention, Co-Construction, and Extension. In the Presentation phase, the instructor orally presents the selected story, focusing students' attention on its meaning. According to Adair-Hauck and Donato, the

Presentation phase should include pre-storytelling, while-storytelling, and post-storytelling activities to make meaning clear to learners. These activities "may include focusing on prior knowledge, content, cultural references, key vocabulary, dramatization, pair-work comprehension checks, or story-retelling exercises" (p. 224). Once students understand the story, instruction moves to the Attention phase, during which learners' attention is focused on a salient form used in the story. The targeted form is highlighted through teacher questions about patterns in the text or presentation of selected phrases from the text with the relevant form highlighted. To help students build conceptual understanding of the targeted form, instruction moves to the Co-Construction phrase. Here, students and instructor engage in "collaborative talk ... to reflect on, hypothesize about, and create understandings about the form, meaning, and function of the new grammar in question" (p. 225). Activities in the Co-Construction phase include asking guiding questions, applying generalizations to new situations, or building on what learners already understand. The instructional sequence concludes with the Extension phase, which allows learners to apply their new grammatical understanding in creative ways. Examples of Extension activities include role-plays, writing projects, interviews, and information-gap activities, all connected to the theme of the story on which the lesson is based.

As in Paesani's (2005) model, the post-reading, or Extension phase of the PACE model serves as a summative assessment because it creates opportunities for learners to use grammar in creative production activities. Such activities therefore provide instructors with a means for assessing learners' ability to use new forms both fluently and accurately. Formative assessments may take place throughout the four phases of the model and may include formal or informal evaluation of a number of the suggested activities. For instance, instructors might formally evaluate learners' ability to understand global meaning in the cultural story through pair-work comprehension checks during the Presentation phase, or they might informally evaluate students' ability to solve problems related to the targeted form through guided questions during the Co-Construction phase.

The final model—the approach to vocabulary instruction in *Français interactif* (Kelton, Guilloteau, & Blyth, 2004)—was developed in response to research indicating that students desire "a clearer and more deliberate progression ... from decontextualized vocabulary words to contextualized discourse" (Blyth & Davis, 2007). It is grounded in concepts related to the lexical approach (Lewis, 1993, 1997a, 1997b) and to processing instruction (Lee & VanPatten, 2003). The *Français interactif* model posits vocabulary as the central organizing principle of the curriculum; it focuses on raising students' awareness about the function of vocabulary in naturally occurring language; it highlights relationships between parts of the language and the whole; it prioritizes the role of context for learning various facets of word meaning; and it moves students from comprehension-based to production-based activities (Guilloteau, 2010; Lewis, 1993). Although this model is not as overtly text based as those presented in Paesani (2005) and Adair-Hauck and Donato (2010), it does emphasize the importance of moving beyond the study of vocabulary words in isolation to provide learners with opportunities to understand and use vocabulary at the sentence and discourse levels.

The *Français interactif* model begins with vocabulary preparation activities, completed as homework and corrected in class, intended to help students establish the basic meaning of vocabulary words associated with a unit or lesson. Examples of activities that establish basic word meaning include listening to and repeating words, writing down words, and translating words into English. Once this basic meaning is established, students then make connections across words by deciding which word does not belong within a subset organized semantically or grammatically (e.g., *brother, sister, uncle, friend*). These vocabulary preparation activities gradually move students from understanding words in isolation toward understanding them within texts. Subsequent stages in the *Français interactif* model include comprehension and production activities at the sentence level, followed by comprehension and production activities at the discourse level. The purpose of each set of activities is to gradually move from word-level understandings developed in the vocabulary preparation stage toward understanding and using vocabulary in contextualized discourse. At the sentence level, students complete activities that require them to do something with language samples that contain words learned in vocabulary preparation activities (e.g., find someone who enjoys each pastime mentioned in a set of statements). They also watch video segments of native speakers explaining vocabulary concepts along with sets of related images, and they complete language production activities that require them to create phrases using the targeted vocabulary. At the discourse level, students once again begin with text-based activities such as answering questions or filling in a form that uses the targeted vocabulary, and continue with watching unstructured interviews with native speakers and carrying out related activities such as filling in a biographical information sheet. This phase of the model ends with students completing activities that require them to produce larger chunks of discourse (e.g., summarizing, making conclusions, writing a description). Assessment can take place at any stage in the model and can be either formative or summative. For example, vocabulary preparation activities can serve as a formative assessment to gauge how well students have grasped the basic meanings of words before moving on to contextualized activities, whereas creative production activities such as writing a description or making a word list can serve as a summative assessment to evaluate how well students use vocabulary words to make meaning in context.

The three pedagogical models outlined in this chapter are summarized in Table 3.1. Although informed by a variety of approaches, these models share a number of commonalities. First, all are examples of meaning-based explicit instruction of language forms: Each one stresses the importance of contextualized language use and of creating connections between form and meaning. In addition, all three prioritize learner involvement in understanding language patterns and relationships between words and phrases through consciousness-raising activities, hypothesizing, and problem solving. Finally, although not explicitly literacy based, each model engages learners in the act of meaning design through interpretation of authentic cultural content and creative production activities based on that content.

TABLE 3.1 Text-Based Models of Form-Focused Instruction

	Paesani (2005)	Adair–Hauck & Donato (2010)	*Français interactif* (2004)
1	Pre-reading (brainstorming, predicting, linking known to new)	Presentation (pre-, while-, post-storytelling activities to focus on meaning)	Vocabulary preparation (establishing basic word meaning and relationships)
2	While-reading (global to detailed comprehension, hypothesis testing, form–meaning connections)	Attention (consciousness raising about forms used in story)	Sentence-level activities (input to output; authentic video)
3	Post-reading (practice of language forms, textual analysis, creative production)	Co-Construction (collaborative talk about grammatical forms)	Discourse-level activities (input to output; authentic video)
4		Expansion (application of new understandings of forms creatively)	

In terms of instructional sequencing, a comparison of the stages summarized in Table 3.1 reveals additional similarities across the models. First, all three include an initial stage that prepares learners to interact with language forms in context. Next, each proposes a progression of activities to move learners from textual interpretation to textual production. Finally, the three models conclude with activities that allow learners to use language forms creatively. With these commonalities in mind, in the next subsection we propose a general format for teaching language forms based on the multiliteracies approach.

2.3 A Template for Organizing Multiliteracies Instruction and Assessment of Language Forms

To effectively implement meaningful grammar and vocabulary instruction grounded in textual interaction and allow students to both learn about and use these language forms, we propose the five-stage template below for designing multiliteracies-oriented, form-focused lessons. This instructional sequence may be used to introduce language forms in an authentic context or to deepen students' understanding of previously studied forms.

1. *Introducing ideas* to access background knowledge and prepare learners to interact with the grammatical and lexical content of the text;
2. *Understanding meaning* to gain global and detailed understanding of the text;
3. *Hypothesizing* to notice language patterns, construct rules, and see connections between parts of language and the whole text;
4. *Establishing relationships* to explore choices related to language forms and understand their effect on textual meaning; and
5. *Applying knowledge* to use new knowledge of language forms in creative production tasks.

At this point, some of you may be concerned about selecting appropriate texts for use with this instructional sequence. Indeed, a common concern among FL instructors is finding what they believe is the rare, perfect text for teaching language forms, one that has multiple examples of a specific grammatical form or that includes a large percentage of the vocabulary words form a particular lesson in the textbook. This lesson plan template can help shift thinking away from finding the perfect text toward developing activities that include a focus on language forms. In other words, if the activities you develop provide linguistic support that targets the grammar and vocabulary that will be the focus of your activities, the actual number or type of forms in the text you select becomes less important. Additional considerations that can help relieve the burden of finding the perfect text include selecting texts that interest both you and your students, that make connections to course content or topics of cultural relevance, that are linguistically accessible to your students, that lend themselves to a multi-stage pedagogy such as the model proposed here, and that can be expanded upon through activities within the pedagogy (Adair-Hauck & Donato, 2010) (see Chapter 2 for additional discussion of text selection).

As we suggested earlier in the "Pedagogical Applications" section, because the lesson plan template is focused on grammar and vocabulary, overt instruction activities (i.e., those that encourage learners to conceptualize information in a text through examination of its formal and functional components) take center stage. Nonetheless, all four pedagogical acts of the multiliteracies framework (situated practice, overt instruction, critical framing, transformed practice) should be implemented to engage students in the learning processes of interpretation, collaboration, problem solving, reflection, and self-reflection and to tap into various Available Designs including, but not limited to, grammar and vocabulary. Examples of learning activities that might be used in each stage of the sequence are provided in Table 3.2. Note that in some cases, the learning activity is reflective of more than one pedagogical act.

2.3.1 INTRODUCING IDEAS. The purpose of the introducing ideas stage is to prepare students to interact with language forms and cultural content in an authentic text. *Brainstorming,* a situated practice activity, achieves this goal by tapping into the knowledge and ideas learners bring to a topic. One way to structure a brainstorming activity is to have learners first write down their initial ideas about a topic on notecards, one idea per notecard. Next, students work in small groups to identify like ideas, name or categorize each group of ideas, and create logical connections between idea groups (Kalantzis & Cope, 2012).

To help students generate initial ideas that are more closely linked to language forms and their contribution to textual meaning, they can *preview using text aids.* Text aids include headings or subheadings, topic sentences, boldfaced or italicized type, charts or tables, and so on. The instructor may select text aids that help students comprehend the content of the text, highlight salient grammatical or lexical forms, or a combination of both. Students then identify the purpose of the text aids and make predictions about the topic of the text. After reading, listening to, or viewing the text, students go back to their predictions

TABLE 3.2 Suggested Learning Activities for Teaching Language Forms

Instructional Stage	Suggested Learning Activities
1 Introducing ideas	Brainstorming (Situated practice)
	Previewing using text aids (Situated practice)
	Word associations (Situated practice / Overt instruction)
2 Understanding meaning	Clink and clunk (Situated practice)
	Reading matrix (Situated practice)
	Selected deletion (Overt instruction / Transformed practice)
3 Hypothesizing	Inductive reasoning (Critical framing)
	Sentence data sets (Overt instruction / Critical framing)
	Text annotation (Overt instruction)
4 Establishing relationships	Extra words (Overt instruction)
	Substitutions (Overt instruction)
	Dictionary work (Overt instruction)
5 Applying knowledge	Imitate the genre (Transformed practice)
	Critical lenses (Critical framing / Transformed practice)
	Revising and editing (Overt instruction)

and compare them with the ideas they gleaned from the text (Kucer & Silva, 2009).

Even more overtly focused on language forms are *word association* activities. Here, students make connections between words from the text and related sets of words, which can include known or new vocabulary. In so doing, students begin to understand how language forms are connected to one another and in subsequent activities can more easily see how selected words contribute to textual meaning.

2.3.2 UNDERSTANDING MEANING. Activities such as clink and clunk, a reading matrix, and selected deletion help learners determine the main facts of a text and link these facts to language use in the understanding meaning stage. *Clink and clunk,* a situated practice activity, assesses what students have learned from a text and what needs to be discussed in more detail. After reading, viewing, or listening to a text for the first time, students list what they understand well in the "clink" column of a table, and they write what they do not understand well in the "clunk" column. In small groups, students discuss and clarify information while the teacher circulates to assess which areas are posing difficulties (Kalantzis & Cope, 2012).

A *reading matrix* also focuses on understanding the facts of a text and furthermore links these facts to language forms. After entering facts, ideas, or scenes from a text into the matrix, students identify language patterns used for expressing these facts, ideas, or scenes. According to Swaffar and Arens (2005), the reading matrix leads "to more informed reading" (p. 87), joins language with ideas, and thus helps avoid the tendency to read word for word (see Chapters 5 and 6 for additional uses of the reading matrix).

Finally, *selected deletion* activities focus even more closely on language forms and their contribution to textual meaning. Students read a version of the text with selected words deleted (e.g., words targeted in the introducing ideas stage, words related to a chapter theme). As they read, they complete the text by inserting a logical word or phrase into each blank space. As a group, students then share ideas and discuss which is the most plausible insertion for each blank (Kucer & Silva, 2009). This activity thus encourages students to use context to help them understand words in the text and furthermore targets specific language forms and how they affect textual meaning.

2.3.3 HYPOTHESIZING. In the hypothesizing stage, learners interact with a text more carefully to identify language patterns and to understand how the Available Designs of grammar and vocabulary connect with other parts of the text to make meaning. *Inductive reasoning,* a critical framing activity, is similar to the inductive and dialogic approaches you have already read about. Students' attention is drawn to specific features of the text, and they are asked to draw conclusions about language patterns or rules based on these features.

Sentence data sets activities are similar to inductive reasoning because learners generalize language patterns and rules based on various sets of features from the text. For instance, students may identify and classify simple and compound sentences and then determine a general pattern or rule for each set of sentences based on the way they are used in the text.

Finally, in *text annotation* activities, students mark up the text as they read it to focus on various language features. For instance, they might underline words or phrases that advance the chronology of the story, put a question mark next to a vocabulary word that is unclear to them, color code words or phrases that are related to one another semantically or morphologically, or circle words that refer to one or more characters in the story. Each of these activities draws students' attention to language forms and encourages them to hypothesize about their function within the text.

2.3.4 EXPLORING RELATIONSHIPS. Students continue to look closely at language forms and delve more deeply into their effect on textual meaning during the exploring relationships phase. In *extra words* activities, students work with their instructor to determine which words are less essential to a text and discuss how overall textual meaning changes if these extra words are eliminated. In some cases, the instructor may direct students to focus on specific extra words (e.g., adjectives, adverbs); in other cases, students determine on their own which words they think may be deleted (Kucer & Silva, 2009).

Similarly, in *substitution* activities, students focus on aspects of grammar by identifying a particular feature and substituting an alternative. For instance, if focusing on pronouns, students might change a text from third person to first person. Students then consider the effects of the change on the text's meaning (Kalantzis & Cope, 2012).

Finally, *dictionary work* can take a number of forms. Beyond looking up unknown words, students can use the dictionary to explore alternate definitions and see which fits best with the way the word is used in context. Alternatively, they can define targeted vocabulary in their own words and then compare their definition with that of the dictionary. In all of these overt instruction activities, students are mindfully reflecting on how the Available Designs of grammar and vocabulary are used to present ideas, and how textual meaning changes as a result of their modification.

2.3.5 APPLYING KNOWLEDGE. Imitate the genre, critical lenses, and revising and editing are all activities that require students to apply knowledge related to grammar and vocabulary through language production. *Imitate the genre,* a transformed practice activity, requires students to create an original text based on the genre they have read, viewed, or listened to. In each case, the text students create makes use of the Available Designs targeted in previous activities. For instance, if students read a poem that features relative pronouns, they then write a poem of the same type on a topic of their choice; if they watch a television interview show, they then create a similar program that incorporates interrogative structures.

Exploring textual meaning through different points of view is the purpose of *critical lenses* activities. Here, students may retell a story from the perspective of a different character, or they may analyze a text targeted to young people from the perspective of older populations. Because such activities require students to step back from the text to explore different viewpoints as well as apply new knowledge creatively, critical lenses activities span both critical framing and transformed practice (Kalantzis & Cope, 2012).

Finally, an applying knowledge activity that focuses on overt instruction is *revising and editing.* Kern (2000) suggests that instructors lead whole-class discussion of student work to teach learners how to edit expression of ideas, textual organization, grammar, and so on. He furthermore proposes a number of strategies to treat in such discussions, including paragraphing, sentence combining, and rereading.

2.3.6 ASSESSMENT. The five-stage lesson plan template can also serve as a model for designing multiliteracies-based exams that focus on students' ability to use grammar and vocabulary accurately and fluently through interaction with a written text. Such an exam might have the following format: (1) the introducing ideas activity of word associations to target vocabulary in the text; (2) the understanding meaning activity of selected deletion that targets vocabulary from the word associations activity; (3) the hypothesizing activity of sentence data sets to classify phrases using the targeted vocabulary into logical groupings; (4) the establishing relationships activity of substitutions in which students replace targeted words with items from the word associations list and comment on how this changes overall meaning; and (5) the applying knowledge activity of critical lenses in which students explore the text from a different viewpoint.

To ensure student success in meaningfully using language forms, exams should be based on a text they have already read, the continuation of a text they have already read, or a text that treats a similar topic to one treated in class.

In addition to serving as a model for creating formal tests, this template provides opportunities for various formative and summative assessments. A number of the suggested introducing ideas, understanding meaning, hypothesizing, and establishing relationships activities can function as formative assessments carried out through in-class discussion or homework. Moreover, the suggested applying knowledge activities may serve as summative assessments that conclude the treatment of particular language forms. A sample lesson plan that targets both grammar and vocabulary and provides examples of assessment activities is presented in the next section.

2.4 Sample Form-Focused Lesson Plan

In Table 3.3, we present a sample lesson plan based on Barrette, Paesani, and Vinall (2010) and organized according to the template presented earlier. Activities implemented in the lesson represent one of the three illustrative activity types presented in Table 3.2 for each stage in the template. This lesson is intended for use in a third- or fourth-semester intermediate Spanish course during an instructional unit on narrating in the past. The goals of this lesson are to enable students to formulate hypotheses about, understand, and use the preterit and imperfect verb forms, to recognize contextually dependent uses of the preterit and imperfect in the text, to understand and use transition words to advance a narrative story, and to interpret and reproduce the genre of a narrative short story. The text that forms the basis of the lesson is the short story *Apocalipsis* (*Apocalypse*) (Denevi, 1974), which recounts the disappearance of the human race at the end of the thirty-second century (see Appendix). Interestingly, this resolution is presented in the first sentence of the story, and is followed by the events leading up to it. In the last sentence of the story, the narrator—one of the machines who destroyed the human race—reveals its identity. This "non-traditional narrative sequence shifts the focus in the development of the story from what happens to how it happens" (Barrette, Paesani, & Vinall, 2010, p. 219). Moreover, the use of the imperfect to narrate most of the story, rather than the preterit, "accentuates the ongoing process of the actions as opposed to their finality" (p. 220). Students are likely to be familiar with the apocalypse theme from movies, television, and fiction and will furthermore have an understanding of the form and expected uses of the preterit and imperfect prior to reading the text.

The activities in this five-stage lesson plan allow students to learn about language forms and use them in a meaningful context. Indeed, language use, one of the seven principles of literacy, is foregrounded in the lesson plan in activities that encourage hypothesizing, reflection, analysis, and establishing connections related to transition words and preterit and imperfect verb forms used in the text. By implementing activities that reflect all four pedagogical acts, students also engage in the act of meaning design: They explore form–meaning connections through textual interpretation and creation; they work with the linguistic

TABLE 3.3 Sample Instructional Sequence, Form-Focused Lesson: *Apocalipsis*

Instructional Stage	Learning Activities
1 Introducing ideas	a Students and teacher work together to *brainstorm* ideas about characteristics of the science fiction genre: common themes, characters, events, chronology. Next, in small groups, students are given the title of the short story and they *brainstorm* characters, events, and chronology specific to the science fiction theme of the apocalypse. During follow up, the teacher makes a master list of ideas, organized by category, on the board. (Situated practice)
	b Next, students complete a *word associations* activity based on an instructor-provided list of transition words common in narrative texts (e.g., *in the beginning*, *next*, *later*, *finally*). In small groups, students classify items in the word list according to whether they introduce an idea or event, move the story along, or conclude an idea or event. The instructor provides a second set of transition words from the text and students then add these words to the categories they have created, justifying their choices during whole-class follow up. (Situated practice / Overt instruction)
2 Understanding meaning	a To focus students on the characters, events, and chronology of the story, they read the text and individually complete a *reading matrix*. Students compare their matrix with a partner, reaching a consensus on the important characters, events, and chronology of the story, and then together identify language patterns or samples in the text used to express this information. During follow-up discussion, the instructor and students highlight the unusual chronology in the story as well as the fact that the narrator is a machine, linking both ideas to language samples from the text. (Situated practice)
	b Students then read the text a second time, with all of the transition words deleted. During this *selected deletion* activity, students work on their own to insert logical transition words from the list provided in the word associations activity. In small groups, students then share their choices and discuss which is most plausible. During follow up, students present their choices, compare them with the transition words used in the original text, and discuss how these choices affect overall textual meaning. (Overt instruction / Transformed practice)

(*Continued*)

TABLE 3.3 Sample Instructional Sequence, Form-Focused Lesson: *Apocalipsis*

Instructional Stage	Learning Activities
3 Hypothesizing	a To focus on verb forms used in the text, students return to their reading matrix and identify language samples that include instances of the preterit and imperfect. The instructor then leads an *inductive reasoning* activity during which students draw conclusions about how these verb forms are used within the context of the text. (Critical framing)
	b To deepen their understanding of how past tense forms are used in the text, students engage in *text annotation* by rereading the text and underlining all examples of the preterit and imperfect. They then determine whether all uses of these verb forms reflect the conclusions made in the inductive reasoning activity. They furthermore note any uses of the preterit and imperfect that differ from what they have already learned about these forms. (Overt instruction)
4 Establishing relationships	a To highlight the unusual use of the imperfect in the text, students complete a *substitutions* activity, changing all examples of the imperfect to the preterit. During follow-up discussion, the instructor guides students in considering the effects of this change on the overall meaning of the text. (Overt instruction)
5 Applying knowledge	a Students complete a *critical lenses* activity and retell the story in the past from the point of view of a human. Students are instructed to include information about characters, events, and chronology based on their reading matrix, including the language samples they have culled. They are furthermore encouraged to use transition words they learned during the lesson. (Critical framing / Transformed practice)
	b The teacher provides feedback on students' drafts, focusing on the appropriate use of the preterit and imperfect, words and phrases from the reading matrix, and transition words. Students then *revise and edit* their story retelling and share it with their classmates in a subsequent class period. (Overt instruction)

and schematic resources that contribute to the text's meaning; and they draw on their own background knowledge about the genre they read. Furthermore, the instructional sequence engages students in the learning processes of interpretation, collaboration, problem solving, and reflection. Students interpret the effect of Available Designs on overall textual meaning; they collaborate by interacting with the text and other learners to design meaning; they solve problems by figuring out relationships between words and between words and textual content; and they reflect on language patterns, meaning, and their own writing.

This sample lesson affords a number of opportunities for both formative and summative assessment. For instance, instructors can provide formative feedback after the word associations, selected deletion, and text annotation activities to ensure that students understand both the form and meaning of the targeted grammar and vocabulary. Likewise, instructors may wish to provide formative feedback during the follow-up part of the reading matrix activity when students explain why they have associated specific pieces of language from the text with information about the characters, events, and chronology of the story. Each of these activities can also be completed as homework and assigned a grade for completion and accuracy related to form–meaning connections. Finally, the writing and revising activities from the applying knowledge phase of the lesson plan can serve as a summative assessment for the instructional sequence. Instructor feedback and evaluation would focus not only on accurate use of transition words and past tense forms, but also on how the preterit and imperfect affect narration, how well students expressed the characters, events, and chronology of the story, and how effectively they narrated the story from a different point of view.

To help you reflect on this sample form-focused lesson plan, read through it a second time and find answers to the following questions:

1. What are the objectives of the lesson and how do they fit within the course curriculum?
2. Is the selected text appropriate to meet these objectives? What elements of the text might be challenging for FL learners to understand?
3. In what ways do students both learn about and use language forms in the lesson? How do they establish form–meaning connections through the various activities in the lesson?
4. Why are the different lesson plan activities labeled as situated practice, overt instruction, critical framing, or transformed practice?
5. Are the basic elements of instruction—conventions, cultural knowledge, and language use—represented in the lesson?
6. Are the learning processes of interpretation, collaboration, problem solving, and reflection/self-reflection represented in the lesson?

As you think about planning your own form-focused lesson plans and assessments using the template above, come back to these questions as a way to help you organize your ideas and apply your understanding of multiliteracies-based pedagogy to the teaching of grammar and vocabulary. Learning Activity 3.5 will help get you started.

LEARNING ACTIVITY 3.5

Developing a Form-Focused Lesson Plan

Go back to the lesson plans you analyzed in Learning Activity 3.4 and create a revised lesson using the multiliteracies-oriented template presented here. Before beginning this task, first evaluate the effectiveness of the lessons by asking the questions presented above. Once you have identified areas that need improvement, create a revised lesson using the five-stage model and suggested learning activities in Tables 3.2 and 3.3. When the lesson plan is finished, ask yourself the same set of questions above to help you justify your pedagogical choices.

3. FINAL CONSIDERATIONS

In this chapter, we established a conceptual base for considering the teaching of FL grammar and vocabulary within the multiliteracies framework. Essential to this base is the idea that language forms are more than sets of rules or lists and that their meaning is contextually dependent. We further established that grammar and vocabulary are meaning-making resources that help learners make form-meaning relationships and engage in the act of meaning design.

This conceptual base informed the form-focused pedagogy we developed in this chapter, a pedagogy whose primary goal is simultaneously to help students learn about language forms and use language in culturally authentic contexts. This pedagogy is grounded in the multiliteracies-based concepts of meaning design, language use, and Available Designs. Through activities reflecting the four pedagogical acts of situated practice, overt instruction, critical framing, and transformed practice, students not only establish form–meaning connections, but they also interpret, collaborate, solve problems, and reflect about the language and content of FL texts.

As you read the remaining chapters of this book, keep in mind that grammar and vocabulary are two among a number of Available Designs that learners tap into to interpret and transform FL texts. As such, grammar and vocabulary—although essential for successful FL learning—are not the only aspects of language use that contribute to learning, nor is language use the only element of instruction on which we should focus our efforts. Instruction of language forms should be balanced with other aspects of language use, such as phonetic systems, organizational patterns, or genre, and with other elements of instruction such as conventions and cultural knowledge. Indeed, to communicate effectively, students need a working knowledge of grammar and vocabulary, but without contextualizing these resources within specific cultural contexts or textual genres, they are devoid of meaning. We hope that you will remember this final consideration as you reflect on the content of this chapter and move ahead to explore the content of Chapter 4, "Scaffolding Oral Language Use in the Classroom."

4. TRANSFORMING KNOWLEDGE

4.1 Reflective Journal Entry

What are the benefits and pitfalls of teaching grammar and vocabulary through FL texts? Is a multiliteracies approach to teaching language forms consistent with the beliefs and experiences related to FL teaching and learning you identified in Chapter 1 or in Learning Activity 3.1? How have your views about teaching and learning grammar and vocabulary changed as a result of reading this chapter?

4.2 Researching Grammar and Vocabulary

Examine the way grammar and vocabulary are presented and practiced in two or three introductory-level textbooks for the language you teach. What is the approach to teaching grammar in each textbook? What is the approach to teaching vocabulary? Are the approaches in each reflective of grammar-based approaches, CLT-oriented approaches, literacy-oriented approaches, or a combination of these? Are there commonalities or differences across the textbooks surveyed? What overall conclusions can you make about the view of grammar instruction in commercially available FL textbooks based upon your research? What overall conclusions can you make about the view of vocabulary instruction in commercially available FL textbooks based upon your research?

Key Resources

Adair-Hauck, B., & Donato, R. (2010). Using a story-based approach to teach grammar. In J. Shrum & E. Glisan (Authors), *Teacher's handbook: Contextualized foreign language instruction* (4th ed., pp. 216–243). Boston, MA: Heinle.

This chapter of *Teacher's Handbook* outlines the PACE model for teaching grammar in FL classrooms. To set up the model, Adair-Hauck and Donato first discuss issues related to communicatively oriented grammar instruction and to inductive and deductive teaching approaches. They then argue that a dialogic approach to grammar instruction, in which teacher and learners collaborate to construct grammar rules and explanations, is ideal. The PACE model—Presentation, Attention, Co-Construction, Evaluation—exemplifies this dialogic approach and grounds grammar teaching in authentic cultural stories. After explaining the model and providing a sample lesson plan, the authors conclude by highlighting advantages of the PACE model over traditional approaches to grammar instruction and providing suggestions for implementing the model in the FL classroom.

Guilloteau, N. (2010). Vocabulary. In C. Blyth (Ed.), *Foreign language teaching methods*. Austin, TX: Texas Language Technology Center, University of Texas at Austin. Retrieved from www.coerll.utexas.edu/methods/.

This module on vocabulary is part of the online methods course, Foreign Language Teaching Methods, at the University of Texas at Austin. Guilloteau guides course participants through a number of theoretical and practical issues related to the teaching and learning of vocabulary, including pitfalls associated with training instructors to teach vocabulary, teaching vocabulary in context, the lexical approach to vocabulary instruction, vocabulary practice activities, and input-to-output activities. Throughout, Guilloteau uses the approach to vocabulary instruction in *Français interactif* (Kelton, Guilloteau, & Blyth, 2004) to illustrate key concepts and teaching techniques. The module includes both print and video elements and has a number of reflective activities for course participants to complete as they progress through the module.

Maxim, H. H. (2009). Developing advanced formal language abilities along a genre-based curriculum. In S. L. Katz & J. Watzinger-Tharp (Eds.), *Conceptions of L2 grammar: Theoretical approaches and their application in the L2 classroom* (pp. 172–188). Boston, MA: Heinle.

In this chapter, Maxim argues for a view of grammar in which form and meaning are merged to discover a text's communicative purpose. He then proposes a three-part genre-based pedagogy for implementing texts in the FL curriculum. The purpose of the pedagogy is to lead students to understand the purpose, function, context, and resources associated with a text or genre and to then construct their own version of the genre in writing. Focusing on an advanced-level German course, Maxim suggests organizing the curriculum using a narrative–expository continuum that moves students from private to public spheres. The chapter includes an example of how the course is organized as well as sample instructional sequences for four genres (personal letter, diary entry, film review, literary analysis) based on the proposed three-part pedagogy.

For Further Reading

Nassaji, H., & Fotos, S. (2011). *Teaching grammar in second language classrooms: Integrating form-focused instruction in communicative context*. New York, NY: Routledge.

Nation, I. S. P. (2008). *Teaching vocabulary: Techniques and strategies*. Boston, MA: Heinle.

Paesani, K. (2009). Exploring the stylistic content of *Exercices de style*. *The French Review, 82*, 1268–1280.

Spada, N. (2011). Beyond form-focused instruction: Reflections on past, present and future research. *Language Teaching, 44*, 225–236.

APPENDIX

Apocalipsis

La extinción de la raza de los hombres se sitúa aproximadamente a fines del siglo XXXII. La cosa ocurrió así: las máquinas habían alcanzado tal perfección que los hombres ya no necesitaban comer, ni dormir, ni hablar, ni leer, ni escribir, ni pensar, ni hacer nada. Les bastaba apretar un botón y las máquinas lo hacían todo por ellos. Gradualmente fueron desapareciendo las mesas, las sillas, las rosas, los discos con las nueve sinfonías de Beethoven, las tiendas de antigüedades, los vinos de Burdeos, las golondrinas, los tapices flamencos, todo Verdi, el ajedrez, los telescopios, las catedrales góticas, los estadios de fútbol, la Piedad de Miguel Ángel, los mapas, las ruinas del Foro Trajano, los automóviles, el arroz, las sequoias gigantes, el Partenón. Sólo había máquinas. Después los hombres empezaron a notar que ellos mismos iban desapareciendo paulatinamente y que en cambio las máquinas se multiplicaban. Bastó poco tiempo para que el número de los hombres quedase reducido a la mitad y el de las máquinas se duplicase. Las máquinas terminaron por ocupar todos los sitios disponibles. No se podía dar un paso ni hacer un ademán sin tropezarse con una de ellas. Finalmente los hombres fueron eliminados. Como el último se olvidó de desconectar las máquinas, desde entonces seguimos funcionando (Denevi, 1974, p. 113).

Apocalypse

The extinction of the human race occurred around the end of the thirty-second century. It happened like this: machines had become so perfect that men no longer needed to eat, drink, speak, read, write, think, or do anything. They only had to press a button and the machines did everything for them. Tables, chairs, roses, records with Beethoven's nine symphonies, antique stores, Bordeaux wines, swallows, Flemish tapestries, all of Verdi's work, the game of chess, telescopes, gothic cathedrals, soccer stadiums, Michelangelo's Pietà, maps, the ruins of Trajan's Forum, cars, rice, giant sequoias, and the Parthenon all gradually disappeared. There were only machines. The humans began to notice that they too were gradually disappearing, while the number of machines continued to multiply. Little time passed before the number of humans on Earth was cut in half, and the machines doubled in population. The machines occupied every available space. You could not make a move or take a step without coming across one of them. In the end, the humans were eliminated. Since the last one forgot to unplug the machines, we have remained on ever since.

CHAPTER 4

Scaffolding Oral Language Use in the Classroom

Up to now, you have explored the concept of literacy and the importance of text-based language teaching and learning, familiarized yourself with theoretical and pedagogical aspects of the multiliteracies framework, identified goals, objectives, and assessments for introductory and intermediate foreign language (FL) contexts, and used these ideas to reconsider the teaching of grammar and vocabulary. In this chapter, we explore applications of the multiliteracies approach to classroom oral language use. Given the importance of texts within this framework, in contrast to the strong emphasis on oral communication typical in lower-level language courses, you may be wondering how literacy development and FL speaking fit together. Recall that our broad definition of literacy, presented in the Introduction, places primary importance on the interpretation and creation of multiple text types from various perspectives; the spoken language samples learners hear and produce thus provide examples of oral texts. Moreover, our conceptualization of communication includes linguistic, cognitive, and sociocultural dimensions and entails not only language use, but also a consideration of how meaning is constructed and negotiated in a range of contexts and textual genres.

Our broad view of literacy and communication differs from the communicative language teaching (CLT) orientation we explored in the Introduction, in which heavy emphasis is placed upon development of functional oral language use in generic contexts. This means that communication often involves using language in predictable patterns, focusing on expression of personal opinions, and studying scripted dialogues as models of oral input and vehicles for oral production. Moreover, traditional teacher-led oral communication often follows a controlled question-and-answer format that does not provide students the opportunity to learn characteristics of typical authentic conversations and use them in interactive settings (McCarthy & O'Keefe, 2004; Shrum & Glisan, 2010). Schulz (2006) underscored these shortcomings, arguing that the goal of communicative competence is not sufficient for introductory and intermediate language courses "because short-lived, communicative survival skills are taught without intellectually challenging content and do not provide those intellectually enriching insights into language-related factors that would indeed justify such study as a requirement for all students" (p. 254).

Whereas CLT-oriented approaches tease out speaking, listening, reading, and writing into separate skills, our broad conceptualization of communication and literacy prioritizes the complementarity of these language modalities. Because speaking overlaps with listening, reading, and writing, it is helpful to adopt terminology from the framework of communicative modes (National Standards, 2006)—specifically interpersonal and presentational communication—to talk about the kind of oral language that characterizes FL classrooms. Although this framework is focused on how language is used in oral communication more than on the sociocultural contexts in which communication takes place, learner roles in speaking tasks, or discourse, it serves as a useful starting point for considering oral language use from a multiliteracies perspective. As you learned in the Introduction, *interpersonal communication* involves interactive, spontaneous oral language use between two or more speakers (e.g., telephone conversation, job interview). Such interactions have a communicative purpose and seek "to emulate real conversation without artificial instructional rules such as 'answer in a complete sentence' when that is not necessary" (Phillips, 2008, p. 96). *Presentational communication* involves planned, one-way oral language use during which interaction with one's audience is limited or impossible. This mode requires "an ability to present cross-cultural information based on the background of the audience" (Shrum & Glisan, 2010, pp. 300–301) and generally follows conventions related to the presentational genre (e.g., oral report, news broadcast).

The purpose of this chapter is to develop our understanding of interpersonal and presentational communication from a multiliteracies perspective as it pertains to oral language use in the FL classroom. We begin the "Conceptual Background" section by exploring key issues in second language acquisition (SLA) research related to oral language use, including the differences between oral and written discourse, interactionist approaches to speaking, and the nature of classroom discourse. We then consider classroom discourse from a multiliteracies perspective, including the concepts of scaffolding and communities of practice, and how this perspective can facilitate more meaningful oral communication. In the "Pedagogical Applications" section, we first discuss general considerations for structuring speaking activities, followed by an overview of text-based models of teaching and assessing oral language use. We then present a template for designing multiliteracies-based speaking lessons and provide a sample lesson plan intended for use in a lower-level language class. By the end of this chapter, you will have a clearer understanding of the relationship between oral communication and literacy development and of how the multiliteracies approach can facilitate meaningful oral language use in your classroom context. To activate your background knowledge about the chapter's content, complete Learning Activity 4.1.

LEARNING ACTIVITY 4.1

Oral Language Use and Literacy Development

Reflect on how you use language to communicate orally in your daily life. What kinds of interpersonal interactions do you have? What is the purpose of these interactions? Do you engage in presentational communication? If so, in what contexts and for what purposes? Complete the first column of the table with examples of how you use oral language to communicate. Then classify the examples based on whether they represent interpersonal or presentational communication, whether the examples you identified typically occur in the context of a FL classroom, and how they contribute to FL literacy development.

Example	Interpersonal or Presentational?	Occur in FL Classroom?	Contribution to Literacy Development

1. CONCEPTUAL BACKGROUND

Before presenting SLA research related to classroom oral language use, it is important to introduce several concepts that frame our discussion. The first of these is *discourse,* or "the process of meaning–creation and interaction, whether in writing or speech" (McCarthy, 2001, p. 96), which entails relationships between language forms and socially situated communicative practices (e.g., textual organization, turn taking, formulaic expressions) (Hicks, 2003). The product of discourse is oral and written texts. Oral and written texts are often distinguished along a continuum rather than according to opposing categories, and are categorized based on their degree of "spokenness" and "writtenness" (Flowerdew & Miller, 2005, p. 48). For example, a casual conversation between friends may fall on the spoken end of the scale, an email message to a family member may fall somewhere in the middle, and a news broadcast may fall on the written end of the scale.

Classroom discourse is one form of oral language use that includes interactions between teachers and students and among students. According to Hall (2001), it is through these interactions that students and teachers create common understandings about source content, build relationships, and determine expectations and patterns of behavior; successful learning therefore results from competent participation in classroom discourse. The way classroom discourse is constructed has implications for student expectations regarding how to communicate both within and beyond a FL course and regarding what is important to learn and how that learning will be assessed. For example, a classroom in which students are expected to provide correctly formed full-sentence answers to questions implies that accuracy is more important than expression of meaning, whereas a classroom in which students are encouraged to expand on answers, ask follow-up questions, or respond to classmates' comments implies that expression of meaning is more important than accuracy.

Three additional concepts that recur in SLA research related to classroom oral language use are fluency, accuracy, and complexity; together, these concepts characterize proficient speech. *Fluency* entails rate of speech (e.g., syllables or words per minute), the use of naturally placed pauses, an absence of restarts due communication breakdown, and the like. *Accuracy* not only includes grammatically appropriate use of language forms and their associated meanings, it also refers to socioculturally appropriate uses of form and meaning. Finally, *complexity* has two dimensions: Syntactic complexity is characterized by more developed phrase structures (e.g., use of subordination, coordination), whereas lexical complexity is linked to lexical density, or the proportion of lexical items to the total number of words or clauses in an utterance (Halliday, 1987; Housen, Kuiken, & Vedder, 2012; Skehan, 2009).

With this base established, in the remainder of the "Conceptual Background" section we summarize SLA research related to oral language use. We focus first on interactionist approaches and the role of input, interaction, output, negotiation of meaning, and feedback. We then overview research on the nature of classroom discourse, including teacher–student and student–student interactions. The section ends with a consideration of concepts related to oral language use from a multiliteracies perspective. To prepare you to read about this research, complete Learning Activity 4.2.

LEARNING ACTIVITY 4.2

Key Concepts in Research on Oral Language Use

Part 1. Below is a list of key concepts in SLA research on oral language use. Before reading the remainder of the "Conceptual Background" section, brainstorm a list of words you associate with each concept.

Input / Output / Interaction / Negotiation / Feedback / Correction / Classroom discourse / Initiation–Response–Evaluation (IRE) / Instructional conversations / Scaffolding / Scaffolded interaction / Community of practice / Multimodality

Part 2. When you finish reading the "Conceptual Background" section, come back to the list of words you associated with each concept. Do these words accurately reflect the concepts based on your understanding of them after reading? Do you need to add or delete words from any of the concepts? If so, cross out any words you feel are no longer appropriate to characterize a concept and add additional words you feel are needed to characterize it more fully.

1.1 Interactionist Approaches to Oral Language Use

As you have likely surmised based on your personal experiences as well as what you have learned up to this point about discourse, communication, and literacy, interaction is a key component of oral language development. Indeed, "it is now commonly accepted within the SLA literature that there is a robust connection between interaction and learning" (Gass & Mackey, 2007, p. 176).

Long's Interaction Hypothesis (1981, 1983, 1985) and the interactionist approaches resulting from it were initially influenced by Krashen's (1982, 1985) Input Hypothesis and Swain's (1985, 1995, 2005) Output Hypothesis. Key concepts related to these approaches are input, output, and interaction. *Input* is the information a learner receives, or the language addressed to learners, and it provides positive evidence for what is possible in a language (i.e., correct forms). Krashen (1982, 1985) argued that exposure to comprehensible input is both necessary and sufficient for FL learning to take place and that speaking is a result of acquisition and not its cause. Swain (1985, 1995, 2005) argued that language production, or *output,* is what allows learners to completely process and develop grammatical and morphological forms in a FL. Pushing learners to produce output has a number of benefits, including practice of language forms and functions, the ability to notice gaps in one's own FL system, opportunities to test hypotheses and experiment with the language, and development of a metalanguage to talk about language forms and functions (Mitchell, Myles, & Marsden, 2013). Contrary to Krashen and Swain, Long (1981, 1983, 1985) hypothesized that FL development arises from conversational interactions and modifications that occur when communication breaks down. *Interaction* refers to the oral exchanges in which learners are involved; it is within these exchanges that learners receive negative evidence, or feedback regarding what is not possible in a language (i.e., incorrect forms). *Negotiation of meaning* is a key concept associated with the Interaction Hypothesis, which, according to Long (1996), includes "adjustments to linguistic form, conversational structure, message content, or all three" when communication breaks down "until an acceptable level of understanding is achieved" (p. 418).

The Interaction Hypothesis, from which arose current interactionist research in SLA, therefore brings together input and output in productive ways through meaning negotiation (Long, 1996). Indeed, all three contribute to the fluency, accuracy, and complexity of learner language.

Interactionist researchers have been particularly interested in the types of discourse that take place during negotiation of meaning, including interactional modifications, feedback, and learner repair or reformulation of errors.

Interactional modifications, also referred to as negotiation strategies, include confirmation checks (e.g., *Is this what you mean?*), clarification requests (e.g., *What did you say?*), and comprehension checks (e.g., *Do you understand?*) (Gass & Mackey, 2007). These negotiation strategies are forms of implicit *feedback* intended to keep the conversation moving forward and to resolve any communication breakdown related to the meaning or structure of the conversation. Corrective feedback, which can be either implicit or explicit, is a response to the formal features (e.g., grammar, vocabulary) of FL learners' speech. Types of corrective feedback include explicit correction, recasts, metalinguistic feedback, elicitation or reformulation, and repetition (Lyster & Ranta, 1997). Although results of research in this area are mixed, particularly with respect to recasts (i.e., teacher reformulation of a learner utterance, minus the error), in general, feedback that includes explicit correction is least effective and feedback requiring learners to reformulate or correct their output (e.g., elicitation and metalinguistic feedback) is most effective in increasing learner accuracy of target language forms (Lyster & Ranta, 1997; Lyster & Saito, 2010; Russell & Spada, 2006).

The implications of interactionist research on meaning negotiation and feedback are far reaching. For instance, this research supports the idea that group work and classroom conversations that involve exchange of ideas help students learn language forms and increase the accuracy, fluency, and complexity of their oral language output. In spite of its significant contributions, however, interactionist research has been criticized as too narrow. Some critics argue that the interactionist tradition centers too much on native-like acquisition of specific grammatical forms and negotiation or feedback strategies. Other critics claim that interactionist approaches are too narrowly focused on cognitive aspects of language development and "uncovering the ways interlocutors unwrap linguistic messages and achieve literal comprehension through requests for clarification and comprehension checking" (Donato & Brooks, 1994, p. 262), rather than on the role of social context in language development (e.g., Cook, 1999; Donato & Brooks, 1994; Firth & Wagner, 1997, 2007). These criticisms have led researchers to suggest that distinctions between language acquisition and learning (i.e., mastery of the linguistic code) and language use or doing (i.e., expression of meaning in a social context) may no longer be useful or easily maintained (Firth, 2009; Firth & Wagner, 2007).

1.2 The Nature of Classroom Discourse

Research on classroom discourse investigates interactions between instructors and their students as well as interactions between students in pair and group activities. Much of this research is based in classroom observation data and seeks to identify the types of interactions that take place, the kind of language or discourse moves used during these interactions, and whether these interactions contribute to FL learning. This research therefore has obvious connections to topics investigated in the interactionist research just summarized. We explore three aspects of research on classroom discourse here: the

Initiation–Response–Evaluation pattern of teacher–student interactions; collaborative talk in teacher–student interactions; and the nature of student–student interactions. As you will see, these three strands of research move along a continuum of teacher-focused to student-focused oral language use and of narrowly to broadly conceived ideas about classroom communication.

1.2.1 INITIATION–RESPONSE–EVALUATION. The *Initiation–Response–Evaluation* (IRE) pattern of teacher–student classroom discourse is the classic question-and-answer format you may have encountered in your educational experiences. Indeed, this pattern typifies many classrooms, FL and otherwise (Hall, 2001; Thoms, 2012). The three-part pattern works as follows:

1. the teacher *initiates* an oral interaction, usually by asking students a question;
2. a student *responds* to the question; and
3. the teacher *evaluates* the student's response by providing positive feedback (e.g., *Very good, Interesting*), negative feedback (e.g., *Not exactly, That's incorrect*) or, in some cases, a follow-up question or statement (e.g., *Can you give an example? What do you mean?*).[1]

Often in IRE exchanges, the instructor asks a question to which he or she already knows the answer (e.g., *What is the date today?, How are Queen Elizabeth and Prince William related to one another?*). Moreover, what students are asked to produce is often limited to tasks such as listing, labeling, or practicing lexical or grammatical items through unrelated questions (Hall 1995, 2004; Hicks, 2003). As a result, there is usually a 2:1 ratio of teacher turns to student turns in IRE exchanges, and teacher turns are usually much longer than student turns (Mehan, 1985; Weissberg, 2006).

Studies investigating the IRE discourse pattern reveal that it does present learning opportunities, but that these opportunities are predominantly mechanical, disjointed, and controlled by the teacher rather than meaningful, contextualized, and controlled by the student (e.g., Barnes, 1992; Cazden, 1988; Hall, 1995, 1998, 2004). The overall conclusion from this research is that IRE exchanges "fail to give opportunities for tackling the complex demands of everyday conversation, especially since teachers usually exercise the follow-up role, while learners often remain in passive, respondent roles" (McCarthy & O'Keefe, 2004, p. 30).

A number of researchers have suggested that changing the nature of the E part of the IRE pattern can affect the oral language students produce (Donato & Brooks, 2004; Hall, 2001; Mantero, 2002; Polio & Zyzik, 2009; Waring, 2009). Rather than provide a positive or negative evaluation of learner answers, teachers should instead elicit reactions to classmates' contributions or ask follow-up

---

[1]The IRE pattern is also referred to as Initiation–Response–Feedback (IRF). Many researchers use these terms interchangeably, whereas others differentiate them. For the purposes of this discussion, we use the term IRE to refer to both.

questions that encourage students to elaborate. Such opportunities for extended discourse not only enhance learning, but they also provide students with opportunities to engage in more culturally authentic conversational exchanges. Indeed, "development of interactional competence is promoted by participation in exchanges that are spontaneous, topically coherent, and extend over multiple turns, which are characteristics of conversations outside the classroom" (Todhunter, 2007, p. 605). In the next subsection we overview research that investigates how to increase student participation and authenticity in teacher–student interactions and thus overcome the shortcomings of the IRE pattern presented here.

1.2.2 INCREASING STUDENT PARTICIPATION IN TEACHER–STUDENT EXCHANGES. As we pointed out earlier, interactionist approaches to oral language development have been criticized as simultaneously too cognitively based and too focused on discrete language forms and negotiation strategies. The IRE pattern of classroom discourse is one example of narrowly focused conversational exchanges that target development of FL accuracy. Nonetheless, you have learned that conversational interactions are essential for language development; the success of teacher–student classroom conversations in improving FL fluency, accuracy, and complexity depends on how the teacher manages interactions. One way to create successful interactions is to balance a cognitive, form-focused orientation with a socially situated orientation in which instructors facilitate FL learning by modeling characteristics of authentic conversations, making challenging content accessible to learners, and mediating communication in a way that yields fruitful learner interaction (Toth, 2011).

Research with this more social orientation investigates collaborative teacher–student discourse rather than the teacher-controlled discourse of the IRE pattern. For instance, Toth (2011) investigated teacher-led discourse in two introductory university Spanish courses, one in which corrective feedback was used to address accuracy during conversational interactions, and another in which collaborative problem solving was used. Results showed that collaborative problem solving facilitated classroom oral discourse more than corrective feedback, but that "successful implementation requires complex decision making at a number of interrelated levels, from broader discourse goals that link turns together to initiations and feedback that determine the range of addressees and the nature of desirable responses" (p. 18). One instructional technique that provides opportunities for extended and collaborative teacher–student discourse is instructional conversations.

Instructional conversations (ICs) are natural-sounding teacher-managed conversations with a pedagogical purpose; they merge conversational characteristics such as open-ended questions and responsiveness with instructional characteristics such as thematic focus, promotion of language development, and direct instruction (Tharp & Gallimore, 1988, 1991; Todhunter, 2007; Weissberg, 2006). The purpose of ICs is to help students understand and communicate about concepts and language features that are central to their learning. Although the instructor is responsible for structuring teacher–student interactions in ICs, they are different from the IRE pattern of classroom discourse because "students are allowed to build on each other's previous utterances with less intrusion from the teacher. The teacher asks fewer known-answer questions and more . . . for which there is no pre-determined answer" (Weissberg, 2006, p. 60). As a result, the content and language used in ICs is less predictable than that of the IRE pattern. Furthermore, students take more turns, their turns are longer, and the instructor acknowledges and builds on students' contributions and links known to new knowledge (Todhunter, 2007; van Lier, 1996; Weissberg, 2006).

Research investigating ICs in FL classrooms looks at their features and the role of the teacher in their implementation, on the one hand, and the nature of learner participation in ICs and the impact of this participation on learning, on the other hand. Features of ICs include a specific thematic focus, connected discourse (e.g., topical coherence, equal distribution of speaking turns), direct teaching, questions with unpredictable answers, promotion of language expression (e.g., prompts that lead to more accurate and appropriate language use), and responsiveness (Goldenberg, 1991; Todhunter, 1997). In addition, empirical research shows that teachers initiate communicative actions that facilitate students' participation in ICs, such as directing attention to turn-taking (e.g., how and when to take the floor), allowing wait time for students to respond, modeling conversational behaviors, providing feedback to guide students away from errors and toward increased understanding and performance, using authentic questions to assist rather than assess or evaluate students, and practicing uptake by deliberately incorporating students' comments into follow-up questions and comments (Boyd & Rubin, 2002; Cazden, 1988; Hall, 2001; Nystrand, 1997; Rubin, 2002; Tharp & Gallimore, 1998; Weissberg, 2006). Finally, research investigating learner participation in ICs and the contribution of this participation to learning shows that when guided by their teacher to communicate, students increase the fluency, accuracy, and complexity of their oral language use through negotiation of meaning and appropriation of more complex concepts and communication strategies (Hall, 2001; Todhunter, 2007).

1.2.3 STUDENT–STUDENT INTERACTIONS IN THE CLASSROOM. You have already read about the negotiation strategies observed in student–student interactions from an interactionist perspective. Here, we summarize socioculturally oriented approaches to investigating student–student classroom interactions. These approaches view language as a tool for negotiating speaking tasks; the focus is on the nature of the interaction and how that interaction drives language learning. This viewpoint differs from cognitively oriented interactionist perspectives, which tend to be more focused on how oral interaction drives acquisition of language forms. Researchers with a sociocultural orientation claim that speaking "simultaneously constitutes the content of an interaction (an *inter* personal communicative function) as well as constructs the very means by which an individual plans for and sustains involvement in a task (an *intra* personal communicative function)" (Brooks, Donato, & McGlone, 1997, p. 526, emphasis in the original).

Jigsaw and information gap activities, in which learners must share two different sets of information with one another, are a common context for socioculturally oriented studies of student–student interaction. For example, Brooks, Donato, and McGlone (1997) found that intermediate-level learners of Spanish used strategies such as metatalk (speaking about one's linguistic resources), metacognition (speaking about the task), and self-talk (whispering) that enabled their participation in jigsaw activities and improved their ability to interact with peers. Likewise, Brooks and Donato (1994), investigating exchanges between third-year high school Spanish learners participating in information gap activities, discovered the following:

> When allowed to structure the procedures of the activity and discuss the language of the task and its goals, even in English, these learners were able to orient themselves jointly, thus allowing them to regulate themselves during the problem-solving activity. (p. 272)

Both studies revealed that allowing students to complete similarly structured activities over time increased their familiarity with the task, reduced their reliance on the strategies identified above, and provided opportunities for spontaneous extended discourse.

The discussion of research perspectives on classroom interaction and discourse up to this point has progressed from being form focused to communication focused and from being cognitively oriented to socioculturally oriented. With socioculturally oriented communication in mind, we now consider oral language use within the multiliteracies framework. To prepare you to read this final part of the "Conceptual Background" section, complete Learning Activity 4.3.

LEARNING ACTIVITY 4.3

Objectives for Oral Language Use in Lower-Level FL Courses

1. Now that you have a better understanding of the nature of classroom discourse, the kinds of oral interactions that promote language proficiency, and the role of cognition and social interaction in oral language development, reflect on what the objectives for oral language use should be in literacy-based lower-level FL courses. Draw on your knowledge of the concept of literacy (developed in the Introduction), the multiliteracies framework (developed in Chapter 1), and instructional goals and objectives (developed in Chapter 2). Brainstorm a list of three or four program-level objectives for interpersonal and presentational oral language use.
2. Compare your list of objectives with a classmate. In what ways are your objectives similar or different? How do your objectives reflect an expanded definition of communication? What aspects of literacy development do your objectives address? How do your goals link oral language use with concepts from the multiliteracies framework (meaning design, Available

Designs, the learning processes of interpretation, collaboration, problem solving, and reflection, etc.)? How do your objectives link oral language use with other language modalities or FL texts?

1.3 Oral Language Use and the Multiliteracies Framework

The definition of communication we foregrounded in the introduction to this chapter, which entails not only language use but also a consideration of how meaning is constructed and negotiated in a range of contexts, is consistent with both the literacy orientation of this book and sociocultural perspectives on oral language use. A literacy orientation emphasizes the linguistic, cognitive, and sociocultural dimensions of learning as well as the interdependence of language forms, language modalities, and literary–cultural content.

> A [sociocultural perspective on language learning] views speaking as the very instrument that simultaneously constitutes and constructs learners' interactions in the target language with respect to the target language itself, the task as it is presented and understood by the participants, the goals learners set for completing tasks, and their orientation to the task and to each other. (Brooks & Donato, 1994, p. 264)

Speaking is therefore an act of meaning design and is consistent with the design features we identified in Chapter 1. It is a dynamic process of discovering meaning through textual creation; it includes both the creation of oral language (process) and the text that results from it (product); it is characterized by linguistic, schematic, and gestural resources that contribute to meaning making; it involves attention to social and cultural knowledge and experiences; and it engages students in the learning processes of interpretation, collaboration, problem solving, and reflection. This perspective on speaking differs from the functional orientation of CLT approaches. Instead, oral language use involves participating in a classroom community, linking together language practice and meaning making, using language patterns in new and creative ways, and communicating about literary–cultural content.

Texts thus play a central role in speaking, both as the discourse students create and as the basis for oral language use. For instance, learners must develop awareness of the features of spoken genres, such as debates, conversations, or oral narratives, to effectively use language to communicate in such contexts. Authentic textual models of spoken language to which students are exposed are thus crucial to oral language development. Yet in many lower-level FL textbooks, it is still common practice to provide scripted dialogues that are devoid of authentic conversational features as models of oral language use (Burns, 1998; Jaén & Bastanta, 2009). There are a number of disadvantages to this practice. For example, because dialogues usually foreground particular language forms (i.e., targeted grammar and vocabulary), "the natural order of spoken discourse, from meaning to form, is reversed" (Burns, 1998, p. 106). Moreover, these scripted texts do not model extended discourse and thus provide a limited view of what conversational language use entails. Finally, many authentic oral texts, such as film, television, podcasts, or even conversation, are multimodal in nature, combining image, sound, text, or gesture; however, the textual models to which students are exposed do not always reflect this reality (Jaén & Bastanta, 2009).

Multimodality is not only a relevant concept related to the nature of oral texts, it also underscores the interrelatedness of speaking, listening, reading, and writing. It is easy to see, for instance, that speaking and listening overlap during interpersonal communication. Yet interpersonal speaking can also overlap with writing if learners work together to brainstorm ideas and vocabulary, or with reading if learners collaborate to create an oral text summary. Likewise, in presentational communication, speaking may overlap with reading as learners research a topic or with writing as they prepare a PowerPoint presentation. Oral language use is thus contingent on listening, reading, and writing, not separate from them as we saw with CLT-oriented approaches. Furthermore, reading, writing, and listening may support speaking tasks and contribute to FL speaking proficiency, just as speaking may support reading, writing, and listening tasks and contribute to FL proficiency in those modalities (Belcher & Hirvela, 2008; Mendelson, 2010; Nystrand, 2006; Van den Branden, 2000; Vandergrift, 2006; Weissberg, 2006; Williams, 2008).

Two important concepts related to oral language use from a multiliteracies perspective are communities of practice (Lave & Wenger, 1991)[2] and scaffolding (Wood, Bruner, & Ross, 1976). Because learning within a multiliteracies perspective is viewed as socially situated and collaborative, it necessarily involves creating a classroom context in which students can simultaneously build knowledge of language and communicate in the FL in a range if contexts and activities (Hall, 2001). Building a *community of practice* in the FL classroom, in which learning is a socially situated mode of participation that entails shared membership in and collaboration with a group, allows learners to develop linguistic, cognitive, and sociocultural dimensions of literacy and engages them in the acts of interpretation, collaboration, problem solving, and reflection. Within a community of practice, students are apprentices who learn the necessary tools to participate in classroom activities, including conventions, language forms, or genres, through collaboration with peers and their instructor to interpret and create textual meaning. Oral language use within a community of practice therefore entails more than practicing speaking; it also includes participation in collaborative activities to solve problems and reflect on language and learning experiences (Hall, 2001; Haneda, 1997; Wenger, 1998).

Key to successful participation in classroom communities of practice is *scaffolding*, or guided assistance by a peer or more capable other. Based on Wood, Bruner, and Ross's (1976) proposed strategies for providing scaffolded assistance, Hall (2001) summarized successful scaffolding as "focusing learners'

---

[2]Gee (2005) proposes the concept of *affinity spaces* as an alternative to communities of practice. Affinity spaces are informal spaces or contexts in which people interact, commonly, but not always, online, that do not entail membership in a community (see Chapter 8).

attention on the task, directing their attention to essential and relevant features, modeling expected behaviors, and keeping the learners motivated throughout" (p. 33). A number of studies point to the importance of scaffolding for oral language development. For instance, Antón (1999), who investigated discourse moves in teacher- and learner-centered introductory Italian and French classes, found that scaffolded assistance in the student-focused class can "lead learners to become highly involved in the negotiation of meaning, linguistic form, and rules for classroom behavior" (p. 314). These opportunities were drastically reduced in the teacher-focused class. Studies investigating scaffolded assistance prior to participation in classroom oral language show that students' autonomous participation in discussions about textual content increased (Mendelson, 2010) and that students' level of accuracy in oral productions increased (Mochizuki & Ortega, 2008).

Communication, meaning design, texts, multimodality, communities of practice, and scaffolding all play an important role as we consider the pedagogical applications of a multiliteracies perspective on oral language use. Before moving on to this next section of the chapter, complete Part 2 of Learning Activity 4.2 to solidify your understanding of the concepts presented up to this point.

2. PEDAGOGICAL APPLICATIONS

With our conceptual background established, it is now time to consider practical applications of research related to oral language use in FL classrooms. We have shown that moving beyond the traditional teacher-led IRE format is crucial to developing the fluency, accuracy, and complexity of learners' oral language, that providing learners opportunities to produce extended discourse furthers language development, and that speaking engages learners in the act of meaning design through creation and interpretation of FL texts. The goal of teaching speaking from a multiliteracies perspective is thus to promote interpersonal and presentational oral communication through exposure to authentic discourse, participation in scaffolded and collaborative speaking tasks, and engagement with target language texts representing various genres and modalities. The question we explore in this section is how to design speaking-oriented lessons grounded in multiliteracies pedagogy as a means of achieving this goal.

General suggestions for organizing speaking activities in FL classrooms are provided in pedagogy textbooks (e.g., Brandl, 2008; Shrum & Glisan, 2010), and a number of these are relevant for teaching speaking within the multiliteracies framework. For instance, learners should be linguistically and cognitively prepared to participate in oral language tasks. Empirical research in this area shows that when learners are given time to participate in pre-speaking activities, they produce more fluent and complex oral language (Mochizuki & Ortega, 2008; Yuan & Ellis, 2003) and participate more autonomously and frequently in conversations about texts (Mendelson, 2010). Equally important is the content with which learners interact. For example, culturally relevant topics that are of interest to students can contribute to the success of speaking activities, and speaking activities designed around authentic texts provide more purpose to the work students carry out. Goals and accountability are other key components of classroom speaking activities; when students know what the goal of an activity is at its outset and are required to do something with the information they gather during the activity, they are more likely to stay focused on the task. Research into the use of information gap and jigsaw activities supports this idea, showing that learners are more engaged and use conversational and negotiation strategies more frequently (e.g., Doughty & Pica, 1986; Platt & Brooks, 2002). Given that meaning negotiation is crucial to language development, another suggestion for organizing speaking activities is to teach students conversational strategies such as clarification requests, follow-up questions, and requesting and giving information. Naughton (2006) found that students who were given training in these strategies increased the amount of time they talked, the number of follow-up questions and clarification requests they made, and their overall ability to request and give help.

In the following subsections, we consider how to organize multiliteracies-oriented instructional activities and assessments that develop students' oral language use. To do so, we draw on text-based models from pedagogical research and propose a template for creating speaking-focused lessons. We then provide a sample lesson plan and suggest literacy-based formative and summative assessments based on that template. To prepare to read this next part of the chapter, complete Learning Activity 4.4.

LEARNING ACTIVITY 4.4

Reflections on FL Speaking Activities and Objectives

You have learned that successful multiliteracies-oriented speaking activities have certain characteristics. They should be goal oriented and text based, include pre-task planning time and scaffolded assistance, provide accountability for learners, include opportunities for extended discourse, and take place within a socially situated collaborative environment (i.e., communities of practice). With these ideas in mind, reflect on the following sets of questions:

1. As you were learning to speak in a FL, did your teachers implement speaking activities that included characteristics of multiliteracies-oriented instruction? How did these activities contribute to your ability to use authentic discourse in interpersonal and presentational modes? How did they contribute to the fluency, accuracy, and complexity of your oral language use?
2. Review the objectives you prepared for Learning Activity 4.3. Do these objectives reflect characteristics of multiliteracies-oriented instruction? How do these objectives contribute to students' ability to use authentic discourse in interpersonal and presentational modes? How do these objectives contribute to the fluency, accuracy, and complexity of students' oral language use?

2.1 Text-Based Models of Speaking Instruction and Assessment

In this section we outline three approaches to speaking-oriented instruction and assessment grounded in texts. First, we present Bueno's (2006) instructional sequence for teaching film that incorporates interpersonal and presentational speaking activities. Next, we outline Johnson's (2003) lesson for advanced ESL learners, which uses project-based learning to develop presentational speaking competence. Finally, we discuss Redmann's (2005) literacy-based *Stationlernen* model. Although focused on interpreting literary texts, this model incorporates multiple opportunities for interpersonal and presentational oral language use.

Grounded in the interactionist-based concepts of input, output, and meaning negotiation, Bueno (2006) described the integration of videotexts with interpersonal and presentational communication in a third-year conversation and composition course. Two Spanish-language films, *Camila* (Baldo, Gallardo, Imbert, & Bemberg, 1984) and *Yerma* (Fragua & Távora, 2003), served as a source of input to students and the basis for various in- and out-of-class activities. In-class interpersonal speaking activities prepared students to interact with the content of the films, whereas out-of-class presentational speaking activities provided opportunities for creative production after watching the films.

The instructional sequence for both films followed the same general format. First, students' background knowledge was activated through brief instructor presentations followed by small-group activities focused on interpreting secondary texts related to each film's content. For instance, students completed small-group jigsaw activities in which they became experts on one aspect of a topic and presented their findings orally to the class, followed by textual interpretation activities in which students identified themes or symbols in the text that overlapped with the film they were to watch. This group work was followed by panel discussions in which students presented hypotheses about themes or characters in the text, and written compositions in which students explored these hypotheses in greater detail. With this background knowledge solidified, students then completed interpretation activities related to the films outside of class. This work involved viewing film segments, answering comprehension questions, and posting to an online bulletin board to discuss questions with classmates. The sequence culminated with presentational speaking in which students videotaped oral journal entries addressing a topic presented in the film or retelling part of the story from another character's perspective. Bueno concluded that the combination of in- and out-of-class activities centered on textual content positively affected learners' FL speaking abilities.

Various activities in Bueno's instructional sequence may serve as formative and summative assessments of students' oral language use. For instance, the jigsaw presentation and panel discussion provide opportunities for informal formative assessment to gauge how well students have understood information prior to viewing a film and how well they can express this information orally. An example of a formal summative assessment is the video journal, which not only provides evidence of students' oral language use, but also demonstrates their understanding of the film, their interpretation of the film's themes and characters, and their ability to use language creatively to express meaning.

Johnson (2003) presented a lesson plan for advanced ESL learners focused on learning how to purchase a car in the United States. The lesson is grounded in principles of project-based learning, whose goal is to provide students opportunities to be active participants in their learning, to become self-directed learners, and to create a realistic and meaningful project. The approach therefore reflects some of the multiliteracies principles with which you are familiar, such as discovery learning, collaboration, reflection, and sociocultural relevance. The four-part lesson (Needs Assessment, Research, Negotiating, Oral Presentation) weaves together speaking, listening, reading, and writing, equips students with negotiation strategies, and provides linguistic support related to car vocabulary and conversational negotiation. The texts with which students interact include car-purchasing web sites, classified ads, and authentic dialogue.

The first part of the lesson, Needs Assessment, prepares learners to participate in interpersonal and presentational speaking activities by providing them with the necessary vocabulary and resources to purchase a car. Learners determine what features they would like in a car (e.g., size, type, make), their budget constraints, which dealerships they will work with, and so on. To help them carry out this task, students work in teams to research a list of instructor-provided terms related to cars (e.g., sedan, keyless entry, financing, torque) and create a semantic map showing how the terms are related. In addition, learners work individually and visit web sites that provide car-buying advice and report their findings to the class. Part 2 of the lesson involves researching print and internet resources to find information based on the needs assessment created in Part 1. To help students in this task, they complete two activities. First, the teacher provides a list of useful web sites and guiding questions to help students get the information they need from each site. Second, students read and interpret sample classified ads in small groups or with their instructor. Based on their research, students then create a written research report that includes the names of helpful web sites they consulted, any pertinent vocabulary or phrases they found, locations for buying a car, and a summary of general information related to car shopping. In Part 3 of the lesson, Negotiating, learners complete a negotiation worksheet designed to help them discuss topics that come up when they meet with a salesperson, determine a position they expect to take during negotiations, and anticipate questions the salesperson might ask. Linguistic support activities focus on reviewing intonation patterns in questions, studying expressions related to asking for clarification, restating an idea, paraphrasing, comprehension checking, and identifying these features in a dialogue between a salesperson and a client. This part of the lesson concludes with telephone and face-to-face meetings with a car salesperson. In the last part of the lesson, students give a multimedia oral presentation that highlights all aspects of their car-buying experience. This includes reviewing the needs assessment and research reports, describing what happened during the preliminary telephone interview and the face-to-face negotiation, and reflecting on their ability to manage the activities involved in the project. To help students prepare an effective presentation, they are provided with the evaluation rubric at the start of this part of the lesson.

The oral presentation students complete in Part 4 of the lesson is a clear example of a summative assessment. An alternative summative assessment would be for students to describe the car they purchased (or attempted to purchase) and to explain why it was the right car for them. The lesson also affords a number of opportunities for formative assessment. For instance, the needs assessment and research report might serve as a formal formative assessment to determine how well students understand targeted vocabulary in the texts they have read. The telephone meeting with a car salesperson might serve as an informal formative assessment to prepare learners for the subsequent face-to-face negotiation.

Although not focused on speaking development per se, Redmann's (2005) pedagogical model targets FL literacy development through collaborative oral and written engagement with target language texts using *Stationlernen*. *Stationlernen,* or learning stations, create a "laboratory-like setting [in which] students rotate between various stations, completing tasks related to an assigned text" (p. 136). Stations typically deal with aspects of a particular theme or topic, and students complete them in whatever order they choose, sometimes working in groups, other times working alone. Reading, writing, and interpersonal and presentational speaking overlap during *Stationlernen* activities, which are scaffolded to accommodate different learning styles and proficiency levels. As such, *Stationlernen* provide "an ideal alternative to large and small group discussions in working with texts" because they "allow for multiple opportunities to foster literacy development in foreign language students" (p. 138).

Redmann described two examples of *Stationlernen* used in intermediate- and advanced-level German courses. In both cases, *Stationlernen* activities took place after students had a general understanding of the text they were studying; these activities thus focused on textual interpretation and transformation, rather than on surface-level comprehension. For example, in the intermediate-level course, working with the youth novel *Grenzgäner* (Günther, 2001), students completed a number of stations that required close reading to support their interpretation of the text as well as creative transformation of the text. Activities included completing a table with information about characters in the text, finding and analyzing quotes that reflected three symbolic elements in the text, creating a map of characters' travels in the text with information about the towns visited, writing a dairy entry from the perspective of the text's main character, and writing a postcard to a second character in the text. After completing the stations, the lesson concluded with oral summaries and reflections regarding the information students had gathered at the stations. According to Redmann, all students in the intermediate-level class "worked actively and intently with the text and communicated in German for the entire hour" (p. 139).

The *Stationlernen* model provides ample opportunities for formative and summative assessment. For instance, formative assessment might include checking the accuracy of information about the story's characters provided in the table or verifying the route students traced on a map. An additional formative assessment would be to evaluate students' interpersonal language use at the various stations and provide suggestions for increasing the quality and quantity of their participation. The oral summary and reflection students provide at the end of the class period might serve as a summative assessment to evaluate students' understanding of the text and their ability to express that understanding presentationally.

The three pedagogical models outlined in this chapter are summarized in Table 4.1. Although informed by a variety of approaches, these models share a number of commonalities. First, all provide examples of interpersonal and presentational oral language use centered on authentic texts and thus on design of meaning through textual interpretation and creation. In addition, in each model, speaking overlaps with the language modalities of listening, reading, and writing. Finally, the three models exemplify scaffolded and collaborative speaking activities that allow students to learn the tools necessary for effective communication, to support and learn from one another, to stay motivated throughout the instructional sequence, and to improve the quality and quantity of their spoken production.

In terms of instructional sequencing, on the surface, the three models seem decidedly dissimilar. In Bueno's model, speaking precedes and follows video viewing; in Johnson's model, speaking follows interaction with textual content; and in Redmann's model, speaking is intertwined with textual interpretation and activities are non-sequential. Nonetheless, all three share common features: They include an initial stage that prepares learners to speak, read, write, and listen effectively; they propose a variety of activities that build learners' linguistic competence and textual understanding; and they conclude

TABLE 4.1 Text-Based Models of Speaking Instruction

	Bueno (2006)	Johnson (2003)	Redmann (2005)
1	Background knowledge activation (jigsaw, oral summary, theme identification, panel discussion, composition)	Needs assessment (semantic map, buying advice)	Initial comprehension activities
2	Video interpretation (comprehension questions, online discussion forum)	Research (guiding questions, internet research, classified ads)	Close reading activities (character analysis, mapping)
3	Oral journal entry	Negotiating (intonation patterns, negotiation strategies, telephone and face-to-face meetings)	Creative transformation activities (diary entry, postcard)
4		Oral presentation (summary, description, reflection)	Oral summary and reflection

with an activity that allows learners to use oral language creatively. With these commonalities in mind, in the next subsection we propose a general format for teaching speaking based on the multiliteracies approach.

2.2 A Template for Organizing Multiliteracies Instruction and Assessment of Oral Language Use

To effectively organize multiliteracies-oriented instructional activities and assessments that promote extended oral discourse in interpersonal and presentational modes, participation in scaffolded and collaborative speaking tasks, and engagement with target language texts, we propose the following four-stage lesson plan template:

1. *Pre-speaking* to access background knowledge and provide linguistic support for speaking tasks organized around textual content;
2. *Textual interpretation* to gather information about lesson content and explore language details;
3. *Knowledge application* to demonstrate textual understanding through interpersonal and presentational oral transformation activities; and
4. *Summary and reflection* to discuss knowledge gained and learning experiences.

The activities to be implemented at each stage should reflect the four pedagogical acts of the multiliteracies framework and engage learners in the processes of interpretation, collaboration, problem solving, and reflection and self-reflection. To review, situated practice activities allow learners to experience a text, idea, or concept through immersion in communicative tasks; overt instruction activities encourage learners to conceptualize information by examining form-meaning connections; critical framing activities foster analysis of textual content by helping students understand the multiple interpretations of an idea or concept and apply background knowledge about the context of the text; and transformed practice activities allow students to apply what they have learned and articulate their perspectives on a text in new or creative ways (see Chapter 1 for a detailed discussion).

Examples of learning activities that might be used in each stage of the lesson plan template are provided in Table 4.2. Note that in some cases, the learning activity corresponds to more than one pedagogical act.

2.2.1 PRE-SPEAKING. The purpose of pre-speaking activities is to build a knowledge base that will help students participate in subsequent speaking activities. This knowledge base can include background information about topics to be explored, language forms and functions that will help learners use language appropriately, or a combination of the two. Activities such as instructional conversations, polling, and teaching gambits provide learners with scaffolded assistance that directs their attention to essential concepts and language features and helps keep them motivated throughout the instructional sequence.

As we discussed in the "Conceptual Background" section, *instructional conversations* (ICs) are teacher-managed discussions that help students

TABLE 4.2 Suggested Learning Activities for Teaching Oral Language Use

Instructional Stage	Suggested Learning Activities
1 Pre-speaking	Instructional conversations (Critical framing) Polling (Situated practice / Critical framing) Teaching gambits (Overt instruction)
2 Textual interpretation	Semantic mapping (Overt instruction) Jigsaw (Situated practice) 3–2–1 summary (Critical framing / Transformed practice)
3 Knowledge application	Video or audio interview (Situated practice) PowerPoint presentation (Transformed practice) Debates (Critical framing / Transformed practice)
4 Summary and reflection	Talking journals (Transformed practice) Think–pair–share (Situated practice) Personal action plan (Transformed practice)

understand and communicate about concepts and language features that are central to their learning. ICs are characterized by open-ended questions, connected discourse, responsiveness to student comments and questions, thematic focus, promotion of language development, and direct instruction. As a critical framing activity, ICs can help students understand, analyze, and apply background knowledge about the topic to be explored in subsequent activities and the language forms they must use to successfully carry out these activities. *Polling* is another way to activate learners' background knowledge about a topic. Polling furthermore encourages students to express their point of view on a topic and to consider the points of view of their classmates. In the FL classroom, polling can be implemented as an interpersonal speaking activity during which students walk around the room to ask *yes/no,* multiple choice, or rating-scale questions from an instructor-provided opinion poll. Once students have collected answers, they report back to the class and the teacher compiles data related to class points of view on the topic under discussion (Kalantzis & Cope, 2012). To add a critical framing component to this activity, students can propose reasons for the class results, using cultural information and background knowledge to support their analyses. A final pre-speaking activity that focuses on the overt instruction of formulaic expressions used in authentic conversations is *teaching gambits* (Keller & Warner, 2005; Rossiter, Derwing, Manimtim, & Thomson, 2010; Wray, 2002). Gambits are expressions, words, or phrases whose role is to frame conversational information and guide listeners through a conversational turn. Examples of gambits include *supposedly, in reality, um, well, lots of people think,* and so on. One strategy for teaching gambits is to provide students with an authentic dialogue for analysis. Students then identify words and phrases from a teacher-provided list of gambits and hypothesize about their meaning and use. Finally, students role play using the gambits they identified in the text. Teaching gambits provides learners with linguistic tools that will help them carry out subsequent interpersonal speaking activities and contributes to the fluency of their oral language use.

2.2.2 TEXTUAL INTERPRETATION. Textual interpretation activities, such as semantic mapping, jigsaw, or 3–2–1 summaries, provide additional scaffolded assistance that allows students to explore in detail topics and language features that will form the basis of interpersonal and presentational speaking activities. The texts that form the basis of textual interpretation activities can be written, oral, or visual.

As an overt instruction activity, *semantic mapping* allows learners to explore ideas or language features in the texts they read, listen to, or view. There are multiple ways to use semantic maps for textual interpretation. As we saw in Johnson's (2003) pedagogical model, learners can create a semantic map of teacher-provided vocabulary to show how terms found in a text are related to one another. Students might also create a semantic map of text-based ideas to develop understanding of a topic. The map can show how these ideas are related to one another, how they are developed within the text using specific vocabulary words, how they relate to a character in the text, and so on (Hall, 2001; Kern, 2000). In *jigsaw* activities students become experts about one aspect of a topic and share this information with others to construct a complete picture of the topic. Students are divided into groups, each of which is responsible for interpreting one portion of a written, oral, visual, or audiovisual text. Students then regroup with one person from each of the expert groups and they learn about the other parts of the text by listening to and sharing information with each expert (Kagan, 1989). Jigsaws thus engage students in meaning design through situated practice as they immerse themselves in the text to search for relevant information to share with others. Moreover, jigsaws encourage interpersonal communication, interpretation, collaboration, and problem solving. *3–2–1 summaries* also engage students in meaning design through summarizing and analyzing knowledge gleaned from a text; 3–2–1 summaries therefore reflect both transformed practice and critical framing. The basic format of a 3–2–1 summary is to have students summarize the text in three sentences; identify two interesting ideas, controversial issues, topics to explore in detail, and so on; and state one connection between what they learned in the text and what they already know, one question about the text, one concept or skill they have mastered as result of interacting with the text, and so on. The types of information students provide in each part of the summary will depend on the goals of the lesson, the learners' proficiency level, and the text with which they are interacting.

2.2.3 KNOWLEDGE APPLICATION. During the knowledge application phase, students apply linguistic and cultural knowledge collected during pre-speaking and textual interpretation activities to creative interpersonal and presentational oral language use. This phase of the lesson plan template is thus conducive to transformed practice; however, activities in this part of the template can span all four pedagogical acts.

An example of a situated practice knowledge application activity is conducting a *video or audio interview* about information collected during pre-speaking and textual interpretation activities. Such interviews can take place with classmates, family members, friends, professors, or members of the community at large. Interviews allow students to prepare discussion topics and questions in advance and to make comparisons across interviewees (Kalantzis & Cope, 2012). *PowerPoint presentations* are transformed practice activities that allow learners to apply knowledge in a multimodal format through text, image, and sound. Because learners refer to visual aids as they speak, they do not have to read from a script but rather can speak from notes. Not only does this kind of knowledge application activity allow learners to highlight everything they have learned throughout the lesson, but it also equips them with a skill set they can apply to presentational speaking in other disciplines or in future professional situations. *Debates* are another example of transformed practice that also includes a critical framing component. In a debate, students are presented with two sides of an issue explored during pre-speaking and textual interpretation activities and must argue in favor of one or the other. Working in groups, students prepare arguments for their side, grounded in the text they have interpreted, and predict counterarguments from the opposing side. During the debate, student groups present an argument, the opposing side proposes a counterargument, and the original group follows up with a response. This interpersonal speaking activity thus encourages meaning design through transformation of knowledge, interpretation, and collaboration.

2.2.4 SUMMARY AND REFLECTION. The lesson plan template for developing oral language use closes with summary and reflection activities, whose purpose is to provide an overview of the knowledge students have gained during the lesson and to reflect on their learning. This stage therefore hones in on the learning processes of reflection and self-reflection. Moreover, this stage shows that the scaffolded assistance learners have received throughout the lesson can result in their autonomous participation in speaking activities related to textual content.

Examples of summary and reflection activities include talking journals, think–pair–share, and personal action plans. *Talking journals* are similar to the oral journal entries in Bueno's (2006) pedagogical model described earlier, although their function can be much broader. As Bueno proposed, in talking journals students can address a topic presented in a text they have read or retell part of a story from another character's perspective. Another way to use talking journals is as a transformed practice activity in which students respond to teacher-provided prompts that encourage summary and reflection about what was learned, how students experienced a text, or their opinion of issues related to the text that came up in previous activities. *Think–pair–share* is a collaborative situated practice activity that serves a similar purpose to talking journals. Students think individually about an instructor-provided question or statement, pair with a classmate to discuss and compare their response, and share their discussion with the whole class (Kagan, 1989). During the pair phase, learners can be directed to pick out ideas they have in common, the most original or convincing ideas each person had, questions that came up during their discussion, and the like. After students share their ideas with the group, the instructor can facilitate class discussion about common ideas, experiences, opinions, or questions. Finally, a *personal action plan* is a written transformed practice activity that encourages both summary and reflection. According to Kalantzis and Cope (2012), the purpose of a personal action plan is to turn an idea into action. Within the context of the lesson plan template proposed here, the action plan can be specific to the text students have interpreted or it can be a form of self-assessment resulting from their work in knowledge application activities. Students begin their personal action plan by identifying a goal. Next, they lay out a series of action steps to complete en route to meeting their goal. With these steps in place, students list the resources and support they will need to meet their goal (e.g., web sites, dictionary, teacher feedback) as well as possible barriers to achieving their goal. The action plan concludes with a list of performance measures to help learners determine whether they have met their goal (e.g., research paper, oral presentation, proficiency test).

2.2.5 ASSESSMENT. The four-stage lesson plan template described here can also serve as a model for designing multiliteracies-oriented tests focused on assessing students' oral language use. Such a test might have the following format: (1) the pre-speaking activity of polling classmates to gather information about a topic; (2) the textual interpretation activity of semantic mapping to relate topics from the poll to textual content; (3) the knowledge transformation activity of a PowerPoint presentation to present conclusions from the poll and link these to textual understanding; and (4) the summary and reflection activity of think–pair–share to summarize information from student PowerPoint presentations and make overall conclusions about the text.

In addition to providing a template for creating formal tests, this speaking model affords opportunities for various formative and summative assessments. A number of the suggested pre-speaking and textual interpretation activities can function as formative assessments carried out through in-class discussion or homework. In addition, the suggested knowledge application and summary and reflection activities may serve as summative assessments that conclude the treatment of a particular text and assess the accuracy, fluency, and complexity of students' oral productions.

2.3 Sample Speaking-Focused Lesson Plan

The lesson plan template for teaching oral language use presented above, organized around the four pedagogical acts, makes it possible for lower-level FL learners to engage in interpersonal and presentational speaking grounded in textual content. Because content-oriented speaking activities require more than expressing personal opinions and viewpoints, the template reflects the broad view of communication we have developed in this chapter and furthermore contributes to students' FL literacy development. Moreover, the instructional stages within the template provide students with the scaffolded assistance and linguistic support necessary to move toward autonomous participation in speaking activities and improved language proficiency. Learners can engage with a variety of oral, written, visual, audiovisual, and digital texts using this lesson template and carry out a number of meaningful activities focused on both form and meaning across language modalities.

In Table 4.3, we present a sample lesson plan organized according to the template above. Activities implemented in the lesson represent one of the three illustrative activity types listed in Table 4.2 for each stage in the model. This lesson is intended for use in a third- or fourth-semester intermediate Spanish course during an instructional unit on health and nutrition. The lesson objectives are to enable students to understand and use vocabulary related to food, health, and nutrition; to understand, compare, and critically evaluate cultural practices related to food and nutrition in both target and home cultures; and to further their ability to engage in extended discourse in interpersonal and presentational modes. Students interact with a number of visual and written texts in this lesson plan. One set of texts includes photos and profiles of four families (two from the United States, one from Mexico, one from Ecuador) depicted in *Hungry Planet: What the World Eats* (Menzel & D'Aluisio, 2005). Each photo is of a family and the food they eat in a typical week; the profile summarizes food items and expenditures. The second set of texts comprises food pyramids or nutritional guidelines from the countries represented in the photos. For the United States, students study the *MyPlate* food guidelines (U.S. Department of Agriculture, 2010); for Mexico, students examine *El plato del bien comer* (Norma Oficial Mexicana para la promoción y educación para la salud en materia alimentaria, 2005); and for Ecuador, students read *La pirámide de la dieta latinoamericana* (Oldways Preservation Trust, 2009). Students work as a class to interpret the texts related to families and nutritional guidelines in the United States and then in small groups to interpret the texts related to either Mexico or Ecuador. The knowledge students gain from these texts forms the basis for interpersonal and presentational speaking activities throughout the lesson.

This four-stage lesson plan facilitates interpersonal and presentational communication through scaffolded activities grounded in textual content. Not only do learners tap into the cultural content of the written and visual texts they analyze, but they also use the FL to understand concepts related to food, health, and nutrition in three different sociocultural contexts. The activities in this lesson engage students in the literacy-based learning processes of interpretation, collaboration, problem solving, and reflection. Students interpret the cultural content of written and visual texts and how the cultural perspectives within these texts relate to one another; they collaborate by interacting with the texts, the instructor, and other learners to interpret and transform meaning; they solve problems by relating vocabulary to textual meaning; and they reflect on cross-cultural differences and similarities. Additionally, this lesson promotes a multimodal approach to oral communication: Speaking is not learned in a vacuum, but rather is intertwined with listening, reading, and writing.

TABLE 4.3 Sample Instructional Sequence, Speaking-Focused Lesson: *Hungry Planet*

Instructional Stage		Learning Activities
1 Pre-speaking	a	Students *poll their classmates* about one or two teacher-provided statements related to food, health, and nutrition in the United States (e.g., Americans eat a healthy diet. Americans eat more junk food than people in Spanish-speaking countries.). Responses are recorded on a five-point rating scale. (Situated practice) Follow up includes tallying class responses and analyzing why the class responded the way it did based on characteristics of U.S. culture. (Critical framing)
	b	Using a PowerPoint presentation, the teacher leads an *instructional conversation* about *Hungry Planet* photos and profiles of U.S. families and *MyPlate* nutrition recommendations. Students make connections between the poll results and information in the photos, profiles, and nutrition recommendations and draw conclusions about food, health, and nutrition in the United States. (Critical framing)
2 Textual interpretation	a	Students work in groups of four to carry out a *jigsaw* activity based on the Mexican or Ecuadorian photos, profiles, and nutrition guidelines. Two students from each group work with the photo and profile and two students with the guidelines; the expert groups come together to share the information they collected. (Situated practice)
	b	Working together, the four students create a *semantic map* of concepts related to food, health, and nutrition in the assigned culture. The instructor provides a brief list of concepts as a starting point based on pre-speaking activities; students fill in the gaps with information from the texts they have discussed. (Overt instruction)
	c	In their same groups, students write a *3–2–1 summary* of what they have learned about food, health, and nutrition in their assigned culture: three sentences that summarize what they learned in the jigsaw and semantic map activities; two comparisons to food, health, and nutrition in the United States; and one question related to food, health, and nutrition in the target culture. (Critical framing / Transformed practice)
3 Knowledge application	a	As a group, students create a *PowerPoint presentation* that integrates information collected during the textual interpretation phase and present their findings to the class. Each student is responsible for presenting one set of information: image of the target culture family, nutrition guidelines from the target culture, semantic map, 3–2–1 summary. (Transformed practice)

(*Continued*)

TABLE 4.3 Sample Instructional Sequence, Speaking-Focused Lesson: *Hungry Planet*

Instructional Stage	Learning Activities
4 Summary and reflection	a Working with a different partner, students complete a *think–pair–share* activity in which they summarize what they learned in previous activities and reflect on cross-cultural similarities and differences related to food, health, and nutrition. During the share portion of the activity, students present the two most important pieces of information they learned, one cultural similarity, and one cultural difference. (Situated practice)
	b Students record a *talking journal* entry in which they summarize what they learned about representations of food, health, and nutrition in the three cultures studied, compare conceptions of food and nutrition across cultures, and speculate as to why these cross-cultural similarities and differences exist. (Transformed practice)

This sample lesson affords a number of opportunities for formative and summative assessment. For instance, instructors can provide formative feedback on both the semantic map and the 3–2–1 summary students create in their groups to clarify any vocabulary misunderstandings or verify textual understanding. After receiving in-class feedback on these activities, students could revise their map and summary at home and then earn a grade based on the completion and accuracy of their revision. The think–pair–share activity at the close of the lesson is another opportunity for formative assessment. Here, individuals can receive informal feedback from the instructor that can facilitate more successful completion of the talking journal. Both the PowerPoint presentation and the talking journal can serve as summative assessments for the lesson. For the PowerPoint presentation, students could receive a group grade based on their collaborative efforts as well as an individual grade based on their portion of the presentation. For the talking journal, students could be assessed on the accuracy of their summary and the soundness of their cultural comparisons. In both cases, students can also be evaluated based on the fluency, accuracy, and complexity of their oral language use.

To help you reflect on this sample speaking-focused lesson plan, read through it a second time and find answers to the following questions:

1. What are the objectives of this lesson and how do they fit within the course curriculum?
2. Are the interpersonal and presentational speaking activities appropriate to meet these objectives? What elements of these activities might be challenging for FL learners to undertake?
3. How does this lesson reflect the conceptualization of communication put forth in this chapter? How does this lesson scaffold oral communication?

4. Why are the different lesson plan activities labeled as situated practice, overt instruction, critical framing, or transformed practice?
5. Are the basic elements of instruction, or the what of multiliteracies pedagogy—conventions, cultural knowledge, and language use—represented in the lesson?
6. Are the learning processes of interpretation, collaboration, problem solving, and reflection and self-reflection (i.e., the how of multiliteracies pedagogy) represented in the lesson?

As you think about creating lesson plans and assessments that focus on oral language development using the template above, come back to these questions as a way to help you to organize your ideas and apply your understanding of multiliteracies-based pedagogy. Learning Activity 4.5 will help you get started.

LEARNING ACTIVITY 4.5

Modifying Textbook-Based Speaking Activities

Select a speaking activity from the textbook you are currently using and modify it using the multiliteracies-based lesson plan template presented in this chapter. Before beginning this task, evaluate the effectiveness of the speaking activity by asking the questions presented above. Once you have identified areas that need improvement, select one or two authentic texts that reflect the content of the speaking activity and then redesign the activity using the four-stage model and suggested learning activities in Tables 4.2 and 4.3. When the lesson plan is finished, ask yourself the same set of questions above as a way to help you justify your pedagogical choices.

3. FINAL CONSIDERATIONS

In this chapter, we have established a conceptual base for considering oral language development in a FL within the multiliteracies framework. Essential to this base are our understanding of communication as language use and meaning design within various sociocultural contexts; the overlapping or multimodal nature of oral language use with listening, reading, and writing; classroom communities of practice in which learning is socially situated and collaborative; and scaffolded assistance that keeps learners focused and motivated, directs their attention to form and meaning, and models expected behaviors. Together, these concepts contribute to FL literacy development and the fluency, accuracy, and complexity of students' oral language use.

This conceptual base informed the approach to FL speaking instruction we developed in this chapter, an approach whose main goal is to promote interpersonal and presentational oral communication through exposure to authentic discourse, participation in scaffolded and collaborative speaking tasks, opportunities to produce extended discourse, and engagement with target language texts representing various genres and modalities. This pedagogy is informed by existing text-based instructional models and is grounded in the four pedagogical acts (situated practice, overt instruction, critical framing, transformed practice) that comprise multiliteracies-based instruction.

We close this chapter by looking ahead to Chapter 5, "Teaching Reading as Constructing Meaning From Texts." We have highlighted throughout this chapter that language modalities are overlapping and intertwined rather than separate. We have furthermore provided a glimpse into the teaching of reading in the textual interpretation stage of the lesson plan template. As you prepare to read Chapter 5, reflect on the following questions: What is the relationship between speaking and reading? In what ways does reading overlap with or complement the other language modalities? What instructional strategies or activities for teaching oral language use apply to the teaching of reading? Which of the multiliteracies concepts you have learned thus far are most important when considering FL reading?

4. TRANSFORMING KNOWLEDGE

4.1 Reflective Journal Entry

For this entry, we ask you to return to the concept map you created after reading Chapter 1 and revised after reading Chapter 2. Now that you have developed an understanding of oral language use, its role in FL literacy development, and its link to the concept of communication, reflect on how speaking and concepts related to it fit within your concept map. Does speaking play a role in only part of the multiliteracies framework as you have conceptualized it or does it play a role in all aspects of the framework? How will you connect oral language use to existing concepts within the map? Are there concepts that you need to add to or delete from your map? Modify your concept map as necessary and use it as a tool as you reflect on the multiliteracies framework and on language forms and other language modalities in subsequent chapters of the book.

4.2 Researching Oral Language Use: Personal Action Plan

Identify a goal or problem area related to teaching speaking and create a personal action plan. Use the table below to lay out your plan, then implement the plan in your teaching. Use your performance measures to collect information that helps determine whether you have met your goal or solved your stated problem. If you have achieved your goal, what are the implications for your approach to teaching speaking? If you have not achieved your goal, how can you modify your action plan to help you move forward in this area of your teaching? You can find a description of the parts of a personal action plan in the "Pedagogical Applications" section of this chapter.

Goal or Problem	
Action Step 1	
Action Step 2	
Action Step 3	
Action Step 4	
Resources and Support	
Possible Barriers	
Performance Measures	

Key Resources

Donato, R., & Brooks, F. C. (2004). Literary discussions and advanced speaking functions: Researching the (dis)connection. *Foreign Language Annals, 37,* 183–199.

The purpose of this qualitative study was to determine how classroom discussion provides opportunities to describe, narrate, use extended discourse, share opinions, explore alternatives, and hypothesize in the context of an advanced Spanish literature course. Through examination of transcripts from classroom observations and interviews with the instructor, the researchers found that simply having a literary discussion does not ensure that students will be pushed to use the language in advanced ways, even when faced with tasks requiring critical thinking and advanced language use. Instead, for students to speak at advanced levels, discussions must enable complex thinking in complex language. As a result, literature instructors should be aware of the discourse opportunities that arise in literary discussions, should make expectations and advanced functions clear, and should monitor language use during discussions. The study's findings not only have implications for how to teach in advanced literature courses, they also suggest that attention must be paid to developing advanced speaking functions from the beginning of FL study.

Hall, J. K. (2001). *Methods for teaching foreign languages: Creating a community of learners in the classroom.* Upper Saddle River, NJ: Prentice Hall.

Chapter 6, "The Interpersonal Mode," presents concepts related to interpersonal speaking and writing and summarizes guidelines for designing effective instructional activities using the four pedagogical acts of situated practice, overt instruction, critical framing, and transformed practice. Hall stresses that the purpose of interpersonal communication is to establish relationships; through interpersonal communication we seek to be understood by others and to understand others so we can behave appropriately toward them. She furthermore underscores the importance of the concept of community and the communities of practice in which the target language is used to communicate interpersonally, both within and outside of the FL classroom. The chapter provides a number of suggested activities to develop interpersonal communication according to the pedagogical acts and concludes with a brief discussion of assessment tools.

McCarthy, M., & O'Keefe, A. (2004). Research in the teaching of speaking. *Annual Review of Applied Linguistics, 24,* 26–43.

This article reviews research and pedagogical practice related to the teaching of speaking. Topics explored in the review include authenticity in spoken materials, understanding the role of speaking in the classroom, which aspects of speaking to teach, and methods and materials for teaching speaking. The review concludes with suggestions for future research, including the role of context in designing speaking activities and of technology in speaking pedagogy.

For Further Reading

Bueno, K. (2006). Stepping out of the comfort zone: Profiles of third-year Spanish students' attempts to develop their speaking skills. *Foreign Language Annals, 39,* 451–470.

Mackey, A., Abbuhl, R., & Gass, S. M. (2012). Interactionist approach. In S. M. Gass, & A. Mackey (Eds.), *The Routledge handbook of second language acquisition* (pp. 7–23). New York, NY: Routledge.

Schulz, R. A. (2006). Reevaluating communicative competence as a major goal in post-secondary language requirement courses. *Modern Language Journal, 90,* 252–255.

Todhunter, S. (2007). Instructional conversations in a high school Spanish class. *Foreign Language Annals, 40,* 604–621.

CHAPTER 5

Teaching Reading as Constructing Meaning From Texts

When confronted with teaching reading in lower-level foreign language (FL) classrooms, instructors often have questions: How can students with limited linguistic competencies read authentic texts? Will I have enough time to integrate authentic texts into my course and develop students' reading competencies as well as to teach grammar and vocabulary? If this is a language class, then shouldn't my primary focus be on developing students' oral communication abilities? Many of these questions reflect communicatively oriented views of reading in lower-level FL courses, in which reading entails decoding words, grammatical forms, and writing systems (Hall, 2001). Several important consequences for reading instruction result from this viewpoint: (1) functional, oral language use takes precedence over interaction with texts; (2) reading is seen as a way to practice language forms rather than to interpret textual meaning; (3) reading is considered distinct from other linguistic modalities such as speaking, listening, viewing, or writing; (4) texts serve primarily as examples of correct vocabulary and grammar; and (5) interaction with texts is often postponed until students have gained some degree of linguistic mastery. This approach to reading, grounded in communicative language teaching (CLT), is often accompanied by a lack of effective articulation between lower- and upper-level courses due to the perception that lower-level courses serve to prepare students linguistically for the literary–cultural content they will learn in upper-level courses. As discussed in the Introduction, this disconnect between the two ends of the undergraduate FL curriculum fuels instructor frustration regarding the teaching of texts, including literature, in lower-level courses. It also creates student frustration regarding the expectation that once they have completed lower-level courses, they are considered ready to interpret and analyze intellectually and linguistically challenging texts, both literary and non-literary.

Yet, as we have seen in the preceding chapters, even students in the first semester of FL study can interact with authentic texts, and the multiliteracies framework provides the tools to design and implement reading-focused activities that make these texts accessible. Indeed, a multiliteracies approach to reading makes possible the integration of texts at all levels of the curriculum, thereby increasing the amount of textual content with which students interact in lower-level courses and preparing them to read a variety of text types (e.g., literature, historical documents, current events) as they progress through the undergraduate curriculum. Moreover, the integration of language and cultural content through multiliteracies-based curricula and instruction makes possible a holistic approach to students' linguistic development, such that reading is viewed as complementary to other modalities (e.g., speaking, listening, viewing, writing) rather than distinct from them.

The purpose of this chapter, therefore, is to explore the teaching and learning of FL reading within the multiliteracies framework. Although we focus primarily on constructing meaning from texts in lower-level language courses, the concepts and applications discussed are relevant across curricular levels, including advanced literature courses. In the "Conceptual Background" section, we overview the treatment of FL reading in previous research, focusing on concepts related to reading ability and cognitive processing models that have informed CLT-based approaches to reading. We then introduce concepts relevant to an integrated, multiliteracies-oriented approach, such as the sociocultural dimension of reading and reading as meaning design. In the "Pedagogical Applications" section, we first consider goals of reading instruction within the multiliteracies framework to organize instructional activities based on the four pedagogical acts of situated practice, overt instruction, critical framing, and transformed practice. We follow with an overview of literacy-based approaches to teaching and assessing textual interpretation and present a model for designing reading-oriented lesson plans. The section concludes with a walk-through of a sample instructional sequence and related assessments based on this model. By the end of this chapter, you should have a clearer understanding of why a multiliteracies approach to constructing meaning from written texts is a viable alternative to CLT-based approaches and how it can be implemented in your classroom context.

1. CONCEPTUAL BACKGROUND

This section provides an overview of second language acquisition (SLA) research on and models of FL reading that have informed both CLT- and multiliteracies-based approaches. Although we elaborate a definition of reading consistent with the concept of literacy and the multiliteracies framework later in this section, we begin by summarizing some common conceptualizations of FL reading within the classroom context. For instance, reading can be understood as having students read aloud paragraphs from a textbook or carry out word-for-word translation with the goal of fostering overall textual understanding. Reading is also often considered a private act of textual decoding that students carry out on their own to comprehend surface-level facts before coming to class. Finally, as explained in the Introduction, reading is frequently seen as a support skill for the purpose of practicing language forms. Some of these viewpoints are remnants of traditional approaches to FL instruction, such as grammar translation or audiolingualism; others result from the predominance of CLT-oriented approaches and the purpose of reading within them. This brief discussion of the concept of reading serves as a backdrop for exploring factors that affect learners' ability to read in a FL, cognitive processes involved in reading, and sociocultural dimensions of reading. After establishing this foundation, we then consider textual interpretation within the multiliteracies framework, focusing on the design of meaning and the goals of reading-focused instruction. To help you interact with this conceptual background information, complete Learning Activity 5.1.

LEARNING ACTIVITY 5.1

My Opinions About Reading in a FL

Part 1. Before reading the "Conceptual Background" section, jot down your opinion regarding each of the statements below related to foreign language reading.

STATEMENT 1: Comprehension and interpretation are two distinct components of reading.

STATEMENT 2: FL learners cannot read successfully when their linguistic proficiency is low.

STATEMENT 3: Being a strong reader in your first language leads to being a strong reader in a FL.

STATEMENT 4: It is more important for lower-level readers to focus first on the individual pieces of a text (e.g., words, phrase, sentences), and then on the overall meaning of the text.

STATEMENT 5: Reading effectively is tied to the ability to understand culturally dependent viewpoints, beliefs, and practices.

STATEMENT 6: A multiliteracies approach to FL reading places primary importance on language features and secondary importance on textual meaning.

Part 2. After reading the "Conceptual Background" section, come back to this activity and complete the table below. First, indicate whether your opinion about statements 1–6 above was supported or contradicted. Then, provide one piece of evidence from the text to support or refute your decision. Finally, reflect on how this new information has contributed to your conceptual understanding related to reading, in particular, and to the multiliteracies framework, in general.

Statement	Opinion Supported or Contradicted?	Evidence From Reading
1		
2		
3		
4		
5		
6		

1.1 Factors Affecting Foreign Language Reading

Although the layperson may assume that the most important factor affecting students' ability to read in a FL is their proficiency in the FL, SLA researchers who study reading have found that linguistic competency is only part of the story. In fact, this research shows that background knowledge, genre familiarity, and first language (L1) reading experiences can positively impact textual interpretation and comprehension, even if FL ability is relatively low (e.g., Bernhardt, 1991; Carrell & Eisterhold, 1983; Chen & Donin, 1997; Hammadou, 1991). Based on a large body of research evidence, Bernhardt (2005) proposed a model of the knowledge base necessary for FL reading that includes L1 literacy, FL knowledge, and unexplained variance. Unexplained variance, which includes factors such as strategy use, background knowledge, interest, and motivation, plays an increasingly important role as learners' FL proficiency improves. As the model in Figure 5.1 illustrates, these "knowledge sources are not additive, but rather operate synchronically, interactively, and synergistically" and, as a result, they "assist or take over for other knowledge sources that are inadequate or nonexistent" (Bernhardt, 2005, p. 140). For instance, knowledge that falls within the unexplained variance category can facilitate vocabulary understanding even if this knowledge is underdeveloped in the L1 or FL.

SLA research further highlights that FL reading is not as simple as transferring L1 reading ability to the FL. Likewise, as Kucer (2009) argued, reading does not involve "a set of subskills that can be easily isolated, practiced, mastered, and then used with the same degree of proficiency or facility from one text to the next" (p. 132). These conclusions suggest that successful readers are not just literate in the L1 and linguistically capable in the FL, but they are also adept at using existing knowledge to make sense of new information, asking questions before, during, and after reading, drawing inferences from a text, monitoring their comprehension, using compensatory strategies when meaning breaks down, determining what is important in a text, and synthesizing

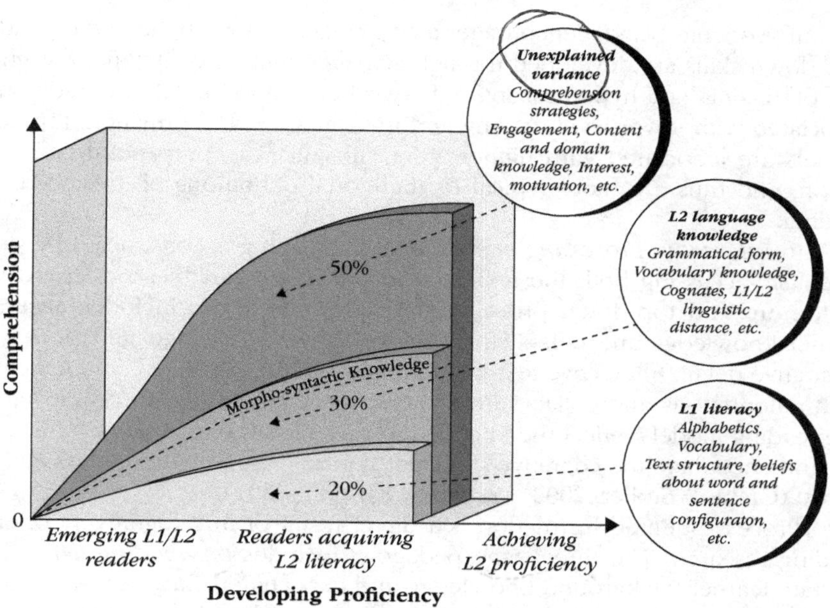

FIGURE 5.1 Bernhardt's Compensatory Model of Second Language Reading (2005, p. 140)

information (Kucer, 2009). Any approach to FL reading instruction, therefore, must encourage these kinds of behaviors and thus play into the unexplained variance category of Bernhardt's model. An understanding of the cognitive processes contributing to the act of reading forms an important component of such an approach.

1.2 Cognitive Reading Processes

In addition to determining the knowledge base required to read successfully in a FL, much of the SLA research related to comprehending written texts has focused on cognitive aspects of the act of reading. This research is mainly interested in studying the psychological processes underlying reading and has identified reading models that characterize these processes. The most common of these models are bottom-up, top-down, and interactive.

Bottom-up processing models are text-driven; that is, textual meaning is constructed from the bottom up through letters, words, phrases, and sentences. This type of processing is primarily linear and discrete and usually involves learners working autonomously to construct meaning. Bottom-up skills are developed through activities such as word segmentation, syntactic feature recognition, and decoding. As such, bottom-up processing typifies the traditional view of lower-level reading discussed in the introduction to this chapter.

Top-down processing models are reader driven: that is, textual meaning is constructed by accessing background knowledge and drawing inferences about the text. In contrast to bottom-up models, top-down processing is holistic and discourse oriented, and it encourages active collaboration on the part of readers. Top-down skills are developed through activities such as contextualized guessing, predicting, and hypothesizing. Whereas bottom-up models are traditionally associated with lower-level reading and transmission of information, top-down models are associated with higher-order subskills and purposeful communication, and thus are more typical of traditional definitions of advanced-level reading.

In *interactive processing models*, textual meaning is constructed by simultaneously accessing both the text- and reader-based variables associated with bottom-up and top-down processing. Reading therefore includes accessing learner knowledge and perspectives, as well as surface language features and illustrative detail. Interactive text processing is multidimensional, and it includes both autonomous and collaborative interaction with a text. Moreover, interactive reading models reflect the knowledge base required for successful FL reading and encourage the cognitive strategies typical of successful readers outlined above (Grabe & Stoller, 2002; Hedgcock & Ferris, 2009).

Process-oriented instruction is a direct result of this cognitively oriented reading research. The three-stage pedagogy includes *pre-reading activities* to activate learner background knowledge and expectations, *while-reading activities* that move from global to detailed text comprehension, and *post-reading activities* that encourage learners to productively use language forms and ideas from the text. These pedagogical activities focus on developing the cognitive skills and strategies necessary to effectively process FL texts from both the top down and the bottom up. For example, when reading a personal ad, learners might be asked in pre-reading to identify features of personal ads they have read previously; in while reading to answer true–false questions about the content of the text and then decode several words or phrases in the text; and finally in post-reading to write a personal ad using these words or phrases. Process-oriented instruction and the models on which it is based have had a profound impact on CLT-based approaches to reading. Yet because of its nearly exclusive cognitive focus, process-oriented approaches leave aside the social and contextual factors essential to language learning and to the multiliteracies framework. To prepare you to learn about the multiliteracies approach to constructing meaning from texts, take a few moments to complete Learning Activity 5.2.

LEARNING ACTIVITY 5.2

Evaluating and Analyzing Conclusions

The conclusion to Section 1.2 that a cognitive approach to reading is insufficient because it does not attend to the sociocultural dimension of learning. Based on what you have understood from reading the chapter up to this point and your background knowledge related to the multiliteracies framework, complete the following tasks:

1. Make a list of shortcomings associated with an exclusive focus on cognitive processes related to reading and why you see these as shortcomings. Try to relate these shortcomings to your experiences as a FL reader or teacher.
2. Indicate which specific traits, concepts, or ideas related to the multiliteracies framework might address each of the shortcomings you identified.

As you read Section 1.3, "Reading and the Multiliteracies Framework," check to see if your proposed multiliteracies solutions are featured in the discussion. Are there elements of the multiliteracies framework presented in the chapter that you did not include in your list? Did you include elements that were absent from the chapter discussion? Why do you think this is the case?

1.3 Reading and the Multiliteracies Framework

As we stated at the start of the "Conceptual Background" section, in more traditional approaches to FL instruction, reading is viewed as a solitary act aimed to develop surface-level factual understanding and to practice language forms. Moreover, process-oriented instruction, which has informed approaches to reading within CLT, is motivated by research on the cognitive processes an individual undergoes during the act of reading. Within the multiliteracies framework, reading has a cognitive dimension, but it is also associated with a broader range of purposes and practices and is viewed as an act of constructing meaning from a text (Hedgcock & Ferris, 2009; Swaffar, Arens, & Byrnes, 1991). The following definition highlights the interpretive and collaborative nature of meaning construction inherent in a multiliteracies-based view of reading:

> Reading is a process undertaken to reduce uncertainty about meanings a text conveys; the process results from a negotiation of meaning between the text and its reader; the knowledge, expectations, and strategies a reader uses to uncover textual meaning all play decisive roles [in the] way the reader negotiates with the text's meaning. (www.coerll.utexas.edu/methods/modules/reading/01/)

Several important concepts emerge from this definition. First, because reading is a process, it is a *recursive act* that involves interaction between text and reader (Swaffar & Arens, 2005, Swaffar, Arens, & Byrnes, 1991). This interaction may include rereading part or all of a text to construct meaning; it may include changing one's interpretation of the text after gathering more information; or it may involve revisiting the text to find evidence of opinions or ideas. Second, because it is a recursive, interactive act of meaning construction, reading involves *interpretation,* or moving beyond surface-level facts to reveal cultural perspectives, points of view, and personal opinions. This kind of textual interpretation involves the ability to engage in *inferencing,* defined as "a thinking process that involves reasoning a step beyond the text, using generalization, synthesis, and/or explanation" (Hammadou, 2002, p. 219). Finally, as we saw in top-down processing models, reading involves the ability to bring one's own *background knowledge* and ideas to a text to contribute to meaning construction. This background knowledge may be topical, linguistic, or rhetorical; that is, to interpret a FL text, learners may tap into knowledge of lived experiences, language forms and functions from their first language or other languages to which they have been exposed, or textual organization and genre features. As you have seen in previous chapters and will see again in future chapters, concepts such as recursiveness, interpretation, and background knowledge characterize not only reading, but also other, complementary language modalities such as writing and listening.

The ideas in the definition presented here reflect the multiliteracies perspective that reading, or any kind of textual interaction, is an act of meaning design. That is, reading is not merely a receptive skill that involves decoding the linguistic features of a text, but rather a communicative process that involves creating and interpreting meaning (Kern, 2000). Moreover, reading is a social and cultural act that includes cognitive processing and understanding of discourse features. In other words, the act of constructing meaning and creating discourse from texts reflects the three dimensions of literacy—cognitive, linguistic, and sociocultural—outlined in the Introduction to this book. As a result, the act of reading is "not fixed and universal, but is instead characterized by contextually appropriate practices" (Kern, 2000, p. 121).

As we have already seen, the cognitive dimension of reading is focused on the individual and how that individual deals with a written text. Key components of this dimension are the psychological processes, strategies, and problem-solving skills a reader uses to construct textual meaning (Kern, 2000; Kucer & Silva, 2006). The linguistic dimension of reading involves recognizing graphic and lexical features of a text and understanding conventions that contribute to the ways in which these elements are combined to create phrases, sentences, paragraphs, and so on (Kern, 2000). In other words, the linguistic dimension of reading "represents all the reader . . . understands about how language operates as a vehicle for communication" (Kucer & Silva, 2006, p. 7). Although the processing models outlined in the previous section include the cognitive and, to a degree, the linguistic dimensions of reading, absent is the sociocultural dimension of reading. This last dimension is crucial in making reading from a multiliteracies perspective unique.

The sociocultural dimension of the multiliteracies framework makes reading more than an act of language use and cognition; it is also a set of patterned literacy practices that are tied to and reflect a group, community, or culture (Kucer & Silva, 2006). This multidimensional view means that reading becomes a socially situated act that connects learners to the world around them. Linked to the sociocultural dimension of literacy is the idea that readers must determine an appropriate context for interpreting a written text, a context that is in part created by the features of a particular text or genre. The ability to appropriately interpret these features is an activity "involving relationships, shared assumptions, and conventions" (Kern, 2000, p. 111) or, put more simply, it is a socially situated activity. Taken together, the three dimensions of literacy allow for interaction between the sociocultural and individual processes that take place as readers interact with the formal and content-oriented features of a text to create meaning.

This multidimensional view of reading and literacy development has grown out of work in reader-response and schema theories. *Reader-response theory* (Fish, 1980; Holland, 1975; Iser, 1974), which informs the sociocultural dimension of the multiliteracies framework, assumes that readers have an active role in determining the meaning of a text. Meaning is not extracted from a monolithic, static text, but is instead interpreted and constructed from a reader's perspectives and ideas and is justified based on evidence found in the text. This active engagement with a text means that interpretation is dependent on the reader, the cultural context, belief systems, and so on, such that the reading of a text is always changing. Central to reader-response theory is the notion of making learners aware of these culturally dependent viewpoints and understanding how cultural norms and beliefs are reflected in various interpretations. Within the context of FL reading, it is important to keep in mind that it is unrealistic to expect learners to have native-like interpretations of a text, given that their own sociocultural frame of reference is different from that of both the text's author and its intended audience. Rather, readers should be made aware that their interpretation of a FL text will likely be different from that of a native speaker and furthermore that even among native speakers from the same target culture, the interpretation of a text may vary considerably (Kern, 2000). It is in identifying these various possible interpretations that learners can recognize sociocultural differences between groups. For instance, returning to our example of a personal ad, readers may find that the kind of information included (e.g., personality or physical traits, activity preferences) differs from one culture to another. Students can use their own culturally situated expectations of such a text and together build alternative or modified interpretations.

Schema theory (Bartlett, 1932; Carrell & Eisterhold, 1983; Rumelhart, 1981) plays a central role in the cognitive reading models outlined earlier and informs the cognitive dimension of reading in the multiliteracies framework. Schema theory models how knowledge is organized in the brain and how this knowledge is used in interpreting a written text. This knowledge organization is systematic; that is, it is constructed of networks of structures, or *schemata*. Not only are schemata related to background or content knowledge and experiences, but they are also formal (e.g., organizational patterns, genre conventions) and linguistic (e.g., syntactic structures, textual coherence and cohesion). Indeed, in multiliteracies parlance, formal and linguistic schemata are examples of some of the Available Designs that come into play during textual interaction. In reading FL texts, learners must tap into these existing Available Designs and at the same time identify gaps in their knowledge. Moreover, because background knowledge is culturally determined, readers must also learn to recognize mismatches between their schemata and the cultural context of the text. The personal ad example illustrates exactly this idea. Learners having certain socially situated expectations about the form and content of a personal ad may encounter mismatches when reading a personal ad from another culture. Learning to recognize these mismatches can help readers gain insight into the cultural implications of such texts and add to their existing Available Designs. It is through interaction with multiple and various FL texts as well as through structured instructional activities that learners develop these socioculturally appropriate schemata (Kern, 2000).

1.4 Reading as Meaning Design

As suggested in the previous section, background knowledge and an understanding of textual features (i.e., Available Designs) make an important contribution to a reader's ability to engage in the socially situated construction of textual meaning. Indeed, within the multiliteracies framework, reading is seen as an act of meaning design, or the "active, dynamic process of creating form–meaning connections through interpretation or creation of texts" (Allen & Paesani, 2010, p. 122). As you learned in Chapter 1, engaging in meaning design involves attending to various Available Designs, or linguistic, schematic, visual, audio, gestural, and spatial resources, of a text and drawing on existing knowledge to construct textual meaning. To interpret a text, a learner uses these Available Designs to engage in Designing, or the "process of shaping emergent meaning [that] involves re-presentation and recontextualization" (New London Group, 1996, p. 75). Designing is therefore a process of applying and recycling known concepts and ideas in new ways. To review your conceptual knowledge of Available Designs and prepare you to think about the role of meaning design in teaching reading, complete Learning Activity 5.3.

As you learned in Chapter 1, linguistic, schematic, visual, audio, gestural, and spatial Available Designs are reflected in three of the seven principles of literacy: conventions, cultural knowledge, and language use. These three principles comprise the basic elements of instruction, or the what of multiliteracies-based FL reading instruction. The remaining four principles of literacy—interpretation, collaboration, problem solving, and reflection and self-reflection—represent the learning processes in which readers engage, or the how of multiliteracies-based FL reading instruction (Kern, 2000). To solidify your understanding of reading-related concepts, complete Part 2 of Learning Activity 5.1.

2. PEDAGOGICAL APPLICATIONS

As we begin our discussion of pedagogical applications of the multiliteracies framework to FL reading instruction, we are again faced with questions: What should a multiliteracies-based lesson focused on interpreting textual meaning look like? How do we design reading-focused lessons that develop students' linguistic competencies and cultural knowledge simultaneously? How do we implement these lessons to meet curricular and course goals and objectives? What kinds of literacy-oriented tasks do we want learners to be able to carry out? What do we want students to learn from analyzing written FL texts? How do we assess students' ability to construct meaning from texts? To help you find answers to these questions, complete Learning Activity 5.4.

LEARNING ACTIVITY 5.3

Accessing Available Designs

Consider the following cartoon. What Available Designs (e.g., linguistic, schematic, visual, spatial resources) must a reader access to interpret this text's meaning? In what ways are these Available Designs socially, culturally, and contextually determined? What areas might cause difficulties for non-native language learners reading this text for the first time?

"You're either too hot or too cold.
Why can't you be just right?"

Source: andrewgenn/Fotolia

LEARNING ACTIVITY 5.4

Think Sheet

To help you to think about teaching FL students to construct meaning from written texts, generate a list of questions that are related to classroom implementation, and then brainstorm possible answers based on what you already know about multiliteracies pedagogy. As you read the "Pedagogical Applications" section, complete the table with information from the chapter that further answers these questions. If there are questions you cannot answer by reading the chapter, consult the references in the "Key Resources" and "For Further Reading" sections at the end of this chapter or discuss the questions with a colleague, classmate, or professor.

My Questions	My Thoughts—What I Already Know	Text Ideas—Additional Answers From the Chapter
should verb tenses/ grammar play a role in my decision?	no-depends on my activities.	
should length be taken into consideration at all?	not necessarily	
how important is genre?	depends on your goal	
how much should students be able to understand?	?	

To ground our discussion, it is important to first consider goals of reading-focused FL instruction and assessment within the multiliteracies framework. Because reading entails meaning design, an important goal of FL reading within the multiliteracies framework is to merge the "communicative" and "textual analysis" sides of the undergraduate curriculum (Kern, 2000). However, traditional approaches to FL reading instruction have impeded integration of text-based learning across the curriculum by separating these two instructional goals. For example, in CLT-oriented approaches, lower-level courses typically focus on functional, oral language use with reading as an add-on skill, whereas advanced-level courses focus on interpretation and analysis of literary–cultural texts. A curriculum grounded in the multiliteracies framework helps to overcome this separation by encouraging learners to interact with FL texts from the beginning of instruction. Merging communication and textual analysis in this way has important implications for FL study. Not only does the multiliteracies framework contribute to creating more coherent curricula, it also contributes to the goal of developing students' linguistic abilities, interpretive skills, and academic literacy. Moreover, linking communication with textual interpretation and analysis encourages a more holistic, multimodal view of language, and can lead to more effective FL use through speaking and writing about the Available Designs within texts (see Chapter 4 for a discussion of oral language use and Chapter 6 for a discussion of writing).

Empirical research specific to creating meaning from texts in lower-level FL courses supports the goal of merging communication and textual analysis across the curriculum. Maxim (2002, 2006) argued in favor of integrating into lower levels "an approach to reading that expands learners' existing reading abilities so that they can gain experience in comprehending and expressing meaning in the imagined world of texts they will encounter at the upper level" (2006, p. 21). He studied the implementation of literacy-based pedagogy in a first-semester German course and found that students who spent half of class time reading a full-length romance novel and half of class time completing communicative language practice fared just as well on language-focused departmental exams as students who did not read the novel and did only communicative language practice in class. Findings from two studies by Scott and Huntington

(2007, 2008) specific to literature instruction in lower-level FL courses revealed that students are not only able to engage in interpretive processes at this level, but that through reading literary texts students are able to connect more fully with cultural content and themes. Similarly, a study on the use of a novel at the intermediate level by Stewart and Santiago (2006) found that engaging in FL reading activities centered on a literary text resulted in complex cultural understandings that had a lasting impact on students. Taken together, this empirical research on literacy development at lower levels of the undergraduate FL curriculum shows that it is not only feasible to merge communication and textual analysis, but that doing so contributes to the development of students' interpretive abilities, sociocultural understanding, and linguistic competencies.

In what follows, we consider how to organize instructional activities and assessments following a multiliteracies framework that meets the goals we have outlined here and engages learners in constructing meaning from written texts. To do so, we propose a template for creating reading-focused lessons synthesized from existing literacy-oriented models present in pedagogical research and provide a sample lesson plan that illustrates its use. We further suggest literacy-based formative and summative assessments that complement the lesson plan and evaluate students' ability to construct meaning from texts.

2.1 Literacy-Oriented Models of Reading Instruction and Assessment

In this section, we outline four approaches to reading-oriented instruction and assessment grounded within the concept of literacy. First, we present Hedgcock and Ferris's (2009) instructional sequence for intensive reading; next we outline two integrated approaches, one from Swaffar and Arens (2005) and the other from Maxim (2006); finally, we discuss Kern's (2000) approach to constructing meaning from texts, organized around the four pedagogical acts.

Framed within a sociocultural and cognitive approach to literacy, Hedgcock and Ferris (2009) present a process-oriented instructional sequence for intensive reading in ESL (English as a Second Language) and EFL (English as a Foreign Language) contexts. Each stage in their three-part pedagogy is broken down into distinct pedagogical activities. The pre-reading stage includes four types of these activities. In the first activity, getting ready to read, learners activate key schemata related to a text and establish a purpose for reading. Next, students survey the text to get a sense of important features, text length, and text organization. Based on the information gathered in these two activities, learners then make predictions and hypotheses and ask questions about the content of the text. The final pre-reading activity involves introducing key vocabulary that could potentially impede comprehension when students engage in while-reading tasks. The while-reading stage is also broken down into four activities. During a first reading of the text, students confirm or disconfirm predictions made during pre-reading and develop a sense of the main facts of the text. Next, students engage in focused re-reading of the text during which the instructor facilitates comprehension and helps develop effective reading strategies. Examples of re-reading activities include highlighting, annotating, outlining, or questioning. The third while-reading activity includes looking closely at the language of the text to analyze vocabulary, syntax, or style. Finally, readers consider the rhetorical organization of the text and how it contributes to an author's purpose and a reader's comprehension. The final stage of Hedgcock and Ferris's instructional sequence is post-reading, which includes three activities. First, students engage in summarizing. This task allows students to review textual facts and details and instructors to check comprehension. Next, students think critically about the text. This work can include questioning ideas in the text or linking ideas to readers' personal experiences. Finally, to establish reading–writing connections, students might write a compare-and-contrast essay, creatively interpret the text, or carry out a research project. According to Hedgcock and Ferris, not all activities within each stage of their pedagogy are required for every text. In fact, they argue that when making decisions about what types of reading activities to include in a lesson, it is most important for instructors to be conscious of "*why* such activities are valuable [and] *how* they may be most effectively implemented" (p. 192, enphasis in the original).

Hedgcock and Ferris argue that by engaging students in this kind of recursive, process-oriented reading pedagogy, instructors have ample opportunities for formative assessment of student progress because "assessing reading is teaching reading" (p. 326). Examples of such formative assessments may be found among the tasks learners carry out in the instructional sequence. For instance, surveying the text to identify main ideas or topics allows instructors to assess learners' progress related to global understanding of a text; reading the text carefully to make connections between vocabulary and textual meaning allows instructors to gauge how well students read closely for specific information. Examinations, homework, or participation-based assessments might include a number of these task types. Hedgcock and Ferris do point out, however, that assessment of student learning is best carried out in the post-reading phase, as it "make[s] the internal reading process and its outcomes more transparent" (p. 184). From the examples provided above, the summarizing activity might be an appropriate summative assessment to gauge students' ability to interpret and analyze the text before moving on to assessing their knowledge through a compare-and-contrast essay or a research project. Finally, Hedgcock and Ferris suggest several alternative assessments, including reading journals, literacy portfolios, and student self-assessments that may complement more traditional tasks, engage learners more fully in the assessment process, and more closely integrate instruction and assessment practices.

The models of literacy-oriented FL reading pedagogy presented in Swaffar and Arens (2005) and Maxim (2006) both draw on the integrative, procedural approach to texts developed in Swaffar, Arens, and Byrnes (1991). For Swaffar and Arens, reading in a FL is seen "as the key to cultural and language literacies" (p. 78) and they propose a pedagogy organized around a reading matrix that makes even challenging texts such as literature accessible to lower-level learners. The first stage in this pedagogy is pre-reading to help readers tap into background knowledge, generate predictions about textual genre, make use of existing literacies, and prepare them for subsequent reading activities. Next, initial reading of the text helps learners identify patterns and focus on global comprehension. One task that facilitates this kind of comprehension is a directed reading thinking activity (DRTA) (Stauffer, 1975) during which students can confirm or refute hypotheses, make predictions about what will come next in the text, or identify how a text presents information. This initial reading stage can lead to a focused look at specific literacies (e.g., linguistic, cultural), depending on the goals of the course or lesson, by building on what readers already know about the text. To do this, Swaffar and Arens propose the use of a reading matrix (see Figure 5.2), which guides students "to more informed reading—a rereading—that establishes the meaning of text structures as logics (keyed visually) and as data sets" (p. 87). In this matrix, readers look at specific scenes played out in "La muerte" (Anderson Imbert, 1976), a fantastical short story about an everyday, familiar situation that, according to Swaffar and Arens "allows a particularly fruitful meeting place between two cultures, which even beginning FL readers can uncover" (p. 81). Readers look at specific scenes listed in the matrix and add to it textual language that expresses familiar and unexpected details about each scene. Based on this matrix, learners can identify patterns in language used for expressing ideas. This type of pattern recognition, Swaffar and Arens argue, can help avoid the tendency to read word for word because it joins language with ideas. The reading matrix can be completed collaboratively in class or, alternatively, may be completed as homework. In this way, the matrix serves as a formative assessment activity that is further elaborated during in-class discussion and through feedback from the instructor. The focus of this feedback should be on appropriate expression of messages found in the text as well as on accurate use of textual language.

Scenes	***Familiar***	***Unexpected***
Picking up a hitchhiker	*la automovilista* ("driver")	*negro, negro, negros, pálida* ("black, black, black, pale")
Conversing	*varias preguntas* ("various questions")	"¿pero no tienes miedo?" (repetition of the question "Aren't you afraid?" and denial three times)
Dying	*el auto se desbarranca;* *la muchacha queda muerta* ("the automobile crashed; the girl lay dead")	voz cavernosa; automovilista desapareció ("sonorous voice"; "driver has vanished")

FIGURE 5.2 Sample Reading Matrix (Swaffar & Arens, 2005, p. 87)

Production tasks follow completion of the reading matrix, and the nature of these tasks is again dependent on course or lesson goals. Language production should begin first at the sentence level and then move to more creative production tasks. Information collected in the reading matrix serves as a basis for these production tasks, which can include transforming the text itself, using language forms from the text to engage in deeper interpretation, or telling the story from a different perspective. For example, Swaffar and Arens suggest asking students to use information from the matrix to describe two characters in the story, thereby transforming the grammar of the text and changing the point of view in the discourse. A final production task might ask students to make conclusions and express their opinion about the content of the text based on this transformed discourse. This last writing task may also serve as a summative assessment to gauge student learning based on the reading.

Maxim (2006), like Swaffar and Arens, argues that "engaging texts at the discursive level does not need to be postponed until learners' linguistic competence has reached an advanced level" (p. 21) given collegiate-level FL learners' cognitive maturity. He therefore proposes a literacy-based approach to the reading of a full-length novel in a first-semester German course that follows a similar sequence to that of Swaffar and Arens. Maxim's pedagogical approach begins with pre-reading to orient students to the novel and activate background knowledge. This is carried out through brainstorming activities about the textual genre and making predictions about textual content based on the title. Next, students engage in an initial reading of the text (in his case, one chapter of the novel at a time) during which they identify major events and attend to how these events are presented and organized in the text. In the next stage, students re-read to identify "microdetails in the text and their accompanying textual language" (p. 23). Two types of production tasks follow these while-reading activities. First, to review students' understanding of textual details and the language used to express them, they write one-paragraph chapter summaries that incorporate specific words and phrases from the text. This activity serves as a formal assessment in the course to measure students' understanding of textual content, their ability to express that content by recycling and transforming textual language, and their overall grammatical accuracy. Next, to conclude the lesson and further develop language production abilities, students analyze the cultural implications of the text by relating textual information to their own cultural perspectives and determining the importance of the story's characters and their behaviors. Although this final stage of the pedagogy takes the form of in-class discussion, the task could be transformed into a written summative assessment such as a reading reaction journal or a short position paper.

The final literacy-based instructional model in Kern (2000) is most reflective of the multiliteracies framework we have outlined in this book because instructional activities are organized around the four pedagogical acts of situated practice, overt instruction, critical framing, and transformed practice. Kern (2000) walks through a five-stage integrative lesson plan for lower-level learners that aims to develop students' FL literacy by focusing on both the product and process of reading and by merging reading with other language competencies, including speaking and writing. In the first stage, linking form and communicative intent, learners interact with the text to gain global understanding. Kern's sample lesson begins with a situated practice activity in which students read a modified, shortened version of a text to make predictions regarding its purpose. Students then scan the original text to identify similar information and to verify if their predictions are borne out. To conclude this stage, readers engage in critical reflection about the text's genre, purpose, topic, and intended audience. In the next stage, students link language to content to establish the facts of the text and prepare them for deeper interpretation in subsequent activities. To carry this out, Kern proposes a situated practice activity in which students identify the who, what, where, and when of a story and find evidence for their answers in the text itself. Next, students link form and meaning by looking more closely at the language features of the text. This stage might begin with an overt instruction activity in which students comment on the use of a particular language feature (e.g., definite versus indefinite articles) and be followed by a critical framing activity in which students are asked to link the use of the targeted forms to textual meaning and the author's intent. In stage four, students explore how ideas and information are organized in a text to get a sense of its rhetorical features. One strategy for achieving this is to have students engage in an overt instruction activity that has them map textual information structures or relationships onto a table or graph format. Kern's model concludes with assessing students' understanding and interpretation of a text through transformed practice activities. Examples of possible transformations include summaries, retellings, or story expansions.

Not only can these transformation activities serve as summative assessments of students' ability to construct meaning from texts, Kern further proposes that the sample lesson plan can serve as the basis for a heuristic reading test that focuses on the process of reading, assesses learners' understanding of language use, conventions, and cultural knowledge, and engages learners in the acts of interpretation, collaboration, problem solving, and reflection. Following the same format as the sample lesson plan, Kern outlines a series of test activities that meet these goals. To link form and intent, readers scan the text and answer global comprehension questions; to link language to content, they answer true–false questions or complete an informational grid to identify the facts of the text; to link form and meaning, students explain why a certain word is repeated multiple times in the text and determine whether it is used differently in different examples; to focus on organization of ideas, readers complete a concept map to show how information expressed in the text relates to two or more central ideas; and to transform knowledge, students write a short summary of the text. To encourage reflection, Kern adds an additional self-evaluation component to the heuristic reading test: Students are asked to comment on difficulties encountered while reading the text and what they learned from reading it.

TABLE 5.1 Literacy-Oriented Models of Reading Instruction

	Hedgcock & Ferris (2009)	Swaffar & Arens (2005)	Maxim (2006)	Kern (2000)
1	Pre-reading (get ready to read, survey the text, make predictions, study vocabulary)	Pre-reading to access existing knowledge	Pre-reading orientation to the text	Link form and intent at the global level
2	While-reading (read for facts, re-read for details, look at language, look at text organization)	Initial reading to identify patterns and build on pre-reading	Initial reading for major events	Link language to content to establish the facts of the text
3	Post-reading (summarize text, think critically, establish reading-writing connections)	Reading matrix to identify textual patterns through language	Location of microdetails	Link form and meaning to explore linguistic choices
4		Sentence-level language production	Reproduction of textual language	Focus on organization of ideas
5		Creative language production and textual transformation	Knowledge application	Transformation based on knowledge gained

The four literacy-oriented reading sequences outlined here are summarized in Table 5.1. A quick look at this table reveals that the four models share a number of similarities. Although Hedgcock and Ferris present a three-stage pedagogy and the other three researchers a five-stage pedagogy, all four models include pre-reading activities that access existing knowledge and orient readers to the text; initial reading activities that encourage students to read for global comprehension; re-reading activities that attend to textual details; critical analysis activities that focus on rhetorical organization, cultural content, or textual analysis; and post-reading activities that require readers to apply their knowledge, most often through writing. These commonalities suggest a general format for reading-focused lessons that we detail in the next subsection.

2.2 A Template for Organizing Multiliteracies Reading Instruction and Assessment

To effectively merge communication with textual analysis and engage FL readers in the process of meaning design, we propose the following five-stage model for designing multiliteracies-oriented reading lessons:

1. *Pre-reading* to access background knowledge and make predictions about the text;
2. *Initial reading* to develop global comprehension of the facts or major events of the text;
3. *Detailed reading* to link meaning with language forms used in the text;
4. *Critical reading* to explore rhetorical organization and genre features found in the text, evaluate knowledge gained from reading the text, or explore cultural concepts related to the text; and
5. *Knowledge application* to demonstrate textual interpretation through transformation activities.

The activities to be implemented at each stage should reflect the four pedagogical acts of the multiliteracies framework and engage learners in the processes of interpretation, collaboration, problem solving, and reflection and self-reflection. To review, situated practice activities allow learners to experience the text through immersion in communicative tasks; overt instruction activities encourage learners to conceptualize information in the text through the examination of its formal and functional components; critical framing activities foster textual analysis by helping readers understand the multiple interpretations of a text and apply background knowledge about the context of the text; and transformed practice activities allow students to apply what they have learned from the text, as well as articulate their own perspectives on the text in new or creative ways (see Chapter 1 for detailed discussion). The guidelines for text selection presented in Chapters 2 and 3 are useful in helping to find appropriate texts for use with this template.

Examples of learning activities that might be used in each stage of the pedagogy are provided in Table 5.2. Note that in some cases, the learning activity corresponds to more than one pedagogical act.

2.2.1 PRE-READING. Making predictions, participating in instructional conversations, and scanning a text for information are provided as examples of pre-reading activities because all of them activate learners' background knowledge, prepare them to interpret the text, and begin to draw their attention to the Available Designs in a text.

To encourage readers to *make predictions* about a text, they should be presented with clues such as the text's title, words from the text, or images related to the text that help them guess what the topic is and why they think that. Predicting not only draws on learners' background knowledge and experiences, it also helps them link knowledge and experiences to cultural messages found in a text (Hall, 2001). At times, texts related to cultural phenomena completely unknown to students can make pre-reading activities such as predicting very challenging. In those instances, *instructional conversations* can be used to provide learners with key cultural information. This can be achieved through a teacher-led conversation regarding background information that is culturally unknown or inaccessible to students. This information may be related to the author, the time or place the text was created, or the importance of

TABLE 5.2 Suggested Learning Activities for Reading Instruction

Instructional Stage	Suggested Learning Activities
1 Pre-reading	Predicting (Situated practice / Critical framing)
	Instructional conversations (Situated practice / Critical framing)
	Scanning for information (Situated practice)
2 Initial reading	Sequencing of text elements (Situated practice)
	Reader's theater (Situated practice / Critical framing)
	Information mapping (Overt instruction)
3 Detailed reading	Reading text signals (Overt instruction)
	Synonym substitution (Overt instruction)
	Focusing on relationships (Overt instruction)
4 Critical reading	Multiple interpretations (Critical framing)
	Textual comparison (Overt instruction)
	Critical focus questions (Critical framing)
5 Knowledge application	Reading journal (Situated practice / Critical framing)
	Text elaboration (Transformed practice)
	Story retelling (Transformed practice)

the text within the target culture. These instructional conversations, therefore, add to students' content schemata to fill gaps in their knowledge and make the content of a text more accessible in subsequent activities (see Chapter 4 for detailed discussion). Finally, when learners *scan a text for information,* they can focus on a variety of Available Designs including vocabulary, genre features, writing conventions, and so on. Scanning can also be linked to other pre-reading activities, such as predicting, where learners scan the text to determine if their predictions are borne out (Kucer & Silva, 2006).

2.2.2 INITIAL READING. Sequencing text elements, reader's theater, and information mapping are appropriate initial reading activities because they focus on global text comprehension and on linking that comprehension to a text's Available Designs. *Sequencing text elements* is a way of synthesizing and organizing the facts of a written text. This situated practice activity involves giving students slips of paper, each with a key event in the story, and then having them sequence those events in chronological order. As they read the text for the first time, learners verify whether their sequencing is correct and make any necessary changes (Kucer & Silva, 2006). *Reader's theater* allows learners to work collaboratively to convert texts into scripts with multiple voices without modifying the original text. First, students identify the parts or characters of the script they will create. Then, as they read, they color code sentences and phrases according to these parts or characters. The script, then, is the original text, be it prose or dialogue, with each phrase or sentence assigned to a part or character as determined by the students. To conclude the activity, student groups perform their scripted text for the class. To add a critical framing component to this situated practice activity, groups can justify the choices they made regarding the various parts and language examples from the text (Kern, 2000). The last example of initial reading activities is *information mapping,* in which students represent the main events or facts of a text in a table, diagram, semantic web, or illustration. However the text is represented, readers should be able to justify their choices with specific examples from the text (Hall, 2001).

2.2.3 DETAILED READING. Examples of detailed reading activities include reading text signals, synonym substitution, and focusing on relationships. Each of these activities requires that learners carry out a focused reading of the text and link their understandings to textual language.

Activities focused on *reading text signals* involve identifying words and phrases that establish relationships between ideas expressed by an author. This overt instruction activity therefore focuses on coherence and cohesion devices and how they are used to express meaning in the text. For FL readers in first- or second-semester courses, the instructor can signal specific connective words in the text and ask learners to explain their meaning; for more experienced readers, learners can find the words themselves and make generalizations about their use and the relationships they signal (Kucer & Silva, 2006). *Synonym substitution* is another overt instruction activity focused on vocabulary. In one type of synonym substitution activity, readers can be provided with a list of known words and asked to find their equivalents in a text; in another type of synonym substitution activity, readers can rewrite words and expressions from the original text in their own words. In both cases, learners reread the text using the new vocabulary and comment on any changes in the way the text might be interpreted. Synonym substitution thus allows learners to explore a text's meaning in detail and to understand why certain words are chosen over others. *Focusing on relationships* involves examining the lexical, syntactic, or discourse features of a text and understanding relationships among these elements, and between these elements and textual meaning. In examining discourse relationships, for example, readers can establish a structure for a text (e.g., transform a prose text into dialogue) or note discourse markers or cues that indicate turn changes or relationships between text parts. In implementing these kinds of activities, instructors should focus students' attention by asking them to justify their answers based on textual information (Kern, 2000).

2.2.4 CRITICAL READING. Critical reading activities focus on exploring the rhetorical organization and genre features of a text, evaluating knowledge gained from reading, or exploring cultural concepts. Three activity types serve to exemplify critical reading: multiple interpretations, textual comparison, and critical focus questions.

Multiple interpretations activities encourage learners to identify their understanding of a particular feature of a text and then to push that understanding further by exploring other possible interpretations. In this critical framing activity, learners identify a phrase or idea in the text that is unclear to them and jot down their best guess regarding its interpretation. Students then carry out a classroom version of crowdsourcing: They walk around the room and ask classmates for their interpretations of the phrase or idea. To end the activity, learners draw conclusions about the appropriate interpretation of the phrase or idea and justify their decision based on the input received (Kucer & Silva, 2006). In *textual comparison* activities, readers are presented with a second, related text and asked to make connections between how information is organized in each text and how this organization affects their understanding of textual meaning and purpose, intended audience, cultural perspectives, and so on (Kern, 2000). For instance, in a reading lesson focused on a restaurant review, learners might also read a menu from that restaurant and be asked to identify features that distinguish the two texts. They might further be asked to explain how similar ideas (e.g., distinct menu items) are expressed and organized in the two texts. The third example of critical reading, *critical focus questions,* is intended to raise students' awareness of the kinds of lexical, grammatical, and rhetorical choices authors make, and what effect these choices have on meaning. Questions should focus on ideas the reader associates with certain words and phrases and the effect those words and phrases have on their overall interpretation of the text (Kern, 2000).

2.2.5 KNOWLEDGE APPLICATION. In the final stage of the pedagogical sequence, learners apply the knowledge they have gained from pre-reading, initial reading, detailed reading, and critical reading activities. Examples of knowledge application include reading journals, text elaboration, and story retelling.

Reading journals allow learners to reflect on a text and what they have learned from it. According to Kern (2000), a journal entry should include a summary of the text, the reader's personal response to the text, and some reflection regarding the process of reading the text (e.g., areas of difficulty, new words learned). To add a critical framing component to this situated practice activity, readers might also be asked to situate the text within their own cultural context or lived experiences in order to highlight similarities or differences. *Text elaboration,* a transformed practice activity, involves adding to the original text words, phrases, or sentences that express ideas or intentions that are implied but not overtly stated. It is the learner who decides what this additional information is and where it is to be inserted in the original text. This activity demonstrates readers' interpretation of the text by encouraging them to use their knowledge in creative ways. The final example of knowledge application is *story retelling*. This transformed practice activity may take place orally or in writing, and can involve retelling a story in one's own words or even retelling a story from the perspective of a different character or reader. This activity and the others proposed for the knowledge application stage "raise the cognitive complexity of the student's task while maintaining a focus on interpretation of the original text" (Kern, 2000, pp. 164–165).

2.2.6 ASSESSMENT. The five-stage reading model summarized above can also serve as a template for designing multiliteracies-oriented reading tests, which might have the following format: (1) the pre-reading activity of predicting the content of a text based on its title; (2) the initial reading activity of sequencing text elements to indicate the text's chronology; (3) the detailed reading activity of synonym substitution to focus on familiar vocabulary; (4) the critical reading activity of critical focus questions to encourage textual analysis; and (5) the knowledge application activity of story retelling in which learners transform the text from another character's perspective. Using this model, students might be tested on their ability to construct meaning from a text they have already read, from the continuation of a text they have already read, or from a text that treats a topic similar to one treated in class, perhaps in a different genre (e.g., a review of a book read in class; a verse version of story read in class; the menu of a restaurant for which they read a review).

In addition to providing a template for creating formal tests, this reading model provides opportunities for various formative and summative assessments. A number of the suggested pre-reading, initial reading, detailed reading, and critical reading activities can function as formative assessments carried out through in-class discussion or homework. In addition, the suggested knowledge application activities may serve as summative assessments that conclude the treatment of a particular text or that form part of a literacy portfolio that students assemble throughout the semester and turn in at the end of the course.

2.3 Sample Reading-Focused Lesson Plan

The lesson plan temple for FL reading instruction grounded in activities reflecting the four pedagogical acts makes it possible for lower-level FL learners to engage with a variety of text types and carry out a number of meaningful activities focused on both textual form and meaning. In Table 5.3, we present a sample lesson plan (based on Allen & Paesani, 2010) organized according to this template. Activities implemented in the lesson represent one of the three illustrative activity types presented in Table 5.2 for each stage in the model. This lesson is intended for use in a second-semester introductory-level French course during an instructional unit on food in the Francophone world. The goals of this lesson are to enable students to understand and use vocabulary related to food, critically evaluate cultural practices related to food in both target and home cultures, recognize differences between prose and dialogue, and collaboratively construct meaning from a literary text. The written text that forms the basis of the lesson is a short literary vignette entitled "A Sunday Morning Box of Pastries" from *We Could Almost Eat Outside: An Appreciation of Life's Small Pleasures* by the French author Philippe Delerm (1997; see Appendix for English and French versions of the text).[1] The vignette expands on cultural information presented within an instructional unit on food and introduces a specific cultural product (French pastry) based on the author's personal experiences. Because the subject matter of the vignette is therefore accessible to students,

---

[1]The titles have been translated from the original French. The vignette's title is "Le paquet de gâteaux du dimanche matin," and the book's title is *La première gorgée de bière et autres plaisirs minuscules.*

TABLE 5.3 Sample Instructional Sequence, Reading-Focused Lesson: "A Sunday Morning Box of Pastries"

Instructional Stage		Learning Activities
1 Pre-reading	a	Students look at pictures of French pastries represented in the text and match them with the appropriate name, provided by the instructor. (Situated practice)
	b	Students then *scan the text* to find the same pastry names and determine why the pastries might have the names they do. For example, *une mille-feuille* has many layers. (Situated practice)
2 Initial reading	a	Students work in groups to complete a *readers' theater activity*. They transform the vignette into a script with multiple voices using colored pens or markers to identify each voice throughout the text. Students then perform the text in front of the class. (Situated practice)
	b	Instructor-led follow up includes discussion of different interpretations of the text across groups and reasons for the various voices groups chose. (Situated practice / Critical framing)
3 Detailed reading	a	Students focus on linguistic and discourse conventions by *identifying structural relationships* in the text between dialogue (or implied dialogue) and description. (Overt instruction)
	b	Instructor-led follow up includes identifying linguistic differences between dialogue and description and what information the author presents in dialogue versus description form. (Overt instruction)
4 Critical reading	a	The instructor asks *critical focus questions* that examine cultural notions expressed through words in the text such as *gâteau* 'cake,' *paquet* 'package,' or *dimanche* 'Sunday.' To answer these questions, students must focus on relationships between the meanings of the words and their use in the title and within the discourse context of the whole text. (Overt instruction)
	b	To contextualize the text more broadly and tap into learner background knowledge, the instructor then asks students to reflect on whether these notions have a similar meaning in their culture or how these notions may have evolved over time. (Critical framing)
5 Knowledge application	a	Students expand on the reader's theater activity and apply the knowledge they have acquired in stages 1–4 in a small group *text elaboration* activity. They express ideas, intentions, or relations implied but not explicitly stated in the text by adding additional commentary such as a reaction (e.g., *They are beautiful!*), an indication of who said what (e.g., *You respond*), or additional information (e.g., *You hold in your hands. . .*). (Transformed practice)
	b	Students present an oral performance of the elaborated text. (Transformed practice)

the sophisticated vocabulary, structures, and stylistic elements of this literary text should not impede students' ability to construct meaning. Visual texts in the form of pictures of French pastries are also part of the lesson, thus making the literary text more accessible and underscoring the multimodal nature of this literacy-oriented approach to teaching reading.

The activities in this five-stage lesson plan facilitate meaning design: Readers interact with Available Designs of the text, they establish form–meaning connections, and they interpret textual meaning. Furthermore, this instructional sequence includes the basic elements of instruction that form part of the seven principles of literacy. Readers explore conventions related to prose and dialogue; they tap into cultural knowledge about Sunday rituals and French pastry shops; and they use language to understand how vocabulary is used within the text to create discourse. Finally, the activities in this lesson plan engage readers in the learning processes of interpretation, collaboration, problem solving, and reflection. Readers interpret the cultural themes of the text and how those themes are related to language forms; they collaborate by interacting with the text and with other learners to design meaning; they solve problems by figuring out relationships between words in the text and overall textual meaning; and they reflect on the significance of specific cultural notions.

The organization of this reading-based lesson around the four pedagogical acts and seven principles of literacy also facilitates a multimodal approach to constructing meaning from written texts. For example, in addition to reading the cultural vignette, students interpret visual images of French pastries. Moreover, instructional activities engage students in both interpersonal and presentational speaking and writing, all grounded within the language and sociocultural content of the literary text.

This sample lesson affords a number of opportunities for both formative and summative assessment. For instance, instructors can provide formative feedback at the close of the reader's theater activity when groups justify the choices they made related to the voices they identified and answer questions related to the language forms used by each voice. Similarly, activities in which students identify structural relationships and answer critical focus questions create opportunities for providing formative feedback. Each of these activities could also be assigned as homework and graded for completion and accuracy related to both textual meaning and language. Finally, a digital recording of students' performance of their text elaboration can serve as a summative assessment for the instructional sequence.

To help you reflect on this sample reading-focused lesson plan, read through it a second time and find answers to the following questions:

1. What are the objectives of this lesson and how do they fit within the course curriculum?
2. Is the selected text appropriate to meet these objectives? What elements of the text might be challenging for FL learners to understand?
3. In what ways are students designing meaning through the various activities in this lesson?
4. Why are the different lesson plan activities labeled as situated practice, overt instruction, critical framing, or transformed practice?

5. Are the basic elements of instruction, or the what of multiliteracies pedagogy—conventions, cultural knowledge, and language use—represented in the lesson?
6. Are the learning processes of interpretation, collaboration, problem solving, and reflection and self-reflection (i.e., the how of multiliteracies pedagogy) represented in the lesson?

As you think about planning reading-focused lesson plans and assessments using the template above, come back to these questions as a way to help you organize your ideas and apply your understanding of multiliteracies-based reading pedagogy. Learning Activity 5.5 will help you get started.

LEARNING ACTIVITY 5.5

Modifying Textbook-Based Reading Activities

Select a reading passage and accompanying activities from the textbook you are currently using and modify the activities to reflect the multiliteracies-based model presented in this chapter. Before beginning this task, first evaluate the effectiveness of the textbook materials by asking the questions presented above. Once you have identified areas that need improvement, redesign the textbook activities using the five-stage model and suggested learning activities in Tables 5.2 and 5.3. When the lesson plan is finished, ask yourself the same set of questions above to help you justify your pedagogical choices.

3. FINAL CONSIDERATIONS

In this chapter, we have established a conceptual base for considering FL reading instruction within the multiliteracies framework. Essential to this base are the cognitive processes in which FL learners engage when confronted with texts; the linguistic features and conventions that characterize a text and contribute to its ability to communicate a message; and the sociocultural dimension of reading that links textual meaning to the perspectives, values, and beliefs of a particular community. We further established that FL reading is an act of meaning design that entails this multidimensional view of communication and that draws on a variety of Available Designs, both linguistic and schematic.

This conceptual base informed the FL reading pedagogy we developed in this chapter, a pedagogy whose main goal is to merge communication with textual analysis through engagement in literacy-based instructional activities and learning processes. This pedagogy is further grounded in existing pedagogical models intended to foster academic literacy and in the four pedagogical acts essential to multiliteracies instruction: situated practice, overt instruction, critical framing, and transformed practice.

We close the chapter with two thoughts to consider as you apply the principles and activities of reading-focused instruction outlined here. The first comes from Kern (2000), who argues that a basic tenet of literacy-based reading instruction is to control the tasks students are asked to carry out, not the texts they are asked to read. In other words, text selection is only part of the picture: Many texts often deemed too difficult for lower-level learners can be made accessible through the careful design and implementation of pedagogical tasks such as the ones outlined in this chapter. This idea is essential to understanding the importance of merging communication with textual analysis from the beginning of FL instruction, as a common barrier to integrating texts at lower levels has been inaccurate beliefs about students' ability to read difficult texts because of their limited linguistic abilities. The second thought for consideration, also gleaned from Kern, is related to the common tendency to tease apart reading from other language competencies, particularly speaking, listening, and writing, and to view development of these competencies as progressing in a linear fashion. Yet, within the multiliteracies framework, the relationship among these language modalities is overlapping rather than linear and, according to Kern, "it is the overlap that most clearly differentiates a literacy-focused curriculum itself from traditional curricula" (p. 132). Indeed, this overlap is represented in the sample lesson plan presented in Table 5.3, in which reading, writing, speaking, and listening form an integral part of meaning design related to a target language text. We hope that you will reflect on these final considerations not only as you digest the content of this chapter, but also as you interact with the content of Chapter 6, "Teaching Writing as Designing Meaning Through Texts."

4. TRANSFORMING KNOWLEDGE

4.1 Reflective Journal Entry

How did this chapter build on your previous understandings of the multiliteracies framework? How did this chapter build on your previous views about FL reading instruction? Did these understandings and views change after reading this chapter and, if so, how? What ideas from the chapter can you apply to your own teaching context? How has what you have learned in this chapter prepared you to read the next chapter on writing?

4.2 Researching Reading: Problem Solving

Identify a problem related to the teaching or learning of FL reading in your instructional context. Use the table to flesh out the what, where, when, who, and why of the problem, and then use this information, along with your knowledge about multiliteracies-oriented reading, to formulate one or more solutions to the problem. In the classroom, try out one of the solutions you have identified and summarize the results you observe. If you are not currently teaching, collaborate with a colleague who is teaching and observe that instructor implement one of your proposed solutions.

The Problem	
What?	
Where?	
When?	
Who?	
Why?	
Potential Solutions	
How?	
How?	
How?	
Results of Implementation	

Key Resources

Maxim, H. H. (2006). Integrating textual thinking into the introductory college-level foreign language classroom. *Modern Language Journal, 90*, 19–32.

Maxim argues for the development of textual thinking and academic literacy beginning with the first semester of foreign language study. To move toward this goal, his study explored what a literacy-oriented pedagogy entails, whether the pedagogy is feasible, how students responded to the pedagogy, and whether a textual focus took away from development of communicative language skills. To test these ideas, Maxim incorporated a full-length romance novel into a communicatively oriented German curriculum using a four-stage, guided instructional approach. Collaborative reading, analysis, and interpretation took place during half of each class session over a 10-week period. During the other half of each class session, students engaged in contextualized grammar activities related to the linguistic functions and themes covered in the textbook. Results showed that the pedagogy was feasible; that student response to the pedagogy was generally positive; and that students who read the novel performed equally well on communicatively oriented departmental exams as students who did not read the novel.

Swaffar, J. (2004). A template for advanced learner tasks: Staging reading and cultural literacy through the précis. In H. Byrnes & H. H. Maxim (Eds.), *Advanced foreign language learning: A challenge to college programs* (pp. 19–46). Boston, MA: Heinle.

Swaffar presents a literacy-based template for engaging advanced learners with texts focused on using "the précis as a template for pedagogical tasks that integrate comprehension and production practice that can enable learners to identify the messages, obligatory textual moves, and language features of various genres" (p. 19). She claims that the précis facilitates linguistic development within the context of discursive practices, allows learners to uncover textual message systems and link them to language features, and links existing knowledge to a text's content–form patterns.

Swaffar, J., Arens, K., & Byrnes, H. (1991). *Reading for meaning: An integrated approach to language learning.* Englewood Cliffs, NJ: Prentice Hall.

Despite its publication over two decades ago, *Reading for Meaning* remains a significant piece of work on literacy-oriented foreign language reading pedagogy. In this book, the authors propose a procedural model of reading that has been adapted and adopted in numerous subsequent proposals, including Swaffar and Arens's (2005) reading matrix and précis and Maxim's (2002, 2006) guided approach to extensive reading in introductory courses. The central tenet of the pedagogy outlined in *Reading for Meaning* is "to teach the connection between language and the ability to manipulate language to analyze or speculate" and, ultimately, "to comprehend and express the meaning of alternate realities" (p. 2). The authors then lay out a learner-centered approach to texts that promotes learners' ability to comprehend, analyze, speculate about, and express textual meaning en route to the development of academic literacy.

For Further Reading

Arens, K. (2008). Genres and the standards: Teaching the 5 Cs through texts. *German Quarterly, 81*(1), 35–48.

Bridges, E. (2009). Bridging the gap: A literacy-oriented approach to teaching the graphic novel *Der erste frühling. Die Unterrichtspraxis/Teaching German, 42*, 152–161.

Kern, R., & Schultz, J. M. (2005). Beyond orality: Investigating literacy and the literary in second and foreign language instruction. *Modern Language Journal, 89*, 381–392.

Redmann, J. (2005). An interactive reading journal for all levels of the foreign language curriculum. *Foreign Language Annals, 38*, 484–493.

Scott, V. M., & Huntington, J. A. (2007). Literature, the interpretive mode, and novice learners. *Modern Language Journal, 91*, 3–14.

APPENDIX

Le paquet de gâteaux du dimanche matin

Des gâteaux séparés, bien sûr. Une religieuse au café, un paris-brest, deux tartes aux fraises, une mille-feuille. À part pour un ou deux, on sait déjà à qui chacun est destiné – mais quel sera celui-en-supplément-pour-les-gourmands? On égrène les noms sans hâte. De l'autre côté du comptoir, la vendeuse, la pince à gâteaux à la main, plonge avec soumission vers vos désirs; elle ne manifeste même pas d'impatience, quand elle doit changer de carton – la mille-feuille ne tient pas. C'est important ce carton plat, carré, aux bords arrondis, relevés. Il va constituer le socle solide d'un édifice fragile, au destin menacé.

—Ce sera tout!

Alors la vendeuse engloutit le carton plat dans une pyramide de papier rose, bientôt nouée d'un ruban brun. Pendant l'échange de monnaie, on tient le paquet par en dessous, mais dès la porte du magasin franchie, on le saisit par la ficelle, et on l'écarte un peu du corps. C'est ainsi. Les gâteaux du dimanche sont à porter comme on tient un pendule. Sourcier des rites minuscules, on avance sans arrogance, ni fausse modestie. Cette espèce de componction, de sérieux de roi mage, n'est-ce pas ridicule ? Mais non. Si les trottoirs dominicaux ont goût de flânerie, la pyramide suspendue y est pour quelque chose – autant que çà et là quelques poireaux dépassant un cabas.

Paquet de gâteaux à la main, on a la silhouette du professeur Tournesol – celle qu'il faut pour saluer l'effervescence d'après messe et le bouffées de P.M.U., de café, de tabac. Petits dimanches de famille, petits dimanches d'autrefois, petits dimanches d'aujourd'hui, le temps balance en encensoir au bout d'une ficelle brune. Un peu de crème pâtissière a fait juste une tache en haut de la religieuse au café.

A Sunday Morning Box of Pastries

A box full of individual pastries. One coffee *religieuse*, one *paris-brest*, two strawberry tarts, one Napoleon. Except for one or two, you already know for whom each has been chosen—but which will be the extra one for the gluttons? You order each one carefully, without rushing. On the other side of the counter, a pair of pastry tongs in her hand, the salesclerk submissively reaches for the pastries you desire; she doesn't even become impatient when she must change to a larger box because the Napoleon won't fit. The flat, square box with upright rounded sides is significant: It forms the foundation for a fragile structure whose destiny is unsure.

"That'll be all!"

[2]A *religieuse,* literally a nun in habit, is a French pastry made of two choux pastry buns, one larger than the other, filled with cream, topped with chocolate ganache, and decorated with a whipped cream "collar" and cap. A *Paris-Brest* is a French pastry consisting of a baked ring of *choux* pastry that is cut in half and filled with hazelnut cream.

The salesclerk then engulfs the flat box in a pyramid of pink paper, tied at the top with a brown ribbon. As you pay, you hold the box at its base, but as soon as you step out the door, you hold it by the ribbon, swinging it gently away from you. That's better. Sunday morning pastries should be swung like a pendulum. Diviner of tiny rites, you continue on with neither arrogance nor false modesty. This magi-like self-importance is a bit ridiculous, isn't it? But no, this suspended pyramid is just as important to the Sunday morning sidewalks as the leeks one espies peeking out of a shopping bag.

With your box of pastries in hand, you resemble Professor Tournesol—the perfect silhouette for greeting the effervescent crowds leaving Mass and the whiffs of smoke coming from the betting shops, cafés, and tobacconists. Sundays with family, Sundays past, Sundays present. Time hangs in a censer at the end of a brown ribbon. A bit of pastry cream has created a small stain on the box, just above the coffee *religieuse*.

CHAPTER 6

Teaching Writing as Designing Meaning Through Texts

In contemplating the role of writing in the lower-level foreign language (FL) classroom, instructors may question how learners with limited knowledge of lexico–grammatical structures and textual conventions in the FL can be expected to make meaning accurately in writing. Further, they may be uncertain of how this language modality should fit into instructional goals and objectives or how they should assess learners' writing development. In fact, in comparison with other language modalities, writing has historically played a lesser role in lower-level FL learning, seen as "something students will take up after having acquired the language through oral communication and reading" (Racelis & Matsuda, 2013, p. 384). Identifying the purposes and goals of writing for lower-level FL learners has also long been an open question, and we will delve into this issue further in the next section of this chapter.

Although long viewed as a secondary skill in the lower-level FL classroom, as Williams (2012) wrote, in recent years, this perception of writing has shifted, and it has "now come into focus as an activity that may promote as well as reflect [language] development" (p. 321). In fact, research has shown that writing facilitates overall FL acquisition, including acquisition of grammar, oral fluency, and knowledge of rhetorical forms for textual genres (Reichelt, Lefkowitz, Rinnert, & Schultz, 2012). Consistent with these current views on the value of writing for FL development, instructional practices related to FL writing have also begun to shift. Writing-focused instruction is no longer seen merely as a vehicle for language practice based on controlled exercises intended to produce error-free language. Instead, an expanded understanding has emerged that focuses on writing as a purposeful act of meaning making for various purposes and audiences. As Byrnes (2013) explained, writing presents an "advantageous environment to observe and, more important, to foster an ability to mean on the part of [second language] learners" (p. 96). When learners use written language for meaning making in a substantive form, it affords instructors "the opportunity to interact with students' work in a manner quite unlike speaking, reading, and listening . . . [It] can be scrutinized and objectified before it is ultimately evaluated" (O'Donnell, 2007, p. 651).

This chapter explores how these emerging understandings of the value of writing can be aligned to reflect the multiliteracies framework, particularly for lower-level FL courses. As we have seen in Chapter 5 in relation to reading, even lower-level learners can develop language modalities often perceived as complex. Moreover, we have argued throughout that the primary purpose of instruction grounded in the multiliteracies approach is meaning design through interpretation and creation of FL texts. In many ways, this chapter serves as a continuation of the previous one, in the sense that in a multiliteracies approach, reading and writing are seen as complementary processes that are intrinsically linked (Kern, 2000). In the "Conceptual Background" section, we review the treatment of FL writing in previous research and explore how, in a multiliteracies approach, writing, like reading, is understood as an act of meaning design with linguistic, cognitive, and sociocultural dimensions. Next, in the "Pedagogical Applications" section, we outline how writing instruction can be organized in a manner consistent with the multiliteracies framework, highlighting several previous models as well as proposing an instructional sequence for writing-focused activities and assessment based on the four pedagogical acts. By the end of this chapter, you will have a better understanding of the role of writing within the multiliteracies approach and how to design writing-focused FL instruction consistent with this approach. Before reading the "Conceptual Background" section, complete Learning Activity 6.1, which focuses on your current ideas about learning to write in a FL and teaching FL writing.

LEARNING ACTIVITY 6.1

My Ideas About Learning and Teaching FL Writing

Indicate whether you agree or disagree with the following statements regarding writing in a FL. In addition, provide an explanation or justification of your stance on each.

	Statement	Agree / Disagree	Explanation / Justification
1	Writing in a FL is primarily an act of translation involving learning new vocabulary and grammar.		
2	First language (L1) writing expertise has a positive impact on FL writing proficiency.		

	Statement	Agree / Disagree	Explanation / Justification
3	Writing should take place primarily outside of the FL classroom so that class time can be dedicated to oral communicative practice and learning about grammar and culture.		
4	In order to make progress as FL writers, learners must abandon the personal in favor of an impersonal, objective stance in their writing.		
5	Responding to errors in FL learners' writing is of questionable value in improving accuracy.		

When you have read this chapter, you will write a reflection that will require that you come back to this table and think about whether your ideas about each statement were confirmed or not.

1. CONCEPTUAL BACKGROUND

This section provides an overview of research and models related to FL writing. We begin with an exploration of the definition of writing as evidenced in two differing perspectives on its role in FL learning. Understanding these two perspectives serves as the foundation for discussion of factors that influence FL writing development, approaches to FL writing instruction, and assessment of learners' written texts. In the final part of this section, we delve into the definition and role of writing within the multiliteracies framework, focusing in particular on meaning design and the goals of writing-focused instruction.

1.1 Why Write in a Foreign Language?

As stated in the introduction to this chapter, it was long assumed in FL teaching and learning that writing was secondary to other skills, including oral communication and reading. This view was, in part, an extension of the notion that writing is nothing more than speech written down (Hall, 2001). As such, writing was typically limited to controlled exercises to reinforce learning orthography, grammar, or vocabulary (Reichelt et al., 2012), or guided composition wherein students completed sentences or paragraphs that their teacher had begun to write (Racelis & Matsuda, 2013). This idea of writing as primarily a vehicle for language practice has been called the *writing-to-learn* perspective. At the other end of the spectrum lies the *learning-to-write* perspective, in which FL learners have a need to write for academic or professional purposes (Manchón, 2009). As (Reichelt et al. 2012) explained, consistent with this view, "students are taught to write for different purposes and audiences, to address levels of formality, and to be sensitive to discipline- and culture-specific styles, guidelines and prescribed norms" (p. 29). In tandem with this perspective, instruction for lower-level FL learners may not include an explicit focus on writing, based on the assumption that it can be effectively taught only at later stages once students are well along their language-learning trajectory (Williams, 2012). That lower-level FL curricula continue to be dominated by communicative language teaching (CLT) and its emphasis on functional oral language skills further supports a lesser role for writing instruction in the early semesters of language learning. As a result, two different cultures of writing instruction may co-exist in undergraduate FL courses: writing focused on knowledge-telling (i.e., personal experience, description, and language exercise) at lower levels, and writing focused on knowledge-transforming (i.e., analysis, interpretive skills, and critical thinking) at advanced levels (Schultz, 2001). In addition, for some researchers, a meaningful difference exists between *writing,* or the simple encoding of words on paper (or on the computer screen)with the purpose of language practice, versus *composing,* or writing for the purpose of communicating meaning (Williams, 2012). This conception of writing-versus-composing further highlights the fact that uses of writing in FL instruction do not necessarily involve a simultaneous focus on the act of writing and writing as a way of purposefully conveying meaning.

Though the stark contrast between the writing-to-learn and learning-to-write perspectives may be a reductionist manner of representing what is, in reality, a more nuanced state of affairs, it reflects what Reichelt (2001) criticized as a general "lack of a unified sense of purpose of writing within the FL curriculum" (p. 578). She elaborated on this issue by asking:

> Is [the purpose of writing] to work on accuracy in orthography and morphology? to practice various syntactic structures? to provide further experience in purposive use of the TL [target language] through interaction and creating of meaning? to learn to create compositions appropriate for some particular audience or purpose? to learn and communicate about aspects of the TL, including literature and culture? to support acquisition of speaking, reading, and listening skills? (p. 579)

These questions should make clear from the outset that unlike a linguistic modality such as speaking, whose primacy for language learners is nearly unquestionable, the purposes for writing and goals for writing instruction in the FL curriculum, particularly for lower-level learners, is far less obvious.

In addition to the question of the purposes and goals for FL writing raised by the writing-to-learn and learning-to-write perspectives, the learning experiences associated with each of these perspectives (e.g., writing as part of grammatical practice as a lower-level learner versus brainstorming, paraphrasing, or synthesizing in writing to become a more proficient writer as an advanced-level learner) lead us to consider a critical issue for how students learn to write in a FL: Engaging in writing-to-learn types of activities does not necessarily prepare them to communicate meaningfully and appropriately for specific audiences and purposes or to produce extended written discourse (Racelis &Matsuda, 2013). For Kern (2000), this shortcoming represents the most significant weakness of collegiate FL programs characterized by CLT, which have been more successful in promoting students' interactive speaking abilities than they have been in developing their extended discourse competence and writing skills, both essential in academic settings. How, then, can FL instructors help learners develop extended discourse competence in writing? To begin to address this question, we turn our attention to factors involved in learning to write in a FL and what research has revealed concerning those elements that positively impact FL writing development.

1.2 Factors in Foreign Language Writing Development

In this chapter's introduction, we described some of the benefits of writing for FL development, including acquisition of grammar, oral fluency, and knowledge of rhetorical forms for creating and interpreting textual genres. According to Williams (2012), several features of writing distinguish it from other linguistic modalities and lead to its facilitative role in FL development, including its slower pace, the enduring record left by writing, and the need for greater precision in language use. As O'Donnell (2007) explained, the concreteness of writing offers both students and instructors the opportunity to scrutinize and objectify it prior to evaluating it, unlike speaking, reading, or listening. Yet whereas the benefits of engaging FL writing for learners may seem to be a straightforward matter, understanding the factors involved in learning to write well in a FL is decidedly more complicated.

Manchón (2009) described FL writing as "a true problem-solving task [that] . . . entails the solution of numerous linguistic problems and creates a tension in attentional demands" (p. 12). This characterization of FL writing as problem solving captures its complexity well. Whereas many students have the impression that writing well in the FL involves learning new vocabulary and grammar and applying them to composition formats from their own language and culture, this is an erroneous oversimplification of what is, in fact, a multidimensional process of learning to think in another language (Reichelt et al., 2012). According to Hyland (2011), learning to write in another language entails five kinds of knowledge:

1. content knowledge of topical concepts and ideas addressed in the text;
2. context knowledge of reader expectations and cultural preferences;
3. genre knowledge of the communicative purposes of a given text type and its value in a particular context;

4. process knowledge of how to carry out a writing task; and
5. system knowledge of lexis, syntax, and formal conventions of writing.

Developing these varied forms of knowledge and applying them to writing tasks can be a tremendous challenge for FL learners. Unlike English as a second language (ESL) learners who typically have access to authentic language use and native speakers outside the classroom, immersion for FL learners is usually limited to an artificial instructional context and supplemental assignments that may or may not focus on writing (Reichelt et al., 2012).

Although opinions vary as to what social, cognitive, and linguistic elements contribute most to second language (L2) writing development, in broad terms, L1 writing proficiency and overall L2 proficiency are two factors often mentioned in the literature as critical to learners' growing L2 writing expertise (Reichelt et al., 2012; Williams, 2005). However, the notion of *transfer* of L1 writing skills to L2 writing performance (i.e., that these skills would be mapped from the L1 to the L2 automatically and easily) should not be oversimplified, as most researchers support some version of the Language Threshold Hypothesis, which holds that a certain level of L2 knowledge is needed for learners to tap into related L1 skills (Williams, 2005). In other words, L1 writing expertise appears to transfer more in advanced L2 learners, in particular in relation to composing strategies, than in less-advanced learners (Williams, 2005). It is also important to remember, as Shrum and Glisan (2010) have pointed out, that composing in a L1 is a different process than composing in a L2:

> In L1, writers begin by organizing their ideas and putting them into suitable language. They decide which aspects they will consciously attend to—for example, grammar, spelling, and organization. This process differs from the process typically used by L2 writers, which is to collect and organize words and phrases they will need to express ideas; for L2 writers, more time is spent in creating a word inventory and putting phrases and sentences together in the L2 with the help of some thinking in the L1. (p. 302)

Moreover, transfer of L1 writing expertise can represent both a benefit and a drawback for L2 learners. On one hand, this can be a benefit insomuch that in a group of learners with a largely homogenous cultural and educational background, even at lower levels of L2 proficiency, certain assumptions and practices related to writing may be capitalized on in instruction. On the other hand, learners (and teachers) may automatically adhere to the assumptions and practices grounded in their L1 and native culture rather than trying out new formats for writing based on L2 writing norms (Reichelt et al., 2012). Recent work on L2 writing has also emphasized the bidirectional nature of transfer or, as Manchón (2009) explained, "it includes transfer of knowledge, skills, and, very importantly, the use of the writer's total linguistic repertoire at product and process levels" (p. 12). Research has suggested, for example, that experienced FL writers possess merged or hybrid portions of their writing knowledge repertoires that they can draw upon when constructing texts regardless of the language being used (L1 or L2) (Reichelt et al., 2012).

Beyond individual learner factors, another formative element in the development of FL writing expertise is the instructional context in which students learn to write. Manchón (2009) described this influence:

> [Context shapes] their metacognitive knowledge about composing and textual conventions, their conception of writing, motives for writing, and, consequently, their approach to writing. Some educational factors that appear to mediate the development of writing ability include the kinds and amounts of instruction received, as well as the type and amount of writing practice engaged in. (p. 11)

The impact of this influence, according to Hall (2001), extends to both students' conceptions of writing (i.e., as a transcription tool versus as an activity for making and discovering meaning) and the kinds of writers they become beyond the classroom. In summary, learning to write well in a FL goes far beyond learning new vocabulary and grammar and overlaying it on familiar text formats from one's own culture and L1. In addition to factors relating to learners themselves, instructional practices play a crucial role in writing development. Next, we will explore dominant orientations to FL writing instruction and assessment.

1.3. Approaches to Foreign Language Writing Instruction

In the previous section, you were introduced to the notions of writing-to-learn versus learning-to-write, which represent two divergent perspectives on the purposes for FL writing. Those perspectives can be imagined as two ends of a continuum, with the dominant approaches to FL writing instruction (product based, process based, and genre based) occupying points along that continuum, in the sense that the focus of each one reflects certain assumptions associated with either or both perspectives.

Until CLT became the dominant pedagogical approach to FL instruction, the *product-based approach* was long the prevalent orientation to FL writing, emphasizing the grammatical and syntactic accuracy of texts or, more simply, textual form. Above all else, this approach put value on the structural well-formedness of learners' writing while de-emphasizing elements such as addressing an audience or fulfilling a communicative purpose (Kern, 2000). According to Lefkowitz's (2009) study of collegiate FL professors whose teaching practices were consistent with this approach, typical elements of instruction included assigning artificial topics before any writing instruction occurred and designing assignments to elicit grammar points. Given the absence of explicit attention to assisting students in becoming FL writers or focusing on their communicative intent in writing, the product-based approach can be viewed as aligning with the writing-to-learn perspective (Reichelt et al., 2012).

Particularly favored in the United Kingdom and North America, the *process-based approach* to FL writing took hold as CLT became the prevalent instructional paradigm in the 1990s (Kern, 2000). In contrast with the product-based approach and arising in part out of its weaknesses (e.g., empirical research, such as Truscott, 1996, demonstrating that focusing on grammatical accuracy does not in and of itself improve student writing ability), the process-based approach focuses not just on the product of writing (i.e., the text itself), but also on the processes needed to produce a meaningful text (Kern, 2000). These processes include expressions of individuality through writing, participation in problem-solving writing-focused activities, and inclusion of the collaborative, social nature of writing and writing critiques (Racelis & Matsuda, 2013). Early instantiations of the process-based approach tended to view the writing process as linear, moving from planning to drafting to revising to editing, and focused on helping individual learners participate in each step of the process (Racelis & Matsuda, 2013). However, later interpretations of this approach have come to understand the writing process in a more nuanced, sophisticated way: It is seen as exploratory and recursive as learners generate ideas in writing and later refine and edit those ideas as they receive feedback from their peers and teacher (Williams, 2005). Thus, the teacher's task involves helping learners develop their writing processes for specific writing situations rather than prescribing a generalized writing process (Racelis & Matsuda, 2013). Given the process-based approach's explicit focus on helping students become skilled writers in the FL, it can be viewed as aligning with the learning-to-write perspective.

Like the product-based approach, the process-based approach has not been without criticism. Although it has been credited with enabling researchers and teachers to understand how good writers compose and how instructional practices can shape the process of FL writing (Shrum & Glisan, 2010), one concern relates to the role of accuracy and textual form, with some detractors of the approach claiming it "ignore(s) formal accuracy" (Williams, 2005, p. 33). An assumption of this approach is that learners will attend to the form of their writing naturally as they revise their ideas during the drafting and editing process (Kern, 2000). This expectation may or may not be met by learners who may not possess grammatical or syntactic knowledge needed to produce comprehensible and accurate texts. Furthermore, it cannot be assumed that addressing issues of form will transfer to other learning contexts (e.g., timed writing assignment). A second criticism of the process-based approach is that some teachers have appropriated only its surface features, meaning that the often-mentioned stages of pre-writing, drafting, revising, and editing are seen as a rigid, idealized sequence (Williams, 2005).

According to Kern (2000), a final criticism of this approach is its tendency to favor students already familiar with culturally appropriate academic genres. For those who are not, the approach's lack of textual models can make it challenging to discover the expectations associated with different written genres. Put simply, because the process-based approach attempts to foster learner creativity and individual participation in effective writing practices rather than impose prescribed patterns for FL writing, it may be easier to navigate for students who are already aware of stylistic and linguistic conventions relevant to a given context of use than for students who may need more explicit textual models (Kern, 2000). Lacking those models, students may display an overreliance on L1 textual genres and writing practices, which may result in writing that is not consistent or appropriate for specific contexts of use of the FL.

Responding directly to the need to sensitize FL learners to the social context of writing, or how meaning is constructed within socially determined constraints or parameters, is the *genre-based approach,* which has been dominant in Australia and New Zealand (Kern, 2000). According to Reichelt et al. (2012), FL educators in the United States have been slow to embrace this approach, choosing instead to retain the process-based approach. The rationale for the genre-based approach is based on the notion that students bring different identities and habits of meaning making to FL learning and that teachers cannot assume that their previous learning experiences will provide appropriate writing schemata (Hyland, 2007). For example, in the United States, L1 writing instruction at the high school level typically targets modes and formats of writing, such as five-paragraph essays, reports, and expository texts (Reichelt et al., 2012). As a result, American students are strongest with recalling and reproducing factual content in straightforward informative writing tasks, whereas they are weakest with persuasive and imaginative ones (Kern, 2000). Thus, a U.S. collegiate student of Italian as a FL studying the language for the first time would need to learn the moves and conventions involved in producing specific textual genres of writing in Italian to make meaning in ways that would be considered appropriate by Italian discourse communities. In a genre-based approach, value is not placed on individualistic self-expression; instead, learners are sensitized to the fact that their creative freedom is not limitless, but exists within certain parameters (Maxim, 2005). As Hyland (2007) explained, genre-based writing instruction entails going beyond a focus on syntactic structures, vocabulary, and composing strategies:

> [This approach] offers students an explicit understanding of how target texts are structured and why they are written in the ways they are. This explicitness gives teachers and learners something to shoot for making writing outcomes clear rather than relying on hit or miss inductive methods whereby learners are expected to acquire the genres they need from repeated writing experiences or the teacher's notes in the margins of their essays. (p. 151)

Given the genre-based approach's dual focus on both form and meaning—that is, on how certain structures and conventions are used to make meaning in situated, culturally determined ways—it can be viewed as occupying a middle ground on the continuum of the learning-to-write and the writing-to-learn perspectives.

As with the other approaches to FL writing instruction, the genre-based approach also has its detractors. As Kern (2000) pointed out, a possible drawback of focusing on textual models as the basis of FL writing is that genres "can be easily reduced to static formal recipes, taught in prescriptive fashion, reminiscent of traditional product-based teaching" (p. 183). In addition, other scholars have questioned whether exposure and practice in particular genres is truly empowering or whether, instead, it might be oppressive (Cope & Kalantzis, 1993).

In recent years, some have called for reconciling the various approaches to FL writing instruction by weaving together their complementary elements. For example, Racelis and Matsuda (2013) suggested that process- and genre-based approaches could be integrated in the sense that genre analysis of textual features and functions could function as "one of the strategies for learning and writing in the writing process" (p. 389). Similarly, Kern (2000) advocated integrating elements of product-, process-, and genre-based approaches into instruction that attends to the relationships and dependencies among texts, cognitive processing, social factors, and cultural contexts. In Learning Activity 6.2, we ask you to review the three approaches to FL writing instruction that you have just read about and to reflect on each one.

LEARNING ACTIVITY 6.2

Evaluation of Approaches to Foreign Language Writing Instruction

Part 1. Now that you have read an overview of the three major approaches to FL writing instruction, synthesize the features, benefits, and weaknesses of each in the following table, taking the time to reread the preceding section to find needed information.

Approach	Key Features	Benefits	Weaknesses
Product-based			
Process-based			
Genre-based			

Part 2. Now consider your orientation to these three approaches to FL writing instruction: Which one(s) did you experience in your FL learning and, in your opinion, how effective was it/were they in your development as a FL writer? As a teacher, do you favor one approach over the others, or perhaps a combined approach? Why? Jot down your responses to these questions before discussing them with your classmates and instructor.

1.4 Assessment of FL Writing Development

Questions of how to respond to learners' attempts at FL writing and what in their writing merits response have garnered much attention and disagreement, both in published research and classroom practice. This reflects the reality that differing approaches to FL instruction exist, with each prioritizing certain elements of writing and the writing process while de-emphasizing others. The following sub-questions relate to larger issues of how teachers should respond to learners' FL writing and what in learners' texts merits response (Williams, 2005):

1. Should responses address form, content/organization, or both?
2. With multi-draft writing, when is the best time to respond (i.e., on which draft) and should all aspects of writing be addressed on all drafts?
3. How should responses be provided (e.g., in writing, electronically, or face-to-face) and what form should the comments take?
4. Should a grade be attached to teacher response on all drafts?

In addition, we might also add the question of who should respond to FL writing, since the process of obtaining feedback can be envisioned as extending not just to teachers, but also to the students' peers.

These questions deal with matters of both assessment and evaluation, which, as you recall from Chapter 2, entail gathering information on student learning and performance and assigning a value, interpreting, and judging the results of assessment. Although it is beyond the scope of this chapter to give responses to each of the questions listed here, they are provided to highlight that assessing and evaluating FL writing are complicated matters, and opinions differ as to how they ought to be carried out. That stated, research on the teaching of writing offers a number of insights into best practices that are salient to our discussion of FL writing.

Teachers' corrective feedback on student writing and, in particular, written corrective feedback (WCF) is the subject of a growing body of research; however, results from empirical studies of the impact of WCF on student writing are varied and inconclusive (Vyatkina, 2011). Although few would dispute that surface-level grammatical and linguistic errors have historically been and continue to be the primary focus of instructors' WCF, some researchers claim that it is of limited value or even harmful, whereas others contend it has a positive influence on students' accuracy in writing (O'Donnell, 2007; Vyatkina, 2011).

Researchers tend to agree on two recommended WCF practices: first, that it is more beneficial to focus on error patterns rather than isolated, random errors; and, second, that indirect correction (i.e., pointing out the location of errors with or without coding the type of error) rather than providing the corrected forms is preferable (O'Donnell, 2007). That said, based on Vyatkina's (2011) survey of WCF practices in university FL programs, indirect correction should be used only with errors that students can realistically be expected to self-correct at their current stage of linguistic development; for other errors, the teachers' direct suggestions can be more beneficial. Students are most likely to correct problems in their texts that are easily resolved (e.g., straightforward editing changes), whereas they tend to ignore WCF that is general and contains suggestions that are difficult to follow. Just as grappling with indirect correction puts students in the role of active problem solvers as they attempt to understand the nature of their writing errors and correct them based on WCF, students can also contribute to the feedback process by annotating their writing, or pointing out places where they have experienced difficulty while producing their text (Williams, 2005).

Best practices in FL writing instruction include the establishment of clear criteria for assessing students' texts so that consistent standards are used to judge performance fairly and communicate criteria transparently to students (Hyland, 2007). Two options for evaluating student writing are *holistic rubrics,* which use multiple criteria to produce an overall score, and *analytic rubrics,* which isolate specific features and use criteria for evaluating and scoring each feature (Hall, 2001). According to O'Donnell 2007), the use of analytic scales may be preferable since they provide more reliability in scoring and give students more detailed information on the strengths and weaknesses of their writing.

1.5 Writing and the Multiliteracies Framework

As you are aware, varying conceptions exist regarding the role of writing in FL learning and the approach used to teach it. Whereas for some, writing is seen as straightforward information transfer—mobilizing one's linguistic resources by finding the right words to convey a message—this is not the case for the multiliteracies perspective. Instead, writing is viewed as a communicative act wherein meaning is mediated and transformed rather than merely transferred from one individual or group to another (Kern, 2000). Thus, writing is understood not only as an act of meaning design based on the use of linguistic Available Designs (e.g., grammar, vocabulary, writing systems), but also one that entails cognitive and sociocultural dimensions. The cognitive dimension of writing promotes the development of deliberate thinking about language use and the mental processes involved in writing, such as strategies for planning and organizing a text (Hall, 2001). The sociocultural dimension of writing is of particular importance in relation to the multiliteracies perspective for several reasons. First, the knowledge of when and how to use L2 schematic Available Designs (e.g., genre and style) is essential for learners to write in ways that would be considered appropriate by users of the language in L2 communities. Second, various cultural elements, including one's background knowledge and the classroom culture, are influential in shaping writing practices and related ideologies, assumptions, and values. Both of these points underscore the notion that writing is an individual, personal act that involves creativity, emotions, and imagination, as well as a collaborative activity that involves shared assumptions, relationships, and conventions (Kern, 2000).

From a multiliteracies perspective, writing is viewed not as a distinct language skill, but as a modality closely intertwined with reading. Not only are writers readers of their own work (Kern, 2000), writing and reading share a number of characteristics that lend to their complementary nature. As Swaffar and Arens (2005) pointed out, unlike speaking and listening, which demand immediacy, writing and reading entail similar cognitive processes as recursive acts that allow attention to linguistic detail and use of the text as "an accessible, reviewable language source" (p. 33). Further, writing and reading both involve knowledge of Available Designs in meaning making, or, as Kern explained, "the residual voices and language forms we have internalized, our knowledge of rhetorical and stylistic devices, genres, formatting conventions, and soon—as resources in a dialogic negotiation between internal and external representations of meaning" (p. 171).

Beyond their numerous shared characteristics, reading and writing differentiate themselves as the former involves representing meaning to oneself, whereas the latter entails representing meaning to others (Cope & Kalantzis, 2009). This act of representing meaning to others offers learners a number of benefits, whether or not FL writing is part of their future plans. According to Kern, these include: organizing and expressing feelings, ideas, and thoughts in ways that align with envisioned readers' expectations; creating and reshaping meaning by manipulating forms and reflecting on the effect that such manipulation has on meaning; taking the time to process meaning free of constraints such as turn taking or pronunciation; and engaging in language use that goes beyond functional communication "to create imagined worlds of [learners'] own design" (2000, p. 172). As such, these elements enrich learners' communicative repertoire, facilitating more effective writing practices, including in the L1, in other academic and professional contexts.

Now that you have begun to familiarize yourself with a literacy-oriented view of FL writing, complete Learning Activity 6.3, which requires you to apply this new knowledge to an analysis of two sample writing activities.

LEARNING ACTIVITY 6.3

The Three Dimensions of Foreign Language Writing

In the preceding section, you learned that based on the multiliteracies perspective, writing is an act of meaning design that includes linguistic, cognitive, and sociocultural dimensions. To complete this Learning Activity, reflect on the role that each of these dimensions might play in two sample FL writing activities. First, review in the previous section what the three dimensions of writing entail and then read the description of the activity prompts below. Brainstorm what students would need to know about each dimension to complete the assignment successfully.

Prompt #1: How did you spend your summer vacation? For this writing assignment, describe what you did, where you were, and who you spent the vacation with, and include one specific anecdote that relates something fun or interesting that happened to you last summer. Be sure to use past tenses correctly in context, distinguishing between narration and description.

Prompt #2: Imagine that you have decided to join an online social networking site. For your writing assignment, create a personal ad to increase your popularity ranking on the site. Your ad should contain information on your appearance, personality, origins, interests, and the type of people who interest you.

After completing your reflection on the roles of the three dimensions of writing in the sample activities, discuss the following question with your classmates: Which writing activity do you think is more reflective of the multiliteracies approach and why?

2. PEDAGOGICAL APPLICATIONS

Based on the multiliteracies-oriented conceptions of writing outlined above, what does a parallel pedagogy of FL writing instruction entail? Above all else, the focus of instruction is on meaning making and helping learners develop the ability to become competent, multilingual creators of written texts (Byrnes, 2013). In addition, as Maxim (2005) explained, beyond learning how to design meaning in culturally and situationally appropriate ways, learners also "reflect on and critique how the real world itself makes meaning" (p. 86). Hall (2001) explained that this process, which she compared to an apprenticeship, involves coming to understand what is considered appropriate and accurate in a given context of writing, including rhetorical and structural forms and strategic processes, and developing a sense of what make writing effective and interesting. This apprenticeship incorporates elements of all three approaches to writing instruction overviewed earlier in this chapter: product based, process based, and genre based. Kern (2000) described this literacy-based orientation as a holistic, student-centered approach that not only develops students' understandings of grammar, vocabulary, textual organization, and so on, but also of the relationships among texts, cognitive processes, social factors, and cultural context and how they work together to make meaning. In other words, this approach recognizes the necessity for teaching linguistic Available Designs, such as vocabulary and grammar, which are of particular importance for learners with limited experience using the FL; schematic Available Designs like genre conventions; and the act of meaning design itself, or writing processes. This approach to writing targets the linguistic, sociocultural, and cognitive dimensions of literacy. It also addresses the types of knowledge involved in the process of learning to write, including context knowledge of reader expectations and cultural preferences, genre knowledge, process knowledge of how to carry out a writing task, and system knowledge of vocabulary, grammar, and formal conventions of writing (Hyland, 2011). That stated, this does not mean that every writing-focused activity in which learners engage entails equal emphasis on all of these elements; rather, instruction includes a continuum of activities, ranging from those that focus on formal accuracy (e.g., dictation, translation) to those that emphasize content and ideas (e.g., creative writing, letter writing, journal writing) (Kern, 2000).

Another parallel between how writing is conceived of in a multiliteracies framework and how it is taught relates to the complementarity of reading and writing. As Kern (2000) explained, traditionally, reading and writing were conceived of as activities completed by students on their own outside the classroom so that class time could be dedicated to oral communication. The typical linear sequence of instruction included reading before class, discussion in class, and writing about what was read and discussed after class. However, as you learned in Chapter 5, in a multiliteracies approach, reading is viewed as both an individual and a collaborative act of meaning design, and, as such, takes place in class so that students can both engage in joint negotiation of meaning about texts and receive direct help in reading from their instructor. The same can also be said of writing: It is brought into the classroom as both an individual and a social act that takes place in a context wherein students can profit from instructor assistance and peer feedback as they construct texts. Therefore, in a multiliteracies approach, reading, writing, and speaking are integrated and often overlap within the same activity, following no linear sequence.

As previously mentioned, FL writing instruction from a multiliteracies perspective entails a continuum of activities, some focusing on formal accuracy, others focusing on the communication of ideas, and some incorporating elements of both of these ends of the spectrum. Table 6.1 summarizes the role of the four pedagogical acts in writing-focused instruction and activities reflective of each (based on Kern, 2000).

This summary of multiliteracies-based instructional activities includes numerous uses for writing, ranging from some that focus primarily on the personal expression of ideas (e.g., letter writing) to others that emphasize the writing process (e.g., peer editing) or the linguistic or schematic properties of written texts (e.g., genre reformulation). In addition, the sample activities listed in Table 6.1 highlight the notion that writing is not seen as a stand-alone activity, but rather as a means of communication interwoven with both reading and speaking, as existing texts serve as a point of departure for new meaning making through or about writing. Transformed practice sample activities also

TABLE 6.1 The Four Pedagogical Acts and FL Writing Instruction

Pedagogical Act	Goal in Writing Instruction	Sample Activities
Situated practice	Immersing learners in writing as an act of meaning design: focusing on fluency and the expression of personal ideas and thoughts	Creative writing Journal writing Letter writing
Overt instruction	Providing direct instruction to learners in generating, organizing, and expressing ideas and editing effectively	Mapping ideas Revising and editing texts Teaching textual genres
Critical framing	Sensitizing learners to the relationships between linguistic forms and the social contexts and purposes of texts	Analytical essay Peer editing Reflective journaling
Transformed practice	Creating new texts or adapting existing ones to new contextual parameters	Genre reformulation Story continuation Writing for speaking

underscore the notion introduced in Chapter 2 that in multiliteracies-based teaching, instruction and assessment are tightly interwoven: Reading and analyzing FL texts helps to familiarize learners with linguistic and schematic Available Designs used in specific contexts before they are asked to create their own written texts in activities such as genre or stylistic reformulation. Before proceeding to the next section, which summarizes several literacy-oriented models of FL writing instruction and assessment, complete Learning Activity 6.4, which asks you to synthesize your current knowledge of multiliteracies-based writing instruction.

LEARNING ACTIVITY 6.4

Idea Map of Multiliteracies-Based FL Writing

Use a graphic organizer to map your understanding of the concepts that undergird multiliteracies-based FL writing instruction and how they relate to one another (google the phrase *graphic organizer* to get an idea of what one looks like and how it is constructed). Your graphic organizer, entitled "Multiliteracies-based FL writing" should include all of the concepts listed below plus any other concept or concepts you view as relevant. Once you have completed your graphic organizer, you will have the opportunity to compare and discuss it with your colleagues and instructor.

apprenticeship	Available Designs*	3 dimensions of writing*
4 pedagogical acts*	meaning design	reading-writing interface
writing processes		

* For these concepts, tease out individual sub-concepts as necessary for mapping purposes (e.g., schematic Available Designs, overt instruction).

2.1 Literacy-Oriented Models of Writing Instruction and Assessment

In this section, we outline three models for writing-focused FL instruction and assessment consistent with the multiliteracies framework. First, we present Schultz's (2001) model for creative writing, wherein the author makes a strong case for using elements of both genre- and process-based approaches combined with creative writing to advance learners' development as both readers and writers. Next, we summarize Maxim's (2009) approach to reading and writing development, which proposes textual borrowing as the key element in learner appropriation of textual features in their written production. Finally, we describe Kern's (2000) model for writing-focused instruction, which highlights the integration of reading, writing, and speaking, and the important role that collaboration and oral communication among learners and between learners and their teacher play in scaffolding a reading-to-writing sequence of instruction. You may notice as you begin to read about these writing-focused models that in comparison to those introduced in Chapters 3, 4, and 5 for speaking- and reading-oriented instruction, they may appear to be more complex. In fact, the writing-focused models share many common features with other literacy-based models for FL instruction, including introductory activities to familiarize learners with linguistic and schematic Available Designs germane to the lesson's focus and integration of reading, writing, and speaking throughout the instructional sequence. What distinguishes writing-focused models from others in this book is that they include a detailed treatment of the steps involved in creating a written text; thus, they tend to break transformed practice activities, for example, into more stages than models focused on other language modalities.

The first writing-focused model (Schultz, 2001) is designed in light of the practice in university-level FL curricula of privileging academic forms of writing over creative ones, particularly as learners move into content-focused courses. As Schultz wrote, "there is a deep-seated belief . . . that progress cannot be made without an eventual abandonment of the personal in favor of a rigorous attention to the detached, impersonal, and the objective" (2001, p. 94). She holds a different view, however, arguing that "creative writing can feed positively into the language learning experience in multiple ways" (p. 95). The author names a number of benefits of creative writing in a FL, including its focus, which encourages students to "form and shape the raw material of experience into an artistic and compellingly executed format"; its liberating effect, which lowers learner anxiety and fosters an atmosphere conducive to language acquisition; and the personal commitment required, which necessitates making progress toward mastering lexico–grammatical structures "most appropriate to their authorial intentions and goals" (pp. 95, 96).

The approach to creative writing Schultz (2001) describes is based on three precepts common to many forms of artistic expression: (1) studying textual models representative of specific genres; (2) analyzing narrative techniques illustrated in literary models; and (3) practicing these techniques through a well-defined series of activities. As students analyze and discuss textual models, they focus on "the ways in which authors create the effects that their texts produce" (p. 99). Although they are not constrained to follow these models rigidly in their writing, students draw inspiration from them in shaping their texts. Schultz (2001) provides a sample instructional sequence for a course on French short stories. As students read and analyze a text by Flaubert, they engage in activities to help them incorporate indirect free style (i.e., a direct representation of a character's thoughts without a narrator's mediation) into their writing. First, they present a physical description of a fictional character they have imagined, focusing on details of his or her appearance and their relation to the character's personality. Next, students participate in several activities that move them from presenting the character's thoughts in an internal and external monologue and then telling the character's story as first-person narrator and retelling it from the perspective of an observer. These activities culminate with students using the third-person omniscient narrator and indirect free style technique. This progression, according to Schultz, involves a constant recycling of the same core material of the story but "from different angles and with increasingly sophisticated elaboration" (p. 100), providing students the opportunity to perfect linguistic aspects of their writing.

Schultz's (2001) model also incorporates process-based writing. For example, activities include small-group peer review of initial drafts of creative writing texts and a read-aloud activity wherein all students respond in writing to a student's finished text. As such, students' writing does not "move unidirectionally from author to teacher/reader, falling into a readership void" (p.103). Instead, peers become an essential part of students' readership, transforming the nature of audience. Representative of this notion is the fact that students collectively compile their best creative writing at term's end into a class anthology, whose preparation they oversee themselves, making choices such as format, cover art, and text order. This model potentially incorporates elements of both formative and summative assessment—the former in relation to practicing a narrative technique activity and peer review, and the latter in relation to the drafts and revisions of the creative writing text. Whereas Schultz (2001) did not provide specific assessment criteria for this model, consistent with literacy-based instruction, a holistic rubric might be used to evaluate students' writing with criteria related to content and form, including, for instance, whether the texts produced reflected indirect free style and other conventions associated with the textual model studied.

In the next model, Maxim (2009) presents an approach to reading and writing development used in a genre-based, literacy-oriented German curriculum. Broadly, this curriculum's aim is "exposing learners to a range of textual environments . . . making them aware of how these environments use language to respond to particular contexts . . . [and] encouraging their appropriation of others' language for their own purposes" (p. 102). Thus, texts play a critical role in writing development, as they are viewed not as individual instances of language production, but as "genres that represent a socially situated and culturally embedded use of language in a specific context . . . from which learners can borrow and appropriate language for their own use" (p. 99). Maxim calls this link between reading and writing *textual borrowing,* or "the appropriate integration and documentation of other texts into one's own language use" (p. 100). This borrowing, which the author views as an essential element of FL learning, does not entail the appropriation of textual content per se, but of "particular language features that provide for opportunities to foster the construction of thought" (p. 103). Maxim is careful to point out that learners are encouraged to appropriate language that suits the meanings they wish to make in the FL while, at the same time, recognizing the "limits placed on borrowing by generic conventions" (p. 103).

Maxim describes several examples of his model in the context of an intensive advanced German course organized into four thematic units on modern German history as reflected in personal and public stories. Students read four to six texts per unit as "carriers of content and models of language use" (p. 103), with emphasis on thematically marked lexico–grammatical structures in the texts. Each unit culminates in two summative assessments—writing and speaking tasks that allow students to use the "generic, content, and language knowledge" (p. 104) acquired during the unit. For the first unit on immediate post-war Germany, for instance, students read four personal narratives of Germans' experiences at the end of the war and one descriptive text about care packages, after which they write their own letter to the giver of a care package using the same historical context from the readings.

The steps in Maxim's instructional sequence include: (1) reading each text to identify key events and themes, which are subsequently discussed in class; (2) retelling the story's chronology; (3) searching the text for salient lexical structures that correspond to semantic fields developed in class; and (4) discussing the text's cultural significance. As students retell the story and work to develop a set of useful words and expressions on the topic of war's end, they are guided to incorporate two language features into their work to link events causally or temporally. Next, students move toward creating their own text based on a task sheet that specifies the genre, content focus, and language features to be incorporated at discourse, sentence, and lexico–grammatical levels. Students are explicitly encouraged to borrow specific textual elements (e.g., temporal and causal constructions) as they draft and, later, revise their thank-you letter. The three areas specified in the task sheet serve as criteria for evaluation.

Particularly compelling in Maxim's (2009) model is that beyond a description of its use, the author conducted an empirical study of its implementation in four writing tasks for six students of German. Based on classroom observations, learner interviews, and writing data, he investigated participants' approach toward, type, degree, and development of textual borrowing. His results indicated that learner comprehension of textual models was primarily content oriented rather than language related, bolstering the case for genre-based writing tasks and a carefully scaffolded reading-to-writing instructional sequence. As Maxim concluded, exposure to textual models alone is insufficient for learner appropriation of linguistic features specific to particular genres of writing; instead, "students need explicit guidance in identifying important items to borrow and in understanding how to use them" (2009, p. 116). An additional attractive element of this model is its applicability to a range of curricular levels, including lower-level courses. For example, in Maxim (2005), the author describes a writing assignment in a module called "The Place You Call Home," in which students prepare an article on their hometown after reading several descriptive texts from a German newspaper (p. 92). Despite differences in curricular level between this example and the one previously described, the pedagogy is identical, as is the way that the writing task is structured and evaluated.

In the final writing-focused model, Kern (2000) reinterprets a pedagogical sequence originally designed for English native speakers reading Tennyson's poem "Mariana" and writing an essay on setting as a reflection of character. He uses the four pedagogical acts to structure activities with the goal of developing students' ability to collaboratively construct meaning from texts and, eventually, to read and write more independently. Of particular interest in this approach are the roles of collaboration and problem solving and the ways that reading, writing, and speaking overlap and recur.

Kern's (2000) instructional sequence begins with two situated practice activities to sensitize students to the notions of setting and protagonist and the relationship between them. In the first activity, linked to the television show *Magnum, P.I.,* while the teacher asks guiding questions, students collaboratively create a map of relationships among elements of the show's setting, the protagonist's characteristics, and students' associations with both the setting and main character. In the second activity, students focus on how setting reflects character in their respective lives and homes by preparing a written list of household items and what the items say about them before passing the list to several classmates, each of whom interprets the significance of the first student's items without seeing others' interpretations. Afterwards, each student reads classmates' interpretations of their items before engaging in a related discussion.

Next, students engage in an activity involving both situated practice and transformed practice as they rewrite a simple descriptive statement as a more elaborated descriptive narrative that expresses the same ideas directly (Kern, 2000). To do so, they use verbal description to show but not tell the following: "The state of her house made it clear that she had long since stopped caring about herself" (p. 215). After a 15-minute period of individual in-class writing, students share their descriptive narratives aloud so they can observe the diversity of their classmates' responses.

Students participate next in several situated practice and critical framing activities related to the Tennyson poem about isolation. First, the teacher reads the text aloud while students follow along on a printed copy, underlining elements describing the setting and the protagonist's psychological state. Students then move to paraphrasing the poem and identifying its themes, using a chart to summarize relationships between elements of the setting, its relationship to the main character, and interpretations of the author's intent in choosing certain details of the poem.

To complete the sequence, students take part in transformed practice and critical framing activities as they plan and draft their analytical essays. First, each student develops a thesis statement and three potential introductions, which are read aloud and discussed, with a focus on the potential effects on the reader. Next, students draft their essays. Finally, they engage in peer editing, revise their drafts, and submit a final essay. Although the author does not provide specific assessment criteria, the two drafts of the essay could be evaluated using an analytic rubric that would include equal emphasis on meaning and form.

Kern's (2000) model for FL writing typifies several elements of effective multiliteracies-based instruction. First, it illustrates how writing functions as both a social and individual act of meaning design. For example, the lesson's second situated practice activity includes both individual and collaborative writing. In addition, this model provides an example of how the traditional read-discuss-write sequence can be rethought in favor of activities in which linguistic modalities overlap and recur. For instance, prior to drafting their essays, students reread the summary chart they made in relation to the poem, write and then read aloud to their classmates several potential introductions to their texts, and discuss their readers' responses to those introductions. Finally, Kern's model demonstrates how writing-focused activities can be adapted to fit the goals of different pedagogical acts. For example, mapping ideas can be used in overt instruction to brainstorm and organize words and phrases as a pre-writing activity or, as described in relation to this model, in situated practice as a pre-speaking activity. This is also the case with many of the sample activities listed in Table 6.1, including creative writing, journal writing, and peer editing.

The three writing models described above are summarized in Table 6.2. As you can see, they share several similarities. First, all three incorporate text-based activities as a precursor to writing, whether the texts that students ultimately create reflect the same genre as that previously read, as in Schultz's (2001) and Maxim's (2009) models, or whether the text read serves as content for written interpretation in a text of a different genre, as in Kern's (2000) model. Second, each model includes in-class pre-writing activities with a targeted focus on one or more specific writing elements prior to students drafting a complete text, so that they receive direct assistance while practicing specific writing techniques. During these activities, teachers provide explicit strategies for FL writing rather than relying on students' own intuitions about how a written text should be constructed. Finally, the three models use process-based writing activities to

TABLE 6.2 Literacy-Oriented Models of Writing Instruction

	Schultz (2001)	Maxim (2009)	Kern (2000)
1	Reading a textual model	Reading a textual model to identify key events and themes	Sensitizing students to the theme of the writing assignment through mapping and writing to speak
2	Analyzing narrative techniques in textual model	Retelling the text's chronology	Practicing writing techniques (e.g., Narration versus description)
3	Practicing narrative techniques	Searching the text for lexical structures that correspond to semantic fields	Reading-focused activities, including paraphrasing and completing a summary chart
4	Drafting a new text	Discussing the text's cultural significance	Initial writing activities, e.g., Drafting several introductions to a text and seeking peer input on them
5	Peer review	Drafting a new text and borrowing specific elements from the text read in step 1	Drafting a new text
6	Revising text	Revising text	Peer review
7	Reading student texts aloud		Revising text

allow students multiple opportunities for feedback and refinement of their texts. These commonalities suggest a general format for writing-focused lessons that we detail in the next subsection.

2.2 A Template for Organizing Multiliteracies-Based Writing Instruction and Assessment

Based on the common elements of the three models summarized above and other principles of the multiliteracies approach related to writing summarized at the end of the "Conceptual Background" section, we propose the following four-step model for writing-focused FL instruction:

1. *Introduction to model texts* to sensitize students to the context or content of texts representing a specific textual genre;
2. *Textual comparison* to immerse students in genre by exposing them to more than one instantiation of a textual genre and helping them establish comprehension of those texts' major events;
3. *Textual interpretation* to facilitate learner awareness of specific linguistic and schematic Available Designs used to design meaning in the model texts and form-meaning connections; and
4. *Textual creation* to provide learners with opportunities to use their new Available Designs in transformation activities.

The activities implemented in each stage of this model should reflect the four pedagogical acts of the multiliteracies framework and engage learners in the processes of interpretation, collaboration, problem solving, and reflection and self-reflection. To review, situated practice activities immerse learners in communicative activities and meaning design that focuses on the expression of personal thoughts and ideas; overt instruction activities provide direct instruction aimed at helping learners to generate, organize, or express ideas effectively; critical framing activities sensitize learners to the relationships between linguistic forms and the social contexts and purposes of texts; and transformed practice activities allow students to apply what they have learned by creating new texts or adapting existing ones to new contextual parameters (see Chapter 1 for a detailed discussion).

This model approximates the one described in Allen (2009) and Allen and Paesani (in press), in which reading and analyzing a specific literary genre served as a precursor to creative writing, based on a four-stage instructional sequence that culminated in advanced-level learners writing their own short story (Allen, 2009) and prose poem (Allen & Paesani, in press). However, different from those examples, the sample lesson plan we describe in the next subsection is adapted for use with a non-literary textual genre and lower-level FL learners. Indeed, one appealing aspect of this lesson plan template is its applicability to a range of courses and instructional goals and objectives.

Examples of learning activities that might be used in each stage of the pedagogy are provided in Table 6.3. Note that in some cases, the learning activity corresponds to more than one pedagogical act.

TABLE 6.3 Suggested Learning Activities for Writing Instruction

	Instructional Stage	Suggested Learning Activities
1	Introduction to model texts	Think-pair-share (Situated practice / Critical framing) Instructional conversations (Situated practice / Critical framing) Predicting (Situated practice)
2	Textual comparison	Summary writing (Situated practice) Reading matrix, Part 1 (Situated practice) Instructional conversations (Situated practice / Critical framing)
3	Textual interpretation	Reading matrix, Part 2 (Overt instruction) Focusing on relationships (Overt instruction) Practicing writing techniques (Overt instruction/ Situated practice)
4	Textual creation	Mapping (Situated practice /Transformed practice) Drafting (Situated practice /Transformed practice) Peer review (Critical framing / Overt instruction) Revising and editing (Overt instruction) Reflecting on the writing process (Critical framing)

2.2.1 INTRODUCTION TO MODEL TEXTS. Think-pair-share, participation in instructional conversations, and predicting activate learners' existing knowledge about the textual model to be read and, eventually, created by them. These activities also provide new information (linguistic, schematic, or cultural) to prepare students to understand texts that they will encounter in the next stage of instruction. Common to these activities is two-way communication, both among learners and between learners (collectively) and their teacher, rather than one-way transfer of background information about texts from the teacher to the students.

To engage in a *think-pair-share* activity (Lyman, 1981), students individually think about and take notes on a question from their teacher designed to target the textual genre or thematic focus of the text, then collaborate with a peer to compare their ideas while using their written notes to facilitate oral communication, and finally share and synthesize ideas orally and in writing with a larger peer group or the entire class. An *instructional conversation,* as presented in Chapters 4 and 5, is useful for providing learners with unknown content schemata through an interactive, teacher-led conversation, structured in a manner that minimizes initiation-response-evaluation (IRE) discourse patterns in favor of fewer known-answer questions and more turn-taking on the part of learners. *Predicting,* which you read about in Chapter 5, involves giving clues about information in a text such as its title, key words or expressions, or associated images to activate learners' related Available Designs and facilitate sharing and comparing of their ideas about the text with those of their peers.

2.2.2 TEXTUAL COMPARISON. The activities in the second stage of the model involve comparison of pairs of texts on a common topic or theme to help students identify what characterizes a given genre (Kern, 2000). Providing more than one textual model is also helpful to illustrate variation within a genre, giving students more potential choices for textual borrowing in later redesign of meaning when they create their own text. Summary writing, completing a reading matrix, and participating in a second instructional conversation all engage students in reading-focused activities and concentrating on global comprehension of the main events or chronology of texts.

In *summary writing,* teachers guide students to participate first in an oral collaborative summary of each text before moving on to a written collaborative summary and, finally, written summaries created by each student. In this way, students are assisted in simplifying textual language and gradually work up to a written paraphrase based on their own point of view. Completing a *reading matrix* (Swaffar & Arens, 2005), an activity you were introduced to in Chapter 5, facilitates students "join[ing] syntax and general (macro-) propositions with supporting details or micropropositions that elaborate them in the text" (p. 87). In this way, students move from a general comprehension activity to one that focuses on both main ideas and details. Both of these activities can be followed up with an *instructional conversation* concentrating on interpretation of textual meaning, which is the design of new meanings based on learners' personal readings of the texts.

2.2.3 TEXTUAL INTERPRETATION. The third stage of the model requires learners to analyze the model texts anew, targeting specific linguistic and schematic Available Designs through completing a second part of the reading matrix, focusing on relationships, and practicing writing techniques. Common to these activities is the objective of helping students gain a vocabulary or metalanguage to talk about the process of meaning making as well as new Available Designs for creating their own texts (Kern, 2000).

Returning to the *reading matrix* tool can be useful to locate specific linguistic and stylistic features of the model texts and compare them across texts to find commonalities and differences in how form is used to express meaning. In addition, to concentrate even more closely on form-meaning connections, a *focusing-on-relationships* activity can be used to examine word relationships, syntactic relationships, or how discourse is organized within a text. Such an activity involves close analysis of textual language through a series of targeted questions (e.g., *What are the connotations associated with the word . . . ?, Which sentences directly support the main idea?*). A last activity in this stage begins to move learners from a reading to a writing focus, as they engage in *practicing writing techniques,* using the model texts as examples of how a specific element of writing is instantiated (e.g., narration in the past or reported speech) before practicing those same techniques themselves.

2.2.4 TEXTUAL CREATION. Following learners' exposure to and analysis of textual models and their embedded linguistic and schematic Available Designs, they now begin the work of creating a new text. After the teacher provides an instruction sheet on the writing assignment and criteria for evaluation, students complete a *mapping* activity to brainstorm initial ideas for their texts in a non-linear fashion by clustering them in the way that makes the most intuitive sense. Depending on the level and focus of the course, the teacher might provide categories or themes as a starting point for this activity. A second, optional component of this activity, also dependent on learner level, can entail students exchanging initial ideas for their texts and offering suggestions to one another using their idea maps. The remainder of this stage is dedicated to a recursive cycle of students *drafting* their texts, participating in structured *peer review* activities in class and *revising and editing* their texts based on WCF from their teacher and suggestions from their peers. At the completion of this cycle, along with their final draft, students can also turn in a *reflection* (in either their native language or the FL, depending on their level) on their perceptions of participating in this writing assignment, the challenges they faced, and the aspects of their writing that they felt were strongest.

2.2.5 ASSESSMENT. The four-stage writing model summarized here provides opportunities for a variety of assessment types. Evidently, transformed practice activities in the textual creation stage culminate with summative assessment of students' written texts. Evaluation would be conducted using an analytic rubric with criteria related to both form (i.e., linguistic Available Designs such as vocabulary and grammar and schematic Available Designs such as adherence to genre-specific conventions) and meaning, or the thematic content communicated through the text. Alternative assessment is incorporated through students' reflections at the end of this last stage of the lesson plan template and could take on an expanded role if students' written texts, reflections, and other forms of assessment from the instructional sequence were to be compiled as part of a writing portfolio. Finally, several written artifacts from the first three stages of the model could serve as formative assessments (e.g., reading matrix or idea maps) and evaluated using a simple holistic rubric for task completion and appropriateness of information included.

2.3 Sample Writing-Focused Lesson Plan

The lesson plan template for FL writing presented here, grounded in activities reflecting the four pedagogical acts, makes it possible for lower-level FL learners to create a written text based on analysis of both meaning and form in existing textual models. It moves from reading-focused to writing-focused activities and from a primary focus on critical framing and situated practice to activities that concentrate on overt instruction (i.e., raising awareness of text-based linguistic and schematic Available Designs) and, finally, transformed practice as learners draft, edit, and revise their texts.

In Table 6.4, we present a sample lesson plan organized according to the model instructional sequence above. Activities implemented in the lesson represent one of the illustrative activity types presented in Table 6.3 for each stage

TABLE 6.4 Sample Instructional Sequence, Writing-Focused Lesson: My Childhood Place

Instructional Stage		Learning Activities
1 Introduction to model texts	a	Students participate in a *think-pair-share* activity, in which they make a list of childhood favorites (e.g., a possession, food, person, place) and associated descriptions; they compare their lists orally with a peer and then with the rest of the class. (Situated practice)
	b	The instructor projects the title "Mon lieu d'enfance" as the precursor for a *predicting* activity, in which students collaboratively respond to a series of questions that take the text title as a point of departure and are designed to transition the focus of instruction from the students' cultural frame of reference to that of the texts while the instructor notes students' ideas on the board. (Critical framing)
2 Textual comparison	a	Students read one of two model texts (half of the class reads Text A, the other half reads Text B), participate in a whole-class *summary* of the texts both orally and then in writing, and finally write a summary of one text based on their understanding of its meaning. (Situated practice)
	b	Students read the other model text (e.g., Text B if they had read Text A before and vice versa) and complete the first part of a *reading matrix* to link the main elements of each text (what, where, when, with whom) with supporting details or micropropositions. (Situated practice)
	c	Instructor-led follow up includes verification of comprehension of elements in the text matrix and discussion of similarities and differences in textual meaning and form in the two articles. (Situated practice / Critical framing)
3 Textual interpretation	a	Students now complete the second part of the *reading matrix* for excerpts from both model texts, focusing on both linguistic Available Designs (e.g., identifying instances where one of three different verb tenses is used to either narrate or describe in the past or present and a brief rationale for that tense) and schematic Available Designs (e.g., conventions they observe in the text for a first-person narrative text); instructor-led follow up accompanies this activity. (Overt instruction)
	b	Using two introductory phrases from the articles as models, students *practice a writing technique* (i.e., description in the past) and rewrite the introductions of both articles to reflect the childhood place article they will create in the next stage; they then read both introductions aloud to a peer and listen to his or her feedback before changing roles and providing feedback on the peer's introductions. (Overt instruction / Situated practice / Critical framing)

(*Continued*)

TABLE 6.4 Sample Instructional Sequence, Writing-Focused Lesson: My Childhood Place

Instructional Stage	Learning Activities
4 Textual creation	a Students complete a *mapping* activity, using a graphic organizer to visually represent the what, where, with whom, and when of their "Childhood Place" and to brainstorm key vocabulary and structures necessary for what they want to communicate in their text. (Transformed practice / Situated practice)
	b Using their map, students *draft* a text that describes their childhood place in detail, its significance for them as a child, and its continued importance in their current life, making appropriate use of past and present tenses in context. (Transformed practice)
	c Students take part in a structured *peer-review* activity, in which they read a peer's text and complete a written summary report on it before engaging in a discussion structured by their summary report to give and receive oral feedback on the texts. (Situated practice / Critical framing)
	d Based on peer feedback and written corrective feedback from their instructor, students *revise and edit* their texts. (Situated practice / Overt instruction)
	e Students *reflect* in writing in the L1 about their participation in this assignment and turn in their reflection with the final draft of their text. (Critical framing)

in the model. This lesson is intended for use in a second-semester introductory-level French course during an instructional unit on childhood and narration in the past. The goals of this lesson are to enable students to understand and use vocabulary related to childhood memories, to recognize how the *passé composé* 'preterit' and *imparfait* 'imperfect' are used in past-tense narration and description, to collaboratively construct meaning from two journalistic texts, and to write their own article based on the textual models. The texts that serve as models for student writing and the basis for reading-focused activities in stages 2 and 3 of the instructional sequence are two short articles from a French weekly magazine entitled *Télérama* that were part of a four-part series called "Mon lieu d'enfance" 'My childhood place,' wherein well-known personalities from French culture describe a place that was special to them when they were young and that continues to play a role in their personal or professional identity. The first text, "Pour Olivia Ruiz, c'était chocolat-tartines au comptoir" (published on July 12, 2008), deals with a singer's memories of her family's café (Text A). The second text, "Bertrand Tavernier habitait au 4, rue Chambovet, à Lyon" (published on July 19, 2008), presents a filmmaker's memories of his childhood home (Text B). Because the subject matter of these texts is concrete, visual, and therefore accessible to students, the fact that they include some sophisticated vocabulary and cultural references that are most likely unknown to learners should not impede students' ability to construct meaning. (To find these texts online, google the terms "télérama" and "mon lieu d'enfance" or go to www.telerama.fr and search using the article titles.)

The activities in this four-stage lesson plan facilitate meaning design through both reading- and writing-focused activities, incorporate the seven principles of literacy (Kern, 2000), and develop learner awareness of the three dimensions of writing (linguistic, sociocultural, and cognitive). Before engaging in reading activities, learners use language to access and share existing Available Designs on the lesson's theme and to predict the content of the model texts, tapping into previous personal experience and cultural knowledge. Next, learners interact with the Available Designs of the two texts, beginning with a focus on meaning and moving to form-meaning connections and why certain linguistic and schematic resources are used in this textual genre. In so doing, they interpret the themes of the texts and how those themes are related to language forms; they collaborate by interacting with the texts and with other learners to design meaning; and they solve problems by figuring out relationships between words in the text and overall textual meaning. They then move from reading-focused to writing-focused activities, using the texts they have analyzed as models for the types of linguistic (e.g., use of certain verb tenses to narrate and describe in the past) and schematic (e.g., conventions such as alternating between the third-person and first-person narrative mode to describe place as well as the narrator's relation to place) Available Designs they should use in their text. Pre-writing activities include practicing one specific writing technique and mapping initial ideas for the text's content in a nonlinear manner, further instantiations of language use and problem solving that facilitate a gradual process of constructing a text. After learners have created a first draft of their text, collaboration takes place as they become readers of others' texts, providing feedback to their peers on their writing. Finally, at the conclusion of the writing process, when they have produced a revised text, students reflect on what they have learned through participation in this reading-to-writing instructional sequence.

The organization of this writing-focused lesson around the four pedagogical acts also facilitates a multimodal approach to constructing meaning from written texts. Students interact with texts through both reading and listening to the text read aloud (e.g., the practicing a writing technique activity) and participate in numerous structured oral activities. Moreover, this instructional sequence engages students in all three modes of communication (interpersonal, interpretive, and presentational), all grounded in text-oriented activities.

To help you reflect on this sample writing-focused lesson plan, read through it a second time and find answers to the following questions:

1. What are the objectives of this lesson and how do they fit within the course curriculum?
2. Are the selected texts appropriate to meet these objectives? What elements of these texts might be challenging for FL learners to understand?
3. In what ways are students designing meaning through the various activities in this lesson?

4. Why are the different lesson plan activities labeled as situated practice, overt instruction, critical framing, or transformed practice?
5. Are the basic elements of instruction, or the what of multiliteracies pedagogy—conventions, cultural knowledge, and language use—represented in the lesson?
6. Are the learning processes of interpretation, collaboration, problem solving, and reflection and self-reflection (i.e., the how of multiliteracies pedagogy) represented in the lesson?

As you think about planning your own writing-focused lesson plans and assessments using the template above, come back to these questions as a way to help you to organize your ideas and apply your understanding of multiliteracies-based writing pedagogy. Learning Activity 6.5 will help you get started.

LEARNING ACTIVITY 6.5

Design of a Multiliteracies-Based Reading-to-Writing Activity Sequence

Create an instructional sequence based on an existing writing activity from your FL textbook that culminates in a summative, genre-based writing assignment. This instructional sequence should be based on the four-step model described here and linked to the themes and lexico–grammatical and cultural objectives of your course. Before beginning this task, review the themes and objectives you need to keep in mind for the unit or chapter for which you will design your instructional sequence. Next, select a textual genre and two model texts on which you will build your activities that are consistent with the themes and objectives of the unit. Once you have selected the texts, design the instructional sequence using the four-stage model and suggested learning activities in Tables 6.3 and 6.4. When the lesson plan is finished, ask yourself the questions above as a way to help you justify your pedagogical choices.

3. FINAL CONSIDERATIONS

In this chapter, we have established a conceptual base for considering FL writing instruction within the multiliteracies framework. Essential to this base is the notion that writing is more than speech written down and thus involves more than saying it with the right words. In addition to the linguistic dimension of writing, which is undoubtedly an area for which FL learners need significant assistance, the multiliteracies framework recognizes the critical role of the sociocultural and cognitive dimensions of writing as learners grapple with understanding the conventionalized nature of written texts and how they function within a discourse community and use various cognitive processes to design meaning in the FL.

We further established that teaching FL learners to write following the multiliteracies framework should reflect an integrated approach, incorporating elements of product-, process-, and genre-based instruction. The related pedagogy we developed in this chapter has as its main goal to facilitate

FL writing development through a text-based reading-to-writing model and engagement in literacy-based instructional activities and learning processes. Thus, we have highlighted the importance of using authentic FL texts as a starting point for teaching learners to use linguistic and schematic Available Designs accurately and appropriately in their writing. As Kern (2000) explained, studying these Available Designs through textual models allows learners to recognize how their use is constrained in a particular genre and also how they allow for new ways of creative personal expression. This pedagogy is further grounded in existing instructional models intended to foster academic literacy and in the four pedagogical acts essential to multiliteracies instruction: situated practice, overt instruction, critical framing, and transformed practice.

To conclude, as previously noted, writing was long considered a secondary skill, particularly in the lower-level FL curriculum, wherein it was traditionally used as a vehicle for language practice. However, in recent years, researchers have recognized the role of writing in facilitating FL development. The pedagogy for FL writing that you have learned about in this chapter is, in fact, intended to go beyond practicing lexico–grammatical structures or even expressing personal thoughts and opinions. Instead, in line with the definition of literacy that we have laid out in this book, writing instruction serves as a means of teaching both language and culture as students learn new meaning-making practices based on existing textual models. As such, we hope that you have come to view writing as a language modality of primary importance in your students' language-learning experience.

4. TRANSFORMING KNOWLEDGE

4.1 Reflective Journal Entry

How did this chapter build on your previous understandings of the multiliteracies framework? How did this chapter build on your previous views about writing and FL writing instruction? Did these change after reading this chapter and, if so, how? What specific ideas from the chapter can you apply to your own teaching context? Before completing this journal entry, return to Learning Activity 6.1 and review your responses to it.

4.2 Researching Writing: Personal Action Plan

Identify a goal or problem area related to teaching writing in your instructional context and create a personal action plan. Use the table below to lay out your plan, then implement the plan in your teaching and use your performance measures to collect information that helps determine whether you have met your goal or solved your stated problem. If you have achieved your goal, what are the implications for your approach to teaching writing? If you have not achieved your goal, how can you modify your action plan to help you move forward in this area of your teaching? You can find a description of the parts of a personal action plan in the "Pedagogical Applications" section of Chapter 4.

Goal or Problem	
Action Step 1	
Action Step 2	
Action Step 3	
Action Step 4	
Resources and Support	
Possible Barriers	
Performance Measures	

Key Resources

Kern, R. (2000). *Literacy and language teaching.* Oxford, England: Oxford University Press.

Chapter 6, "Writing as Design," presents a literacy-oriented definition of writing as an act of meaning design that includes linguistic, sociocultural, and cognitive dimensions. After reviewing factors involved in writing in an L2, Kern reviews the three major orientations to teaching writing (product-, process-, and genre-based approaches) and argues for weaving together different elements of these approaches to emphasize Available Designs and interdependencies among cognitive processes, textual products, social factors, and cultural contexts. Chapter 7, "Teaching Writing as Design," lays out what a literacy-oriented pedagogy of FL writing instruction entails—integrating the teaching of Available Designs with the teaching of meaning design. This pedagogy is described in relation to the four pedagogical acts, with three to six learning activity types given for each pedagogical act. The chapter concludes with a sample teaching sequence that illustrates this pedagogy.

Maxim, H. H. (2009). "It's made to match": Linking L2 reading and writing through textual borrowing. In C. Brantmeier (Ed.), *Crossing languages and research methods* (pp. 97–122). Charlotte, NC: Information Age Publishing.

This chapter focuses on the notion of textual borrowing, or the appropriation of textual language into writing and speaking at the lexico–grammatical, sentential, and textual level. Maxim argues for a comprehensive reconsideration of textual borrowing's role in language learning, locating it within the "gradual appropriation by all learners of a range of L2 textual features into their language use" (p. 97). In addition to outlining a pedagogical sequence for reading and writing development that includes textual borrowing, the chapter also presents data from a study of textual borrowing practices by six advanced FL learners.

Reichelt, M., Lefkowitz, N., Rinnert, C., & Schultz, J. M. (2012). Key issues in foreign language writing. *Foreign Language Annals, 45*, 22–41.

In this review article, four L2 writing specialists representing varied backgrounds address several questions on writing instruction related to the following topics: differences between FL and ESL writing; the sociolinguistic role of a given FL and its influence in the writing curriculum; the role that writing should play in the FL classroom; and the possible purposes for students writing in FLs. The authors argue that methods for teaching English and ESL cannot be overlaid in FL writing contexts and that specific training should be provided to FL teachers in writing instruction. They further argue for a focus on teaching writing in the FL classroom to facilitate overall language acquisition.

For Further Reading

Allen, H. W. (2009). A literacy-based approach to the advanced French writing course. *The French Review, 83*(2), 368–387.

Hyland, K. (2011). Learning to write: Issues in theory, research, and pedagogy. In R. M. Manchón (Ed.), *Learning to write and writing to learn in an additional language* (pp. 17–35). Amsterdam, Netherlands: John Benjamins.

Maxim, H. (2005). Articulating foreign language writing development at the collegiate level: A curriculum-based approach. In C. Barrette & K. Paesani (Eds.), *Language program articulation: Developing a theoretical foundation* (pp. 78–93). Boston, MA: Heinle.

CHAPTER 7

Teaching Video-Mediated Listening as Constructing Meaning From Texts

Foreign language (FL) instructors have long regarded videotexts as essential resources for instruction. In the last two decades, publishers have responded to instructor demand by increasingly including videotexts, albeit more often simulated than authentic, as part of the ancillary package accompanying their textbooks. Despite this development, authentic FL videotexts, due to "technological, pedagogical and sociological factors" (Kaiser, 2011, p. 232), have made only limited inroads in the FL curriculum over that same time period. Due to a recent confluence of trends, however, a number of changes are taking place in the FL classroom.

Taking advantage of advances in internet technology, news reporting and commentary have been moving to the web at an unprecedented pace, and popular video-sharing web sites such as YouTube, Google Video, and Hulu have been making the internet the go-to place for the distribution of commercials, documentaries, music videos, short films, and so forth. At the same time, the report of the MLA Ad Hoc Committee on Foreign Languages (2007) underscored that the goal of language study should be translingual and transcultural competence, defined as "the ability to operate between languages" (pp. 3–4), and it identified videotexts as one important resource for challenging "students' imaginations and helping them consider alternative ways of seeing, feeling, and understanding things" and teaching them "differences in meaning, mentality, and worldview as expressed in American English and in the target language" (p. 4). With broadened access to a growing supply of a wide range of authentic videotexts, which can be used to promote translingual and transcultural competence both inside and outside the FL classroom, instructors are progressively making greater use of these resources in their teaching, although more readily so in advanced-level than in lower-level courses. Many FL instructors still express doubt regarding the appropriateness of these materials for lower-level learners. When considering teaching video-mediated listening (Gruba, 2004, 2006; Shrum & Glisan, 2010) in lower-level classrooms, FL instructors often ask the following questions: In authentic videotexts, people speak very fast, so how can I use them with students whose linguistic abilities are limited? Can I use authentic videotexts for something other than providing background knowledge and important vocabulary and grammar to my students? In a language class, shouldn't my primary focus be on helping my students develop their oral communicative competence? Overall, these questions reflect traditional views of video-mediated listening in the lower-level FL classroom, wherein the focus is largely on recognizing and understanding different linguistic elements. The consequences of such a viewpoint for lower-level FL video-mediated listening instruction are threefold: Videotexts are primarily used for (1) preparing students for subsequent oral tasks, rather than for meaningfully engaging them with the genre and content of the videotexts themselves; (2) providing students with examples of correct vocabulary and grammar for later use; and (3) indirectly assessing students' knowledge of vocabulary and grammar. Interaction with videotexts and interpretation of their textual meaning are usually postponed until later, when students have developed higher levels of language proficiency. Until then, videotexts are used at the service of something else, rather than for themselves; that is, their meaningful and culturally situated elements are often secondary to the set of linguistic structures targeted in the text, a phenomenon reflective of the curricular dissonance found in many FL departments (see Introduction).

However, as we have seen in previous chapters, even first-semester FL students can interact with and interpret authentic texts, including videotexts; the multiliteracies framework examined in this book provides the tools to design video-mediated listening activities that make these videotexts accessible. In this respect, a multiliteracies-oriented approach to video-mediated listening makes it possible to integrate authentic videotexts into instruction throughout the undergraduate FL curriculum, thereby increasing the amount of textual content with which lower-level students interact while preparing them to comprehend and interpret a variety of videotexts (e.g., film, documentaries, news reports, music videos, commercials) as they make their way through the four-year sequence.

In this chapter, we examine the teaching and learning of FL video-mediated listening within the multiliteracies framework. Several reasons prompted us to focus on video-mediated listening, rather than audio-mediated listening. First is the overall consensus among researchers and practitioners that compared to an audio medium, videotexts provide considerable enhancement in terms of context, discourse, paralinguistic features, and aspects of culture (Alm 2008; Altman, 1989; Buck, 2001; Bueno, 2009; Cross, 2011; Hammer & Swaffar, 2012; Kramsch, 1993, 1999; Swaffar & Vlatten, 1997) because they offer an ideal way for raising students' awareness of discursive practices in target language societies and of how these discursive practices are both historically and culturally situated. Additionally, the wide array of Available Designs (e.g., audio, visual, linguistic, gestural, and spatial resources) within videotexts makes their comprehension and interpretation less challenging than that of audiotexts, which contain only a small subset of these meaning-making resources (Cross, 2009; Rivens-Mompean & Guichon, 2009; Rubin, 1995b). Next, the digitization of videotexts and the ability to manipulate them on a computer with greater ease opens up new avenues for teaching video-mediated FL listening. Finally, videotexts are ubiquitous in our contemporary culture. Their widespread use, especially among the digital natives (Prensky, 2001) enrolled in our classrooms who have never known a world without computers, digitally mediated texts, or the internet, increases the likelihood that learners will listen to another language through this multimodal medium (Guichon & McLornan, 2008).

Our choice of the word videotext rather than video is deliberate and purposeful. Typically, when we hear or read the word *video,* it is the technology of the medium that first comes to mind, namely its ability to dynamically combine visual and audio elements in a contiguous sequence (Gruba, 2004, p. 55). However, as noted by Gruba, in the field of applied linguistics, our attention ought to be directed to textual features and literacy practices, rather than to the technology itself. Expanding on Joiner (1990), who introduced the term *videotext* after arguing that video "is as deserving of the label *text* as is a written document" (p. 54, emphasis in the original), Gruba calls our attention to the need to consider the use of cohesive devices, style nuances, composition and narrative structure, and underlying viewpoints of videotexts. Videotext genres fall on a continuum, with entertainment (e.g., movies, cartoons, music videos) on one end and information (e.g., documentaries, news) on the other. Broadly speaking, videotexts also vary in their degree of structure with movies, cartoons, and music videos at the less structured end of the continuum and news, talk shows, comedies, and soap operas at the more structured end. Further, although similarities may be found in the formats of more structured videotexts, their production and construction will reflect the sociocultural norms, values, and perspectives of their country of origin (Meinhof, 1998). When a videotext is seen as a text, "questions can be asked about authorship, intended audience, the presentation of a worldview or the influence of specific textual features" (Gruba 2005, p. 9). Thinking of videotexts in this fashion is especially meaningful within the context of multiliteracies-oriented teaching and learning.

Our primary focus in this chapter is on constructing meaning from videotexts in lower-level language classes. The concepts and applications considered herein, however, are germane to higher curricular levels as well, including advanced-level cinema courses. In the "Conceptual Background" section, we overview a small but growing body of research on FL video-mediated listening focusing on concepts related to listening/viewing ability and the contributions of various Available Designs, especially visual resources, and cognitive processing models. Next, we turn our attention to concepts aligned with an integrated, multiliteracies-oriented approach to video-mediated listening, including its sociocultural dimensions, and video-mediated listening as an act of meaning design. In the "Pedagogical Applications" section, we start by examining the goals of video-mediated listening instruction within a multiliteracies-oriented approach to guide the organization of instructional activities anchored in the four pedagogical acts. Next, we overview four current literacy-based approaches to teaching and assessing videotext-based comprehension and interpretation, and we present a model for designing and implementing video-mediated listening lesson plans in lower-level FL classrooms. We conclude this section with a walk-through of a sample lower-level, video-mediated listening lesson plan guided by this model and provide sample assessments related to it. By the end of this chapter, you will have a better understanding of why a multiliteracies-oriented approach to constructing meaning from authentic videotexts is a viable alternative to more traditional models and how it can be implemented in your classroom context. To interact with the notions introduced in this chapter, take a few minutes to complete Learning Activity 7.1.

LEARNING ACTIVITY 7.1

My Experience With Video-Mediated Listening as a FL Learner

Part 1. Before continuing to read this chapter, reflect on the use of videotexts in the beginning FL classes you took. Use the following questions to guide your reflection:

1. How often were videotexts used in the beginning FL classes you took? How much time was typically devoted to viewing videotexts in class?
2. What kinds of videotexts were typically used in your beginning FL classes? Were these videotexts used in their entirety or were only clips shown? On average, how long were these videotexts?
3. What kinds of video-mediated listening activities did you engage in? What was the main focus of these activities? What do you think the purpose of these activities was? Did you find these activities effective for learning?
4. Did the way videotexts were used and the type of activities proposed reflect a multiliteracies-approach to teaching and learning?

Part 2. Once you have completed this chapter, reread your answers to these questions. Using the new understandings you developed in relation to video-mediated listening in a multiliteracies-oriented approach, add any final thoughts you have.

1. CONCEPTUAL BACKGROUND

In this section, we overview theoretical research and models related to FL video-mediated listening. We begin by examining the definition of video-mediated listening, followed by a discussion of various factors known to play a role in learners' ability to engage with videotexts, cognitive processes involved in video-mediated listening, and sociocultural dimensions of video-mediated listening. Next, after highlighting similarities and differences between reading and video-mediated listening, we examine notions of visual literacy. Finally, we use this foundation to consider textual interpretation of videotexts, focusing on meaning design and the goals of FL video-mediated listening within multiliteracies-oriented teaching and learning. To help you interact more effectively with the notions included in the "Conceptual Background" section, take a moment to work through Learning Activity 7.2

LEARNING ACTIVITY 7.2

My Ideas About Video-Mediated Listening in a FL

Part 1. Before reading this section, consider the following statements related to video-mediated listening and reflect on the degree to which you agree or disagree with each one.

1 = strongly agree 2 = agree 3 = slightly agree 4 = slightly disagree 5 = disagree 6 = strongly disagree							
	Statement	**Degree of Agreement**					
1	Compared with other language modalities, video-mediated listening is a passive activity.	1	2	3	4	5	6
2	Video-mediated listening means understanding all of the spoken words in a videotext.	1	2	3	4	5	6
3	FL learners with limited language proficiency cannot engage with authentic videotexts.	1	2	3	4	5	6
4	An effective listener-viewer is able to understand the meanings attached to both verbal and visual elements.	1	2	3	4	5	6
5	Visual, gestural, spatial, and textual elements (captions and subtitles) are useful in FL video-mediated listening.	1	2	3	4	5	6

Part 2. When you have completed reading the "Conceptual Background" section, come back to these statements and decide whether your ideas about them were confirmed or not. Locate in this section one piece of evidence that supports or refutes your ideas. How has the new information found in this section contributed to your conceptual understanding of video-mediated listening in particular and refined your understanding of multiliteracies-oriented teaching and learning in general?

1.1 What Is Video-Mediated Listening?

According to Gruba (2005, 2006), "no single definition of video-mediated listening comprehension has become established" (p. 77). One key conceptual issue has revolved around the role that visual elements play in video-mediated listening comprehension, with some scholars downplaying their importance (Kellerman, 1992) and others acknowledging their contribution (e.g., Cross, 2009, 2011; Ginther 2002; Gruba, 2004, 2005, 2006, 2007; Ockey, 2007; Seo, 2002; Sueyoshi & Hardison, 2005; Vandergrift & Goh, 2012; Wagner 2007, 2008, 2010a; 2010b). For the purpose of this chapter and to better capture what *video-mediated listening* is in a multiliteracies approach, we choose to follow Rubin (1995a), who describes it as an "active process in which listeners select and interpret information which comes from auditory and visual cues in order to define what is going on" (p. 7). In other words, visual and verbal elements are not separated; both make contributions in the video-mediated listening process. More importantly, this definition underscores the constructive nature of video-mediated listening, the critical role played by the listener–viewer, and the interaction between the listener–viewer's knowledge and the videotext. Much like reading, video-mediated listening is a process, a recursive act that involves interaction between the videotext and the listener–viewer. The nature of this interaction is variable. The listener–viewer can pause and replay the whole videotext or segments of it to construct meaning, examine specific points to confirm, revise an initial understanding, or gather concrete evidence to support it. Further, because video-mediated listening is a recursive and interactive act of meaning construction, it encompasses more than the comprehension of surface-level facts; it also involves inferencing to understand particular points of view and perspectives. Finally, video-mediated listening involves the listener–viewer being able to link what he or she hears/views to his or her background knowledge to construct meaning.

The ideas in Rubin's (1995a) definition reflect the multiliteracies perspective of video-mediated listening as an act of meaning design. This means that video-mediated listening, much like reading, is not an act during which the listener–viewer passively absorbs information that resides in the videotext to arrive at one single possible interpretation. Instead, it is an act that includes dynamic involvement on the listener–viewer's part as he or she interacts with visual, audio, gestural, spatial, and verbal features of the videotext, selects those deemed important for processing the information, and uses them to reconstruct and interpret the meaning of the videotext. Furthermore, as an act of meaning design, video-mediated listening, much like reading, involves an interplay between social and personal dimensions. In other words, video-mediated listening is both a social and individual process in addition to being a cognitive one, a dimension that will be examined next as we consider factors known to affect learners' ability to comprehend and interpret FL videotexts.

1.2 Factors Affecting Foreign Language Video-Mediated Listening

At the beginning of this chapter, we included questions commonly asked by teachers about video-mediated listening in the lower-level FL classroom. One underlying assumption common to these questions is that FL learners' language proficiency is a determining factor in their ability to engage in video-mediated listening. Although second language acquisition (SLA) scholars focusing on this area of research do not contest that FL learners' language proficiency plays a role, they also underscore that learners' language proficiency is far from the whole story. In fact, these scholars (e.g., Altman, 1989; Cross, 2011; Ginther 2002; Rubin, 1995a; Seo, 2002; Sueyoshi & Hardison, 2005; Vandergrift & Goh, 2012) outline several factors involved in effective comprehension and interpretation of videotexts: prior knowledge, which is organized into schemata (see Chapter 5 for more information); knowledge of the FL; knowledge of the videotext genre; the ability to hold information in short-term memory while engaging with texts; and the ability to use listening–viewing strategies such as predicting, monitoring, inferencing, elaborating, and contextualizing. In video-mediated listening, FL learners tap into these types of knowledge and abilities as they engage in comprehension and interpretation of videotexts. We now turn our attention to understanding the contributions these cognitive processes make to the act of video-mediated listening.

1.3 Cognitive Video-Mediated Listening Processes

To date most of the research on video-mediated listening is cognitively based. Studying the cognitive processes involved in the act of video-mediated listening and elaborating models that best capture these processes and the way they operate has been the primary focus of this research. Three common models have emerged from this research: bottom-up, top-down, and interactive. Because these models have already been discussed in Chapter 5 in relation to reading, for this chapter we will revisit them briefly in the context of video-mediated listening.

Bottom-up processing models are text oriented, which means that the listener–viewer autonomously constructs textual meaning in a linear and sequential fashion from individual sounds and phonological features to words, phrases, and sentences and, eventually, to the whole videotext. Bottom-up sub-skills are developed through individual activities, such as sound discrimination, intonation cues recognition, and sentence structure analysis, which are emblematic of the traditional view of video-mediated listening in lower-level FL classrooms.

Top-down processing models are listener–viewer oriented, which means that the listener–viewer constructs textual meaning through the use of contextual clues and activation of prior knowledge about the content and organizational structure of the videotext. Top-down sub-skills are developed through collaborative activities, such as predicting content, identifying key ideas, and guessing meaning, which represent the traditional view of video-mediated listening in upper-level FL classrooms.

Interactive processing models call on both bottom-up and top-down processing, operating simultaneously rather than sequentially, to construct textual meaning. In these models, video-mediated listening is both listener–viewer and text driven, and it includes both individual and collaborative interaction with videotext.

Research on cognitive processes related to video-mediated listening has had a direct influence on process-oriented instruction (see Chapter 5 for more information). Three distinct phases characterize this pedagogy: a *pre-viewing phase,* which commonly includes activities meant to activate learner background knowledge and expectations about the videotext; a *while-viewing phase*, which typically consists of activities meant to move the learner from comprehending the gist to grasping the details of the videotext; and a *post-viewing phase*, which generally includes activities meant to involve learners in actively using the vocabulary, grammar, and content from the videotext. The purpose of these activities is to help learners process videotexts from both the top down and the bottom up by prompting them to use specific cognitive skills and strategies to regulate their comprehension. The impact of process-oriented pedagogy on video-mediated listening has been profound and lasting. If you examine current FL textbooks, most of which are based on communicative language teaching (CLT) principles (see Introduction), you will find that the three-stage pedagogy outlined above is commonplace as an approach to video-mediated listening. Yet, because of their emphasis on cognitive processes, process-oriented approaches to video-mediated listening instruction tend to overlook the social, contextual, and use-related factors that are essential in video-mediated listening as meaning design. A multiliteracies-oriented approach to video-mediated listening, however, encompasses the full complexity of language as the linguistic, cognitive, and sociocultural dimensions of literacy interact with one another to make video-mediated listening a social and cultural act. To help you prepare for examining in greater depth what a multiliteracies-oriented approach to designing meaning from videotexts entails, complete Learning Activity 7.3.

LEARNING ACTIVITY 7.3

(Re)considering Video-Mediated Listening

In our conclusion to this section, we suggested that the cognitive approach and its related three-phase pedagogy to video-mediated listening are inadequate. Using your knowledge of the multiliteracies framework developed in this chapter and those that precede it, identify an authentic videotext included in the textbook you use and complete the following tasks:

1. List the sequence of instructional phases for this videotext and their focus.
2. Indicate the shortcomings you see in each of these instructional phases.
3. Suggest solutions for addressing these shortcomings consistent with the multiliteracies framework.

As you read the remainder of the "Conceptual Background" section, check back on these ideas and revise as needed based on the discussion of video-mediated listening and the multiliteracies framework.

1.4 Differences Between Reading and Video-Mediated Listening

Throughout the previous section, we alluded to the similarities between reading and video-mediated listening in terms of the types of cognitive processes involved in successful interpretation of both authentic written texts and videotexts. However, differences also exist, especially in terms of textual features that constrain learners' memory capacity and interpretative ability when working with videotexts.

Printed texts afford learners control over the pace of information flow, the ability to reread if needed, and time to dwell on a passage, all of which facilitate the processing of language and content. In contrast, with videotexts the pace of information flow is rapid and learners' ability to process both language and content can be reduced. Even so, we must acknowledge that technology is changing the ways we now interact with videotexts. Since the early 2000s, videotexts are increasingly digitized and, when played on a computer, offer more precise control and nonlinear access. For learners, this means that they can stop to concentrate on key areas, start again, rewind to go over poorly understood areas, or move quickly over a videotext to get a sense of its overall structure and organization. Furthermore, visual, gestural, spatial, and textual (titles, captions, and subtitles) elements that complement the audio track can provide valuable support to FL listener–viewers, particularly in the case of beginning FL learners. Rubin (1995b) explains that visual elements in videotexts can provide assistance to listener–viewers through the display of props, action, and interaction. She further outlines the ways in which these supports can be used: (1) to narrow interpretations when listener–viewers observe the physical settings in which the action takes place; (2) to validate hypotheses when listener–viewers make sense of what takes place; and (3) to judge emotional states when listener–viewers view interactions on screen. Textual elements in the form of captions and subtitles can also be beneficial in various ways, including word recognition, vocabulary building, and text comprehension (Danan, 2004; Vanderplank, 2010). In contrast to live viewing, digitized videotexts, by transforming live context into analyzable text, place fewer constraints on FL learners' memory capacity, an especially valuable feature for learners in lower-level courses.

Videotexts present other challenges to learners, particularly in relation to multimodal patterns of meaning. In the living context, linguistic Available Designs acquire their meaning by pointing to gestural, audio, spatial, and visual Available Designs; in a videotext they do as well, but they are inevitably filtered through the filmmaker and the camera and its lens (Kramsch & Andersen, 1999). Filmmakers rely on movie techniques to impose a particular style onto a videotext through selective shot types, camera movements, variations in lighting, color palette, and special effects to signify different meanings and thus influence the treatment and understanding of content. For a productive engagement with videotexts, learners need to understand how language interacts with other Available Designs, including cinematic ones (Kramsch & Andersen, 1999). Videotexts both "reenact the original, lived context in which language was used and transform it into readable "discourse" or text" (Kramsch & Andersen, 1999, p. 40). They give us the ability to make words and events durable and identifiable as the same at every replay: We can come back to them; we can share them with multiple audiences; we can stop, fast forward, or rewind them and take time to scrutinize them; we can cut, remix, and swap scenes and juxtapose/superimpose gestures, words, and actions that were experienced separately; and so on. Videotexts have made it possible for speech and images to be objectified, textualized, interpreted, and reinterpreted just as much as printed texts. In sum, videotexts transform lived contexts into analyzable texts. The task of the instructor is, therefore, to not only "contextualize the videotext but also textualize the contexts presented on the screen" (Kramsch & Andersen, 1999, p. 40); that is, to help students read the videotext, which entails linking the words heard to the actions seen on the screen and to the background knowledge students have developed.

1.5 Video-Mediated Listening and the Multiliteracies Framework

Video-mediated listening within the multiliteracies framework is viewed as a socially embedded communicative act that involves the three dimensions of literacy—linguistic, cognitive, and sociocultural—dynamically interacting as meaning is created from videotexts.

As presented in the previous section, processing models include the cognitive, and to some extent, the linguistic dimensions of video-mediated listening but leave out its sociocultural dimension, which is a key dimension of the multiliteracies framework. Video-mediated listening is more than an ability to decode aural elements and use strategies to construct meaning from a videotext; it is also a socially situated practice that calls on learners to bring context and text together. As listener–viewers interact with the context and text of a videotext to make meaning, the three dimensions of the multiliteracies framework interact.

1.6 Video-Mediated Listening as Meaning Design

As previously discussed, videotexts can pose a number of challenges for lower-level FL learners as they view and try to comprehend and interpret them (Cross, 2009; Kaiser, 2011; Swaffar & Vlatten, 1997). In FL videotexts, learners may be confronted with new patterns of discourse, prosody, and syntactic structures; fast rates of speech; different language varieties and accent patterns; high content density; multiple semiotic systems that interact simultaneously; and intertextuality. Furthermore, other challenges may arise when learners do not have needed background knowledge and are unfamiliar with certain contexts and cultural norms (Cross, 2009; Meinhof, 1998). As suggested in the previous section, prior knowledge and an understanding of textual features play a significant role in a listener–viewer's ability to engage in constructing meaning from videotexts. We examined how video-mediated listening within the multiliteracies framework is an act of meaning design, during which the learner draws from Available Designs to construct meaning from videotext. These Available Designs may be linguistic (e.g., delivery, accents, dialects, registers), visual (e.g., colors, perspectives, lighting), audio (e.g., music, sound effects), or gestural (e.g., facial expressions, body spacing and posture, shot types, camera movements, edits). In Designing, the learner creates a new design. In other words, as the listener–viewer watches a videotext, he or she puts Available Designs to use; he or she is not simply recycling found designs but is creating a new design, a personal expression, which draws from the array of meaning making resources he or she happened to find in his or her context and culture. A learner's Designing becomes the Redesigned, a new resource for meaning, available to all. Before exploring pedagogical applications of video-mediated listening from a multiliteracies perspective, return to Learning Activity 7.2 and completed Part 2, then move on to Learning Activity 7.4, which reviews your conceptual understanding of Available Designs.

LEARNING ACTIVITY 7.4

Available Designs in Videotexts

Consider the following screenshot of a rally held in June 2014 outside the Federal Energy Regulatory Commission. What Available Designs would a listener–viewer need to access to interpret its meaning? How are these Available Designs socially and contextually determined? What elements might prove most challenging for non-native language learners viewing this screenshot? If you are having trouble remembering the different linguistic, schematic, visual, gestural, spatial, and other Available Designs, review section 2.1 in Chapter 1.

Source: Bill Clark/CQ-Roll Call Group/Getty Images

2. PEDAGOGICAL APPLICATIONS

As we turn our attention to the application of the multiliteracies framework to video-mediated listening in the FL classroom, several questions come to mind: What should a multiliteracies-oriented lesson focused on interpreting a videotext look like? How do we create video-mediated listening lessons that promote the concurrent development of students' language abilities and cultural knowledge? What kind of literacy-oriented tasks do we want students to engage in?

What do we want students to learn from analyzing and interpreting videotexts? What are meaningful ways to assess students' ability to construct meaning from videotexts in a multiliteracies approach? To answer these questions, let us first consider the goals of video-mediated listening instruction and assessment within the multiliteracies framework.

Video-mediated listening involves constructing meaning from text. An important goal of FL video-mediated listening within the multiliteracies framework, therefore, is to help learners interpret the textual representation of the lived context of culture presented on the screen. Teaching and learning language is not only teaching and learning what people say and how they say it correctly and appropriately, but why people say this rather than that to whom, and for which purpose, and how they express it in the lived context of culture. It is about going "beyond the here-and-now of the interaction," which is typically the focus of CLT-based, lower-level courses, to reflect on the "broader attitudes, values and beliefs" of the target community and culture (Kramsch & Andersen, 1999, p. 40), which is a common focus of video-mediated listening in advanced-level courses. A multiliteracies-oriented approach to videotexts not only contributes to smoothing out the curricular dissonance found in many four-year FL curricula; it also contributes to the goal of developing learners' linguistic, cultural, and interpretive abilities, as well as their academic literacy as they engage with various forms of multimodal discourse.

Published research related to designing meaning from videotexts in lower-level FL courses, which can lend support to the merging of communication and textual analysis at all levels of the FL curriculum, comes primarily in the forms of position papers and descriptive reports (e.g., Bueno, 2009; Dubreil, 2011; Eken, 2001; Etienne & Vanbaelen, 2006; Kaiser, 2011; Swaffar & Vlatten, 2007; Zhang, 2011); empirical studies, however, are almost nonexistent. We found one recent study that examined FL learners' ability to recognize cultural patterns in verbal and nonverbal information in videotexts and interpret that information. Hammer and Swaffar (2012) investigated the impact of four episodes of a popular German television show, *Lindenstraße,* on fourth-semester students' strategic ability to negotiate details of cultural knowledge and sociolinguistic content. They found that the majority of the students in their study were able to expand "their reading and articulating of images and cultural content they viewed in the televised text" and that "for most, repeated exposure to the video led to increased awareness and ability to articulate a variety of cultural similarities and differences" (p. 219). One empirical study is certainly not enough, but Hammer and Swaffar have led the way in demonstrating that it is possible to merge communication and textual analysis at lower levels of the undergraduate FL curriculum. In classrooms where this holistic approach is in place, students who are guided to observe and choose culturally relevant features of the context and to relate linguistic features to other features can develop their ability to read and interpret videotexts by making connections between text and context.

In the section that follows, we consider how best to organize literacy-oriented instructional tasks and assessments that engage students in designing meaning from videotexts. To help you create literacy-oriented, video-mediated listening lessons, we propose a template that combines elements of relevant pedagogical models published in the research literature and provide a sample lesson plan putting the proposed template into practice. Further, we outline several literacy-based formative and summative assessments that align with the lesson plan and evaluate students' ability to construct meaning from videotexts.

2.1 Literacy-Oriented Models of Video-Mediated Listening Instruction and Assessment

Four literacy-oriented models of video-mediated listening instruction and assessment are presented in this section. We first present a framework proposed by the Center for Media Literacy (2003) that is organized around five key questions and four phases. Next we outline three integrated frameworks that focus on the use of film/video in the FL classroom: those of Eken (2001), Zhang (2011), and Swaffar and Vlatten (1997), respectively.

Grounded in a media literacy perspective, the Center for Media Literacy (CML) framework (Thoman & Jolls, 2003) was elaborated to establish "a common ground upon which to build curriculum programs, teaching materials and training services for teaching in an increasingly mediated world" (p. 12), and to reflect the impact of the internet and new multimedia technology on learning. The cornerstone of this framework is Five Key Questions related to five core concepts, presented in Table 7.1, which allow for the analysis and evaluation of a wide array of media texts including videotexts.

To organize media literacy lessons, the CML framework proposes four phases: (1) Awareness; (2) Analysis; (3) Reflection; and (4) Action. In the Awareness phase, students engage in activities that lead them to observe and make personal connections, gain insight, and activate core schemata related to the media text and the goal for viewing. Ultimately, these Awareness activities are meant to generate moments of insight whose purpose is to "unlock a spiral of critical inquiry and exploration that is the foundation of media literacy" (Thoman & Jolls, 2003, p. 31). In the Analysis phase, the Five Key Questions and their subsets of guiding questions are implemented to help students understand the complexity of the issue examined in the videotext selected. In this phase, students figure out the ins and outs of the issue as they grapple with "how the *construction* of a media [text] influences and contributes to the meaning [they] make of it" (Thoman & Jolls, 2003, p. 31, emphasis in the original). In the Reflection phase, students reflect and ask *So what? or What ought I do or think?* The activities in phases 2 and 3 can serve as formative assessments. Finally, in the Action phase, students have the opportunity to learn by doing as they engage in activities that lead them to apply their new knowledge in a different and purposeful context. In this final phase, the activities can be used as summative assessments.

Drawing from a variety of models, Eken (2001) proposed an integrated framework for video-mediated listening to help students concurrently develop a deeper understanding of the target language and culture and a keener awareness of how films are designed. Adopting a three-part framework for video-mediated

TABLE 7.1 Center for Media Literacy Framework: Key Questions and Core Concepts (based on Thoman & Jolls, 2003)

Core concept #1: Media messages are constructed.

Key question #1: Who is the author of this message?

Guiding questions #1: What kind of text is it? What are the different elements that make up the whole text? How similar or different is this text to others that belong to the same genre? Which technologies are employed to create this text? How different would this text be if an alternative medium had been used? What choices were made that might have been made differently? How many people contributed to the creation of this message? What are their various roles?

Core concept #2: Media messages are constructed using a creative language that has its own rules.

Key question #2: What techniques are employed to catch my attention?

Guiding questions #2: Is there something noteworthy about the way the message is constructed? Sound effects? Music? Silence? Colors and shapes? Props, sets, clothes? Lighting? Dialogue or narration? Where is the camera? What is the viewpoint? How is the story told? What are people doing? Are there any visual symbols or metaphors? What is the emotional appeal? What are the persuasive devices used? What makes it seem real?

Core concept #3: Different people experience the same media message differently.

Key question #3: How might others understand this message differently than me?

Guiding questions #3: Have you ever had an experience like this? How close does it come to a real-life experience you have had? What did you learn from this media text? What did you learn about yourself from this media text? What did you learn from other people's responses to this media text? How many different interpretations could there be? How can you explain these different interpretations? Are other interpretations as valid as mine?

Core concept #4: Values and points of view are embedded in media messages.

Key question #4: What lifestyles, values, and viewpoints are represented in, or left out from, this message?

Guiding questions #4: How is the person characterized? What kinds of actions/consequences are presented? What type of the person is the reader/watcher/listener invited to identify with? What questions come to mind as you watch/read/listen? What ideas or values are being sold in this message? What political or economic ideas are communicated in the message? What judgments or statements are made about how we treat other people? What is the overall worldview? Are any ideas or perspectives left out? How would you find out what might be missing?

Core concept #5: Most media messages are organized to gain profit and/or power.

Key question #5: Why was this message sent?

Guiding questions #5: Who is in control of the creation and transmission of this message? Why is the person sending it? How do you know? Who is served by, profits, or benefits from this message? The public? Private interests? Individuals? Institutions? Who wins? Who loses? Who decides? What economic decisions may have influenced the construction or transmission of the message?

listening, Eken proposed a sequence of lessons. The first lesson focuses on the literary aspects of films; in other words, aspects that film and literature share, including narrative, characters, setting, theme, signs (i.e., objects, sounds, persons, and colors of significance beyond their usual function and meaning), and genre. In the second lesson, the focus is on the dramatic aspects of film—acting, costumes, make-up—all examined from the perspective of the contribution they make to the film. The last lesson focuses on cinematic aspects—camera shots, movements, and positions; music, sound effects, and visuals; and lighting—each being considered for the way they affect our understanding of the film. Within each lesson, Eken integrates small-group and class-based discussions during which students use the questions included in his framework to guide their film analysis. Furthermore, students read and write film reviews after having done extensive work on this genre's features. He concludes the lesson sequence with a six-hour film workshop, in which students have the opportunity to apply their newly developed knowledge. Students work in small groups on one aspect of a selected film and create activities for analysis, lead discussions, and ask questions when needed to elicit further answers from their peer audience. The activities learners engage in throughout the instructional video-mediated listening sequence outlined here may be used as formative assessments, whereas the film workshop can serve as a summative assessment at the end of a unit.

Zhang (2011) proposed a three-phase framework in which "the goal of the activities is to engage students to examine how meanings are constructed and conveyed through language, to explore . . . cultural perspectives embedded in discourse, and to interpret cultural assumptions and ideologies rooted in power relations" (p. 213). The framework includes the following three phases: Pre-Viewing; Viewing and Discussion; and Post-Viewing. In step 1 of the Pre-Viewing phase, students are shown a screenshot that appears at the beginning of the movie and that is connected to its title. The purpose is for students to "read the silent language created by [the screenshot]" (p. 216) so that it can lead them to make predictions about the theme of the conversation taking place in the videotext and notice relevant cultural features. In step 2, learners are presented with a screenshot of the main scene of the videotext[1] and are provided with a written synopsis of it. They are guided to look for elements in the scene that are different from what they expected and are asked to hypothesize about the reason for these differences. In this second step, activities are meant to guide learners to consider their experiences and living environment and how these affect their assumptions and expectations. The next phase, Viewing and Discussion, starts off with learners listening to the videotext without visuals several times. This listening task is meant to sensitize learners to the roles held by the various participants in the conversation (i.e., *Who has the most turns? Who asks the most questions? What is the tone of the conversation and why?*). Next, learners are guided to imagine what the main issue might be and recreate the

---

[1]Zhang (2011) uses a three-minute film clip from the full-length feature film *Blue Paper Crane,* directed by Xiaohua Li.

dialogue of the scene, which requires them to think about word choices and discourse strategies. The purpose of the activity is to lead learners to reflect on how cultural perspectives and assumptions from their first language (L1) affect what they choose to include in the dialogue. In the third step of Viewing and Discussion, learners experience the conversation in the scene visually, aurally, and in print. The activities included in this step are meant to help learners notice how language forms spoken in the videotexts reflect certain values, assumptions, and ideologies. They are further guided to compare and contrast their dialogue with that in the scene and examine how different forms carry different meanings. In the final phase, Post-Viewing, students are asked to put themselves into the scene, reflect on it, and interpret it from their viewpoint. Suggested activities can include writing a narrative from one of the character's perspectives, re-enacting the scene in learners' L1 cultural context, viewing a videotext from the learners' culture on the same topic and predict what people from the FL culture would have difficulty understanding, and so forth. "Through contextualization, interaction, comparison, and interpretation, students come to recognize differences" (Zhang, 2011, p. 227) between their native culture and that of the FL.

The final literacy-oriented instructional model is most reflective of the multiliteracies framework. Its instructional activities focus both on the process and product dimensions of video-mediated listening; integrate viewing, listening, thinking, writing, and discussing; and promote a wide array of literacies from the lower to advanced levels of the curriculum. Swaffar and Vlatten's (1997) model of FL viewing pedagogy draws on an integrative, procedural approach to videotexts, which makes it possible for lower-level learners to view videos of varying length without "frustration and with clearly articulated learning objectives" (p. 177). Their five-stage model moves from an initial focus on "a film's images and sound effects" in stages 1 and 2, "toward comprehension of detail; that is, word choice, content, and grammatical features" (p. 176) in stages 3, 4, and 5. Underlying this model is the belief that students learn more easily and more efficiently from videotexts when related tasks that connect visual systems to verbal ones are hierarchically organized. Furthermore, their model illustrates how multiple modalities can be sequentially integrated into the FL acquisition process. Stage 1 (How Genres Tell Stories) of their model includes a first silent viewing whose purpose is to avoid having learners feel overwhelmed and frustrated by too much unfamiliar language and to help foster *visual literacy,* or "the ability to read picture sequences as meaningful systems," and "recognize that visual images . . . suggest a pattern of values" (p. 175). In this first silent viewing, students tap into their background knowledge and make connections with what they already know about a videotext genre type, using the visual literacies they developed through their experience as U.S. viewers.

Two possible activities are suggested to follow-up to this first silent viewing. One activity engages students in sorting scrambled descriptive phrases or sentences of scenes in the FL and rearranging them in the order in which they appeared in the video they just viewed. Students can then use these sentences and phrases to discuss what they saw. Another activity leads students to think about words or phrases they expect to hear in the video. Both activities have students look for "the distinct message systems generated by the images presented" (p. 179).

In stage 1, students identify and discuss how information is coded in the visual elements of a video; in stage 2 (Identifying Cultural Difference in Visual Relationships), they are prompted to examine what they consider to be normal or different in the video and are asked to identify cultural differences in the visual elements of a video. Swaffar and Vlatten underscore the importance of these first two stages in which students are encouraged "to concentrate their attention on two different message potentials: the sequence of events or the message systems that mark cultural features" (p. 179). For this second stage, Swaffar and Vlatten suggest using activities that direct students' attention to particular cultural elements, introduce related vocabulary words articulated in the videotext itself, and use this as a basis for discussion wherein students can "begin to establish visual–sematic fields appropriate to the unfamiliar language and its cultures" (p. 179). Stage 1 and stage 2 activities provide a basis for students to move on to the next set of stages wherein activities increasingly link visual elements and textual content.

In stage 3 (Verbalizing Visual Themes), students view the videotext with sound for the first time and are asked to grasp main ideas by confirming or disconfirming their visual comprehension against what they hear. For example, they might be asked to match key words or phrases they grasped with key actions, which later helps them discuss the videotext even though their language competencies are limited.

In stage 4 (Identifying Minimal Linguistic Differences as Difference in Meaning), students are asked to focus on isolated elements through repeated video viewings. The purpose of the activities included in this stage is to help students monitor "their understanding of small but meaningful semantic or morphosyntactic distinctions" (p. 181) as they view a videotext. Swaffar and Vlatten underscore that these activities are particularly well suited for introductory-level learners as they do not require a spoken command of the language; rather, they are just a different kind of comprehension task.

Finally, in stage 5 (Information as the Basis for Student Perspectives), after students have been carefully prepared through the first four stages, they are ready to "develop individual insights into the FL, about the FL culture, or both" (p. 181) using the videotext as a basis. Examples of activities at this stage include "role playing and small group discussions, in conjunction with written work such as story prequels and sequels, interview scenarios, and essay topics" (p. 181), which can lead later to compare and contrast essays or investigative reporting. In this final stage, activities are meant to lead students to confront otherness and consider other ways of viewing and talking about an event.

At each stage, the carefully tailored videotext-based activities lead to repeated viewing with the purpose of having students gather additional information. Repeated viewing teaches students how to identify some, but not necessarily all, of the ideas expressed in fast-paced authentic videotexts. It does so by directing learners' attention to discrete modalities from visual to sound to verbal, and thus highlighting how "textual messages are coded in the visual images as well as in the language and music" (p. 176) of most videotexts. Activities in stages 1, 2, 3, and 4 of this video-mediated listening sequence may be used as formative assessments. Summative assessment is best carried out in stage 5 when learners have had a chance to view the videotext multiple times and develop insights into the foreign language and culture.

The four literacy-oriented video-viewing sequences outlined in this section are summarized in Table 7.2. A quick look at this table reveals that these models share a number of features. Although the number of steps included in

TABLE 7.2 Literacy-Oriented Models of Video-Viewing Instruction

	Thoman & Jolls (2003)	Eken (2001)	Zhang (2011)	Swaffar & Vlatten (1997)
1	Awareness (survey videotext; make connections and predictions about genre; set goals for viewing)	Repeated viewing (view videotext to identify literary, dramatic, and cinematic aspects)	Pre-Viewing/ Silent viewing (access existing knowledge; identify cultural differences)	Silent viewing (access existing knowledge about videotext genre, type, topic)
2	Analysis (view videotext to gather facts, identify how construction of videotext influences and contributes to meaning)	Film review (read to identify content and features of the genre; look at language; think critically; establish viewing, reading, and writing connections)	Viewing and Discussion (make connections between visual images, dialogue, word choices, and conversation strategies)	Silent viewing (identify cultural differences in visual elements)
3	Reflection (view the videotext to identify and interpret viewpoints; think critically)	Film workshop (view videotext to prepare tasks to lead discussion and analysis with peer audience)	Post-Viewing (put oneself into the video script, reflect on it, and interpret from one's viewpoint)	Viewing with sound (confirm or disconfirm visual comprehension against spoken word)
4	Action (share exploration, new insights, and reflection in writing, performing, etc.)			Word or sentence level comprehension and interpretation
5				Creative language use and transformation

each model differs, all four include pre-viewing activities that allow listener–viewers to tap into their existing knowledge and orient themselves to the videotext; initial viewing activities that guide students to comprehend the gist; additional viewing activities that prompt students to focus on textual details; critical analysis activities that lead students to pay attention to the construction of videotext and their cultural content; and post-viewing activities that provide opportunities for listener–viewers to apply their newly developed knowledge, primarily through speaking or writing. The common elements found across all four models suggest a general template for creating videotext-based lessons, which is detailed in the next subsection.

2.2 A Template for Organizing Multiliteracies Video-Mediated Listening Instruction and Assessment

Based on our examination of current models of video-mediated listening, we propose the following six-stage model for designing multiliteracies-oriented video-mediated listening lessons wherein communication and textual analysis are merged and learners are engaged in designing meaning from videotexts:

1. *Initial silent viewing* to identify genre structure, access background knowledge on the topic, and make predictions about the videotext;
2. *Second silent viewing* to identify cultural differences in visual elements;
3. *Initial viewing with sound* to develop global comprehension of essential events and facts by confirming or disconfirming hypotheses elaborated in two previous stages;
4. *Detailed viewing with sound* to link key lexical, grammatical, or discourse features to the cultural perspectives they carry;
5. *Critical viewing with sound* to examine the construction of a videotext, take stock of knowledge developed from the videotext, and explore sociocultural notions; and
6. *Knowledge application* to demonstrate textual interpretation through multimodal transformation activities.

For each stage, the activities to be implemented should reflect the four pedagogical acts of the multiliteracies framework and Kern's (2000) seven principles of literacy (see Chapter 1 for a detailed discussion).

In Table 7.3, we present examples of learning activities that might be used at each stage of the video-mediated listening template for instruction. In several instances, a learning activity may be reflective of more than one of the four pedagogical acts.

2.2.1 INITIAL SILENT VIEWING. In the initial silent viewing stage, the focus is on guiding students to identify and talk about the way information is structured in the videotext. Sample activities include making predictions, participating in instructional conversations, and sequencing events. Their primary purpose is to activate learners' knowledge of videotext genre or type, draw their attention to the range of modes of meaning, and lay the groundwork for their interpretation of the videotext.

TABLE 7.3 Suggested Learning Activities for Video-Mediated Listening Instruction

Instructional Stage	Suggested Learning Activities
1 Initial silent viewing	Videotext orientation and predictions (Situated practice / Critical framing)
	Instructional conversations (Situated practice / Critical framing)
	Caption strategy (Situated practice)
2 Second silent viewing	Mapping cultural visual information (Overt instruction)
	Participant observation (Situated practice / Critical framing)
	Classifying by concepts (Overt instruction / Critical framing)
3 Initial viewing with sound	Matching verbal and visual signals (Overt instruction)
	Camera shot types, movements, and meanings (Overt instruction / Critical framing)
4 Detailed viewing with sound	Focusing on relationships (Overt instruction)
	Identify minimal linguistic differences as differences in meaning (Overt instruction)
5 Critical viewing with sound	Multiple interpretations (Critical framing)
	Critical literacy and multiliteracies (Critical framing)
	Critical focus questions (Critical framing)
6 Knowledge application	Online fanfiction (Situated practice / Critical framing)
	Role playing (Transformed practice)
	Story retelling (Transformed practice)

For learners to *orient themselves and make predictions* about a videotext, it is best to start with presenting relevant clues such as the videotext's title, the name of the filmmaker, some quotes from the videotext, and an initial meaningful scene (e.g., three to four minutes long), which often set style and tone. Such clues will help learners guess the videotext type or genre, its organizational macrostructure, topic, and the language register likely to be used, and explain what allowed them to reach these conclusions. In addition to allowing learners to tap into their background knowledge and experiences as viewers, another advantage of orienting themselves and making predictions is that it can help them make meaningful connections between specific scenes or settings and their cultural meanings. Although FL videotexts subject to global influences often come with a relatively predictable sequence of images, they often retain conventions and patterns that characterize media from the FL culture. In those instances, students can find orienting themselves and making predictions quite challenging. Led by the teacher, *instructional conversations* (see Chapter 4) can provide learners with key information about the videotext type or genre and composition features that are country specific and that may be unfamiliar to the learner. The goal of instructional conversations is to fill the knowledge gaps learners may have and give them access to the context of the videotext before they engage in the upcoming video-mediated listening activities. Finally, *caption strategy* allows students to extract key ideas, concepts, and moments in a way that makes sense to them personally, and to get a feel for the videotext might be about. One way to carry out such an activity is first to provide students with screenshots of key scenes in the videotext and ask them to write a caption for each screenshot that captures its essence. Next, students compare and discuss the captions they have proposed with peers. As they view the videotext silently for the second time, students update their captions as needed.

2.2.2 SECOND SILENT VIEWING. In this stage, students are prompted to examine the visuals in the videotext and construct meaning from them. Sample activities in this step include cultural information mapping, participant observation, and concept classification activities.

Cultural information mapping activities direct students' attention to particular cultural topics and words related to them that may be articulated in a scene of the videotext. In this way students begin to develop visual/gestural/spatial-semantic fields in the FL and its cultures. The cultural information map can lead next to a *participant observation* activity in which students select cultural notions unfamiliar to them represented in the map and suggest possible interpretations. A final activity appropriate for this stage is *classifying by concepts,* during which students group like and unlike words, images, or objects by their common or related characteristics.

2.2.3 INITIAL VIEWING WITH SOUND. In this stage, learners develop a general understanding of key events and facts. Examples of initial viewing with sound activities include matching verbal and visual signals and identifying the connotative meaning of camera shot types and movements.

In activities focused on *matching verbal and visual signals,* students engage in connecting key words or sentences with related visuals. This overt instruction activity focuses students' attention on how verbal and visual elements work together to create meaning in videotext. A follow-up overt instruction/critical framing activity prompts students to make *connections between camera shot types, movements, and their connotative meanings* en route to developing their media literacy. In this activity students examine select scenes in the videotext, identify camera shots and movements used, and explain ways in which these techniques of tradecraft work together with the script to create meaning. These activities lead students to understand how a videotext is not a simple recording of reality, but rather a complex blending of various elements skillfully manipulated by the filmmaker.

2.2.4 DETAILED VIEWING WITH SOUND. In this stage, students make connections between key lexical, grammatical, or discourse features and the cultural meanings associated with them. Focusing on relationships and identifying minimal linguistic differences as difference of meaning are two examples of detailed viewing with sound activities.

Focusing on relationships activities engage students in looking closely at lexical, grammatical, or discourse features used by key characters in the videotext and discovering how cultural perspectives, assumptions, and ideologies are woven into the "questions, statements, phrases or words, parts of speech, performance of speech acts, topic control, and responses to previous turns" (Zhang, 2011, p. 228). A second overt instruction activity, *minimal linguistic differences as difference of meaning,* involves students in selecting a written item that matches the spoken words; in doing so, students become aware of the importance of paying attention to small differences in language exchanges in videotexts.

2.2.5 CRITICAL VIEWING WITH SOUND. Activities in the critical viewing with sound phase focus learners' attention on the Available Designs of a videotext, lead them to evaluate the knowledge they gained from viewing it, or explore cultural concepts found in it. Appropriate activities for this stage include multiple interpretations, critical literacy and multiliteracies, and critical focus questions.

When engaged in *multiple interpretation* activities, learners examine their understanding of a scene and consider all possible interpretations. For this critical framing activity, learners select a scene that proves challenging to them, identify words and phrases spoken by characters that are unclear, and consider visual, audio, gestural, and spatial elements, shifting from one mode to another, to come up with a possible interpretation. Sharing their interpretation with other classmates, who might have different interpretations, leads learners to realize how social-cultural reality shapes their understandings. When engaged in *critical literacy and multiliteracies* activities, students ask themselves how the videotext works to position the listener–viewer, which Available Designs the filmmaker chose to use, and what their purpose is. A final critical framing activity appropriate for this stage is *critical focus questions,* which raise learners' awareness of a script writer's or filmmaker's choices regarding the Available Designs that characterize a videotext. Questions should focus on ideas the viewer–listener associated with specific features of the videotext and the effect these features have the overall interpretation of the videotext.

2.2.6 KNOWLEDGE APPLICATION. In the final stage of the lesson plan template, learners apply the knowledge gained from completing activities in the previous four stages. Knowledge application activities in this stage include online fanfiction, role playing, and story retelling.

In *online fanfiction* activities, learners choose a favorite character or setting in the videotext, come up with a new storyline and add a unique and interesting element, create their own videotext based on it by mixing old and new elements, and share it with fellow fans. Learners can draw on linguistic as well as visual, audio, gestural, and spatial forms and patterns, and combine any or all of these Available Designs into their videotexts, which allows them to augment their words with other modes of expression and convey more sophisticated meanings. Furthermore it gives them access to the target community. In online fanfiction activities learners demonstrate their interpretation of the original videotext and use their new knowledge in creative ways. Another transformed practice activity is *role playing*, which requires learners to put themselves into the script of a scene they chose to reenact. It prompts them to interpret the chosen scene from their viewpoint and reflect on the challenges they will face in playing it. Asking learners to situate the scene in their cultural context adds a critical framing dimension to the activity as it allows learners to further grasp the similarities and differences between the target culture perspectives and their own, and helps them understand what makes them who they are through the lens of the target culture. *Story retelling* is the last suggested knowledge application activity. It engages learners in retelling the same story but from a different perspective while using their own Available Designs. We suggest that the retelling be carried out using video as the medium so that learners are allowed to go beyond monomodal ways of representing learning and engage in new and multimodal textual practices.

2.2.7 ASSESSMENT. The six-phase video-mediated listening pedagogical model described above can also guide the development of multiliteracies-oriented tests. For example, the test could include the following stages: (1) the initial silent viewing activity of predicting the content of a videotext based on a title or screenshot of an initial scene; (2) the second silent viewing activity of mapping cultural visual information with semantic fields; (3) the initial viewing with sound activity of matching verbal and visual signals to demonstrate students' understanding of the gist; (4) the detailed viewing activity of focusing on relationships between linguistic elements and cultural perspectives; (5) the critical viewing activity of critical focus questions to guide learners' analysis of the videotext; and (6) the knowledge application activity of story retelling in which learners reproduce the story using their own words. The videotext to be used for this assessment could be a scene following the one they already viewed in class or a different videotext that treats the same topic but from a different perspective.

Not only can the video-mediated listening model we proposed be used as a template to guide the development of formal tests, but the activities suggested in its first five stages can be used as formative assessments. Furthermore, the knowledge applications activities can serve as summative assessments after the work on the selected videotext is completed.

2.3 Sample Video-Mediated Listening Lesson Plan

Grounded in activities that reflect the four pedagogical acts, the instructional sequence we have outlined makes it possible for lower-level language learners to engage in viewing a variety of videotext types and participate in meaningful activities that lead them to closely examine textual form and meaning. Sample activities that learners might carry out include viewing a TV commercial and examining how a product commonly available for purchase in both cultures is represented, viewing a newscast and summarizing its content in writing, and viewing a TV series and tweeting about it, which would allow learners to record their progress overtime.

In Table 7.4, we present a sample video-based lesson plan organized according to the lesson plan template and suggested learning activities detailed in the model above. This lesson is intended for use in a first-semester lower-level German course during an instructional unit on clothing, body parts, and body care in the German-speaking world. The goals of this lesson are for students to comprehend and use vocabulary related to clothing items, body features, and body care products, become aware of German press and media reporting style, critically evaluate cultural practices related to commercials in German and home cultures and the concept of *Schadenfreude,* and work together to construct meaning from a 2013 Nivea TV commercial. The videotext used as a basis for the lesson is entitled *Stresstest* (see Appendix for English and German versions of the script and link to the videotext). Expanding on information previously presented in the course, the videotext introduces students to Nivea, a globally recognized German brand of facial and body care products. Students should not find it overly challenging to construct meaning from the text as they will most likely be familiar with the brand and some of its products as well as the videotext genre. Further, the videotext's multimodal and intertextual elements should make the commercial accessible and enable the viewer to understand how meaning is shaped.

Outlined in this six-stage lesson plan are activities that facilitate students' design of meaning. Throughout the lesson, listener–viewers interact with the broad range of Available Designs used in the videotext, they make form–meaning connections, and they engage in textual interpretation. Further, this lesson plan is organized around not only the four pedagogical acts, but also the basic instructional elements and learning processes that are part of the seven principles of literacy. Viewers tap into cultural knowledge about dress and grooming as well as body language, facial expressions, or body spacing as message systems particular to a culture; they examine conventions related to personal descriptions, news headlines, and commercial slogans; and they use language to understand how lexical and grammatical forms are used in both spoken and written contexts to create discourse in the videotext. Viewers furthermore interpret the interplay of codes present in the commercial; they collaborate by interacting with the videotext and with other learners when designing textual meaning; they solve problems by teasing out relationships between lexical and grammatical forms and overall textual meaning; and they reflect on the significance of the use of various semiotic systems that work together to make a successful sales pitch.

Included in this sample lesson plan are several opportunities for both formative and summative assessments. Throughout the silent viewing phase, instructors can provide formative feedback after each predicting activity

TABLE 7.4 Sample Instructional Sequence, Videotext-Based Lesson: *Stresstest* by Nivea

Instructional Stage		Learning Activities
1 Initial silent viewing[2]	a	Students watch the initial scene of the videotext (0:00–0:11) to *orient themselves* and *make connections* with it. (Situated practice)
	b	Before watching the entire videotext silently, students are provided with screenshots of key scenes and *write captions* that represent the essence of each screenshot. Next, students compare and discuss the captions they have proposed with peers. Finally, students watch the videotext silently and update their captions as needed. (Situated practice)
	c	The instructor leads an *instructional conversation* during which students discuss the genre of the video and the notion of *Schadenfreude*. (Situated practice / Critical framing)
	d	Finally, students are provided with a list of words or expressions, some of which are in the commercial, and are asked to *predict the words or expressions* they are likely to hear. (Situated practice)
2 Second silent viewing	a	Students watch the videotext a second time and *map cultural information* by identifying cultural elements that lead them to determine whether the commercial was shot in the United States or Germany. Students are directed to focus on dress and grooming, as well as on body language, facial expressions, gestures, body spacing, and so forth. (Overt instruction)
3 Initial viewing with sound	a	After a third viewing, students engage in *matching verbal and visual signals*. Students focus on the verbal descriptions given of individuals and the visuals of the corresponding individuals themselves. (Situated practice / Overt instruction)
4 Detailed viewing with sound	a	Students view the video a fourth time and *identify minimal linguistic differences as differences in meaning*: They are provided with pairs of sentences and are asked to identify the sentence that is actually spoken in the videotext. (Overt instruction)

(continued)

[2]When using videotexts, you may want to provide students, at least initially, with a list of the kinds of cinematic techniques and camera usage that comprise narrative video grammar and their connotative meanings.

TABLE 7.4 Sample Instructional Sequence, Videotext-Based Lesson: *Stresstest* by Nivea

Instructional Stage		Learning Activities
5 Critical viewing with sound	a	Students view the video a fifth time and using *critical focus questions* are guided to examine how the commercial is constructed, focusing on its multiple meaning resources (e.g., linguistic, audio, visual, gestural, spatial) and how they work together in a sales pitch. (Overt instruction / Critical framing)
6 Knowledge application	a	In small groups students chose one individual in the commercial and engage in *story retelling* by thinking about how their selected individual would retell what took place and convey what they were thinking/feeling at the time. This activity culminates in an oral performance of the retelling in an interview format. (Transformed practice)

by asking students to identify the elements behind the choices they made. In the viewing phases, activities that ask students to make verbal and visual connections or answer critical focus questions are additional opportunities for instructors to provide formative feedback. At the end of the lesson, the oral performance of students retelling what happened and how they felt in an interview format can serve as a summative assessment of this instructional sequence.

To help you reflect on this sample videotext-based lesson plan, read through it a second time and find answers to the following questions:

1. What are the objectives of this lesson and how do they fit within the course curriculum?
2. Is the selected videotext appropriate to meet these objectives? What elements of the videotext might be challenging for FL learners to understand?
3. In what ways are students designing meaning through the various activities in this lesson?
4. Why are the different lesson plan activities labeled as situated practice, overt instruction, critical framing, transformed practice?
5. Are the basic elements of instruction, or the what of multiliteracies pedagogy—conventions, cultural knowledge, and language use—represented in the lesson?
6. Are the learning processes of interpretation, collaboration, problem solving, and reflection and self-reflection (i.e., the how of multiliteracies pedagogy) represented in the lesson?

As you think about planning your own video-viewing lesson plans and assessments using the template above, come back to these questions as a way to help you to organize your ideas and apply your understanding of multiliteracies-based videotext pedagogy. Learning Activity 7.5 will help you get started.

LEARNING ACTIVITY 7.5

Designing a Videotext-Based Lesson

Identify an authentic videotext that would be appropriate for one of the themes included in your textbook and create activities for each of the steps found in the model detailed in this chapter. In selecting an authentic videotext, keep in mind the following criteria, adapted from Joiner (1990): Select a videotext that does not require extensive background knowledge, contains a variety of locations, speakers and elements of tradecraft, is professionally produced, and represents distinct levels of difficulty. Next, start planning your lesson and design appropriate activities following the six-step model and the learning activities suggested in Tables 7.3 and 7.4. Once you have completed your lesson plan, ask yourself the same set of questions as a way to help you justify your pedagogical choices.

3. FINAL CONSIDERATIONS

In this chapter, we started with laying out the conceptual base for FL video-viewing instruction within the multiliteracies framework. The critical elements undergirding this base include the cognitive processes in which FL learners engage when viewing videotexts and the multimodal Available Designs in videotexts that allow for their creation and interpretation.

The FL video-viewing pedagogy outlined in this chapter rests on this conceptual base and has as its main goal the merging of communication with textual analysis, which takes place as students engage in the planned multiliteracies-oriented instructional viewing activities. This video-viewing pedagogy is grounded in essential elements and processes of multiliteracies instruction, namely the four pedagogical acts and the seven principles of literacy.

As we bring this chapter to a close, we leave you with some final ideas to consider. Although Swaffar and Vlatten (1997) acknowledge that viewing authentic FL videotexts can be challenging on many levels for beginning students, they disagree with the solution most commonly adopted to deal with this challenge: to limit selections to short, scripted videotexts. They argue that authentic videotexts, often thought of as too challenging for lower-level learners with limited language abilities, can in fact be made accessible by implementing lessons with a hierarchy of well-designed pedagogical tasks that "connect visual systems to verbal ones" (p. 176). Swaffar and Vlatten's idea echoes Kern's (2000) proposal for written texts; namely, that in multiliteracies-oriented teaching it is important to control the tasks students carry out, not the texts with which they interact. It is an idea that may have struck you as counterintuitive the first time you encountered it in Chapter 5, since using adapted texts, regardless of the media, has been so much a part of lower-level FL instruction. However, this is a crucial idea in that it lends support to the possibility of integrating videotexts at lower levels and the feasibility of merging communication with textual analysis from the first semester of FL instruction. Another important idea discussed by scholars referenced in this chapter, including Swaffar and Vlatten (1997), is the importance of guiding students to read and interpret visual, audio, gestural, and spatial Available Designs. As underscored by Kress and van Leeuwen (1996), "just as knowledge of other languages can open new perspectives on one's own language, so a knowledge of other semiotic modes can open new perspectives on language" (p. vii). We have entered a new era, one in which we have moved from "telling the world to showing the world" (Kress, 2003, p. 140) and in which language needs to be conceptualized from a broader, socially constructed, multimodal perspective. As you consider this final point and reflect on it in light of the notions presented in this chapter, make sure to keep it at the forefront of your mind as we move to Chapter 8, "Teaching New Literacies: Making Meaning with Web 2.0 Tools."

4. TRANSFORMING KNOWLEDGE

4.1 Reflective Journal Entry

Reread your responses to Part 1 of Learning Activity 7.1, complete Part 2 of that activity, and then reflect on the ways you are engaging your students in video-viewing activities. In what ways are the processes and activities you commonly use congruent with multiliteracies instruction? In what ways do they depart from it? What ideas introduced in this chapter do you think you can readily apply in your local teaching context? What connections do you see between what you have learned in this chapter, in Chapter 5 on reading, and the one coming next, which focuses on new literacies and the affordances brought by Web 2.0?

4.2 Researching Video-Mediated Listening in Your Instructional Context

Identify and outline a problem related to the teaching or learning of FL video viewing that you are faced with in your own instructional context and consider why it is a problem.

SOLUTIONS PROPOSED: Using your knowledge about multiliteracies-oriented video viewing, describe your solution to the problem. Consider the materials you will use, the steps you will take, and the time you will need to implement the solution.

GOALS AND OBJECTIVES OF THIS ACTION RESEARCH: Outline the questions you are seeking answers to and detail the instructional measure you plan on using to answer them.

RESULTS OF IMPLEMENTED SOLUTION: In the classroom, implement your solution and collect the data that you will need to answer your questions. Finally, summarize and reflect on the results that you observe. If you are not currently teaching, collaborate with a colleague who is teaching and observe that instructor implement your solution.

Key Resources

Etienne, C., & Vanbaelen, S. (2006). Paving the way to literary analysis through TV commercials. *Foreign Language Annals, 39*, 87–98.

Etienne and Vanbaelen propose a literacy-oriented three-step lesson sequence (Impressions, Description, Interpretations) in which students are guided to carefully analyze TV commercials. In the description stage, a grid, wherein filmic Available Designs are described, is provided to students to help them examine how the various Available Designs work together to create meaning. The authors propose that the same lesson structure be repurposed for the analysis of literature. They argue that reading the semiotics of TV commercials prepares students for advanced-level courses in literature and culture.

Hammer, J., & Swaffar, J. (2012). Assessing strategic cultural competency: Holistic approaches to student learning through media. *Modern Language Journal, 96*, 209–233.

Hammer and Swaffar present a literacy-based approach for the development of cultural literacy by engaging second-year learners with viewing and reflecting on *Lindenstraße,* a German television series about everyday life on a street in Munich. To realize this goal, the authors propose a sequence of tasks to support student learning: "(a) a preview in the form of a reading assignment: descriptions or pseudo-biographies of characters to be seen in the *Lindenstraße* episode to be shown; (b) a 15-minute preview of the episode in class, with a short discussion of characters' biographies and identification of them in an initial scene from each of the three segments of the episode; (c) a 30-minute viewing of the entire German-language episode without subtitles; (d) a homework assignment to write summary analyses of the episode for the next class hour; and (e) a follow-up at the next class with an hour-long class discussion and review of students' questions and perceptions about the episode and its cultural characteristics" (pp. 210–211). Study results showed that learners developed their ability to read the images and cultural content they saw in the videotext. Sample lesson plans are provided.

Zhang, L. (2011). Teaching Chinese cultural perspectives through film. *L2 Journal, 3*, 201–231.

Zhang argues that teaching cultural perspectives is more challenging than cultural products and behaviors; she proposes a literacy-based model anchored in the four pedagogical acts wherein language is viewed as communicative practice and Available Designs as essential elements of this practice. The author proposes a pedagogical sequence for second and third year Chinese courses, in which activities are divided into four parts: pre-viewing and a synopsis, viewing and discussion 1 and 2, and post-viewing. The purpose of the activities included in the sequence is to "engage students to examine how meanings are constructed and conveyed through language, to explore Chinese cultural perspectives embedded in discourse, and to interpret cultural assumptions and ideologies rooted in power relations" (p. 213). Sample activities are provided.

For Further Reading

Bueno, K. (2009). Got film? Is it a readily accessible window to the target language and culture for your students? *Foreign Language Annals, 42*, 318–339.

Gruba, P. (2005). *Developing media literacy in the L2 classroom*. Sydney, Australia: Macquarie University, National Centre for English Teaching and Research.

Paesani, K. (2006). A process-oriented approach to *Zazie dans le métro*. *The French Review, 79*, 762–778.

APPENDIX

German transcription of Nivea *Stresstest* prank commercial

[The scene of this commercial takes place in a departure lounge at Hamburg Airport. Turned into wanted criminals for Nivea's "Stress Protect" deodorant brand, unsuspecting passengers see their pictures being advertised as "wanted" on fake newspapers, news broadcasts, and the intercom system while waiting for their flights.

[*Newspaper with bolded headline and headshot*] Verdächtiger auf der Flucht!

[*Airport intercom system*] Sehr geehrte Damen und Herren, wir bitten Sie kurz um Ihre Aufmerksamkeit. Die Behörden suchen folgende Person: weiblich, zirka 1,65 groß. Die Gesuchte trägt eine hellgraue Jacke und einen großen Schal. Wenn Ihnen diese Person auffällt verständigen Sie bitte umgehend das Flughafenpersonal.

[*Man in sound room*] Und bitte. . .

[*News anchor*] Guten Morgen meine Damen und Herren. Ich begrüße Sie zu den M-24 Breaking News. Die Polizei bittet um Ihre Mithilfe. Dringend gesucht wird diese Frau. Sie befindet sich seit gestern Vormittag auf der Flucht. Die Verdächtigte ist zirka 1,65m groß, hat dunkelblondes lockiges Haar und trägt eine helle Jacke. Die Flüchtige gilt als unberechenbar und äußerst gefährlich. Bitte versuchen Sie nicht die gesuchte Person festzuhalten [Girl: Ich habe nichts gemacht] oder gar anzusprechen. Für Hinweise zur Ergreifung der Verdächtigen wählen Sie bitte die unten eingeblendete Nummer. Wir melden uns wieder zu den Hauptnachrichten zur vollen Stunde und bis dahin noch einen schönen Tag.

[*Woman with curly hair sitting across man reading a newspaper. She nudges her friend*] Ich bin auf der Zeitung.

[*Airport intercom system*] Die Behörden suchen die folgende Person. Der Gesuchte trägt einen grünen Pulli und hat eine rosa Tasche bei sich. . . . Männlich zirka 1,80 groß. Der Gesuchte trägt eine beige Hose, einen lila Pulli, und eine braune Jacke.

[*News anchor*] Dringend gesucht wird diese Frau. Sie befindet sich seit gestern Vormittag auf der Flucht. Die Flüchtige gilt als unberechenbar und äußerst gefährlich.

[*Police officer*] Guten Morgen, sind Sie gestresst? Sie sehen so gestresst aus. Da hätten wir was für Sie. [*Police officer opens a metal suitcase which contains a spray can of Nivea's "Stress Protect" deodorant.*]

Source: Stresstest, Nivea: www.youtube.com/watch?v=FhkS4Ez4nu8

English translation of Nivea *Stresstest* prank commercial transcript

The scene of this commercial takes place in a departure lounge at Hamburg Airport. Turned into wanted criminals for Nivea's "Stress Protect" deodorant brand, unsuspecting passengers see their pictures being advertised as "wanted" on fake newspapers, news broadcasts, and the intercom system while waiting for their flights.]

[*Newspaper with bolded headline and headshot*] Suspect on the run!

[*Airport intercom system*] Attention please, ladies and gentlemen. The authorities are looking for the following person: female, 1.65m tall, wearing a light gray jacket and a big scarf. If you see this person, please notify the airport authorities immediately.

[*Man in sound room*] Ok, we're live. . .

[*News anchor*] Good morning, ladies and gentlemen. Welcome to N–24 Breaking News. The police are asking for your help. They are searching for this woman. She's been on the run since yesterday morning. The suspect is 1.65m tall, has dark blond curly hair, and is wearing a light jacket. The fugitive is considered unpredictable and extremely dangerous. Please do not attempt to approach or apprehend this person. (Girl: I didn't do anything.) For information leading to the capture of the suspect, please call the number at the bottom of the screen. Back to the main news now and until then have a nice day.

[*Woman with curly hair sitting across man reading a newspaper. She nudges her friend*] I'm in the paper.

[*Airport intercom system*] The authorities are looking for the following person. This suspect is wearing a green sweater and is carrying a pink bag. . . Male, about 1.80m tall. The suspect is wearing beige pants, a purple sweater, and a brown jacket.

[*News anchor*] This woman is wanted by the authorities. She's been on the run since yesterday morning. The fugitive is considered unpredictable and extremely dangerous.

[*Police officer*] Good morning, are you stressed? You look stressed. We have something for you.

[*Police officer opens a metal suitcase which contains a spray can of Nivea's "Stress Protect" deodorant.*]

CHAPTER 8

Teaching New Literacies: Constructing Meaning in Web 2.0 and Beyond

Throughout the previous chapters of this book, you have examined the concept of literacy and the central role that texts play in teaching and learning a foreign language (FL) at all levels of the curriculum. In the process, you have become familiar with conceptual and pedagogical aspects of the multiliteracies framework, and have considered the ideas presented and how to best instantiate them in the introductory and intermediate FL classroom. In this last chapter, we explore the application of the multiliteracies framework to digitally mediated texts. Given current widespread computer use and unprecedented access to networked communication technologies, this book would not have been complete without a close examination of Web 2.0 tools and environments and the profound ways in which they are re-mediating reading and writing. How we read and write, but also our understandings of texts and authors, are affected by this re-mediation. Digital–electronic technologies are expanding our definition of what it means to be literate. Interpreting and authoring digitally mediated texts adds layers of complexity to the already complex processes you learned about in Chapters 5, 6, and 7.

Today, web-based technologies play a ubiquitous role in our everyday life. Recent U.S. survey findings (Lenhart, Purcell, Smith, & Zickhur, 2010) show that over 90% of the population between the ages of 12 and 29 is regularly online. Among this population, three-quarters have profiles on social networking sites (e.g., Facebook), over one-third report sharing self-created content (e.g., photos, podcasts, videos), and about 20% remix content into new artistic creations. In the last decade, the remarkable shift from Web 1.0 to Web 2.0 has meant more than communicating and connecting with others on the web. Whereas Web 1.0 is about disseminating static information created by a few experts with the technical know-how to write and post content to a very large number of users, Web 2.0 is about the publication, by general users, of collaboratively created products, thus highlighting participation over information. Wesch (2007) summarized these differences between Web 1.0 and 2.0 as an evolution from the linking of information to the linking of people. People are still going on the web to access information, but they are increasingly going online to interact, collaborate, play, create, share, and shape its content through feedback and evaluation mechanisms (Coiro, Knobel, Lankshear, & Leu, 2008). Not only are literacies associated with digital–electronic technologies changing the way we make meanings; they are also changing the kinds of social identities we can enact and social relationships we have with others. Some are even saying these literacies are changing the way we think.

The impact of web-based technologies in our everyday life is significant, and the same can be said for FL teaching and learning. In recent years, FL departments have put greater emphasis on the importance of technology use because of the unique opportunities it offers. In 2002, the Modern Language Association (MLA) published a document stating that "information technology is critical to fulfilling the educational and research missions of modern language departments" (2002, para. 1). Five years later, the MLA (2007) published another report, *Foreign Languages and Higher Education: New Structures for a Changed World,* that identified digital media as one important resource for fostering negotiation of meaning across linguistic and cultural boundaries and helping students "consider alternative ways of seeing, feeling, and understanding things" and teaching them "differences in meaning, mentality, and worldview as expressed in American English and in the target language" (p. 4). However, despite the recommendations issued by professional organizations and the ever-increasing presence of web-based technology in our daily lives, the types of technology FL teachers more readily use and the ways in which they use it for teaching and learning often remain somewhat limited. In a survey of 173 college FL teachers, Arnold (2007) reported that while the vast majority of her participants used computer technology in their teaching, they reported using technology mainly in a supportive rather than a teaching/learning role, reflecting a utilitarian attitude toward technology and possibly a lack of conviction regarding its pedagogical benefits. Furthermore, Arnold reported that, when using web-based technology, the responding teachers primarily used basic Web 1.0 tools and environments (e.g., classroom management systems to post homework, web browsers to conduct searches and access authentic documents) and that convenience and enhancement, not transformation, were two notions driving their use of technology. Four years later, Arnold's findings were mirrored in those reported by Lomicka and Williams (2011), whose survey of 171 French teachers found that Web 1.0 platforms and applications (e.g., email, web browsers to conduct searches and access radio and TV shows, newspapers, dictionaries) were used most frequently, that the ways in which respondents used these resources tended to replicate traditional teaching and learning paradigms, and that their use was much more limited in lower-level classes than in advanced-level ones. These findings point to not only a possible digital disconnect between the ways students use the internet in and out of the FL classroom but also a continued reliance on transmission and teacher-centered approaches to FL instruction and a belief that lower-level learners' limited language abilities preclude the use of digital media in meaningful ways. As a result, there are many missed opportunities to engage learners in making meaning. Learners are not experiencing how Web 2.0 tools and environments, through their *affordances* and *constraints,* are reshaping literacy practices, which today "sit within a much wider communication landscape" (Pahl & Roswell, 2006, p. 8). Specifically, the mediated ways in which Web 2.0 tools and environments allow us (affordances) or inhibit our ability (constraints) to do things, make meanings, relate to others, think, and adopt the social identities we want to project, are at the heart of new forms of literacy. Within these new forms of literacy, the written word is no longer the primary carrier of literate meaning (Kress, 2009); the patterns of interaction and participation are different, the ways we experience and think about the world are affected by time and space, the kinds of social identities we can adopt have expanded, and yet many of these new forms of literacy tend to be absent from the FL classroom (Kessler, 2013). Lotherington and Jenson (2011) argued that in FL instruction, the old basics no longer fit and that "assumptions about learners, language form and format, text types, and social discourses must all be reexamined" (p. 227).

The New London Group (1996) argued "that literacy pedagogy now must account for the burgeoning variety of text forms associated with information and multimedia technologies" (p. 60) and called for changing the "'what' of literacy pedagogy" (p. 65) to include six design elements in the meaning-making process: linguistic, visual, audio, gestural, and spatial meaning, and multimodal interplay. New literacies cannot continue to take a back seat in the FL classroom, and waiting until learners develop some level of functionality in the language is not justified. Lower-level FL learners can participate in these new practices, and the multiliteracies framework that lies at the center of this book can provide the tools to design activities using Web 2.0 tools and environments that will make the development of new literacies possible as learners make their way through the four-year undergraduate curriculum.

Our focus in this chapter is on teaching and learning that allows students to interpret and author digitally mediated texts in lower-level FL courses; even so, the concepts and applications examined herein are also relevant to advanced-level courses on a range of foci including literature, film, music, or media arts. In the "Conceptual Background" section, we provide a definition of Web 2.0 and related new literacies. We overview a growing, but still limited, body of research on digitally mediated literacies in second language (L2) contexts, examining more closely concepts related to hypertext, multimodality, interactivity, participation and collaboration, and remix, and the development of new literacy practices, shaped by the various mediational means of Web 2.0 tools and environments. In the "Pedagogical Applications" section, we begin by examining the goals of teaching digitally mediated texts and new literacy practices within a multiliteracies-oriented approach to guide the organization of instructional activities anchored in the four pedagogical acts.

Next, we overview three current multiliteracies-based models to teach and assess FL digitally mediated texts, and we present a model for designing and implementing lesson plans centered on the development of new literacies in lower-level FL classrooms. We conclude the section with a walk-through of a sample lower-level integrated lesson plan guided by this model and provide sample assessments related to it. By the end of this chapter, you will have a better understanding of why a multiliteracies-oriented approach to constructing meaning from and through digitally mediated texts is not only a viable, but also a much needed alternative to the ways in which Web 2.0 is typically used and how it can be implemented in your instructional context. To better interact with the notions introduced in this chapter, complete Learning Activity 8.1.

LEARNING ACTIVITY 8.1

My Experience with Digital–Electronic Technologies as a FL Learner

Reflect on the use of digital–electronic technologies in the lower-level FL classes you took as a student. Use the following questions to guide your reflection:

1. What digital electronic technologies do you recall your instructors using in your lower-level FL classes? How often were they used? Do you think that they enhanced or hindered your lower-level FL learning experiences? Explain.
2. In what kinds of digitally mediated activities did you engage in your lower-level FL classes? What was the main focus of these activities? What do you think the purpose of these activities was?
3. Did the kinds of digitally mediated activities you engaged in reflect a multiliteracies-approach to teaching and learning? Explain.

1. CONCEPTUAL BACKGROUND

In this section, we overview theoretical research on new literacies. We start by defining Web 2.0 and new literacies, and we continue with a discussion of how Web 2.0 affordances and constraints are changing the way we make meanings, the way we relate to other people, and the kinds of social identities we can assume. Next, we highlight key affordances of several Web 2.0 tools and environments, and we focus our attention on how they can affect learners' engagement with digitally mediated texts. We examine the cognitive processes involved in reading and writing online, and we consider their sociocultural dimensions. Using this foundation, we then focus on meaning design in digitally mediated texts and consider how to rethink texts in Web 2.0 tools and environments from a multiliteracies perspective. To help you interact with the notions examined in the "Conceptual Background" section, complete Learning Activity 8.2.

LEARNING ACTIVITY 8.2

My Personal and Professional Use of Web 2.0 Applications

Before reading this section, consider the Web 2.0 tools and environments listed in the table. Check those that you use in your daily life and in your classroom. For Web 2.0 tools and environments common to both contexts, indicate their purpose in each context, and state reasons behind your decision to use them in one context or the other.

Tools and Environments	Context of Use	Purpose in My Daily Life	Purpose in My Classroom	Reasons
Social networking site (e.g.: Facebook; Google+)	Daily life ❑ Classroom ❑			
Microblog (e.g., Twitter, SnapChat)	Daily life ❑ Classroom ❑			
Blog (e.g., Blogger, Wordpress)	Daily life ❑ Classroom ❑			
Wiki (e.g., Wikispaces, Hackpad)	Daily life ❑ Classroom ❑			
Folksonomy (e.g., Delicious, Diigo)	Daily life ❑ Classroom ❑			
Media sharing site (e.g., YouTube, Flickr)	Daily life ❑ Classroom ❑			
Videoconferencing (e.g., Google+ Hangouts, Skype)	Daily life ❑ Classroom ❑			
Content aggregator/ curator (e.g., Storify, Paper.li)	Daily life ❑ Classroom ❑			

1.1 Poke! Web 2.0 and Digital Literacies

In the 1980s and 1990s, while the transformative potential of digital–electronic technologies was not going unnoticed by scholars and practitioners, the majority of the population around the world was not yet accessing the web and very few people had the required technical skills set to create and publish content online. At the time, the web was more of a tool to search for and locate information to solve problems than to collaborate, create, and share content with a wide audience. Today, the landscape has dramatically changed. Internet use has grown and has spread to 2.5 billion users globally. Previous hurdles to online publishing have largely disappeared, and, thanks to new digital technologies, creative, collaboratively produced content can easily be shared. The new types of online communication that have emerged in the last decade or so are referred to as *Web 2.0,* or the read-and-write web as opposed to *Web 1.0,* the predominantly read-only web. Examples of Web 2.0 include social networking sites (e.g., Facebook, Google+, LinkedIn); folksonomies[1] (e.g., Delicious, Diigo); blogs and microblogs (e.g., Blogger, WordPress, Digg, Twitter); wikis (e.g., Wikispaces, Wikia); media sharing sites (e.g., YouTube, Flickr, Slideshare); video conferencing (e.g., Skype, Google+ Hangouts); content aggregation and curation (e.g., Pinterest, Storify, Paper.li, List.ly); or mash-ups (e.g., Google Maps) of content. Although the term Web 2.0 may suggest a new generation of web technology, it actually refers to changes in the communicative uses of the underlying web platform on which innovative applications have been built. Providing examples of sites and applications can be useful as a reference, but one should not lose sight of the fact that our use of the term Web 2.0 in this chapter does not refer to a set of tools and environments that are developed and used at a particular point in time. Rather, this term refers to new and changing forms of social practice and new and changing means of text production, exchange, and distribution that are particular to them. Indeed, according to Thorne (2010), Web 2.0 tools and environments "involve less a wave of technological innovation and more accurately a significant transformation in the types, quality and volume of personal expression, mediated interactivity, and ambient awareness of multiple social networks" (p. 143).

New literacies have to do with the multimodal forms of texts and text production/sharing that have emerged in the wake of the recent tide of digital–electronic technologies. The *new* in new literacies relates to the new "*technical* stuff" and new "*ethos* stuff" that Lankshear and Knobel (2006, 2007, emphases in the original) see as closely interconnected. According to Lankshear and Knobel, for a literacy practice to be regarded as a new literacy, not only does it have to integrate new technical stuff (e.g., screens and pixels versus paper and font type; digital code versus material print), but it also has to privilege certain qualities and values or mindsets currently associated with Web 2.0 (Lankshear & Knobel, 2003, 2006, 2007), including participation, collaboration, distributed expertise, collective intelligence and agreement, tagging and sharing, and relationships. Put another way, knowledge is decentralized, widely accessible, and co-constructed by and among a large swath of users who are as important as the content created. Engaging in new literacies presupposes that the ethos values discussed here are shared. In other words, using a YouTube video to illustrate a concept in a class presentation or bringing up a blog post as an exemplar of an opinion on a current issue, without otherwise engaging in any of the kinds of participation that one has come to expect on such sites

---

[1]A type of collaborative tagging system in which resources (e.g., web pages) are classified by users.

(e.g., tagging and sharing, responding, or remixing), would not be considered a new literacy practice. As underscored by Clark (2010), to foster new literacies, we must move "away from the use of technology as convenient serendipity" (p. 28) and move toward a pedagogy, like the one taking central stage in this book, that carefully guides students to develop understandings of how meaning is made and can be made in Web 2.0.

1.2 Constructing Meaning in Web 2.0

With the development of Web 2.0, reading and writing have been affected in a number of ways. Although the notions and processes examined in Chapters 5 and 6 remain central and relevant here, several scholars (Coiro, 2003; Kress, 2003; Walsh, 2009) have underscored that new media are changing, through their affordances and constraints, the ways in which meaning is made, and therefore require us to think differently about reading and writing, to reconsider our definition of what a reader or a writer is, and to adopt new reading and writing practices.

On a screen, "'reading' may involve viewing, listening and responding, while 'writing' may involve talking, listening, designing and producing" (Walsh, 2009, p. 2). Hypertext is profoundly affecting the way in which writers can structure and organize content, as well as the ways in which readers can navigate through it. Images, audio, or video are increasingly combined with written text, and in many areas of communication, they are actually displacing writing where it used to dominate. Furthermore, in Web 2.0 tools and environments, people are commenting, annotating, and engaging in conversations about texts with author(s) and other users, and in so doing are participating in the texts of others and are also producing their own texts or their own versions of texts. In a nutshell, *digitally mediated texts* are typically nonlinear, inclusive of multimedia elements, and interactive/participatory. New Web 2.0 practices have led to the widespread use of such terms as *produsers* and *produsage* (Bruns, 2008) that highlight how people are both users and producers of texts, and how production of texts is both collaborative and continuous.

It is important to understand what the affordances and constraints of Web 2.0 tools and environments mean for the practices of reading and writing or designing, a term Kress (2003) prefers to characterize the new approach to representation, communication, and interaction that they bring. Let us explore four key elements—hypertext, multimodality, remix, and interactivity/participation/collaboration—in detail and examine their contributions to the development of FL literacies as reported in a number of recent studies.

1.2.1 HYPERTEXT. *Hypertext* is nonlinear, multimedia, electronic text that is hyperlinked internally (i.e., used to link different parts of the same digital document and structure the text internally) or externally (i.e., used to organize a digital document by associating it to other texts on the internet). Weinberger (2009) has equated *hyperlinks* to a new form of punctuation that, unlike most punctuation, tells us how to proceed rather than where to pause or stop. It has led Boardman (2005) to note that "we have a problem with hypertext because in a real sense the narrative is never finished, and there are more ways of navigating the available paths than a reader can pursue in a lifetime" (p. 4). Hyperlinks allow readers to construct from a range of options their personal reading path in a text. The expectation is that readers will make choices and read in a nonlinear fashion, given the many opportunities they have to branch out; the choices they make will largely determine the quality and coherence of the text they are reading (Burbules & Callister, 2000). For writers, hyperlinks provide an array of options to link their text to others on the web to support, elaborate, and lend credence and balance to the point they are making depending on which texts they choose to link to (Dudeney, Hockly, & Pegrum, 2013; Jones & Hafner, 2012; Pegrum, 2011). However, with this affordance comes a new problem for both writers and readers. For writers, there is no guarantee that readers will read through their entire story or argument, as they may wander off to delve in and out of hyperlinked texts and never return to the text they were originally reading. For readers, there is flexibility when it comes to choosing which hyperlinks to click on as they read, yet the choice of which hyperlinks are inserted in a text or not is made by the writer, which in some ways constrains their reading trajectory. Indeed, the complexities and intricacies associated with the process of hypertext reading and writing are changing the way we read, write, and communicate (Coiro & Dobler, 2007; Lankshear & Knobel, 2003; Leu, Kinzer, Coiro, & Cammak, 2004; Leu et al., 2011).

According to Arnold (2007) and Lomicka and Williams (2011), FL teachers incorporate hypertexts in their instruction, yet little research has examined how FL learners read, interpret, or create such texts within the open networked system of the internet. In prior work on hypertext use in FL contexts, the term has typically referred to digitally mediated texts, often written by teachers for learners, that are hyperlinked within a closed electronic system and most often consist of electronic and multimedia glosses and annotations of specific lexical or cultural items. The primary focus of research studies related to the use of hypertexts has been to gather evidence of their effectiveness for learners' vocabulary and cultural knowledge development and textual comprehension. Such hypertexts have little in common with those found on the internet, and their purpose and use are different. In an exploratory study with sixth-grade U.S. students, Coiro and Dobler (2007) found that although hypertext reading was quite similar to reading printed text (e.g., students drew on prior knowledge of the topic and genre), it was also more complex (e.g., students drew on knowledge of web search engines and web site organizational structures). They also found evidence of a higher incidence of multilevel predictive inferential reasoning in hypertext comprehension because texts lying beyond a particular link are not available for scanning. Finally, they were able to observe that hypertexts involve new dimensions of self-regulated reading, and they suggested that currently available descriptions of the self-regulated cycle that takes place when reading printed texts (e.g., making connections, monitoring understanding) do not reflect the "physical process of clicking the mouse, dragging scroll bars, rolling over dynamic images, and navigating pop-up menus that intertwines with [the] cognitive process of planning, predicting, monitoring, and evaluating one's pathway through the open Internet text spaces," all of which happen rather quickly and "across much shorter and disparate units of Internet text" (p. 242).

In a related study, Konishi (2003) examined the strategies used by Japanese students of English as a foreign language (EFL) while reading hypertexts on the internet. She found that her participants used local and global strategies (e.g., activating background knowledge, making inferences, checking coherence within a text, checking consistency between sources, evaluating the importance or truth value of a text) and meta-cognitive strategies (e.g., setting a goal for reading or for searching, monitoring understanding, navigational strategies). Konishi noted that some of the strategies used, such as activating background knowledge, were similar to those used when reading printed texts, whereas others, such as navigational strategies, were unique to reading hypertexts. One interesting finding is that the hypertext environment prompted some participants to read beyond the texts they had been assigned to complete their tasks. In her study of Colombian EFL students' reading of hypertexts, Lugo (2005) also found that participants employed strategies traditionally associated with reading print text, but adapted them to the unique contexts of the internet and the tasks they were carrying out. In a more recent study, Bolanos (2012) compared the comprehension strategies employed by Filipino EFL students while reading hypertexts and print texts. He also found that the reading environment triggered the use and adaptation of specific reading strategies. Participants in these studies displayed the kind of strategic disposition that Kalantzis, Cope, and Harvey (2003) identified as critical to meet the challenges presented by the rapidly changing texts and emerging technologies, and were able to successfully complete the tasks they had been assigned.

FL research on hypertext authoring is just as scant as that on hypertext reading on the internet. In one study, Gonglewski (2001) implemented a digital composition project with advanced German learners and examined how their writing of printed and digitally mediated texts differed. She reported that, for the most part, learners "organized their web documents using the more linear and sequential text organization characteristic of traditional print text" (p. 116). However, being able to hyperlink to other texts found on the web elicited interesting reflections from learners. Most learners reported that using hyperlinks in their web document not only expanded their knowledge of the selected topic, but it also expanded their presentation of that knowledge. One student underscored that choosing and linking sources in her digital text helped "make [her] thinking multidimensional" (p. 118). Learners also included visual elements (e.g., images, colors, textured background) in their hypertext, whereas they did not do so in the print version of their text. Several commented on the power of images and acknowledged that when reaching their web page, readers would get an overview of the content or at least an idea of how the author saw the content. Another interesting finding was that learners were acutely aware of their expanded audience when authoring their web documents; they indicated in their comments that "they made additions and changes based on their perceptions of the needs and interest of the public audience the Web afforded them" (p. 121), as opposed to the single recipient (i.e., their teacher) of their print version. Another study of digital authoring conducted by Kramsch, A'Ness, and Lam (2000, 2001) investigated the creation, by advanced learners of Spanish, of a CD–ROM about Latin American culture, which could be used by future generations of Spanish learners and instructors. Focusing on two Spanish learners and the module they were authoring, Kramsch, A'Ness, and Lam (2000) reported that Lucy and Helen started with a "print literacy mentality" where the printed word has supremacy and images are conceived as supplemental and often ornamental in nature, but soon realized that they were not optimally using multimedia technology and the alternative modes of representation it offers. As Lucy and Helen moved forward in the design of the CD–ROM, they "became more aware of both the technological constraints and the potential of their new medium of representation, they experimented with and adapted more to the medium's logic or rhetoric of representation" (p. 88). Kramsch, A'Ness, and Lam concluded that in this project, "the students were never simply archiving authentic materials but actively recontextualizing them to create new and oftentimes quite personalized effects and alternative readings of Latin American culture" (p. 89), a process that led Helen, after completing her co-authored module with Lucy, to reflect that multimedia "make[s] you think about how knowledge is represented" (p. 89). Both Lucy and Helen were also well aware that in hypertext environments, authorship is shared with users who are free to follow (or not) the intended ordering of the information.

When designing hypertexts, learners must necessarily tap into Available Designs beyond linguistic resources. Further, learners must not only consider the modes (e.g., animations, audio, video) that might be best suited to the expression of certain meaning but also the ways in which the selected modes might combine and interact with one another to create a particular communicative effect (Kern, 2000).

1.2.2 MULTIMODALITY. Written texts have traditionally drawn on more than one mode for meaning making: font, color, spacing, and images. However, with recent technological developments, the multimodal content of texts has increased tremendously. Digitally mediated texts can incorporate multiple-media formats that printed texts cannot—audio, animations, and video—thus making the creation of texts less a matter of writing than a matter of design (Kress & van Leeuwen, 2001). For Kress (2003), the logic behind the way content is organized in page-based and screen-based texts is different. Whereas page-based texts are "organized and dominated by the logic of writing" and are meant to be read from the left to right and top to bottom (in English and many other languages), screen-based texts are "organized and dominated by the image and its logic" (p. 19) and are often organized by regions that contain words, sentences, or images that can be read in any order. In short, page-based texts are linear and sequential, whereas screen-based texts are spatial and simultaneous. The first visual element that one encounters in digitally mediated

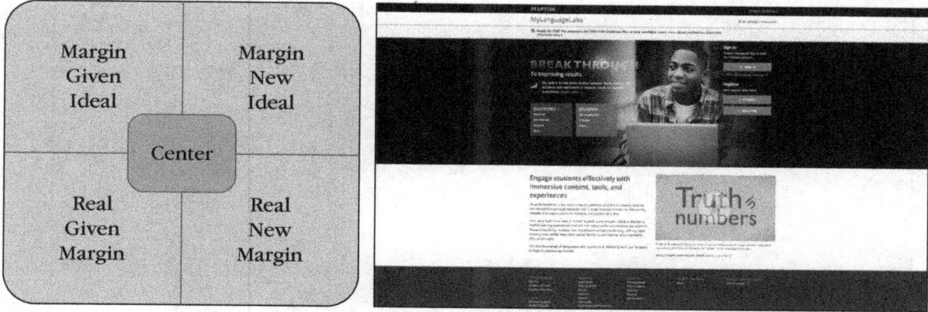

FIGURE 8.1 Meaning Potential of Textual Regions in an Image (based on Kress & van Leeuwen, 2006)

texts is the layout, which Kress and van Leeuwen (2006) suggest can be divided into five textual regions with associated meaning potential (Figure 8.1). In some cases, these different information structures may overlap on a page or screen.

The Pearson MyLanguageLabs login screen in Figure 8.1 presents a clear division between left and right, top and bottom. The left of the screen includes the Pearson and MyLanguageLab logos and the slogan *BREAKTHROUGH, To improving results, Our goal is to help every student succeed. We're working with educators and institutions to improve results for students everywhere,* and the image of signal strength bars, thus indicating that learning can happen without interruption. MyLanguageLab's slogan about students' results and success is further reinforced by a photo of a student logged into MyLanguageLabs. On the right of the screen, we see the sign in and register buttons. They are presented as new, and we need to either register if we are not members yet (something new indeed), or sign in so we can access all the learning tools available to achieve better results and greater learning. The sign in button appears at the top (ideal) with the register button below it (real), suggesting to nonmembers that the ideal of membership is only a short couple of text fields away. At the bottom of the page, we find a series of links with concrete information. They represent the real that is needed to achieve the ideal. Most web pages follow a similar organization pattern, irrespective of content. Sometimes, however, digitally mediated texts can be organized around a dominant element found at the center that gives meaning to other elements on the margin. One good example is the Google homepage (Figure 8.2). In the middle are the logo and the search-field bar, which relates to the company's primary mission of "organiz[ing] the world's information and mak[ing] it universally accessible and useful" (Google, n.d.). All other elements on the page are subservient to this search-field bar. As for the rest of the screen, the divisions right and left, top and bottom are similar to what we observed in the Facebook page. In the upper right margin, there are links to Google services, including the sign-in option, which are presented as new. The banner at the bottom has a

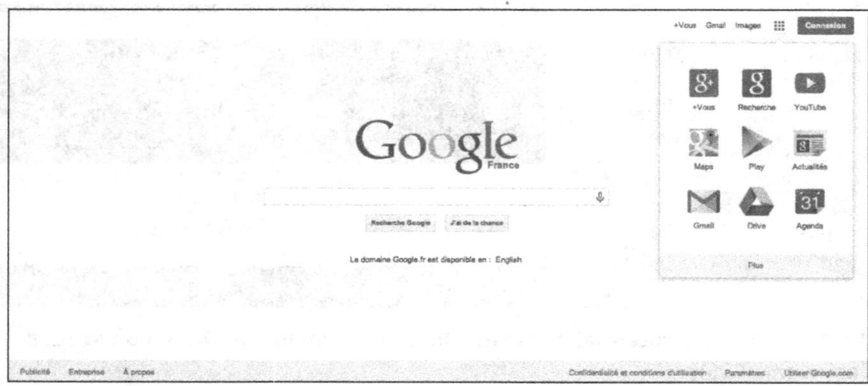

FIGURE 8.2 Google Homepage

left-to-right organization, with the company's information presented as a given on the left and user options presented as new on the right.

Today images, including layout, videos, sounds, and music, are carrying a greater load of the communication of meaning, especially on the web. Kress (2005) underscored that multimedia modes of representation carry cultural, social, and discursive values and norms with them, hence the importance for FL learners to understand how they can draw on these resources to meaningfully interact with and interpret digitally mediated texts.

A small but growing number of studies of multimodal communication (e.g., digital storytelling, web page composing, PowerPoint slide drafting) in FL instructional settings focus on learners' use of multimodal resources, presentation of authorial voice, and identity performance. With respect to the use of multimodal resources, research findings reveal that in the process of authoring digitally mediated texts, FL learners develop awareness and understanding of the synesthetic[2] relationship between multimodal resources for making meaning (Nelson, 2006; Nelson & Hull, 2008; Shin & Cimasko, 2008, Yang, 2012). In some instances, however, findings also show that in authoring digitally mediated texts, learners may continue to use nonlinguistic resources primarily to enhance the core message they constructed using linguistic resources (Shin & Cimasko, 2008), thus not taking full advantage of the meaning potential of these new modalities.

In relation to authorial voice, research shows that FL learners make use of images, language typology and topology, and transduction (i.e., the reshaping of meaning-making resources across modes) to achieve optimal meaning making (Nelson, 2006). Nelson (2006) also reported, however, that learners' authorial voices can at times be constrained by their assumptions about an intended audience's expectations or understandings. Identity performance has

---

[2]Synesthesia refers to the process of shifting between modes and representing again the same thing from one mode to another.

also been investigated in several studies (McGinnis, Goodstein-Stolzenberg, & Saliani, 2007; Tardy, 2005) that report on how learners make use of multimodal resources to represent and display their identity/identities. For example, Tardy (2005) showed how FL learners selected organizational structures, subject-related terminologies, and visuals related to scientific discourses to perform their disciplinary identity and showcase their professionalism in multimodal PowerPoint slides. Although these studies (Nelson, 2006; McGinnis, Goodstein-Stolzenberg, & Saliani, 2007; Tardy, 2005) report that participants made use of multimodal resources and developed an awareness and understanding about the synesthetic relationship among them, in some cases they also report that tension occurred in reading and producing multimodal and traditional print texts. Given the growing importance of multimodal texts on the internet, researchers suggest that exposure to a wide range of multimodal texts and opportunities to produce such texts is critical for FL learners.

1.2.3 REMIX. Writers today have the ability to copy, splice, edit, rework, and mix preexisting digitally mediated texts, images, sound, music, and video to create new texts or artifacts and, as a result, new meanings (Lankshear & Knobel, 2007; Lessig, 2007). Remix practices, which are highly participatory, collaborative, and distributed (Lankshear & Knobel, 2007; Mills, 2010), are considered by many the hallmark of digital culture. One example of remix practices is fanfiction,[3] which promotes the creative use of existing storylines, characters, and model texts to support an author's creation of serialized stories. The stories are then posted on such sites as FanFiction.net, where readers provide suggestions, support, encouragement, and linguistic and stylistic feedback to authors so that they continue to improve the quality of the stories they contribute to the site (Thorne, 2010). In fanfiction, authors "may remix media, combine or flout genre conventions, and use multiple languages and cultural themes" (Thorne, 2010, p. 144). In her case study research of Nanako, an English language learner writing fanfiction on FanFiction.net, Black (2005, 2006, 2008) reported that Nanako initially drew on the storylines, characters, and settings of two *anime* series and "a range of pop cultural resources from different countries, such as Japanese animation, music from the United Kingdom, and novels and motion pictures from the United States to assist her in composing in English" (p. 174) to scaffold her writing. Similarly, Lam (2000), in an ethnographic study, explored how Almon, a Chinese-speaking English language learner, constructed a personal website on Ryoko Hirosue, a young Japanese popular (J-pop) singer. To design his Ryoko page, Almon made use of "materials and sources from magazines and other web sites on J-pop music and celebrities," (p. 470) from which he appropriated, and then remixed, a variety of photos, songs, and video clips. He also included hybrid linguistic resources, using *kanji* and English text.

[3]We suggested fanfiction as a knowledge application activity in the template for video-mediated instruction in Chapter 7.

Reflecting on the potential of internet communities, and fanfiction sites in particular, for FL development, Thorne (2009, 2010) drew on Vygotsky's (1978) Zone of Proximal Development (ZPD), which has traditionally been described as the gap that exists between what an individual can accomplish on his or her own and what the same individual can, through imitation and assistance, accomplish jointly. Thorne highlighted how the existing storylines, characters, settings, and model texts found on fanfiction sites can scaffold an author's creation of a new story, and how the active fanfiction site community can give authors the support they need to revise and improve the texts they post online. Furthermore, Thorne underscored the strong alignment that exists between the remixing practices taking place in fanfiction sites and Bakhtin's (1986) description of FL learning, namely that "we acquire language through a 'process of assimilation'—more or less creative—of others' words (and not the words of a language)" (p. 89). Yet, as the paucity of FL research studies on remix practices indicates, they seem to have made very few inroads in the formal context of the collegiate FL classroom. This gap may be due to concerns about the originality of products students create through remixing practices, which borrow from and build on existing work, in spite of their characterization as "filled with others' words, varying degrees of otherness or varying degrees of our-own-ness" (Bakhtin, 1986, p. 89) and as "tissue[s] of quotations" (Barthes, 1977 p. 146). Practitioners may also be reticent because digital vernaculars stand apart from the traditionally approved formal registers of FL classrooms, and because visual available designs often take precedence over linguistic ones. In one study on remix practices, Gruber-Miller (2013) reported on advanced learners of Latin who were asked to recreate a scene from Vergil's *Aeneid* in the target language. The goals of this culminating project "were to make Vergil's text come alive for [the learners'] generation, to better comprehend the characters, themes, and purposes of Vergil's poem, and to understand how new media, genres, and audiences intersect to deliver a new perspective" (p. 148). Learners' projects used different media and formats (e.g., video, PowerPoint, puppet show); drew on different genres (e.g., documentary footage from National Geographic and the Discovery Channel, epic film series such as *Star Wars* and *Lord of the Rings,* gangster films from the 1930s, children's literature, comics); addressed different audiences (e.g., children, fellow students, general audiences); and had different purposes (e.g., education, entertainment). Each project in this study involved a substantial amount of Latin, some at a complex level. From the learners' final reflective essays, Gruber-Miller was able to gather evidence of their awareness of language, character, audience, and purpose in their remixes.

1.2.4 INTERACTIVITY, PARTICIPATION, AND COLLABORATION. We underscored earlier that the most critical recent technological development has been the move from the read-only Web 1.0 to the read–write Web 2.0. One affordance of Web 2.0 is the opportunity to interact, participate, and collaborate through functions such as the comment field in blogs, the reply button in forums, the discussion page in wikis, the wall in social networking sites (SNS), and so on. Other more elaborate forms of participation include RSS feeds, permalinks, blogrolls, and tags. The functionality of these various interfaces means that they are not simply one-way publication sites, but rather that they have the potential to be highly interactive, participatory, and collaborative as readers comment and writers respond. Although dialogue between writers and readers is not exclusive to digital media, it has become a hallmark feature of online writing.

Research into the integration of blogs and microblogs (e.g., Twitter), forums, wikis, social computing networks (e.g., Facebook), and media self-publishing venues (e.g., YouTube, Flickr) into FL curricula has gained momentum since the early 2000s. Several scholars have advocated their use in the FL classroom because of the potential of interactivity and collaboration allowed by the Web 2.0 functions outlined in this chapter. Recent empirical studies have yielded some interesting results. For example, reading and writing in Web 2.0 environments can contribute to promoting critical reading abilities (blog: Ducate & Lomicka, 2008; Ward, 2004), developing rhetorical strategies (wiki: Bloch, 2007; Bloch & Crosby, 2008; Elola & Oskoz, 2010), and the fluency (blog: Fellner & Apple, 2006; Lee, 2010a; wiki: Lee 2010b) and lexico–grammatical accuracy and complexity (blog: Ducate & Lomicka, 2008; Murray & Hourigan, 2008; wiki: Arnold, Ducate, & Kost, 2009; Ducate, Lomicka, & Moreno, 2011; Kessler, 2009; Kessler & Bikowski, 2010) of writing in the context of formal university settings. Other researchers have examined the usefulness of Web 2.0 in fostering intercultural competence by making it possible for FL learners to connect with peers in the target culture (blog: Diehl & Prins, 2008; Ducate & Lomicka, 2005; Elola & Oskoz, 2008, 2010; forum: Bauer, deBenedette, Furstenberg, Levet, & Waryn, 2006; Furstenberg, Levet, English, & Maillet, 2010; Hanna & de Nooy, 2003; SNS: Blattner & Fiori, 2011; Blattner & Lomicka, 2012; Chun, 2011). Several scholars have investigated the emergence of online writing communities and the development of close relationships over time as a result of the interactivity and participation allowed between readers and writers in Web 2.0 spaces (microblog: Lomicka & Lord, 2012; blog: Ducate & Lomicka, 2008; Hauck & Young, 2008; Micelly, Visocnik, & Kennedy, 2010; forum: Hanna & de Nooy, 2003; SNS: Mills, 2011; Reinhardt & Zander, 2011). However, it must be noted that reading and writing in Web 2.0 spaces does not always support accuracy, as peer feedback may not be consistent (e.g., some students report not feeling comfortable correcting peers or being interested in the topic) or foster high levels of intercultural competence (Ducate & Lomicka, 2008). Furthermore, participation in Web 2.0 spaces does not always promote community building because some students indicate having little time outside of class to post messages or comment on messages posted by peers (Arnold, Ducate, & Kost, 2012; Petersen, Divitni, & Chabert, 2009; Sercu, 2013), or finding the activity of little use as it clashes with what they consider to be legitimate classroom learning practices (Reinhardt & Zander, 2011) or with what they do in other discursive dimensions of their lives (Thorne, 2003). Both van Compernolle and Abraham (2009) and Hanna and de Nooy (2003) agree that blogs and internet forums can be sites of invaluable learning; however, they point out that reducing their use to practicing and assessing a skill basically replicates classroom practices that used to be carried out with pen and paper and, as such, curtails the potential that such new media offer for social and cultural activity. They argue that the focus of tasks students carry out on blogs or forums should be on "authorship as social practice as opposed to a skill" (van Compernolle & Abraham, 2009, p. 209) and that the focus of assessment should be more on the goals and purposes typically valued by blog or forums participants, namely expression of opinions and knowledge and emotions, and less on formal accuracy. Furthermore, they suggest that drawing FL learners' attention to the genre qualities and the language of blogs, or forums in noneducational contexts can serve as a springboard for learners' authorship when using these media (van Compernolle & Abraham, 2009; Reinhardt & Zander, 2011) and can contribute to legitimizing their use for learning (Reinhardt & Zander, 2011). Not only is it essential for teachers to raise FL learners' awareness of the diversity of participation structures, technological affordances, and discourse found in noneducational online writing communities, but teachers should also allow FL learners to join these communities so that they can participate in a social and cultural practice with and on the same terms as local users (Hanna & de Nooy, 2003). Hanna and de Nooy's findings showed that learner participation in open and theme-based internet communities, such as *Le Monde* newspaper discussion forums, has the potential to foster the processes that FL instruction strives so hard to provide, namely the use of language for identity development and meaningful communication for purposes other than practice as typically understood in the formal context of the FL classroom. In online writing communities like *Le Monde* newspaper discussion forums (Hanna & de Nooy, 2003) or FanFiction.net (Black, 2005, 2006, 2008), writing is viewed "more as a collaborative, social activity, where the participative process of writing together is as important as the actual writing itself" (Jones & Hafner, 2012, p. 43) and "success is measured by [participants'] growing ability to meaningfully contribute to ongoing collective activity" (Thorne, 2010). FL learners are allowed to take on "powerful authorial and social roles, even as they learn and develop fluency with multiple textual forms, languages, and online registers" (Thorne & Black, 2007, p. 5).

Online games, another example of collaborative Web 2.0 spaces, have also received growing attention from FL scholars and practitioners since the early 2000s. Online games, which include massively multiplayer online role playing games (MMORPGs) and, more recently, casual social networking games (SNGs), have not only grown in numbers and accessibility, they are also played in many languages, a boon for FL learners who can have the opportunity to interact with native or expert speakers of the target language and culture. Furthermore, as underscored by Reinhardt and Sykes (2012), games "are genuine cultural products, and as such, can be seen to incorporate cultural discourses and narratives that lend themselves to language learning and the development of critical awareness" (p. 35). To communicate with one another during online game play, gamers use synchronous chat tools, asynchronous mail-type tools, or multi-party voice communication tools. Thorne (2010) explained that games provide "unique opportunities, and good reasons for, talk-in-interaction," examples of which include "offering help to someone or receiving assistance or information from someone else, cooperatively engaging in event-driven scenarios that involve situationally responsive language use, communication relating to planning and strategizing, and pragmatically sensitive talk in 'high stakes' scenarios" (p. 149). In this context, communication is purposeful and language is used to jointly accomplish shared goals, something that FL teachers often find difficult to achieve in the classroom.

A small but growing number of exploratory studies have investigated the impact of network-based gaming on FL development (Pasfield-Neofitou, 2011; Rama, Black, Van Es, & Warschauer, 2012; Rankin, Gold, & Gooch, 2006; Rankin, Morrison, McNeal, Gooch, & Shute, 2009; Ryu, 2011; Thorne, 2008; Zheng, Newgarden, & Young 2012). These studies report beneficial effects of participation on language learning, suggesting that interaction in a MMORPG facilitates "situated learning involving collaborative dialog, negotiation, and self-repair" (Peterson, 2010, p. 436). For example, Thorne (2008) examined a multilingual communication (English and Russian) in the *World of Warcraft* between two gamers, one American and the other Ukrainian. Thorne, Black, and Sykes (2009) reported on the transcript of the dialogue between the American and Ukrainian gamers as follows:

> [It] illustrated a number of positive assets for language learning, such as natural and unscripted interaction, reciprocal alterations in expert status, explicit self-correction and other-correction at the level of linguistic form, extensive repair sequences, development of an emotional bond, and exhibition of motivation by both parties for learning the other's language. (p. 811)

Studies conducted by Rankin et al. (2006, 2009) involving groups of ESL learners using *Ever Quest II* reported positive findings on vocabulary learning. Further, they showed evidence of extensive, enhanced FL production involving collaborative interpersonal dialogs.

If the research studies we just examined are any indication, opportunities for the development of FL literacy do exist in these contexts. Nonetheless, scholars and practitioners have raised questions regarding whether open internet communities have a place in the sanctioned formal collegiate FL curriculum and whether they could be successfully integrated. In light of such reticence, Thorne, Black, and Sykes (2009; but also Thorne, 2010 and Thorne & Black, 2007) have argued that:

> As our everyday linguistic and social practices undergo significant shifts as a result of technological mediation, it seems only reasonable that . . . L2 educational practice should also shift to both reflect and provide learners with access to the communicative practices and social formation associated with these changes. (p. 815)

The research examined in this section highlights that, as the practices that thrive in Web 2.0 spaces are slowly incorporated into FL instruction, a shift from a skill focus to a communication focus and from a cognitive orientation to a sociocultural orientation is taking place. This shift provides a natural segue for delving into digitally mediated reading and writing within the multiliteracies framework. To help prepare you to examine more closely what a multiliteracies approach to reading and writing digitally mediated texts entails, complete Learning Activity 8.3.

LEARNING ACTIVITY 8.3

New Literacies

For Learning Activity 8.2, you checked which new Web 2.0 tools or environments you use in your classroom and indicated the ways in which you use them. Reread your responses to Learning Activity 8.2 and reflect on how the new information in the "Conceptual Background" section has contributed to your conceptual understanding of Web 2.0 and new literacies. Consider whether the ways you currently use these tools or environments with your students are consistent with new literacies practices. If they are not, explain what you could change to foster new literacies in your classroom.

1.3 Web 2.0 and the Multiliteracies Framework

Within the multiliteracies framework, reading and authoring in Web 2.0 are viewed as socially embedded communicative acts that bring together the linguistic, cognitive, and sociocultural dimensions of literacy, dynamically interacting together as meaning is created from and through digitally mediated texts.

As examined in the previous section, the opportunities that Web 2.0 offer for developing authentic, interactive reading and authoring of multimodal texts in the classroom are extensive. Furthermore, Web 2.0 tools and environments can be used to foster learners' attention to aspects of language use (e.g., lexical and syntactic choices, rhetorical style, textual structure, genre), ways of conducting social relationships, and practices of socialization. Web 2.0 tools and environments make it possible for learners to draw from a range of Available Designs for making meaning and achieving communicative purpose and to develop, in the process, awareness of the conventions in which the use of written language and multimodal forms of representation are grounded. Available Designs in digitally mediated texts go beyond the linguistic and schematic resources typically found in traditional printed texts and include visual, audio, gestural, and spatial means of designing meaning. Classroom interpretation and authoring of digitally mediated texts that bring together different modes of expression can lead learners to consider how meanings are created and to expand their textual competence in the process (Kern, 2000). Further, as we have seen in several studies, when learners are given the opportunity to examine and use discourse structures and conventions other than those typically found in FL classrooms, they can reflect on what it means to communicate and develop in the process meta-communicative awareness. From a sociocultural perspective, Web 2.0 tools and environments can foster a strong sense of audience and community, which drives the type of feedback and reviews reported in many of the research studies we examined. What these studies' findings show is that the feedback and review practices that take place on the internet have the primary purpose of sustaining social relationships "by tempering critique of form with genuine enthusiasm for content or rhetorical effect, strongly discouraging hostile feedback and attending to the express needs of the author through . . . synchronous and asynchronous communication between writers and [readers/] reviewers" (Black, 2005, p. 127). Studies have also found that Web 2.0 tools and environments allow learners to make connections and participate in communities that cross local and national boundaries and as they do, they learn from and about other cultures and develop the ability to negotiate effective and constructive communication with members of those cultures (Hanna & de Nooy, 2003).

Reading and authoring in Web 2.0 are acts of meaning design and are consistent with the view of learning within the multiliteracies framework, namely a dynamic process of discovering how meaning is made through textual interpretation and creation (see Chapter 1 for elaboration). Multimodal texts are central to the development of new literacies, as they provide a basis for learners to develop awareness of discourse systems in Web 2.0 (e.g., shared conventions, norms of participation, and practices of people who are active participants in them) and of how to effectively use them.

One key concept related to successful communication in Web 2.0 from a multiliteracies perspective is *affinity spaces* (Gee, 2004, 2005). Gee proposed the concept of affinity spaces as an alternative to communities of practice (Lave, 1996; Lave & Wenger, 1991; Rogoff, 1990; Wenger, 1998), which were discussed in Chapter 4 in relation to oral classroom language use, because of its focus on people's interaction within a space rather than on people's membership within a community. Affinity spaces is thus a more appropriate term for describing what happens in Web 2.0 spaces. For Gee, affinity spaces are physical, virtual, or blended spaces that facilitate informal learning in which both newcomers and masters come together and interact around a shared endeavor, interest, or goal. In these spaces, people "affiliate with others to share knowledge and gain knowledge that is distributed and dispersed across many different people, places, Internet sites, and modalities" (Gee, 2004, p. 73). To summarize, affinity spaces instantiate the following features:

- ***Participation.*** Participation in a shared purpose or activity can take "different forms and routes" in affinity spaces (Gee, 2005, p. 228) and can be described as self-directed, multifaceted, and dynamic. Participation in these spaces is also increasingly multimodal and less text based.
- ***Distribution and dispersion of expertise.*** Knowledge is distributed across people, texts, and other mediating devices, and dispersed across sites. Such distributed and dispersed expertise makes it possible for people to know and do more on their own.

- ***Collaboration.*** In affinity spaces, people develop intensive (specialized) and extensive (less specialized, broader, and more widely shared) knowledge. Moreover, within these spaces, participants' knowledge is both collective and individual, such that each person has something special to offer, and therefore can contribute to the growth and dynamic participation found in these spaces.
- ***Relatedness.*** Although the primary motivation for people to engage in an affinity space is participation in a common purpose or goal, not all participation revolves around it. Participation is also about socializing, being and feeling connected to other people, and celebrating with them a passion for something or someone. Socializing plays a crucial role in getting people to regularly come back to the space and participate.

All these features are integral to the mindset of new literacies and central to a socially situated view of learning that can take place within Web 2.0 spaces.

As we now consider the pedagogical applications of the multiliteracies framework to digitally mediated texts, keep in mind the central role the concepts of communication, Available Designs, multimodal texts, discourse systems, and affinity spaces play in designing instruction and assessments to develop new literacies.

2. PEDAGOGICAL APPLICATIONS

With the conceptual background on new literacies now established, we turn our attention to applications of the multiliteracies framework to the teaching of digitally mediated texts in the FL classroom. Although the static informational orientation of Web 1.0 makes it well suited to delivering and consuming content and supporting traditional, transmission-based paradigms of teaching and learning, the social nature of Web 2.0 lends itself to fostering the principles and dimensions of literacy. We have also shown that by limiting the use of technology to Web 1.0 in the FL classroom, we are not allowing learners to be producers of content; thus, we are curbing the potential that Web 2.0 tools and environments hold for transforming, rather than just enhancing, students' learning. In this section, we examine ways to design multiliteracies-based lesson plans that will contribute to the goal of fostering the development of new literacies in lower-level FL learners. Specifically, we draw on relevant models of teaching digitally mediated texts from pedagogical research and then propose a template for creating lesson plans centered on interpreting and creating digitally mediated texts. Next, we provide a sample lesson based on this template and suggest several formative and summative assessments that align with the lesson plan and evaluate students' ability to construct meaning with Web 2.0 tools and environments.

2.1 Literacy-Oriented Models of Digital Text Instruction and Assessment

For this section, we summarize three pedagogical models for teaching digitally mediated texts that are consistent with the multiliteracies-based concepts discussed previously. Although not every model was developed with digitally mediated texts or FL teaching contexts in mind, these models can easily be adapted to teach and assess digitally mediated texts in the FL classroom. We first present van Compernolle and Abraham's (2009) pedagogical model. Based on Herring's (2007) faceted classification scheme (i.e., consisting of clusters of facets) for computer-mediated discourse, this model can be useful in drawing FL learners' attention to the social and communicative goals of various digitally mediated texts. Next, we outline Hyland's (2001) genre awareness teaching–learning model, which can inform the design of instructional activities and assessments around FL digitally mediated texts. Finally, we discuss Reinhardt and Thorne's (2011) bridging activities model, which was designed to "[bring] learners' everyday digital communicative practice into the L2 classroom," and "facilitate the experiential and analytic awareness of digitally mediated student selected or created texts and literacy practices" (p. 270).

Computer-mediated discourse (CMD) is typically classified according to two criteria: modality, or synchronous versus asynchronous discussion; and type, such as blogs, chats, or forums. Herring (2007) argues that this two-pronged classification is inadequate and proposes a faceted classification scheme that additionally takes into account medium and situation factors (see Table 8.1 for details) in a nonhierarchical way to allow for a finer characterization of CMD. Medium factors include features (e.g., synchronicity, message format) of computer-mediated communication systems that impact the creation, sending, receiving, and archiving of texts and situation factors include features (e.g., participation structure, characteristics, purpose, tone) that participants bring to a communication environment. Although some of these medium and situation factors should present no difficulty to learners when they start exploring digitally mediated texts, others, such as participant characteristics, tone, or norms, may require instructor intervention because they tend to vary across languages and CMD types.

The work of van Compernolle and Abraham (2009) extended Herring's model to the FL field and provided guiding questions related to select medium

TABLE 8.1 Classification CMD Scheme (based on Herring, 2007)

Medium Factors	Situation Factors
Synchronicity	Participation structure
Message transmission	Participant characteristics
Persistence of transcript	Purpose
Size of message buffer	Topic/Theme
Channels of communication	Tone
Anonymous messaging	Activity
Private messaging	Norms
Filtering	Code
Quoting	
Message format	

and social factors more pertinent for FL blog reading and writing. The purpose of their guiding questions is to "raise learners' and teachers' awareness of the diversity of blog postings in terms of participation structure, technological affordances, discourse, and so forth" and concurrently enable learners "to understand what strategies, norms, and activities blog writers engage in, which helps them to become better blog writers themselves" (p. 206). The guiding questions, provided in Table 8.2, may shift for other media and social factors.

To organize digital literacy lessons using Herring's CMD classification scheme, van Compernolle and Abraham (2009) propose the following sequence for working with blogs: (1) create a blog corpus, ideally built by learners themselves; (2) engage learners in classifying the blogs they found and coding them using the classification scheme adapted from Herring; (3) ask learners to use the classification of a blog or several blogs to analyze the discourse produced by the author(s), and then relate the discursive practices they found to the medium and social factors they identified while classifying each blog; and (4) use the results of the analysis as a lead-in to student authorship of their own blog. Learners work through steps 1 through 3 with the assistance of the instructor, who can "draw their attention to discursive features that they may not have identified independently" (p. 208), using instructional conversations (See Chapter 4). The activities carried out for steps 2 and 3 can serve as formative assessments. To plan their blog postings in step 4, learners must ask themselves the same questions they "posed for the corpus analysis, but in relation to their own purposes for writing a blog" (p. 208), so that it is a social practice and goal-oriented activity, not simply an exercise in writing. In this last phase, learners have the opportunity to learn by doing as they apply their developed knowledge in a new and purposeful context. The contributions learners make on their blog and/or those of others can be used as summative assessments.

Another model is Hyland's (2001) five-stage genre awareness model (see Figure 8.3). Although originally intended for L2 literacy development in general, this model is easily adapted to digital contexts. Each stage seeks to achieve a different purpose, calling on different types of activities and instructor–learner roles.

The first phase of the cycle, developing the context, involves guiding learners to explore the social and situational features of a text, which include purpose of communication, roles and relationships, audience, and authorship choice. During this phase, learners are supported (i.e., scaffolded, Chapter 4) on an as-needed basis by instructor questioning, direct instruction, and a variety of relevant activities. In the second phase, modeling the text, learners explore with instructor guidance the lexical, grammatical, and rhetorical features found in the text. The purpose of the activities in this phase is to ensure that learners understand and appreciate how stages, purpose, and language work together. In the third phase, jointly negotiating the text, learners work together or with their instructor to produce their own texts, using the knowledge developed in phases 1 and 2. In the fourth phase, independently constructing the text, learners individually create their own texts "in which they combine a knowledge of content, process, language, context, and genre" (Hyland, 2001, p. 136). In the fifth and final phase of the cycle, comparing texts, learners link the text they have constructed to other texts and reflect critically on their similarities and

TABLE 8.2 Guiding Questions Based on Selected Medium (Blog) and Social Factors (based on van Compernolle and Abraham, 2009)

Medium Factors	Source	• What web site is the blog from? • What kind of membership is needed to post on the blog? • Is the blog the main page (e.g., Blogger, Wordpress, Tumblr) or is it part of another type of web site (e.g., Facebook page, commercial web site)? • What is the nature of the blog (e.g., personal or commercial)?
	Private messaging	• Is the blog public or private? • Who can comment on the blog (e.g., everyone or only a select group of people)?
	Anonymous messaging	• Is login required to post a comment on the blog? • Are anonymous comments permitted? • How are authors and commentators identified (e.g., real name, fictitious name)?
	Message format	• How do entries appear? In what order (e.g., newest to oldest)? • Are comments on the main page or is a comments page accessed through a comments link?
Social Factors	Participation structure	• Who posts on the blog? • How is participation balanced or distributed? • How long can each post/comment be? • Do blog authors make rejoinders to comments?
	Participant characteristics	• Who is the author of the blog? What is the author's age, genre, or nationality? • Are the blog authors and commentators students, professionals, etc.?
	Purpose	• Why was this blog created? • Why does the author keep a blog?
	Topic/Theme	• Are the blog or blog entries topic or theme specific?
	Tone	• Is the blog serious? Playful? A bit of both? • What is the tone of the blog (e.g., formal or informal)?
	Activity	• What does the blog author write in each posting? Can posts be debated or commented on? • Is this blog for disseminating information? Writing about personal life? Creative writing? • Are differences between entries within the blog evident?
	Norms	• Are there any identifiable patterns for participant roles? Language use?
	Code	• Is the writing formal or informal? What evidence indicates this? • What fonts are used and when? • Are graphics creatively used (e.g., emoticons, capital letters, punctuation)?

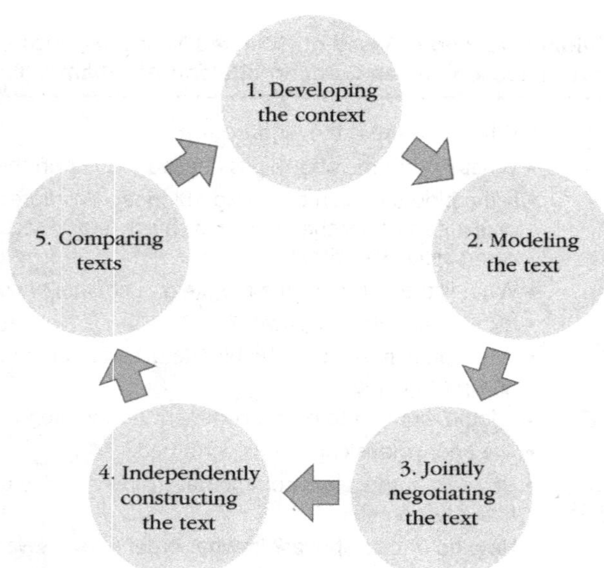

FIGURE 8.3 Genre Awareness Model (based on Hyland, 2001)

differences. Two central aspects of this genre teaching–learning cycle are the examination of language as functional within texts and contexts and the presentation of various genre descriptions from the culture.

Although Hyland's genre awareness model was not conceived with digitally mediated texts in mind, it can easily be adapted to work for Web 2.0 spaces. Continuing with the example of a blog as a digitally mediated text, once learners have considered what they know about blogs, they can explore a blog they selected by focusing on its cultural, situational, functional, and structural elements, paying particular attention to its multimodal qualities. Once students have considered the nature, purpose, and structure of the blog they selected, the instructor can direct their attention to the blog comments and ask them to explore some of the linguistic and schematic Available Designs of the genre. Next, learners can work in small groups or as a class to craft a joint response to a blog comment they found of interest and later examine the rejoinders it generates. Finally, learners can respond individually and bring to their classmates' attention samples of their own and others' participation for further analysis.

Informed by both awareness- and multiliteracies-oriented approaches, Reinhardt and Thorne's (2011) bridging activities model was developed to "facilitate the experiential and analytic awareness of digitally mediated student selected or created texts and literacy practices . . . generated through the use of Web 2.0 technologies" (p. 270). Within their model, Reinhardt and Thorne exploit "the everyday, experiential nature of multimodal, digital mediation as the means of instruction" and use it concomitantly as "the explicit object of analysis" (p. 270). In so doing, the model bridges the world of learners inside and outside the classroom, thus ensuring relevance and building and sustaining motivation, which have been identified as challenges to using Web 2.0 tools and environments in a number of studies (Arnold, Ducate, & Kost, 2012; Petersen, Divitni, & Chabert, 2009; Reinhardt & Zander, 2011; Sercu, 2013; Thorne, 2003). To facilitate the implementation of their model, Reinhardt and Thorne outlined a three-phase instructional cycle to scaffold student learning: (1) observation and collection; (2) exploration and analysis; and (3) creation and participation. Whereas the first step in each phase of their model (observation, exploration, and creation) is based in experiential learning, the second (collection, analysis and participation) is based on analytical learning. Accordingly, activities in the first step are grounded in the internet activities and literacy practices in which learners engage on a daily basis (e.g., browsing, reading, viewing/listening, posting, commenting). In the second step, activities are carefully designed to draw learners' attention to "similarities and differences among technology-mediated practices in their own language and culture and the language and culture being studied" (p. 271). Reinhardt and Zander (2011) implemented this model in an intermediate classroom in an Intensive English Program. The activities they used to guide learners, which were "designed to develop experiential and critical awareness of Facebook practices as a means to learn English in the IEP community" (p. 326), are displayed in Table 8.3.

TABLE 8.3 Sample Instructional Sequence Based on the Bridging Activities Model (based on Reinhardt & Zander, 2011, pp. 334–228)

Focus	Activities	Objectives
Experiential learning	• Biographical survey (included questions on English use and study habits) • Interview and discussion on friendship and the social use of English • Journal entry asking learners to document their use of particular technologies	Situate practice and prompt learners to think about the ways in which they use and study English and use language to socialize.
Critical learning	• Listen to NPR story about Facebook use and privacy concerns; follow-up discussion based on journal entry and SNS use in general • Introduction to the nuts and bolts of Facebook use • Participation in social networking games. Learners explain rules and strategies related to the game selected, report on positive and negative aspects of playing games, report on language they learned while playing, explain whether they would recommend their selected game.	Develop learners' critical awareness regarding technology use, Facebook functionality, and popular practices such as gaming on Facebook.

In this instructional sequence, activities in the experiential learning phase can be used as formative assessments, whereas the final activity in the critical learning phase can be used as a summative assessment.

The three literacy-oriented models for teaching and learning digital literacies examined here are summarized in Table 8.4. It is apparent that these models share a number of similarities, although they may differ in the number of steps. All three models include gathering and immersing activities as a way for learners to tap into what they know about the type of digitally mediated texts under consideration and orient themselves by considering questions related to purpose, authorship, and audience of their digital text(s). In addition, learners engage in analysis activities that prompt them to focus on textual details, such as the language and multimodal features of the digitally mediated text(s) they are exploring; this analysis focuses their attention on the structure and cultural content of the text(s) they are working with. All three models also provide learners opportunities to apply their new knowledge and engage in the creation

TABLE 8.4 Literacy-Oriented Models for Teaching and Learning Digital Literacies

	Van Compernolle & Abraham (2009)	Hyland (2001)		Reinhardt & Thorne (2011)
1	Creation of a corpus of existing digitally mediated texts	Building the context	a	Observation of L2 digitally mediated texts and practices
			b	Collection and critical reflection on learner-selected L2 digitally mediated texts
2	Classification and coding of digitally mediated texts	Modeling and deconstructing the text	a	Exploration and comprehension of collected L2 digitally mediated texts
			b	Analysis of social and lexico–grammatical features of collected L2 digitally mediated texts
3	Analysis and linking of discourse practices found in digitally mediated texts to Herring's (2007) classification scheme (medium and social factors)	Jointly constructing the text	a	Creation of L2 digitally mediated texts comparable to those collected
			b	Participation by sharing own L2 digitally mediated texts and reflecting on responses received
4	Creation/authoring of digitally mediated texts	Independently constructing the text		
5		Linking related texts		

of their own digital text(s). Finally, the last set of activities in each model is designed to allow learners to reflect on what they have learned, how they can use this new knowledge in other areas of the curriculum, and what they would like to learn next. The commonalities found across these three models provides the basis for a general template for teaching digitally mediated texts based on the multiliteracies approach, which we detail in the next subsection.

2.2 A Template for Organizing Multiliteracies-Oriented Instruction of Digitally Mediated Texts and Assessment

To merge communication with the interpretation and creation of digitally mediated texts, we propose the following four-stage model for designing multiliteracies-oriented lessons that develop new literacies.

1. *Textual immersion and familiarization* to collect digitally mediated texts of potential interest for the type under examination (e.g., websites, blogs, forums, chatrooms, online novels, etc.), and immerse and familiarize oneself with medium and social features.
2. *Textual exploration and interpretation* to comprehend the collected digitally mediated texts and examine their linguistic, schematic, multimodal, and sociocultural resources and their contribution to meaning creation.
3. *Knowledge application* to demonstrate understanding of digital practices through creation of original digitally mediated texts.
4. *Evaluation and reflection* to consider what has been learned in the process of working with and creating digitally mediated texts and to entertain ways in which the knowledge gained could be transferred to other areas of academic, professional, and/or personal life.

The activities planned for each phase should reflect the four pedagogical acts of the multiliteracies framework (situated practice, overt instruction, critical framing, and transformed practice) and engage students in the learning processes of interpretation, collaboration, problem solving, reflection, and self-reflection. You will recall that situated practice, typically referred to as immersion in language use, may include activities that involve learners in exploring, observing, or connecting with a text. Overt instruction activities focus learners' attention explicitly on Available Designs (e.g., linguistic, schematic, multimodal) and their contribution to creating certain meanings and not others in a text. Critical framing involves metacognitive reflections on how meaning is made and might include activities that engage learners in comparing, synthesizing, critiquing, or understanding, including analyzing, for example, author purpose in a text. Transformed practice consists of activities in which learners apply what they have learned from a text in new and creative ways.

Examples of learning activities that might be used in each stage of the instructional template are presented in Table 8.5. In several instances, a learning activity may correspond to more than one pedagogical act.

2.2.1 TEXTUAL IMMERSION AND FAMILIARIZATION. The focus of textual immersion and familiarization activities is on building learners' knowledge base

TABLE 8.5 Suggested Learning Activities for Teaching Digitally Mediated Texts

Instructional Stage	Suggested Learning Activities
1 Textual immersion and familiarization	Polling (Situated practice / Critical framing) Connecting with text chart (Situated practice) Annotating (Situated practice)
2 Textual exploration and interpretation	Frames (Overt instruction) Juxtaposition (Overt instruction / Critical framing) Sociogram (Overt instruction / Critical framing)
3 Knowledge application	Kinesthesia (Transformed practice) Storyboard (Transformed practice) Multimodal digital text (Transformed practice)
4 Reflection and evaluation	DEAF (Describe, Evaluate, Analyze, Future Action) thinking (Transformed practice) Knowledge transfer (Transformed practice) Personal action plan (Transformed practice)

by asking them to think about what they know about the type of digitally mediated text under examination, to find such texts on the internet, to familiarize themselves with these texts by immersing themselves in them, and to attend to the texts' medium and social factors so that they can classify them and prepare to interpret them. Activities such as polling, connecting with text, and annotating provide scaffolded guidance that helps direct learners' attention to these factors.

One way to activate learners' background knowledge about the type of digital text to be examined in a unit or lesson is *polling*. Yes/No, multiple choice, rating scale, or open-ended questions can be used to raise learners' awareness about their situated digital practices and those of their classmates. In the classroom, polling can be implemented using an application like Poll Everywhere, which lets the instructor engage learners in real time and display responses live on a screen as learners enter their answers to the instructor-created poll. Asking learners to analyze their class's visualized responses and provide evidence to support their analysis can add a critical framing component to the polling activity. A *connecting with text chart* is another situated practice activity that can be used to activate and build background knowledge. This activity asks learners to record in writing any personal connections they find in the digitally mediated text they are reading. Learners' personal connections may be about similar experiences, images, or texts they have read, information they recall, or people they know. Once students have completed the chart they can share with fellow students and discuss similarities or differences in the connections they made (Kalantzis & Cope, 2012). Finally, another situated practice activity is to ask learners to *annotate* one of the collected digitally mediated texts. Using codes, learners record questions/wonderings (?) they have about what is happening or being reported in the text or the vocabulary being used; underline (___) aspects of the writing style or tone, use of certain images, music, sounds, or colors; note interesting or intriguing moments in the text (!); indicate aspects that they would like to know more about (M) or new information that is given (N), and so forth. Learners next discuss their annotations with a partner, focusing on what is most important or interesting to them, and finally share with the whole class.

2.2.2 TEXTUAL EXPLORATION AND INTERPRETATION. Activities included in this stage are meant to give learners opportunities to explore in detail the themes and topics, structure, and use of different modes of meaning in digitally mediated texts. Examples of textual exploration and interpretation activities include genre framing, text juxtaposition, and sociogram.

As an overt instruction activity, *frames* allows students to explore a digitally mediated text using a frame appropriate for its specific genre (e.g., blog in the form of diary, report, or commentary; digital story in the form of narrative, autobiography, or report) to help understand how this genre is constructed. For example, in the case of a digital narrative, an appropriate frame would focus students' attention on "orientation (characters, setting, starting event), complication (something surprising or interesting that happens, one or more episodes), resolution (how the story ends)" (Kalantzis & Cope, 2012), which then leads them to see how meaning is designed in such texts. To carry out this frames activity, an instructor-created matrix is provided to learners, who fill it out with the appropriate information. In a *juxtaposition* activity, two texts are placed side by side (e.g., a print and digital version of the same text, two digitally mediated texts on the same topic by two authors) with the purpose of comparing and contrasting their content, structure, and features. Through overt instruction, students can focus on Available Designs and discuss form–meaning connections in each text. Asking students to reflect on the contributions these Available Designs make to the feel of each text, for example, promotes critical framing because learners have an opportunity to think about the ways in which Available Designs, communicative situation, and sociocultural context are linked to and interact with one another (Kern, 2000). Finally, as an overt instruction activity, a *sociogram* helps students capture over time the structure and patterns of relationships among characters in literary texts or among people in non-fiction texts, in a way that reflects their understanding. Conventions for developing a sociogram exist (e.g., placing the main character at the center of the sociogram; representing perceived psychological distance between characters/people by increasing or decreasing the physical distance between them; using arrows to represent the direction of a relationship and a brief label to describe its nature) and should be shared with students. Students can work on their sociogram either independently or collaboratively in small groups and later share their sociogram with the whole class. To engage in critical framing, students could be asked to examine, for example, use of lexicon for a given character or person, identify words or expressions that predominate for this character or person, and think about the relations and interactions between character or person, communicative context, and sociocultural context.

2.2.3 KNOWLEDGE APPLICATION. In knowledge application activities, students apply the new knowledge of digitally mediated texts they developed during the textual immersion and familiarization and the textual exploration and interpretation phases to create new digitally mediated texts or to reshape existing texts so that they are appropriate for a context of communication different than the one for which they were originally intended (New London Group, 1996). Knowledge application activities include kinesthesia, storyboard, and multimodal digital text.

In *kinesthesia* activities, learners transfer meanings from one mode to another (e.g., from linguistic to visual, from visual to auditory), or from one medium to another (e.g., from print to video). Learners can also transfer meanings from one setting (e.g., country, time in history) to another and make adjustments to mode and medium accordingly (Kalantzis & Cope, 2012). In *storyboarding,* another transformed practice activity, students plan the sequence of an episode in a real or fictional story and make choices in terms of modes and features, paying attention to continuity of use, based on what was included in earlier episodes of the story they read. In designing a *multimodal digital text,* students can either enhance a digitally mediated text they read in previous stages of a lesson or create a new text using information gleaned in previous activities, in which they mix "modes of meaning (linguistic, visual, gestural, audio, and spatial), media, and genres in an original or hybrid way" (Kalantzis & Cope, 2012).

2.2.4 REFLECTION AND EVALUATION. In this final stage of the pedagogical sequence, activities prompt learners to take stock of what they have learned during the lesson, reflect on their learning, and plan for furthering their learning in areas of interest to them. Three sample activities are proposed: DEAF (Describe, Evaluate, Analyze, Future Action) thinking, knowledge transfer, and personal action plan.

DEAF thinking is a transformed practice activity in which, according to Kalantzis and Cope (2012), students, prompted by instructor-provided questions, describe the scope and nature of their learning experience with the digital text they examined or the one they created. Students then evaluate and analyze aspects of this learning experience that went particularly well and not so well for them, and reflect on the reasons that might have led to these outcomes. They consider what they could have done differently and make suggestions for future action. *Knowledge transfer* is a transformed practice activity in which students are asked to use the new knowledge they have acquired by applying it "in a different setting, to a different subject matter or to a different problem" (Kalantzis & Cope, 2012). For instance, students might consider the similarities and differences that exist between the original and the new context and reflect on implications for knowledge transfer. Finally, a *personal action plan* (see also Chapter 4) is a transformed practice activity that promotes both evaluation and reflection after participation in the lesson. The purpose of this activity is to turn an idea into action (Kalantzis & Cope, 2012). The action plan can be related either to the text students interpreted or to the one they created. Students start off by identifying a goal and laying out the action steps they need to take to reach it. Once the goal and steps are in place, students locate resources (e.g., targeted web sites, online dictionary and thesaurus, images, videos, music and sound, software applications) and support (e.g., feedback provided by teacher, peers, online community) that could be useful to accomplish their goal. Not only must students consider what will be useful to meet their goal, they must also consider what possible hurdles may prevent them from reaching it. Finally, students identify performance measures (e.g., creation of a web page, composition of a digital story, participation in an online discussion) that help determine whether their goal has been met.

2.2.5 ASSESSMENT. The four-phase pedagogical model for working with digitally mediated FL texts described here can also serve as a guide to develop multiliteracies-oriented tests focused on the assessment of students' ability to interpret and create digitally mediated texts. For example, the test could include the following phases: (1) the textual immersion and familiarization activity of a connecting with text chart to access background knowledge and connect personally with the text; (2) the textual exploration and interpretation activity of genre framing to demonstrate how the genre of the digitally mediated text is constructed; (3) the knowledge application activity of storyboarding in which students plan the sequence of an episode in a real or fictional story, make choices in terms of modes and features, and outline the effects sought; (4) the reflection and evaluation activity of knowledge transfer in which students outline how they applied the knowledge they developed in the lesson taught in class to the task on the test.

Not only can this model for teaching digitally mediated FL texts provide a template to develop formal tests, but the activities included in each phase can also function as formative and summative assessments. Several activities suggested for the first two phases of the model can be used as formative assessments carried out through in-class discussions or out-of-class assignments. Further, the activities proposed for the knowledge application and the reflection and evaluation phases can serve as summative assessments that follow the work completed on a particular digitally mediated text and assess students' new literacies.

2.3 Sample Lesson Plan for Digitally Mediated Texts

Built around activities that are representative of the four pedagogical acts, the instructional template proposed in the previous section provides a way to engage lower-level language learners in scaffolded interaction with various types of digitally mediated texts and participation in meaningful activities that allow them to delve into textual content and meaning. In Table 8.6 we present a sample digitally mediated storytelling lesson plan organized according to the template proposed in the previous section. The activities included in each stage of the lesson plan reflect one or more of the three types presented in Table 8.5. The lesson is intended for use in a third- or fourth-semester Italian course during an instructional unit on media. The objectives of this lesson are for

TABLE 8.6 Sample Instructional Sequence, Digitally Mediated Text Lesson: *Alice Inanimata*

	Instructional Stage		Learning Activities
1	Textual immersion and familiarization	a	Students participate in an instructor-created *poll* in Poll Everywhere[4] and respond to statements related to their familiarity and engagement with specific digital practices (Situated practice). Next, students examine the graphs generated in real time, and compare/contrast the class responses to that of published polls conducted on the same topic with the same age group, providing possible explanations for the discrepancies that might be present. (Critical framing)
		b	To help students connect with *Alice Inanimata*, they discuss as a class what they think the title might mean. Next, they record personal connections into a *connecting with text chart* as they read/view/listen/play Episode 1. Personal connections may include similar experiences, the people Alice reminds them of, links to other printed or digitally mediated texts they have read in either the target language or the L1. Students then pair with a peer to compare and discuss the connections they have made. (Situated practice)
		c	Next, students go back to the text and *annotate* Episode 1.[5] Using codes, they record questions/wonderings (?) they have about what is happening in the story and the vocabulary used; underline (___) aspects of the writing style or tone, use of certain images, music, sounds, or colors; note interesting or intriguing moments in the story (!); indicate aspects that they would like to know more about (M) or new information that is given (N), etc. Students discuss their annotations with a partner, focusing on what is most important or interesting to them, and then share with the whole class. (Situated practice)
2	Textual exploration and interpretation	a	Students now look at the text more closely, using a *frame* according to the *Bildungsroman* genre. In groups of four, students discuss elements that narratives, in general, and *Bildungsroman*, in particular, possess (e.g., elements they generally have, elements they can also have, elements that really good ones have). Next, students scan the text to identify the elements from their list that occur in the printed transcript of episode one. The instructor guides students as needed. Next, students share with the whole class. (Situated practice / Overt instruction)
		b	Students read/view Episode 1 again. *Juxtaposing* the printed transcript of Episode 1 and its digital version, students continue to work with their group to generate a list of additional elements that characterize digital narratives. The instructor provides help as needed. As a class, students share their list of additional elements and discuss their experience of reading the print version of Episode 1 versus reading/viewing/listening/playing its digital version and the contribution that the presence or absence of certain elements made to their experience with the text. (Overt instruction / Critical framing)

(Continued)

TABLE 8.6 Sample Instructional Sequence, Digitally Mediated Text Lesson: *Alice Inanimata*

Instructional Stage		Learning Activities
	c	Working in their groups, students are assigned one episode to work with (1, 2, 3, or 4) and fill in a *retrieval chart* in which they identify the modes used in the assigned episode (linguistic, visual, audio, spatial and gestural), its features, and the effects of mode(s) on the narrative. Each group shares its findings. (Overt instruction / Critical framing)
	d	Next, the instructor leads the whole class in a discussion related to the previous activity. Students refer back to the retrieval chart, and highlight the similarities and differences (text structure, style, visuals, music, sounds, etc.) they find across all four episodes and discuss what their presence or absence might mean. If needed, the instructor can guide students as they work with the text. Students share their group's ideas with the class. (Overt instruction / Critical framing)
3 Knowledge application	a	Students are now ready to collaboratively author their own episode of *Alice Inanimata.* They may chose to compose an episode that branches off an existing one as a way to answer some of the questions and wonderings they identified in the annotation activity, retell an episode from another viewpoint, or compose the next episode in the series. In small groups, students *storyboard* the sequence of their episode using inklewriter[6] to facilitate collaboration, participation, and interaction. As they storyboard their sequence, students refer back to the work they did before and bear in mind the conventions of the genre. (Transformed practice)
	b	Students compose a *multimodal digital text* in the form of an episode of *Alice Inanimata* and post it on a class blog or Facebook group and invite comments from peers and the greater community. (Transformed practice)
4 Reflection and evaluation	a	Students engage in a *DEAF thinking* activity. Prompted by instructor-provided questions, students reflect on the scope and nature of their experience as readers/viewers/listeners/players and writers of a digitally mediated text and what they learned from this experience. In pairs, students evaluate and analyze aspects of their learning experience with *Alice Inanimata,* focusing on what they think went well and not so well, and examine the reasons why. In hindsight, they consider what they could have done differently and consider what they could do in the future. (Transformed practice)
	b	Finally, as a class, students consider how they might *transfer the knowledge* they developed as readers/viewers/listeners/players and writers of a digitally mediated text to another project in a different discipline and what it could look like. (Transformed practice)

[4]www.polleverywhere.com/
[5]Students could take screenshots of moments in the story they want to annotate and use ThingLink (www.thinglink.com/) to make multimodal annotations and share these with others in the class.
[6]www.inklestudios.com/inklewriter/

students to identify, become familiar with, and comprehend multiple modes of representation in digitally mediated storytelling and their effects on narrative, and to work collaboratively to create an episode of a transmedia[7] story in development. The transmedia, multilingual novel *Alice Inanimata (Inanimate Alice)* is used as the basis for this lesson (see Appendix for links to English and Italian versions of the novel episodes and scripts). For this lesson, we are expanding on themes and topics (e.g., family, lodgings, travels) that learners have most likely examined in previous semesters and tapping into learners' experiences with digital media. Produced using manipulated images, text, games, music, and sound effects, *Alice Inanimata* is a 10-episode multimedia interactive story of an adventurous young woman in the early years of the twenty-first century. The first time we meet Alice, she is eight years old and living in China, where her father has gone missing, and we follow her until she reaches her mid 20s and is a successful game designer. Most likely familiar with this kind of digital story and its genre, *Bildungsroman,* or a coming-of-age narrative, learners should not have difficulty constructing meaning from the text. Further, the multimodal and intertextual elements found in *Alice Inanimata* will make the story accessible to learners and enable them to understand how the various Available Designs used shape meaning.

In this four-stage lesson plan, we outlined activities that scaffold students' design of meaning as they read, view, listen to, and play the digital novel *Alice Inanimata.* As students engage with this narrative, they interact with a wide range of modes and features, they make form–meaning connections, and they participate in textual interpretation. Organized around the four pedagogical acts of situated practice, overt instruction, critical framing, and transformed practice, the activities included in this lesson plan reflect the basic elements of literacy-based instruction (conventions, cultural knowledge, and language use) and engage students in the literacy-based learning processes of interpretation, collaboration, problem solving, and reflection. Students interpret the form and content of a multimodal, transmedia novel; they collaborate by interacting with the digital novel, their instructor, and peers to interpret and transform meaning in a digital text; they solve problems by relating textual structure and multimodal choices to textual meaning; and they reflect on the effects and significance of the use of a variety of modes and features on the narrative, and on themselves as readers/viewers/listeners/players and writers of digitally mediated texts.

Several opportunities for both formative and summative assessments are included in this sample lesson plan. For example, instructors can provide formative feedback on the frames, the juxtaposition, and the retrieval chart activities by drawing students' attention to certain elements in the text and asking them focused questions to verify textual understanding. Using the feedback they receive, students then amend their list or chart accordingly. The storyboarding activity is another opportunity for formative assessment. Here, by walking through the choices they are making for their story with their teacher, the instructor can facilitate creation of a more successful episode of *Alice Inanimata.* Both the multimodal digital text creation and knowledge transfer activities

---

[7]A transmedia story is told across multiple media platforms and formats using current digital–electronic technologies.

can serve as summative assessments for this lesson. For the multimodal digital episode, students might receive a grade on their collaborative effort and their contribution as writers and creators. Students could be graded on the quality of their narrative structure and their respect of the conventions tied to the genre, the appropriateness of their lexico–grammatical choices, the relevance of the multimodal elements included in their episode, and the overall alignment of their episode with the rest of the *Alice Inanimata* novel. For the knowledge transfer activity, students could be graded on the soundness of what they propose and their ability to explain the choices they make.

To guide your reflection on the sample digitally mediated text lesson plan, closely examine it a second time and answer the following questions. When appropriate, make sure to refer to specific activities in the lesson to support your answer:

1. What are the goals and objectives of this lesson and how do they fit within the course curriculum?
2. Are the activities and texts appropriate to meet the objectives of this lesson? If so, how? What elements of these activities and texts might be challenging for FL learners?
3. How does this lesson reflect the conceptualization of new literacies discussed in this chapter? How does this lesson scaffold development of learners' new literacies?
4. Why are the different lesson plan activities labeled as situated practice, overt instruction, critical framing, or transformed practice?
5. Are the basic elements of instruction, or the what of multiliteracies pedagogy—conventions, cultural knowledge, and language use—represented in the lesson? How?
6. Are the learning processes of interpretation, collaboration, problem solving, and reflection and self-reflection (i.e., the how of multiliteracies pedagogy) represented in the lesson? How?

As you start thinking about planning your own FL digital text-based lesson plans and assessments using the four-stage multiliteracies-based template, keep in mind the key principles that undergird the development of new literacies and refer back to the questions you just considered to help you organize your ideas and apply your understanding of multiliteracies-oriented pedagogy. Learning Activity 8.4 will give you a headstart.

LEARNING ACTIVITY 8.4

Modifying Internet-Based Textbook Activities

Recently, publishers have made a concerted effort to include internet-based activities in FL textbooks. These internet-based activities are typically conceived as supplementary, primarily ask students to look for information to later report to the class, and are usually found on the companion web site of the textbook. Select one of these activities and modify it so that it is reflective of the multiliteracies-based model detailed in this chapter. Before starting, consider whether the activity you selected can effectively promote the development of new literacies based on the key principles that we listed above. Identify places where the activity could be improved and redesign it using the four-stage model and suggested learning activities included in this chapter. When you have completed this lesson plan, ask yourself the same set of questions above as a way to help you justify your pedagogical choices.

3. FINAL CONSIDERATIONS

In this chapter, we have provided a conceptual base for the instruction of digitally mediated FL texts within the multiliteracies framework. Critical to the development of new literacies is the understanding that new literacies means more than mastering the technical aspects of digital tools. It also means using these tools to generate, communicate, and negotiate meanings (1) through language, including the many modes and features that often supersede linguistic expression in digitally mediated texts; and (2) within various affinity spaces where individuals are connected by shared interest or endeavor, where knowledge is dispersed and distributed across people and platforms, and where learning takes place through participation and collaboration with scaffolded assistance provided as needed.

This conceptual base is at the core of the pedagogy for digitally mediated FL texts developed in this chapter. It is a pedagogy whose primary goal is to promote the development of new literacies through exposure to, participation in, and production of digitally mediated texts that represent various genres and call on various modalities. This pedagogy is grounded in essential elements and processes of the multiliteracies framework, namely the four pedagogical acts and the seven principles of literacy.

To conclude, we leave you a few final thoughts to consider. We started this chapter by bringing to your attention the gap that exists between the kinds of formalized interactions that typically take place in the FL classroom and those that occur in the everyday world, including on the internet. Several researchers (Lotherington & Jenson, 2011; Merchant, 2009; Pegrum, 2011; Thorne, 2008; Thorne & Black, 2007; Thorne, Black, & Sykes, 2009) have underscored that we cannot continue to ignore this gap and that FL education "will need to accommodate emerging communication tools, their emergent and plastic cultures of use, as well as their attendant communicative genres that are, and have been for some years, everyday dimensions of competent social and professional activity" (Thorne & Black, 2007, p. 149). Web 2.0 tools and environments can have a profoundly transformative impact on FL teaching and learning when their use is thoughtfully structured and guided by instructors using the multiliteracies pedagogy that we espouse. When used wisely, Web 2.0 tools and environments can potentially boost "the ecological relations between the language practices and identity dispositions developed within instructional L2 contexts and the broader plurilingual communicative contexts of life outside of the academy" (Sykes, Oskoz, & Thorne, 2008, p. 539). The two activities in the "Transforming Knowledge" section will lead you to consider how your FL educational practice can both reflect and provide learners greater access to the communicative and social practices associated with Web 2.0 and in the process be truly transformational.

4. TRANSFORMING KNOWLEDGE

4.1 Reflective Journal Entry

For this final journal entry, we ask you to go back to the concept map you created after reading Chapter 1 and revised after reading Chapters 2 and 4. Now that you have developed an understanding of new literacies and their role in FL literacy development, reflect on how they fit within your concept map. Do they play a role in only part of the multiliteracies framework as you have conceptualized it, or do new literacies play a role in all aspects of the framework? What connections can you make between new literacies and existing concepts within the map? Are there concepts that you need to add to or delete from your map? Modify your concept map as necessary and use it as a tool as you reflect on the multiliteracies framework.

4.2 Researching Digital Literacies in the Classroom Context

"Reducing L2 learning to the flat literacies of paper-based resources in the classroom raises questions of authenticity in L2 learning. If teachers are to meaningfully engage L2 learners in communication as it exists in the social world" (Lotherington & Jenson, 2011, p. 228), the new dimensions of literacy presented in this chapter must be woven into classroom learning. In the context of your FL textbook's chapter whose theme is technology, have your students create and carry out a survey of their digital literacy practices and tally the information collected. Have them next write a summary of their findings and present them to the class. Reflect on your students' findings and draw implications for FL multiliteracies instruction and learning. How do your student's practices compare to the practices in your classroom? What could you do to answer Lotherington and Jenson's call?

Key Resources

Jones, R., & Hafner, C. (2012). *Understanding digital literacies: A practical introduction*. New York, NY: Routledge.

As indicated in the title, this book provides an introduction to digital media and digital literacies with a focus on Web. 2.0. Jones and Haffner provide the tools needed to explore and grasp the linguistic and social impact of a range of digital media texts, environments, and practices and include case studies to illustrate each topic.

Reinhardt, J., & Thorne, S. L. (2011). Beyond comparisons: Frameworks for developing digital L2 literacies. In N. Arnold & L. Ducate (Eds.), *Present and future promises of CALL: From theory and research to new directions in language teaching* (pp. 257–280). San Marcos, TX: CALICO Publications.

In this chapter, Reinhardt and Thorne examine the theories behind the concept of digital literacies and focus on several pedagogical frameworks that can be used for their development in the L2 classroom.

van Compernolle, R., & Abraham, L. (2009). Interactional and discursive features of English-language weblogs for language learning and teaching. In L. Abraham & L. Williams (Eds.), *Electronic discourse in language learning and language teaching* (pp. 193–211). Amsterdam, Netherlands: John Benjamins.

In this chapter, van Compernolle and Abraham discuss the use of authentic blogs in the L2 classroom and offer several recommendations on how to design learning opportunities for L2 learners with the purpose of promoting their development of digital literacies

For Further Reading

Abraham, L., & Williams, L. (Eds.). (2009). *Electronic discourse in language learning and language teaching*. Amsterdam, Netherlands: John Benjamins.

Dudeney, G., Hockly, N., & Pegrum, M. (2013). *Digital literacies*. Harlow, England: Pearson Education.

Lankshear, C., & Knobel, M. (2006). *New literacies: Everyday practices and classroom learning*. (2nd ed.). Milton Keynes, England: Open University Press.

APPENDIX

Website

Inanimate Alice: www.inanimatealice.com/
Transcripts (English/Italian)

English

- *Inanimate Alice,* Episode 1: China
  http://inanimatealice.com/education/scripts/InanimateAliceEp1script_English.pdf
- *Inanimate Alice,* Episode 2: Italy
  http://inanimatealice.com/education/scripts/InanimateAliceEp2script_English.pdf
- *Inanimate Alice,* Episode 3: Russia
  http://inanimatealice.com/education/scripts/InanimateAliceEp3script_English.pdf
- *Inanimate Alice,* Episode 4: Hometown
  http://inanimatealice.com/education/scripts/InanimateAliceEp4script_English.pdf

Italian

- *Alice Inanimata,* Episodio 1: Cina
  http://inanimatealice.com/education/scripts/InanimateAliceEp1script_Italian.pdf
- *Alice Inanimata,* Episodio 2: Italia
  http://inanimatealice.com/education/scripts/InanimateAliceEp2script_Italian.pdf
- *Alice Inanimata,* Episodio 3: Russia
  http://inanimatealice.com/education/scripts/InanimateAliceEp3script_Italian.pdf

AFTERWORD

In this book, we have outlined a multiliteracies framework for collegiate foreign language (FL) teaching. This framework represents a unified approach to curriculum and instruction that brings together the two sides of traditionally bifurcated programs through the simultaneous development of language competencies and engagement with authentic texts. Fostering students' FL literacy, conceptualized broadly as "dynamic, culturally and historically situated practices of using and interpreting diverse written and spoken texts to fulfill particular social purposes" (Kern, 2000, p. 6) is the main goal of this approach, and it motivates our ideas related to organizing goals, objectives, instruction, and assessments in FL programs. Equally important to the multiliteracies framework is the act of meaning design, or the process of discovering form–meaning connections through interpretation and creation of written, oral, visual, audiovisual, and digital texts, which underlies all aspects of the theory and pedagogy developed throughout this book. Indeed, it is the ability to design meaning from texts that advances learners' FL literacy development (Kern, 2000). This unified approach to FL teaching and learning, which aligns theoretical concepts (e.g., meaning design, Available Designs) and pedagogical practice (e.g., principles of literacy, pedagogical acts), has allowed us to meet the goals set out at the start of this book: to create coherence in pedagogical approach, assessment practices, and curriculum design; and to enable more holistic, consistent, and effective professionalization of FL teachers.

Throughout, we have challenged you to rethink what you know about FL curriculum, instruction, and assessment and to frame traditional, communicatively oriented concepts within a literacy orientation. We began by asking you to reconsider communicative language teaching (CLT) itself, and to recognize both its important contributions to language teaching and learning as well its limitations and their impact on the current state of affairs in bifurcated FL programs. Next, we encouraged you to rethink your beliefs, experiences, and assumptions related to FL teaching and learning. This practical knowledge served as a basis for reformulating goals, objectives, and assessments in lower-level FL courses according to a multiliteracies orientation and for reflecting on the impact of this orientation on the overall coherence of the undergraduate curriculum. Finally, we asked you to reconsider the teaching of linguistic forms (e.g., grammar, vocabulary) and language modalities (e.g., speaking, writing, reading, viewing). By treating these parts of language in distinct chapters, we did not wish to imply that they should be taught and learned in isolation, as is often the case in CLT-oriented approaches. Rather, our goal was to highlight key research and practice that informed our approach, which treats these language components as overlapping parts of a whole that contribute equally to development of students' FL literacy. Indeed, as Swaffar and Arens (2005) stated,

> [E]vidence in both first- and second-language learning indicates that thinking in terms of skills is a flawed model for language acquisition, because students' cognitive processing of new information becomes more effective and the language material included becomes more memorable when new information can be introduced through multiple modalities. (p. 15)

For instance, rather than viewing grammar as a set of rules to be memorized, we encouraged you to see it as one of a number of linguistic, schematic, visual, audio, gestural, and spatial Available Designs that comprise students' toolkit for designing meaning from texts. We furthermore asked you to reflect on teaching a language modality such as speaking or reading as involving not only student engagement in the learning processes of interpretation, collaboration, problem solving, and reflection, but also recognition of the multimodal nature of communication and the ways in which language modalities overlap with and complement one another.

Although our focus has been primarily on lower-level FL courses, it is not hard to imagine how the multiliteracies framework may be applied to advanced-level language, literature, and culture courses. Throughout this book, we have provided a number of resources to allow you to explore this possibility. A focus on literacy development is consistent with the mission of many FL programs and prepares learners to participate in diverse discourse communities both at home and in the target culture. Indeed, "a literacy orientation creates an intellectual foundation upon which language and literary-cultural content may be merged at all curricular levels and with which faculty from a department's various subdisciplines can identify" (Paesani & Allen, 2012, p. s67). The multiliteracies framework therefore provides a basis for developing coherent curricula that link FL learning with literary–cultural content; address the needs of diverse educational settings, learners, and languages; and articulate goals and objectives accessible to instructors and students (Byrnes, 2008).

Kern (2004) proposed several elements of a literacy-based curriculum that are common across instructional levels and that reflect many of the ideas we have developed throughout this book. First, a literacy-based curriculum must prepare learners to interpret multiple forms and modes of language in various contexts (e.g., oral, written, formal, informal) and must, furthermore, incorporate a range of oral, written, visual, audiovisual, and digital texts. Next, a literacy-based curriculum must develop learners' ability to communicate in the FL and to interpret and transform texts at all curricular levels. The instructional practices that underlie such a curriculum must therefore integrate communicative and text-based approaches. A literacy-based curriculum must also focus on relationships among text types, their purposes, and their conventions and on critical analysis of language use. In doing so, students engage in problem solving related to language use through the acts of textual interpretation and transformation. Finally, a literacy-oriented curriculum must integrate the linguistic, cognitive, and sociocultural dimensions of literacy while also bringing reading and writing into the classroom (rather than relegating them to homework). An important outcome of this approach to curriculum is that it helps lessen "the isolation of the lower-division courses" (Swaffar & Arens, 2005, p. 29) while at the same time providing the foundation for a coherent instructional approach that can be applied across the four-year undergraduate sequence. Furthermore, this approach encourages development of advanced-level language abilities through careful planning of long-term instructional sequences and facilitates determination of specific learning objectives across the undergraduate FL curriculum (Crane, 2006).

As we stated in the Introduction, the multiliteracies framework is conducive to establishing a long-term model of FL teacher professional development, given that the concept of literacy is consistent with both short-term needs for teaching in lower-level courses and long-term needs for future teaching at more advanced levels. Moreover, because a literacy orientation further challenges us to rethink traditional perceptions of linguistic forms, language modalities, and texts, it equips FL instructors with tools for teaching in multiple contexts and for thinking about instruction and assessment from course-level and curricular perspectives.

Nonetheless, we do not assume or anticipate that you are ready to apply the multiliteracies approach to all aspects of your current and future teaching experiences. Instead, we suggest that even though you have reached the end of this book, you are only at the start of your development as a teacher–scholar. We understand that this is a challenging approach and that you may still be feeling overwhelmed and uncertain about how to apply the theoretical concepts and pedagogical tools you have learned to your daily lesson plans in order to develop your students' FL literacy. Research on conceptual development related to teaching supports the feelings you may have. Indeed, the ability to develop and apply conceptual knowledge is a gradual process requiring sustained and long-term reflection, collaboration with peers and experts, and scaffolded learning (Allen, 2011; Johnson, 2009). In spite of these challenges, an important benefit of implementing the multiliteracies framework in multiple contexts over time is your increased agency related to pedagogical practice. For instance, Allen (2011) found that instructors who had developed conceptual understanding of the multiliteracies approach were better able to respond to the limitations of lower-level textbooks, to apply literacy-based concepts to assessment practices, and to share examples of text-based teaching with peers.

To conclude, we encourage you to gradually apply the multiliteracies-based concepts and tools you have learned in your everyday teaching and to continually reflect on your developing conceptual understanding and pedagogical practices. As a starting point, implement the lessons you developed in Chapters 3 through 8, discuss the teaching challenges and successes you faced with peers and professors, and revise your lessons to incorporate new understandings (Allen & Dupuy, 2013). Likewise, take advantage of opportunities to apply literacy-based concepts and tools to articulation of goals and objectives, curriculum or course design, or creation of course assessments. In doing so, you will contribute to the foundation you have built through reading this book, a foundation that can serve you throughout your career as a teacher–scholar, whether you work as a graduate teaching assistant, a part-time instructor, a professor specializing in literature, a language program director, or an educational researcher.

REFERENCES

Abraham, L., & Williams, L. (Eds.). (2009). *Electronic discourse in language learning and language teaching*. Amsterdam, Netherlands: John Benjamins.

Adair-Hauck, B., & Donato, R. (2010). Using a story-based approach to teach grammar. In J. Shrum & E. Glisan (Authors), *Teachers handbook: Contextualized foreign language instruction* (4th ed.) (pp. 216–243). Boston, MA: Heinle.

Allen, H. W. (2008). Textbook materials and foreign language teaching: Perspectives from the classroom. *The NECTFL Review, 62*, 5–28.

Allen, H. W. (2009). A literacy-based approach to the advanced French writing course. *The French Review, 83*(2), 368–387.

Allen, H. W. (2011). Embracing literacy-based teaching: A longitudinal study of the conceptual development of novice foreign language teachers. In K. E. Johnson & P. R. Golombek (Eds.), *Sociocultural research on second language teacher education: Exploring the complexities of professional development* (pp. 86–101). New York, NY: Routledge.

Allen, H. W., & Dupuy, B. (2013). Evolving notions of literacy-based foreign language teaching: A qualitative study of graduate student instructors. In H. W. Allen & H. H. Maxim (Eds.), *Educating the future foreign language professoriate for the 21st century* (pp. 171–190). Boston, MA: Heinle.

Allen, H. W., & Paesani, K. (2010). Exploring the feasibility of a pedagogy of multiliteracies in introductory foreign language courses. *L2 Journal, 2*(1), 119–142.

Allen, H. W., & Paesani, K. (in press). "Invitation au voyage": A multiliteracies approach to teaching genre. In C. Krueger (Ed.), *Approaches to teaching Baudelaire's prose poems*. New York, NY: Modern Language Association of America.

Alm, A. (2008). Integrating emerging technologies in the foreign language classroom: A case study. *International Journal of Pedagogies and Learning, 4*, 44–60.

Altman, R. (1989). *The video connection: Integrating video in language teaching*. Boston, MA: Houghton Mifflin.

Anderson Imbert, E. (1976). *Cuento en miniature: Antología*. Caracas, Venezuela: Equinoccio, Universidad Simon Bolivar.

Antón, M. (1999). The discourse of a learner-centered classroom: Sociocultural perspectives on teacher-learner interaction in the second-language classroom. *Modern Language Journal, 83*, 303–318.

Arens, K. (2008). Genres and the Standards: Teaching the 5 Cs through texts. *German Quarterly, 81*(1), 35–48.

Arens, K. (2010). The field of culture: The Standards as a model for teaching culture. *Modern Language Journal, 94*, 321–324.

Arnold, N. (2007). Technology-mediated learning 10 years later: Emphasizing pedagogical or utilitarian applications. *Foreign Language Annals, 40*, 161–181.

Arnold, N., Ducate, L., & Kost, C. (2009). Collaborative writing in wikis: Insights from culture in German classes. In L. Lomicka & G. Lord (Eds.), *The next generation: Social networking and online collaboration in foreign language learning* (pp. 115–144). San Marcos, TX: CALICO Publications.

Arnold, N., Ducate, L., & Kost, C. (2012). Collaboration or cooperation? Analyzing group dynamics and revision processes in wikis. *CALICO Journal, 29*, 431–448.

Aski, J. M. (2003). FL textbook activities: Keeping pace with second language acquisition research. *Foreign Language Annals, 36*, 57–65.

Askildon, V. (2008). *What do teachers and students want from a foreign language textbook?* (Unpublished doctoral dissertation). University of Arizona, Tucson, AZ.

Atay, D., & Kurt, G. (2006). Elementary school EFL learners' vocabulary learning: The effects of post-reading activities. *Canadian Modern Language Review, 63*, 255–273.

Bachman, L. F. (1990). *Fundamental considerations in language testing*. Oxford, England: Oxford University Press.

Bachman, L. F. (2000). Modern language testing at the turn of the century: Assuring that what we count counts. *Language Testing 17*, 1–42.

Bachman, L. F., & Palmer, A. S. (1996). *Language testing in practice: Designing and developing useful language tests*. Oxford, England: Oxford University Press.

Bakhtin, M. (1986). *Speech genres and other late essays*. Austin, TX: University of Texas Press.

Baldo, A., Gallardo, H., & Imbert, E. (Producers), & Bemberg, M. L. (Director). (1984). *Camila*. Argentina/Spain: A Gea Cinematográfica–Impala Co-Production.

Barrette, C. M., Paesani, K., & Vinall, K. (2010). Toward an integrated curriculum: Maximizing the use of target language literature. *Foreign Language Annals, 42*, 216-230.

Barnes, D. (1992). *From communicating to curriculum*. Portsmouth, NH: Boynton/Cook.

Barthes, R. (1977). The death of the author. In *Image, music and text: Essays selected and translated by Stephen Heath* (pp. 142–148). London, England: Fontana. Retrieved from www.scribd.com/doc/13270483/Barthes-ImageMusicText

Bartlett, F. C. (1932). *Remembering: A study in experimental and social psychology*. Cambridge, England: Cambridge University Press.

Bauer, B., deBenedette, L., Furstenberg, G., Levet, S., & Waryn, S. (2006). The Cultura project. In J. A. Belz & S. L. Thorne (Eds.), *Internet-mediated intercultural foreign language education. Issues in language program direction* (pp. 31–62). Boston, MA: Heinle.

Belcher, D., & Hirvela, A. (Eds.) (2008). *The oral–literate connection: Perspectives on L2 speaking, writing, and other media interaction*. Ann Arbor, MI: University of Michigan Press.

Bernhardt, E. (1991). *Reading development in a second language*. Norwood, NJ: Ablex.

Bernhardt, E. (2005). Progress and procrastination in second language reading. *Annual Review of Applied Linguistics, 25*, 133–150.

Black, R. (2005). Access and affiliation: The literacy and composition practices of English-language learners in an online fanfiction community. *Journal of Adolescent & Adult Literacy, 48*, 118–128.

Black, R. (2006). Language, culture and identity in online fanfiction. *E–Learning and Digital Media, 3*, 170–184. Retrieved from www.wwwords.co.uk/pdf/validate.asp?j=elea&vol=3&issue=2&year=2006&article=5_Black_ELEA_3_2_web

Black, R. (2008). *Adolescents and online fan fiction*. New York, NY: Peter Lang.

Blattner, G., & Fiori, M. (2011). Virtual social network communities: An investigation of language learners' development of sociopragmatic awareness and multiliteracy skills. *CALICO Journal, 29*, 24–43.

Blattner, G., & Lomicka, L. (2012). Facebook-ing and the social generation: A new era of language learning. *Alsic, 15*, 1–25. Retrieved from http://alsic.revues.org/2413

Bloch, J. (2007). Abdullah's blogging: A generation 1.5 student enters the blogosphere. *Language Learning & Technology, 11*, 128–141. Retrieved from www.llt.msu.edu/vol11num2/bloch/default.html

Bloch, J., & Crosby, C. (2008). Blogging and academic writing development. In F. Zhang & B. Barber (Eds.), *Handbook of research on computer-enhanced language acquisition and learning* (pp. 36–47). Hershey, PA: Information Science Reference.

Blyth, C., & Davis, J. (2007). Using formative evaluation in the development of learner-centered materials. *CALICO Journal, 25*, 48–68.

Boardman, M. (2005). *The language of websites*. New York, NY: Routledge.

Bolanos, E. (2012). A comparison of the reading strategies used by good readers in print and hypertext environments: Implications and recommendations for the improvement of reading instruction. *TESOL Journal, 7*, 2–9.

Bournot-Trites, M., & Séror, J. (2003). Students' and teachers' perceptions about strategies which promote proficiency in second language writing. *Canadian Journal of Applied Linguistics, 6*(2), 129–157.

Boyd, M. P., & Rubin, D. L. (2002). Elaborated student talk in an elementary ESL classroom. *Research in the Teaching of English, 36*, 495–530.

Brandl, K. (2008). *Communicative language teaching in action: Putting principles to work.* Upper Saddle River, NJ: Prentice Hall.

Bridges, E. (2009). Bridging the gap: A literacy-oriented approach to teaching the graphic novel *Die erste frühling*. *Der Unterrichtspraxis/Teaching German, 42*, 152–161.

Broady, E. (2008). Fragmentation and consolidation: Recent articles on vocabulary acquisition. *Language Learning Journal, 36*, 259–265.

Brooks, F. B., & Donato, R. (1994). Vygotskian approaches to understanding foreign language learner discourse during communicative tasks. *Hispania, 77*, 262–274.

Brooks, F. B., Donato, R., & McGlone, J. V. (1997). When are they going to say "it" right? Understanding learner talk during pair-work activity. *Foreign Language Annals, 30*, 524–541.

Brown, D. (2010). What aspects of vocabulary knowledge do textbooks give attention to? *Language Teaching Research, 15*, 83–97.

Bruns, A. (2008). *Blogs, Wikipedia, Second Life, and beyond: From production to produsage.* New York, NY: Peter Lang.

Buck, G. (2001). *Assessing listening.* Cambridge, England: Cambridge University Press.

Bueno, K. (2006). Stepping out of the comfort zone: Profiles of third-year Spanish students' attempts to develop their speaking skills. *Foreign Language Annals, 39*, 451–470.

Bueno, K. (2009). Got film? Is it a readily accessible window to the target language and culture for your students? *Foreign Language Annals, 42*, 318–339.

Burbules, N., & Callister, T. (2000). *Watch IT: The promises and risks of information technologies for education.* Boulder, CO: Westview Press.

Burns, A. (1998). Teaching speaking. *Annual Review of Applied Linguistics, 18*, 102–123.

Byrnes, H. (2001). Articulating foreign language programs: The need for new curricular bases. In C. G. Lally (Ed.), *Foreign language program articulation: Current practice and future prospects* (pp. 63–77). Westport, CT: Bergin & Garvey.

Byrnes, H. (Ed.) (2006). Perspectives: Interrogating communicative competence as a framework for collegiate foreign language study. *Modern Language Journal, 90*, 244–266.

Byrnes, H. (2008). Articulating a foreign language sequence through content: A look at the culture standards. *Language Teaching, 41*, 103–118.

Byrnes, H. (2013). Positioning writing as meaning-making in writing research: An introduction. *Journal of Second Language Writing, 22*, 95–106.

Byrnes, H., Crane, C., Maxim, H. H., & Sprang, K. (2006). Taking text to task: Issues and choices in curriculum construction. *International Journal of Applied Linguistics, 152*, 85–110.

Byrnes, H., Maxim, H. H., & Norris, J. (2010). Realizing advanced foreign language writing development in collegiate education: Curricular design, pedagogy, assessment. *Modern Language Journal, 94*, Supplement, 1–221.

Canale, M. (1983). From communicative competence to communicative language pedagogy. In J. C. Richards & R. W. Schmidt (Eds.), *Language and communication* (pp. 2–27). London, England: Longman.

Canale, M., & Swain, M. (1980). Theoretical bases of communicative approaches to foreign language teaching and testing. *Applied Linguistics, 1*, 1–47.

Carrell, P. L., & Eisterhold, J. C. (1983). Schema theory and ESL reading pedagogy. *TESOL Quarterly, 17*, 553–573.

Cazden, C. B. (1988). *Classroom discourse.* Portsmouth, NH: Heinemann.

Celce-Murcia, M. (1991). Grammar pedagogy in second and foreign language teaching. *TESOL Quarterly, 25*, 459–480.

Celce-Murcia, M. (1995). The elaboration of sociolinguistic competence: Implications for teacher education. In J. E. Alatis, C. A. Straehle, & M. Ronkin (Eds.), *Linguistics and the education of language teachers: Ethnolinguistic, psycholinguistic, and sociolinguistic aspects. Proceedings of the Georgetown University Round Table on Languages and Linguistics* (pp. 699–710). Washington, DC: Georgetown University Press.

Celce-Murcia, M. (2007). Rethinking the role of communicative competence in language teaching. In E. Alcón Soler & M. P. Safont Jordà (Eds.), *Intercultural language use and language learning* (pp. 41–57). Dordrecht, Netherlands: Springer.

Celce-Murcia, M., Dörnyei, Z., & Thurrell, S. (1995). Communicative competence: A pedagogically motivated model with content specifications. *Issues in Applied Linguistics, 6*(2), 5–35.

Chen, Q., & Donin, J. (1997). Discourse processing of first and second language biology texts: Effects of language proficiency and domain-specific knowledge. *Modern Language Journal, 81*, 209–227.

Chun, D. (2011). Developing intercultural communicative competence through online exchanges. *CALICO Journal, 28*, 392–419.

Clark, J. E. (2010). The digital imperative: Making the case for a 21st century pedagogy. *Computers and Composition, 27*, 23–35.

Coiro, J. (2003) Exploring literacy on the Internet. *The Reading Teacher, 56*, 458–464.

Coiro, J., & Dobler, E. (2007). Exploring the online reading comprehension strategies used by sixth-grade skilled readers to search for and locate information on the Internet. *Reading Research Quarterly, 42*, 214–257.

Coiro, J., Knobel, M., Lankshear, C., & Leu, D. J. (2008). *The handbook of research on new literacies*. Mahwah, NJ: Erlbaum.

Cook, V. (1999). Going beyond the native speaker in language teaching. *TESOL Quarterly, 33*, 185–209.

Cope, B., & Kalantzis, M. (1993). Introduction: How a genre approach to literacy can transform the way writing is taught. In B. Cope & M. Kalantiz (Eds.), *The powers of literacy: A genre approach to teaching writing* (pp. 1–21). London, England: The Falmer Press.

Cope, B., & Kalantzis, M. (2009). 'Multiliteracies': New literacies, new learning. *Pedagogies, 4*(3), 164–194.

Crane, C. (2006). Modelling a genre-based foreign language curriculum: Staging advanced L2 learning. In H. Byrnes (Ed.), *Advanced language learning: The contribution of Halliday and Vygotsky* (pp. 227–245). London, England: Continuum.

Cross, J. (2009). Effects of listening strategy instruction on news videotext comprehension. *Language Teaching Research, 13*, 151–176.

Cross, J. (2011). Comprehending news videotexts: The influence of the visual content. *Language Learning & Technology, 15*, 44–68.

Danan, M. (2004). Captioning and subtitling: Undervalued language learning strategies. *Meta, 49*, 67–77.

Delerm, P. (1997). *La première gorgée de bière et autres plaisirs minuscules*. Paris, France: Gallimard.

Denevi, M. (1974). *Salón de lectura*. Buenos Aires, Argentina: Librería Huemal.

Department of German. (2011). Curriculum. *Georgetown University*. Retrieved from http://german.georgetown.edu/undergraduate/curriculum/

Diehl, W., & Prins, E. (2008). Unintended outcomes in Second Life: Intercultural literacy and cultural identity in a virtual world. *Language and Intercultural Communication, 8*, 101–118.

Donato, R., & Brooks, F. C. (2004). Literary discussions and advanced speaking functions: Researching the (dis)connection. *Foreign Language Annals, 37*, 183–199.

Dörnyei, Z. (2009). Communicative language teaching in the 21st century: The 'principled communicative approach.' *Perspectives, 36*(2), 33–43.

Dotson, E. K. (2010). The effects of deductive and guided inductive approaches on the learning of grammar in an advanced college French course. (Unpublished doctoral dissertation). Emory University, Atlanta, GA.

Doughty, C., & Pica, K. (1986). "Information gap" tasks: Do they facilitate second language acquisition? *TESOL Quarterly, 20*, 305–325.

Dubreil, S. (2011). Rebel with a cause: (Re)defining identities and culture in contemporary French cinema. *L2 Journal, 3*, 176–200.

Ducate, L., & Lomicka, L. (2005). Exploring the blogosphere: Use of web logs in the foreign language classroom. *Foreign Language Annals, 38*, 410–422.

Ducate, L., & Lomicka, L. (2008). Adventures in the blogosphere: From blog readers to blog writers. *Computer Assisted Language Learning, 21*, 9–28.

Ducate, L., Lomicka, L., & Moreno, N. (2011). Wading through the world of wikis. *Foreign Language Annals, 44*, 495–524.

Dudeney, G., Hockly, N., & Pegrum, M. (2013). *Digital literacies*. Harlow, England: Pearson Education.

Duff, P. (2014). Communicative language teaching. In M. Celce-Murcia, D. Brinton, & M. A. Snow (Eds.), *Teaching English as a second or foreign language* (4th ed.) (pp. 15–30). Boston, MA: Cengage.

Eken, A. N. (2001). The third eye. *Journal of Adolescent and Adult Literacy, 46*, 220–230.

Ellis, N. (2002). Frequency effects in language processing: A review with implications for theories of implicit and explicit language acquisition. *Studies in Second Language Acquisition, 24*, 143–188.

Ellis, R. (2006). Modelling learning difficulty in second language proficiency: The differential contributions of implicit and explicit knowledge. *Applied Linguistics, 27*, 431–463.

Elola, I., & Oskoz, A. (2008). Blogging: Fostering intercultural competence development in foreign language and study abroad contexts. *Foreign Language Annals, 41*, 421–444.

Elola, I., & Oskoz, A. (2010). Collaborative writing: Fostering foreign language and writing conventions development. *Language Learning & Technology, 14*, 51–71. Retrieved from http://llt.msu.edu/issues/october2010/elolaoskoz.pdf

Etienne, C., & Vanbaelen, S. (2006). Paving the way to literary analysis through TV commercials. *Foreign Language Annals, 39*, 87–98.

Fellner, T., & Apple, M. (2006). Developing writing fluency and lexical complexity with blogs. *The JALT CALL Journal, 2*, 15–26.

Firth, A. (2009). Doing *not* being a foreign language learner: English as a *lingua franca* in the workplace and (some) implications for SLA. *International Review of Applied Linguistics in Language Teaching, 47*, 127–156.

Firth, A., & Wagner, J. (1997). On discourse, communication, and (some) fundamental concepts in SLA research. *Modern Language Journal, 81*, 285–300.

Firth, A., & Wagner, J. (2007). Second/foreign language learning as social accomplishment: Elaborations on a reconceptualized SLA. *Modern Language Journal, 91*, 800–819.

Fish, S. (1980). *Is there a text in this class? The authority of interpretive communities*. Cambridge, MA: Harvard University Press.

Flowerdew, J., & Miller, L. (2005). *Second language listening: Theory and practice*. Cambridge, England: Cambridge University Press.

Fragua, C. (Producer), & Távora, P. (Director). (2004). *Yerma*. Spain: Artimagen: Cenemateca Literaria, Condor Media, Inc.

Furman, N., Goldberg, D., & Lusin, N. (2007). *Enrollments in languages other than English in United States institutions of higher education, Fall 2006*. New York, NY: Modern Language Association of America.

Furman, N., Goldberg, D., & Lusin, N. (2010). *Enrollments in languages other than English in United States institutions of higher education, Fall 2009*. New York, NY: Modern Language Association of America.

Furstenberg, G., Level, S., English, K., & Maillet, K. (2001). Giving a virtual voice to the silent language of culture: The Cultura project. *Language Learning & Technology, 5*, 55–102. Retrieved from www.llt.msu.edu/vol5num1/furstenberg/default.pdf

Gass, S. M., & Mackey, A. (2007). Input, interaction, and output in second language acquisition. In B. VanPatten & J. Williams (Eds.), *Theories in second language acquisition: An introduction* (pp. 175–199). Mahwah, NJ: Lawrence Erlbaum.

Gee, J. P. (2004). *Situated language and learning: A critique of traditional schooling*. New York, NY: Routledge.

Gee, J. P. (2005). Semiotic social spaces and affinity spaces: From the age of mythology to today's schools. In D. Barton & K. Tusting (Eds.), *Beyond communities of practice: Language, power and social context* (pp. 214–232). Cambridge, England: Cambridge University Press.

Gee, J. P. (2011). *Social linguistics and literacies: Ideology in discourses* (4th ed.). New York, NY: Routledge.

Gee, J. P. (2012). *Social linguistics and literacies: Ideology in discourses* (4th ed.). New York, NY: Routledge.

Ginther, A. (2002). Context and content visuals and performance on listening comprehension stimuli. *Language Testing, 19*, 133–167.

Goldenberg, C. (1991). Instructional conversations and their classroom application (Educational Practice Report No. 2). Santa Cruz, CA: National Center for Research on Cultural Diversity and Second Language Learning.

Gonglewski, M. (2001). Hypermedia: Enriching L2 compositions. In G. Brauer (Ed.), *Pedagogy of language learning in higher education: An introduction* (pp. 109–126). Westport, CT: Ablex Publishing.

Grabe, W., & Stoller, F. L. (2002). *Teaching and researching reading*. Harlow, England: Longman/Pearson Education.

Graves, K. (1999). *Designing language courses: A guide for teachers*. Boston, MA: Heinle.

Gruba, P. (2004). Understanding digitized second language videotext. *Computer Assisted Language Learning, 17*, 51–82.

Gruba, P. (2005). *Developing media literacy in the L2 classroom*. Sydney, Australia: Macquarie University, National Centre for English Teaching and Research.

Gruba, P. (2006). Playing the videotext: A media literacy perspective on video-mediated L2 listening. *Language Learning & Technology, 10*, 77–92.

Gruba, P. (2007). Exploring media literacy research in Australian ESL contexts: A review paper. *University of Sydney Papers in TESOL, 2*, 167–191.

Gruber-Miller, J. (2013). Engaging multiple literacies through remix practices: Vergil recomposed. *Teaching Classical Languages, 4*, 141–161.

Guichon, N., & McLornan, S. (2008). The effects of multimodality on L2 learners: Implications for CALL resource design. *System, 36*, 85–93.

Guilloteau, N. (2010). Vocabulary. In C. Blyth (Ed.), *Foreign language teaching methods*. Austin, TX: Texas Language Technology Center, University of Texas at Austin. Retrieved from www.coerll.utexas.edu/methods/

Günther, H. (2001). *Grenzgänger.* Ravensberg, Germany: Ravenburger Buchverlag.

Haight, C. E., Herron, C., & Cole, S. P. (2007). The effect of deductive and guided inductive instructional approaches on the learning of grammar in the elementary foreign language classroom. *Foreign Language Annals, 40*, 288–310.

Hall, J. K. (1995). "Aw, man, where you goin'?": Classroom interaction and the development of L2 interactional competence. *Issues in Applied Linguistics, 6*, 37–62.

Hall, J. K. (1998). Differential teacher attention to student response: The construction of different opportunities for learning in the IRF. *Linguistics and Education, 9*, 287–311.

Hall, J. K. (2001). *Methods for teaching foreign languages: Creating a community of learners in the classroom*. Upper Saddle River, NJ: Prentice Hall.

Hall, J. K. (2004). "Practicing speaking" in Spanish: Lessons from a high school foreign language classroom. In D. Boxer & A. Cohen (Eds.), *Studying speaking to inform second language learning* (pp. 68–87). Clevedon, England: Multilingual Matters.

Halliday, M. A. K. (1978). *Language as social semiotic.* London, England: Edward Arnold.

Halliday, M. A. K. (1987). Spoken and written modes of meaning. In R. Horowitz & S. J. Samuels (Eds.), *Comprehending oral and written language* (pp. 55–82). San Diego, CA: Academic Press, Inc.

Hammadou, J. A. (1991). Interrelationships among prior knowledge, inference, and language proficiency in foreign language reading. *Modern Language Journal, 75*, 27–38.

Hammadou, J. A. (2002). Advanced foreign language readers' inferencing. In J. A. Hammadou (Ed.), *Literacy and the second language learner* (pp. 217–238). Greenwich, CT: Information Age Publishing.

Hammer, J., & Swaffar, J. (2012). Assessing strategic cultural competency: Holistic approaches to student learning through media. *Modern Language Journal, 96*, 209–233.

Haneda, M. (1997). Second language learning in a 'community of practice': A case study of adult Japanese learners. *The Canadian Modern Language Review/La Revue canadienne des langues vivantes, 54*, 11–27.

Hanna, B., & de Nooy, J. (2003). A funny thing happened on the way to the forum: Electronic discussion and foreign language learning. *Language Learning & Technology, 7*, 71–85. Retrieved from http://llt.msu.edu/vol7num1/hanna/default.html

Harley, B., & Swain, M. (1984). The interlanguage of immersion students and its implications for second language teaching. In A. Davies, C. Criper, & A. P. R. Howatt (Eds.), *Interlanguage* (pp. 291–311). Edinburgh, Scotland: Edinburgh University Press.

Harmer, J. (2007). *The practice of English language teaching* (4th ed.). London, England: Longman.

Hauck, M., & Young, B. (2008). Telecollaboration in multimodal environments: The impact on task design and learner interaction. *Computer Assisted Language Learning, 21*, 87–124.

Hedgcock, J. S., & Ferris, D. R. (2009). *Teaching readers of English: Students, texts, and contexts.* New York, NY: Routledge.

Herring, S. C. (2007). A faceted classification scheme for computer-mediated discourse. *Language@Internet, 4*, Article 1. Retrieved from www.languageatinternet.org/articles/2007/761/

Herron, C., & Seay, I. (1991). The effect of authentic oral texts on student listening comprehension in the foreign language classroom. *Foreign Language Annals, 24*, 487–495.

Herron, C., & Tomasello, M. (1992). Acquiring grammatical structures by guided induction. *The French Review, 65*, 708–718.

Hicks, D. (2003). Discourse, teaching and learning. *Open University.* Retrieved from http://labspace.open.ac.uk/course/view.php?id=7134

Holland, N. N. (1975). *5 readers reading.* New Haven, CT: Yale University Press.

Horwitz, E. K. (1988). The beliefs about language learning of beginning university foreign language students. *Modern Language Journal, 72*, 283–294.

Housen, A., Kuiken, F., & Vedder, I. (2012). Complexity, accuracy and fluency: Definitions, measurement, and research. In A. Housen, F. Kuiken, & I. Vedder (Eds.). *Dimensions of L2 performance and proficiency: Complexity, accuracy, and fluency in SLA* (pp. 1–20). Amsterdam, Netherlands: John Benjamins.

Huang, S., Eslami, Z., & Willson, V. (2012). The effects of task involvement load on L2 incidental vocabulary learning: A meta-analytic study. *Modern Language Journal, 96*, 544–557.

Hyland, K. (2001). *Genre and second language writing.* Ann Arbor, MI: University of Michigan Press.

Hyland, K. (2007). Genre pedagogy: Language, literacy, and writing instruction. *Journal of Second Language Writing 16*, 148–164.

Hyland, K. (2011). Learning to write: Issues in theory, research, and pedagogy. In R. M. Manchón, R.M. (Ed.), *Learning to write and writing to learn in an additional language* (pp. 17–35). Amsterdam, Netherlands: John Benjamins.

Hymes, D. (1972). On communicative competence. In J. B. Pride & J. Holmes (Eds.), *Sociolinguistics* (pp. 53–73). Harmondsworth, England: Penguin Books.

Iser, W. (1974). *The implied reader: Patterns of communication in prose fiction from Bunyan to Beckett.* Baltimore, MD: Johns Hopkins University Press.

Jacobs, G. M., & Farrell, T. S. C. (2003). Understanding and implementing the CLT (communicative language teaching) paradigm. *RELC Journal, 34*(1), 5–30.

Jaén, M. M., & Bastanta, C. P. (2009). Developing conversational competence through language awareness and multimodality: The use of DVDs. *ReCALL, 21*, 283–301.

Jean, G., & Simard, D. (2011). Grammar teaching and learning in L2: Necessary but boring? *Foreign Language Annals, 44*, 467–494.

Johnson, K. E. (2003). Let's make a deal: A sample project for advanced ESL learners. *CALPER Pedagogical Materials Project Work, No 1.* The Pennsylvania State University, PA: Center for Advanced Proficiency Education and Research.

Johnson, K. E. (2009). *Second language teacher education: A sociocultural perspective.* New York, NY: Routledge.

Joiner, E. G. (1990). Choosing and using videotexts. *Foreign Language Annals, 23*, 53–64.

Jones, R., & Hafner, C. (2012). *Understanding digital literacies: A practical introduction.* New York, NY: Routledge.

Kagan, S. (1989). *Cooperative learning: Resources for teachers.* San Juan Capistrano, CA: Resources for Teachers.

Kaiser, M. (2011). New approaches to exploiting film in the foreign language classroom. *L2 Journal, 3*, 232–249.

Kalantzis, M., & Cope, B. (n.d.). Kalantzis and Cope on differentiated literacies instruction. Retrieved from www.newlearningonline.com/literacies/chapter-14/kalantzis-and-cope-on-differentiated-literacies-instruction

Kalantzis, M., & Cope, B. (2012) The knowledge processes. *New Learning: Transformational designs for pedagogy and assessment.* Retrieved from www.newlearningonline.com/learning-by-design/the-knowledge-processes

Kalantzis, M., Cope, B., & Harvey, A. (2003). Assessing multiliteracies and the new basics. *Assessment in Education, 10*, 15–26.

Katz, S., & Blyth, C. (2007). *Teaching French grammar in context: Theory and practice.* New Haven, CT: Yale University Press.

Keller, E., & Warner, S. (2005). *Gambits 2: Conversational tools.* Ottawa, Canada: Canada School of Public Service.

Kelton, K., Guilloteau, N., & Blyth, C. (2004). *Français interactif: An online introductory French course.* Retrieved from www.laits.utexas.edu/fi

Kern, R. (2000). *Literacy and language teaching.* Oxford, England: Oxford University Press.

Kern, R. (2002). Reconciling the language–literature split through literacy. *ADFL Bulletin 33*(3), 20–24.

Kern, R. (2003). Literacy as a new organizing principle for foreign language education. In P. C. Patrikis (Ed.), *Reading between the lines: Perspectives on foreign language literacy* (pp. 40–59). New Haven, CT: Yale University Press.

Kern, R. (2004). Literacy and advanced foreign language learning: Rethinking the curriculum. In H. Byrnes & H. H. Maxim (Eds.), *Advanced foreign language learning: A challenge to college programs* (pp. 2–18). Boston, MA: Heinle.

Kern, R. (2008). Making connections through texts in language teaching. *Language Teaching, 41*, 367–387.

Kern, R., & Schultz, J. M. (2005). Beyond orality: Investigating literacy and the literary in second and foreign language instruction. *Modern Language Journal, 89*, 381–392.

Kessler, G. (2009). Student initiated attention to form in wiki based collaborative writing. *Language Learning & Technology, 13*, 79–95. Retrieved from www.llt.msu.edu/vol13num1/kessler.pdf

Kessler, G. (2013). Collaborative language learning in co-constructed participatory culture. *CALICO Journal, 30*, 307–322.

Kessler, G., & Bikowski, D. (2010). Developing collaborative autonomous learning abilities in computer mediated language learning: Attention to meaning among students in wiki space. *Computer Assisted Language Learning, 23*, 41–58.

Konishi, M. (2003). Strategies for reading hypertext by Japanese ESL learners. *The Reading Matrix, 3*, 97–119.

Kramsch, C. (1988). The cultural discourse of FL textbooks. In A. J. Singerman (Ed.), *Toward a new integration of language and culture* (pp. 63–88). Middlebury, VT: Northeast Conference on the Teaching of Foreign Languages.

Kramsch, C. (1993). *Context and culture in language teaching*. Oxford, England: Oxford University Press.

Kramsch, C. (2006). From communicative competence to symbolic competence. *Modern Language Journal, 90*, 249–252.

Kramsch, C., & Andersen, R. (1999). Teaching text and context through multimedia. *Language Learning & Technology,* 2, 31–42.

Kramsch, C., A'Ness, F., & Lam, E. (2000). Authenticity and authorship in the computer-mediated acquisition of L2 literacy. *Language Learning & Technology, 4*, 78–104. Retrieved from http://llt.msu.edu/vol4num2/kramsch/default.html

Kramsch, C., A'Ness, F., & Lam, W. S. E. (2001). Technology, language, and literacy: The new pedagogical challenge. In R. De Cellia, H. J. Krumm, & R. Wodak, (Eds.) *Loss of communication in the information age* (pp. 117–129). Vienna, Austria: Austrian Academy of Sciences.

Krashen, S. (1981). *Second language acquisition and second language learning*. Oxford, England: Oxford University Press.

Krashen, S. (1982). *Principles and practices in second language acquisition*. Oxford, England: Pergamon.

Krashen, S. (1985). *The input hypothesis: Issues and complications*. London, England: Longman.

Kress, G. (2000). Design and transformation: New theories of meaning. In B. Cope & M. Kalantzis (Eds.), *Multiliteracies: Literacy learning and the design of social futures* (pp. 153–161). New York, NY: Routledge.

Kress, G. R. (2003) *Literacy in the new media age*. New York, NY: Routledge.

Kress, G. R. (2005). Gains and losses: New forms of texts, knowledge, and learning. *Computers and Composition, 22*, 5–22.

Kress, G. R. (2009). *Multimodality: A social semiotic approach to contemporary communication*. New York, NY: Routledge.

Kress, G. R., & van Leeuwen, T. (2001). *Multimodal discourse: The modes and media of contemporary communication*. London, England: Edward Arnold.

Kress, G. R., & van Leeuwen, T. (2006). *Reading images: The grammar of visual design* (2nd. ed.). New York, NY: Routledge.

Kucer, S. B. (2009). *Dimensions of literacy: A conceptual base for teaching reading and writing in school settings* (3rd ed.). New York, NY: Routledge.

Kucer, S. B., & Silva, C. (2006). *Teaching the dimensions of literacy.* New York, NY: Routledge.

Kumaravadivelu, B. (1994). The postmethod condition: (E)merging strategies for second/foreign language teaching. *TESOL Quarterly, 28*, 27–48.

Lam, W. S. E. (2000). Second language literacy and the design of the self: A case study of a teenager writing on the Internet. *TESOL Quarterly, 34*, 457–483.

Lankshear, C. (1999). Literacy studies in education: Disciplined developments in a post-disciplinary age. In M. Peters (Ed.), *After the disciplines: The emergence of culture studies* (pp. 199–228). Westport, CT: Greenwood Press.

Lankshear, C., & Knobel, M. (2003). *New literacies: Changing knowledge and classroom learning*. Maidenhead, England: Open University Press.

Lankshear, C., & Knobel, M. (2006). *New literacies: Everyday practices and classroom learning* (2nd ed.) Milton Keynes, England: Open University Press.

Lankshear, C., & Knobel, M. (Eds.). (2007). *A new literacies sampler (New literacies and digital epistemologies)*. New York, NY: Peter Lang.

Lantolf, J. P. (2011). The sociocultural approach to second language acquisition. In D. Atkinson (Ed.). *Alternative approaches to second language acquisition* (pp. 24–47). New York, NY: Routledge.

Lantolf, J. P., & Johnson, K. E. (2007). Extending Firth and Wagner's (1997) ontological perspective to L2 classroom praxis and teacher education. *Modern Language Journal, 91*(s1), 877–892.

Lantolf, J. P., & Thorne, S. L. (2006). *Sociocultural theory and the genesis of L2 development*. Oxford, England: Oxford University Press.

Lapkin, S., Hart, D., & Swain, M. (1991). Early and middle French immersion programs: French-language outcomes. *Canadian Modern Language Review, 48*, 11–40.

Lave, J. (1996). Teaching, as learning, in practice. *Mind, Culture, and Activity, 3*, 149–164.

Lave, J., & Wenger, E. (1991). *Situated learning: Legitimate peripheral participation*. Cambridge, England: Cambridge University Press.

Lee, J., & VanPatten, B. (2003). *Making communicative language teaching happen* (2nd ed.). New York, NY: McGraw-Hill.

Lee, L. (2010a). Fostering reflective writing and interactive exchange through blogging in an advanced language course. *ReCALL, 22*, 212–227.

Lee, L. (2010b). Exploring wiki-mediated collaborative writing: A case study in an elementary Spanish course. *CALICO Journal, 27*, 260–276.

Lefkowitz, N. (2009). The future of foreign language writing. Colloquium paper presented at the Symposium on Second Language Writing, Tempe, AZ.

Lenhart, A., Purcell, K., Smith, A., & Zickhur, K. (2010). Social media and young adults report. Retrieved from www.pewinternet.org/Reports/2010/Social-Media-and-Young-Adults.aspx

Lessig, L. (2007). Laws that choke creativity. TED Talk. Retrieved from www.new.ted.com/talks/larry_lessig_says_the_law_is_strangling_creativity

Leu, D., Kinzer, C. K., Coiro, J., & Cammak, D. (2004). Toward a theory of new literacies emerging from the Internet and other ICT. In R. B. Ruddell & N. Unrau (Eds.), *Theoretical models and processes of reading* (5th ed.) (pp. 1568–1611). Newark, DE: International Reading Association.

Leu, D., McVerry, J. G., O'Byrne, W. I., Kiili, C., Zawilinski, L., Everett-Cacopardo, H., Kennedy, C., & Forzani, E. (2011). The new literacies of online reading comprehension: Expanding the literacy and learning curriculum. *Journal of Adolescent & Adult Literacy, 55*, 5–14.

Levine, G. S., Melin, C., Crane, C., Chavez, M., & Lovik, T. A. (2008). The language program director in curricular and departmental reform. *Profession*, 240–254.

Lewis, M. (1993). *The lexical approach*. Hove, England: Language Teaching Publications.

Lewis, M. (1997a). *Implementing the lexical approach: Putting theory into practice*. Hove, England: Language Teaching Publications.

Lewis, M. (1997b). Pedagogical implications of the lexical approach. In J. Coady & T. Huckin (Eds.), *Second language vocabulary acquisition: A rationale for pedagogy* (pp. 255–270). Cambridge, England: Cambridge University Press.

Littlewood, W. (2011). Communicative language teaching: An expanding concept for a changing world. In E. Hinkel (Ed.), *Handbook of research in second language teaching and learning* (Vol. II) (pp. 541–557). New York, NY: Routledge.

Lomicka, L., & Lord, G. (2012). A tale of tweets: Analyzing microblogging among language learners. *System, 40*, 48–63.

Lomicka, L., & Williams, L. (2011). The use of new technologies in the French curriculum: A national survey. *The French Review, 84*, 764–781.

Long, M. (1981). Input, interaction, and second-language acquisition. *Annals of the New York Academy of Sciences, 379*, 259–278.

Long, M. (1983). Linguistic and conversational adjustments to nonnative speakers. *Studies in Second Language Acquisition, 5*, 177–194.

Long, M. (1985). Input and second language acquisition theory. In S. M. Gass & C. G. Madden (Eds.), *Input in second language acquisition* (pp. 377–393). Rowley, MA: Newbury House.

Long, M. (1991). Focus on form: A design feature in language teaching methodology. In K. deBot, R. Ginsberg, & C. Kramsch (Eds.), *Foreign language research in cross-cultural perspective* (pp. 39–52). Amsterdam, Netherlands: John Benjamins.

Long, M. (1996). The role of the linguistic environment in second language acquisition. In W. Ritchie & T. K. Bhatia (Eds.), *Handbook of language acquisition: Vol. 2. Second language acquisition* (pp. 413–468). San Diego, CA: Academic Press.

Long, M., & Crookes, G. (1992). Three approaches to task-based syllabus design. *TESOL Quarterly, 26*, 27–56.

Long, M., & Robinson, P. (1998). Focus on form: Theory, research, and practice. In C. Doughty & J. Williams (Eds.), *Focus on form in classroom language acquisition* (pp. 15–41). Cambridge, England: Cambridge University Press.

Lotherington, H., & Jenson, J. (2011) Teaching multimodal and digital literacy in L2 settings: New literacies, new basics, new pedagogies. *Annual Review of Applied Linguistics, 31*, 226–246.

Lugo de Usategui, K. (2005). El proceso de lectura de hipertextos. ¿una nueva forma de leer? *Educere - Investigación Arbitrada, 30*, 366–372.

Lyman, F. T., Jr. (1981). The responsive classroom discussion: The inclusion of all students. In A. Anderson (Ed.), *Mainstreaming digest* (pp. 109–113). College Park, MD: The University of Maryland Press.

Lyster, R., & Ranta, L. (1997). Corrective feedback and learner uptake. *Studies in Second Language Acquisition, 19*, 37–66.

Lyster, R., & Saito, K. (2010). Oral feedback in classroom SLA: A meta-analysis. *Studies in Second Language Acquisition, 32*, 265–302.

Mackey, A., Abbuhl, R., & Gass, S. M. (2012). Interactionist approach. In S. M. Gass & A. Mackey (Eds.), *The Routledge handbook of second language acquisition* (pp. 7–23). New York, NY: Routledge.

Manchón, R. (Ed.). (2009). *Writing in foreign language contexts: Learning, teaching, and research*. Bristol, England: Multilingual Matters.

Manley, J. H., & Calk, L. (1997). Grammar instruction for writing skills: Do students perceive grammar as useful? *Foreign Language Annals, 30*, 73–83.

Mantero, M. (2002). Bridging the gap: Discourse in text-based foreign language classrooms. *Foreign Language Annals, 35*, 437–456.

Mantero, M. (2006). Applied literacy in second language education: (Re)framing discourse in literature-based classrooms. *Foreign Language Annals, 39*, 99–114.

Maxim, H. H. (2002). A study into the feasibility and effects of reading extended authentic discourse in the beginning German language classroom. *Modern Language Journal, 86*, 20–35.

Maxim, H. H. (2005). Articulating foreign language writing development at the collegiate level: A curriculum-based approach. In C. Barrette & K. Paesani (Eds.), *Language program articulation: Developing a theoretical foundation* (pp. 78–93). Boston, MA: Heinle.

Maxim, H. H. (2006). Integrating textual thinking into the introductory college-level foreign language classroom. *Modern Language Journal, 90*, 19–32.

Maxim, H. H. (2009). An essay on the role of language in collegiate foreign language programmatic reform. *Die Unterrichtspraxis/Teaching German, 42*, 123–129.

McCarthy, M. (1984). A new look at vocabulary in EFL. *Applied Linguistics,* 5, 12–22.

McCarthy, M. (2001). *Issues in applied linguistics*. Cambridge, England: Cambridge University Press.

McCarthy, M., & O'Keefe, A. (2004). Research in the teaching of speaking. *Annual Review of Applied Linguistics, 24*, 26–43.

McGinnis, T., Goodstein-Stolzenberg, A., & Saliani, E. C. (2007). "indnpride": Online spaces of transnational youth as sites of creative and sophisticated literacy and identity work. *Linguistics and Education, 18*, 283–304.

McQuillan, J. (1994). Reading versus grammar: What students think is pleasurable for language cquisition. *Applied Language Learning, 5*, 85–100.

Mehan, H. (1985). The structure of classroom discourse. In T. van Dijk (Ed.), *Handbook of discourse analysis, Volume 3: Discourse and dialogue* (pp. 119–131). London, England: Academic Press.

Meinhof, U. (1998). *Language learning in the age of satellite television*. Oxford, England: Oxford University Press.

Mendelson, A. (2010). Using online forums to scaffold oral participation in foreign language instruction. *L2 Journal, 2*, 23–44.

Menzel, P., & D'Aluzio, F. (2005). *Hungry planet: What the world eats*. Napa, CA: Material World Books.

Merchant, G. H. (2009) Web 2.0, new literacies, and the idea of learning through participation. *English Teaching: Practice and Critique, 8*, 8–20.

Meyer, C. (2009). The role of thinking on the college language classroom. *ADFL Bulletin, 41*(1), 86–93.

Micelly, T., Visocnik, S., & Kennedy, C. (2010). Using an L2 blog to enhance learners' participation and sense of community. *Computer Assisted Language Learning, 23*, 321–341.

Mills, K. A. (2010). A review of the "digital turn" in the New Literacy Studies. *Review of Educational Research, 80*, 246–271.

Mills, N. (2011). Situated learning through social networking communities: The development of joint enterprise, mutual engagement, and a shared repertoire. *CALICO Journal, 28*, 345–368.

Mitchell, R., Myles, F., & Marsden, E. (2013). *Second language learning theories*. New York, NY: Routledge.

MLA Ad Hoc Committee on Foreign Languages. (2007). Foreign languages and higher education: New structures for a changed world. *Profession,* 234–245.

Mochizuki, N., & Ortega, L. (2008). Balancing communication and grammar in beginning-level foreign language classrooms: A study of guided planning and relativization. *Language Teaching Research, 12*, 11–37.

Modern Language Association. (2002). Guidelines for institutional support of and access to IT for faculty members and students. Retrieved from www.mla.org/it_support

Moeller, A. J., Theiler, J. M., & Wu, C. (2012). Goal setting and student achievement: A longitudinal study. *Modern Language Journal, 96*, 153–169.

Murray, L., & Hourigan, T. (2008). Blogs for specific purposes: Expressivist or socio-cognitivist approach? *ReCALL, 20*, 83–98.

Nassaji, H., & Fotos, S. (2011). *Teaching grammar in second language classrooms: Integrating form-focused instruction in communicative context*. New York, NY: Routledge.

Nation, I. S. P. (2001). *Learning vocabulary in another language*. Cambridge, England: Cambridge University Press.

Nation, I. S. P. (2008). *Teaching vocabulary: Techniques and strategies*. Boston, MA: Heinle.

Nation, I. S. P. (2011). Research into practice: Vocabulary. *Language Teaching, 44*, 529–539.

National Capital Language Resource Center. (2013). Portfolio assessment in the foreign language classroom. Retrieved from www.nclrc.org/portfolio/

National Standards in Foreign Language Education Project (NSFLEP). (2006). *Standards for foreign language learning in the 21st century.* Lawrence, KS: Allen Press.

Naughton, D. (2006). Cooperative strategy training and oral interaction: Enhancing small group communication in the language classroom. *Modern Language Journal, 90*, 169–184.

Nelson, M. E. (2006). Mode, meaning, and synaesthesia in multimedia L2 writing. *Language Learning & Technology, 10*, 56–76. Retrieved from http://llt.msu.edu/vol10num2/nelson/default.html

Nelson, M. E., & Hull, G. (2008). Self-presentation through multimedia: A Bakhtinian perspective on digital storytelling. In Lundby, K. (Ed.), *Digital storytelling, mediatized stories: Self-representations in new media* (pp. 123–144). New York, NY: Peter Lang.

New London Group. (1996). A pedagogy of multiliteracies: Designing social futures. *Harvard Educational Review, 66*(1), 60–92.

Norma Oficial Mexicana para la promoción y educación para la salud en materia alimentaria. (2005). El plato del bien comer. Retrieved from http://promocion.salud.gob.mx/dgps/index.html

Norris, J. M., & Ortega, L. (2001). Effectiveness of L2 instruction: A research synthesis and quantitative meta-analysis. *Language Learning, 50*, 417–528.

Nystrand, M. (1997). Dialogic instruction: When recitation becomes conversation. In M. Nystrand, A. Gamoran, R. Kachur, & C. Prendergast (Eds.), *Opening dialogue: Understanding the dynamics of language learning and teaching in the English classroom* (pp. 1–29). New York, NY: Teachers College Press.

Nystrand, M. (2006). Research on the role of classroom discourse as it affects reading comprehension. *Research in the Teaching of English, 40*, 392–412.

Ockey, G. (2007). Construct implications of including still image or video in computer-based listening texts. *Language Testing, 24*, 517–537.

O'Donnell, M. E. (2007). Policies and practices in foreign language writing at the college level: Survey results and implications. *Foreign Language Annals, 40*, 650–671.

Oldways Preservation Trust. (2009). La piramide de la dieta latinoamericana. Retrieved from http://oldwayspt.org/resources/heritage-pyramids/latino-diet-pyramid/overview

OpenLearn. (2010). *Language and literacy in a changing world.* Retrieved from http://labspace.open.ac.uk/course/view.php?id=7134

Paesani, K. (2005). Literary texts and grammar instruction: Revisiting the inductive presentation. *Foreign Language Annals, 38*, 15–23.

Paesani, K. (2006). A process-oriented approach to *Zazie dans le métro*. *The French Review*, 79, 762–778.

Paesani, K. (2009). Exploring the stylistic content of *Exercices de style*. *The French Review, 82*, 1268–1280.

Paesani, K., & Allen, H. W. (2012). Beyond the language-content divide: Research on advanced foreign language instruction at the postsecondary level. *Foreign Language Annals, 45*(s1), s54–s75.

Pahl, K., & Rowsell, J. (Eds) (2006). *Travel notes from the New Literacy Studies: Instances of practice.* Clevedon, England: Multilingual Matters.

Pasfield-Neofitou, S. (2011). Online domains of language use: Second language learners' experiences of virtual community and foreignness. *Language Learning & Technology, 15*, 92–108. Retrieved from http://llt.msu.edu/issues/june2011/pasfieldneofitou.pdf

Pegrum, M. (2011). Modified, multiplied, and (re-)mixed: Social media and digital literacies. In M. Thomas (Ed.), *Digital education: Opportunities for social collaboration* (pp. 9–35). New York, NY: Palgrave Macmillan.

Pennycook, A. (1994). *The cultural politics of English as an international language.* London, England: Longman.

Petersen, S., Divitini, M., & Chabert, G. (2008). Identity, sense of community and connectedness in a community of mobile language learners. *ReCALL, 20*, 361–379.

Peterson, M. (2010). Massively multiplayer online role-playing games as arenas for second language learning. *Computer Assisted Language Learning, 23*, 429–439.

Phillips, J. K. (2008). Foreign language standards and contexts of communication. *Language Teaching, 41*, 93–102.

Platt, E., & Brooks, F. B. (2002). Task engagement: A turning point in foreign language development. *Language Learning, 52*, 365–400.

Poehner, M. E. (2007). Beyond the test: L2 dynamic assessment and the transcendence of mediated learning. *Modern Language Journal, 91*, 323–340.

Polio, C., & Zyzik, E. (2009). Don Quixote meets *ser* and *estar*: Multiple perspectives on language learning in Spanish literature classes. *Modern Language Journal, 93*, 550–569.

Prensky, M. (2001). Digital natives, digital immigrants. *On the Horizon* 9(5), 1–6. Retrieved from www.marcprensky.com/writing/Prensky%20-%20Digital%20Natives,%20Digital%20Immigrants%20-%20Part1.pdf

Racelis, J. V., & Matsuda, P. K. (2013). Integrating process and genre into the second language writing classroom: Research into practice. *Language Teaching, 46*, 382–393.

Rama, P., Black, R., Van Es, E., & Warschauer, M. (2012). Affordances for second language learning in World of Warcraft. *ReCALL, 24*, 322–338.

Rankin, Y. A., Gold, R., & Gooch, B. (2006). 3D role-playing games as language learning tools. *Proceedings of EuroGraphics 25*(3), 211–225.

Rankin, Y. A., Morrison, D., McNeal, M. K., Gooch, B., & Shute, M. W. (2009). Time will tell: In-game social interactions that facilitate second language acquisition. In Young, R. (Ed.), *Proceedings of the 4th international conference on foundations of digital games* (pp. 161–168). New York, NY: ACM.

Reder, S., & Davila, E. (2005). Context and literacy practices. *Annual Review of Applied Linguistics, 25*, 170–187.

Redmann, J. (2005). An interactive reading journal for all levels of the foreign language curriculum. *Foreign Language Annals, 38*, 484–493.

Redmann, J. (2005). *Stationlernen:* A student-centered approach to working with foreign language texts. *Die Unterrichtspraxis/Teaching German, 38*, 135–142.

Reichelt, M. (2001). A critical review of foreign language writing research on pedagogical approaches. *Modern Language Journal, 85*, 578–598.

Reichelt, M., Lefkowitz, N., Rinnert, C., & Schultz, J. M. (2012). Key issues in foreign language writing. *Foreign Language Annals*, 45, 22–41.

Reinders, H. (2009). Learner uptake and acquisition in three grammar-oriented production activities. *Language Teaching Research, 13*, 201–222.

Reinhardt, J., & Sykes, J. (2012). Conceptualizing digital game-mediated L2 learning and pedagogy: Game-enhanced and game-based research and practice. In H. Reinders (Ed.), *Digital games in language learning and teaching* (pp. 32–49). New York, NY: Palgrave Macmillan.

Reinhardt, J., & Thorne, S. L. (2011). Beyond comparisons: Frameworks for developing digital L2 literacies. In N. Arnold & L. Ducate (Eds.), *Present and future promises of CALL: From theory and research to new directions in language teaching* (pp. 257–280). San Marcos, TX: CALICO Publications.

Reinhardt, J., & Zander, V. (2011). Social networking in an intensive English program classroom: A language socialization perspective. *CALICO Journal, 28*, 326–344.

Richards, J. C. (2006). *Communicative language teaching today.* Cambridge, England: Cambridge University Press.

Richards, J. C., & Rodgers, T. S. (2001). *Approaches and methods in language teaching.* Cambridge, England: Cambridge University Press.

Rivens-Monpean, A., & Guichon, N. (2009). Assessing the use of aids for a computer-mediated task: Taking notes while listening. *JALT CALL Journal, 5*, 45–60.

Rogoff, B. (1990). *Apprenticeship into thinking.* Oxford, England: Oxford University Press.

Rossiter, M. J., Derwing, T. M., Manimtim, L. G., & Thomson, R. I. (2010). Oral fluency: The neglected component in the communicative language classroom. *The Canadian Modern Language Review/La Revue canadienne des langues vivantes, 66*, 583–606.

Rubin, D. L. (2002). A binocular view of communication education. *Communication Education, 51*, 412–419.

Rubin, J. (1995a). An overview to *A guide for the teaching of second language listening*. In D. J. Mendelsohn & J. Rubin (Eds.), *A guide for the teaching of second language listening* (pp. 7–11). San Diego, CA: Dominie Press.

Rubin, J. (1995b). The contribution of video to the development of competence in listening. In D. J. Mendelsohn & J. Rubin (Eds.), *A guide for the teaching of second language listening* (pp. 151–165). San Diego, CA: Dominie Press.

Rumelhart, D. E. (1981). Schemata: The building blocks of cognition. In J. T. Guthrie (Ed.), *Comprehension and teaching: Research reviews* (pp. 3–26). Newark, DE: International Reading Association.

Russell, J., & Spada, N. (2006). The effectiveness of corrective feedback for the acquisition of L2 grammar: A meta-analysis of the research. In J. M. Norris & L. Ortega (Eds.), *Synthesizing research on language learning and teaching* (pp. 133–164). Amsterdam, Netherlands: John Benjamins.

Ryu, D. (2011). Non-native English speakers' multiliteracy learning in beyond-game culture: A sociocultural study. *MERLOT Journal of Online Learning and Teaching, 7*, 231–243.

Salaberry, R. (2010). Grammar. In C. Blyth (Ed.), *Foreign Language Teaching Methods*. Austin, TX: Texas Language Technology Center, University of Texas at Austin. Retrieved from www.coerll.utexas.edu/methods/

Savignon, S. (1972). *Communicative competence: An experiment in foreign-language teaching*. Philadelphia, PA: Center for Curriculum Development.

Savignon, S. (2002). Communicative language teaching: Linguistic theory and classroom practice. In S. Savignon (Ed.), *Interpreting communicative language teaching: Contexts and concerns in teacher education* (pp. 1–27). New Haven, CT: Yale University Press.

Schulz, R. A. (1996). Focus on form in the foreign language classroom: Students' and teachers' views on error correction and the role of grammar. *Foreign Language Annals, 29*, 343–364.

Schulz, R. A. (2001). Cultural differences in student and teacher perceptions concerning the role of grammar instruction and corrective feedback: USA–Colombia. *Modern Language Journal, 85*, 244–258.

Schulz, R. A. (2006). Reevaluating communicative competence as a major goal in postsecondary language requirement courses. *Modern Language Journal, 90*, 252–255.

Scott, V. M., & Huntington, J. A. (2007). Literature, the interpretive mode, and novice learners. *Modern Language Journal, 91*, 3–14.

Scott, V. M., & Huntington, J. A. (2008). Reading culture: Using literature to develop C2 competence. *Foreign Language Annals, 35*, 622–631.

Seo, K. (2002). The effect of visuals on listening comprehension: A study of Japanese learners' listening strategies. *International Journal of Listening, 16*, 57–81.

Sercu, L. (2013). Weblogs in foreign language education. Real and promised benefits. In L. Gómez Chova, A. López Martínez, & I. Candel Torres (Eds.), *Proceedings from INTED2013: The 7th International Technology, Education and Development Conference* (pp. 4355–4366). Valencia, Spain: INTED.

Shaffer, C. (1989). A comparison of inductive and deductive approaches to teaching foreign languages. *Modern Language Journal, 73*, 395–403.

Shin, D., & Cimasko, T. (2008). Multimodal composition in a college ESL class: New tools, traditional norms. *Computers and Composition, 25*, 376–395.

Shrum, J. L., & Glisan, E. W. (2010). *Teacher's handbook: Contextualized language instruction* (4th ed.). Boston, MA: Heinle.

Simon, E., & Taverniers, M. (2011). Advanced EFL learners' beliefs about language learning and teaching: A comparison between grammar, pronunciation, and vocabulary. *English Studies, 8*, 896–922.

Skehan, P. (2009). Modelling second language performance: Integrating complexity, accuracy, fluency, and lexis. *Applied Linguistics, 30*, 510–532.

Sonbul, S., & Schmitt, N. (2010). Direct teaching of vocabulary after reading: Is it worth the effort? *ELT Journal, 64*, 253–260.

Spada, N. (2007). Communicative language teaching: Current status and future prospects. In J. Cummins & C. Davis (Eds.), *International handbook of English language teaching* (pp. 271–288). New York, NY: Springer.

Spada, N. (2011). Beyond form-focused instruction: Reflections on past, present and future research. *Language Teaching, 44*, 225–236.

Spada, N., & Lightbown, P. M. (2008). Form focused instruction: Isolated or integrated? *TESOL Quarterly, 42*, 181–207.

Spada, N., & Tomita, Y. (2010). Interactions between type of instruction and type of feature: A meta-analysis. *Language Learning, 60*, 263–308.

Stauffer, R. G. (1975). *Directing the reading–thinking process*. New York, NY: Harper.

Steward, D. (2006). Report on data from the 2004–05 MLA guide to doctoral programs in English and other modern languages. *ADE Bulletin, 140*, 61–79.

Street, B. (1984). *Literacy in theory and practice*. Cambridge, England: Cambridge University Press.

Street, B. (1997). The implications of the "New Literacy Studies" for literacy education. *English in Education, 31*(3), 45–59.

Street, B. (2000). Introduction. In B. Street (Ed.), *Literacy and development: Ethnographic perspectives* (pp. 7–8). New York, NY: Routledge.

Sueyoshi, A., & Hardison, D. (2005). The role of gestures and facial cues in second language listening comprehension. *Language Learning, 55*, 661–699.

Swaffar, J. K. (2003). Foreign languages: A discipline in crisis. *ADFL Bulletin 35*(1), 20–24.

Swaffar, J. K. (2004). A template for advanced learner tasks: Staging reading and cultural literacy through the précis. In H. Byrnes & H. H. Maxim (Eds.), *Advanced foreign language learning: A challenge to college programs* (pp. 19–46). Boston, MA: Heinle.

Swaffar, J. K. (2006). Terminology and its discontents: Some caveats about communicative competence. *Modern Language Journal, 90*, 246–249.

Swaffar, J. K., & Arens, K. (2005). *Remapping the foreign language curriculum: An approach through multiple literacies*. New York, NY: Modern Language Association of America.

Swaffar, J. K., Arens, K., & Byrnes, H. (1991). *Reading for meaning: An integrated approach to language learning*. Englewood Cliffs, NJ: Prentice Hall.

Swaffar, J. K., & Vlatten, A. (1997). A sequential model for video viewing in the foreign language curriculum. *Modern Language Journal, 81*, 175–188.

Swain, M. (1985). Communicative competence: Some roles of comprehensible input and comprehensible output in its development. In S. Gass & C. Madden (Eds.), *Input in second language acquisition* (pp. 235–253). Rowley, MA: Newbury House.

Swain, M. (1995). Three functions of output in second language learning. In G. Cook & B. Seidlhofer (Eds.), *Principles and practices in applied linguistics* (pp. 125–144). Oxford, England: Oxford University Press.

Swain, M. (2005). The output hypothesis: Theory and research. In E. Hinkel (Ed.), *Handbook on research in second language learning and teaching* (pp. 471–484). Mahwah, NJ: Lawrence Erlbaum Associates.

Sykes, J., Oskoz, A., & Thorne, S. (2008). Web 2.0, immersive environments, and the future of language education. *CALICO Journal, 25*, 528–546.

Tardy, C. (2005) Expressions of disciplinarity and individuality in a multimodal genre. *Computers and Compositions, 22*, 319–336.

Terrell, T. D., Rogers, M. B., Kerr, B. J., & Spielmann, G. (2009). *Deux mondes: A communicative approach* (6th ed.). Boston, MA: McGraw-Hiill.

Tharp, R. G., & Gallimore, R. (1988). *Rousing minds to life: Teaching, schooling, and learning in social context.* Cambridge, England: Cambridge University Press.

Tharp, R. G., & Gallimore, R. (1991). *The instructional conversation: Teaching and learning in social activity* (Research Report No 2). Santa Cruz, CA: National Center for Research on Cultural Diversity and Second Language Learning.

Thoman, E., & Jolls, T. (2003). *Literacy for the 21st century: An overview and orientation guide to media literacy education (Part I: Theory).* Malibu, CA: Center for Media Literacy.

Thoms, J. (2012). Classroom discourse in foreign language classrooms: A review of the literature. *Foreign Language Annals, 45*(s1), s8–s27.

Thorne, S. L. (2003). Artifacts and cultures-of-use in intercultural communication. *Language Learning & Technology, 7,* 38–67. Retrieved from http://llt.msu.edu/vol7num2/thorne/default.html

Thorne, S. L. (2008). Transcultural communication in open Internet environments and massively multiplayer online games. In S. Magnan (Ed.), *Mediating discourse online* (pp. 305–327). Amsterdam, Netherlands: John Benjamins.

Thorne, S. L. (2009). 'Community', semiotic flows, and mediated contribution to activity. *Language Teaching, 42,* 81–94.

Thorne, S. L. (2010). The 'intercultural turn' and language learning in the crucible of new media. In F. Helm & S. Guth (Eds.), *Telecollaboration 2.0 for language and intercultural learning* (pp. 139–164). New York, NY: Peter Lang.

Thorne, S. L., & Black, R. (2007). Language and literacy development in computer-mediated contexts and communities. *Annual Review of Applied Linguistics, 27,* 133–160.

Thorne, S. L., Black, R., & Sykes, J. (2009). Second language use, socialization, and learning in Internet interest communities and online gaming. *Modern Language Journal, 93*(s1), 802–821.

Todhunter, S. (2007). Instructional conversations in a high school Spanish class. *Foreign Language Annals, 40,* 604–621.

Toth, P. D. (2011). Social and cognitive factors in making teacher-led classroom discourse relevant for second language development. *Modern Language Journal, 95,* 1–25.

United States Department of Agriculture. (2010). MyPlate. Retrieved from www.choosemyplate.gov/

van Compernolle, R., & Abraham, L. (2009). Interactional and discursive features of English-language weblogs for language learning and teaching. In L. Abraham & L. Williams (Eds.), *Electronic discourse in language learning and language teaching* (pp. 193–211). Amsterdam, Netherlands: John Benjamins.

Van den Branden, K. (2000). Does negotiation of meaning promote reading comprehension? A study of primary school classes. *Reading Research Quarterly, 35,* 426–444.

van Lier, L. (1996). *Interaction in the language classroom: Awareness, autonomy and authenticity.* New York, NY: Longman.

Vandergrift, L. (2006). Second language listening: Ability or language proficiency? *Modern Language Journal, 90,* 6–18.

Vandergrift, L., & Goh, C. (2012). *Teaching and learning second language listening: Metacognition in action.* New York, NY: Routledge.

Vanderplank, R. (2010). *Déjà vu?* A decade of research on language laboratories, television, and video on language learning. *Language Teaching, 43,* 1–37.

VanPatten, B. (2002). Processing instruction: An update. *Language Learning, 52,* 755–803.

Vyatkina, N. (2011). Writing instruction and policies for written corrective feedback in the basic language sequence. *L2 Journal, 3,* 63–92.

Vygotsky, L. S. (1978). *Mind in society.* Cambridge, MA: Harvard University Press.

Wagner, E. (2007). Are they watching? An investigation of test-taker viewing behavior during an L2 video listening test. *Language Learning & Technology, 11,* 67–86. Retrieved from http://llt.msu.edu/ vol11num1/wagner/default.html

Wagner, E. (2008). Video listening tests: What are they measuring? *Language Assessment Quarterly, 5*, 218–243.

Wagner, E. (2010a). Test-takers' interaction with an L2 video listening test. *System, 38*, 280–291.

Wagner, E. (2010b). How does the use of video texts affect ESL listening test-taker performance? *Language Testing, 27*, 493–510.

Walsh, M. (2009). Pedagogic potential of multimodal literacy. In L. T. W. Hin & R. Subramaniam (Eds.), *Handbook of research on new media literacy at the K–12 Level: Issues and challenges* (pp. 32–47). Hershey, PA: IGI Global.

Walther, I. (2007). Ecological perspectives on language and literacy: Implications for foreign language instruction at the collegiate level. *ADFL Bulletin, 38*(3) & *39*(1), 6–14.

Ward, J. M. (2004). Blog assisted language learning (BALL): Push button publishing for the pupils. *TEFL Web Journal, 3*, 1–16. Retrieved from http://www.esp-world.info/articles_26/push%20button%20publishing%20ward%202004.pdf

Waring, H. Z. (2009). Moving out of IRF (Initiation–Response–Feedback): A single case analysis. *Language Learning, 59*, 796–824.

Weinberger, D. (2009). *Truth and transparency*. New York, NY: Personal Democracy Forum. Retrieved from www.youtube.com/watch?v=o3qSDLF6lU4

Weissberg, R. (2006). *Connecting speaking and writing in second language writing instruction*. Ann Arbor, MI: The University of Michigan Press.

Wenger, E. (1998). *Communities of practice: Learning, meaning and identity*. Cambridge, England: Cambridge University Press.

Wesch, M. (2007). Web 2.0. . .The machine is us/ing us. Retrieved from www.youtube.com/watch?v=6gmP4nk0EOE

Wetzel, C. D., Radtke, P., & Stern, H. W. (1994). *Instructional effectiveness of video media*. Hillsdale, NJ: Lawrence Erlbaum Associates.

Widdowson, H. G. (1978). *Teaching language as communication*. Oxford, England: Oxford University Press.

Wiggins, G., & McTighe, J. (2011). *The understanding by design guide to creating high quality units*. Alexandra, VA: ACSD.

Williams, J. (2005). *Teaching writing in second and foreign language classrooms*. New York, NY: McGraw–Hill.

Williams, J. (2008). The speaking–writing connection in second language and academic literacy development. In D. Belcher & A. Hirvela (Eds.), *The oral-literate connection: Perspectives on L2 speaking, writing, and other media interactions* (pp. 10–25). Ann Arbor, MI: University of Michigan Press.

Williams, J. (2012). The potential role(s) of writing in second language development. *Journal of Second Language Writing, 21*, 321–331.

Wong, W., & VanPatten, B. (2003). The evidence is in: Drills are out. *Foreign Language Annals, 36*, 403–423.

Wood, D., Bruner, J., & Ross, G. (1976). The role of tutoring in problem-solving. *Journal of Child Psychology and Psychiatry in Applied Disciplines, 17*, 89–100.

Wray, A. (2002). *Formulaic language and the lexicon*. Cambridge, England: Cambridge University Press.

Yang, Y. F. (2012). Multimodal composing in digital storytelling. *Computers and Composition, 29*, 221–238.

Yuan, F., & Ellis, R. (2003). The effects of pre-task planning and on-line planning on fluency, complexity, and accuracy in L2 monologic oral production. *Applied Linguistics, 24*, 1–27.

Zhang, D. (2012). Vocabulary and grammar knowledge in second language reading comprehension: A structural equation modeling study. *Modern Language Journal, 96*, 558–575.

Zhang, L. (2011). Teaching Chinese cultural perspectives through film. *L2 Journal, 3*, 201–231.

Zheng, D., Newgarden, K., & Young, M. (2012). Multimodal analysis of language learning in World of Warcraft: Languaging as values-realizing. *ReCALL, 24*, 339–360.

Zyzik, E., & Polio, C. (2008). Incidental focus on form in university Spanish literature courses. *Modern Language Journal, 92*, 53–70.

CREDITS

Introduction

Page 2: Swaffar, J. (2003. p. 20). Foreign languages: A discipline in crisis. *ADFL Bulletin 35 (1)*, 20–24.

Page 2: MLA Ad Hoc Committee on Foreign Languages. (2007. p. 3). Foreign languages and higher education: New structures for a changed world. *Profession*, 234–245.

Page 2: Adapted from Kern, R. (2000). Literacy and language teaching. Oxford, England: Oxford University Press. and Maxim, H. H. (2006). Integrating textual thinking into the introductory college-level foreign language classroom. *Modern Language Journal, 90*, 19–32.

Page 3: Byrnes, H., Maxim, H. H., & Norris, J. (2010. p. 23). Realizing advanced foreign language writing development in collegiate education: Curricular design, pedagogy, assessment. *Modern Language Journal, 94*, Supplement, 1–221.

Page 3: Kern, R. (2003. p. 43). Literacy as a new organizing principle for foreign language education. In P. C. Patrikis (Ed.), *Reading between the lines: Perspectives on foreign language literacy* (pp. 40–59). New Haven, CT: Yale University Press.

Page 3: Kern, R. (2000. p. 6). *Literacy and language teaching*. Oxford, England: Oxford University Press.

Page 4: Duff, P. (2014. p.18). Communicative language teaching. In M. Celce-Murcia, D. Brinton, & M.A. Snow (Eds.), *Teaching English as a second or foreign language* (4th ed., pp. 15–30). Boston, MA: Heinle Cengage.

Page 5: Savignon, S. J. (1972. p. 2). *Communicative competence: An experiment in foreign-language teaching*. Philadelphia, PA: Center for Curriculum Development.

Page 5: Canale, M. (1983). From communicative competence to communicative language pedagogy. In J. C. Richards & R. W. Schmidt (Eds.), *Language and communication* (pp. 2–27). London, England: Longman. p. 7, 9, 10.

Page 6: Celce-Murcia, M. (2007. p. 47, 48). Rethinking the role of communicative competence in language teaching. In E. Alcón Soler & M. P. Safont Jordà (Eds.), *Intercultural language use and language learning* (pp. 41–57). Dordrecht, Netherlands: Springer.

Page 6: Jacobs, G. M. & Farrell, T. S. C. (2003. p. 8.). Understanding and implementing the CLT (communicative language teaching) paradigm. *RELC Journal, 34(1)*, 5–30.

Page 7: Richards, J. C. (2006. p. 22). *Communicative language teaching today*. Cambridge, England: Cambridge University Press.

Page 7: Spada, N. (2007. p. 271). Communicative language teaching: Current status and future prospects. In J. Cummins & C. Davis (Eds.), *International handbook of English language teaching* (pp. 271–288). New York, NY: Springer.

Page 8: Kern, R. (2000. p. 19). *Literacy and language teaching*. Oxford, England: Oxford University Press.

Page 8: Pennycook, A. (1994. p. 311). *The cultural politics of English as an international language*. London, England: Longman.

Page 8: Byrnes, H. (Ed.) (2006. p. 244). Perspectives: Interrogating communicative competence as a framework for collegiate foreign language study. *Modern Language Journal, 90*, 244–266.

Page 8: Richards, J. C. (2006. p. 22). *Communicative language teaching today*. Cambridge, England: Cambridge University Press.

Page 8: Kumaravadivelu, B. (1994). The postmethod condition: (E)merging strategies for second/foreign language teaching. *TESOL Quarterly, 28(1)*, 27–48.

Page 9: Harmer, J. (2007). *The practice of English language teaching*. (4th ed.) London, England: Longman.

Pages 9, 10: Kern, R. (2003. p. 42, 43). Literacy as a new organizing principle for foreign language education. In P. C. Patrikis (Ed.), *Reading between the lines: Perspectives on foreign language literacy* (pp. 40–59). New Haven, CT: Yale University Press.

Page 11: Kern, R. (2000. p. 16). *Literacy and language teaching*. Oxford, England: Oxford University Press.

Page 11: Hall, Joan Kelly, *Methods for teaching foreign languages: Creating a community of learners in the classroom*, 1st Ed., ©2002. Reprinted and electronically reproduced by permission of Pearson Education, Inc., Upper Saddle River, New Jersey.

Page 11: Lantolf, J. P. (2011. pp. 24–47), The sociocultural approach to second language acquisition. In Atkinson, D. (Ed.). *Alternative approaches to second language acquisition*. New York, NY: Routledge.

Pages 12, 12–13: Kucer, S. B. (2009. p. 7, 311). *Dimensions of literacy: A conceptual base for teaching reading and writing in school settings* (3rd ed.). New York, NY: Routledge.

Page 13: Kern, R. (2003. p. 49, 49–50). Literacy as a new organizing principle for foreign language education. In P. C. Patrikis (Ed.), *Reading between the lines: Perspectives on foreign language literacy*. New Haven, CT: Yale University Press.

Page 14: Cope, C., & Kalantzis, M. (2009. p. 15). 'Multiliteracies': New literacies, new learning. *Pedagogies, 4(3)*, 164–194.

Page 14: New London Group. (1996. p. 81). A pedagogy of multiliteracies: Designing social futures. *Harvard Educational Review, 66*, 60–92.

Page 14: OpenLearn. (2010). *Language and literacy in a changing world*. Retrieved from http://labspace.open.ac.uk/course/view.php?id=7134

Page 15: Kern, R. (2000. p. 19). *Literacy and language teaching*. Oxford, England: Oxford University Press.

Page 15: Street, B. (1997. p. 84). The implications of the "New Literacy Studies" for literacy education. *English in Education, 31(3)*, 45–59.

Page 15: Kumaravadivelu, B. (1994. p. 39). The postmethod condition: (E)merging strategies for second/foreign language teaching. *TESOL Quarterly, 28(1)*, 27–48.

Page 16: Kern, R. (2003. p. 51). Literacy as a new organizing principle for foreign language education. In P. C. Patrikis (Ed.), *Reading between the lines: Perspectives on foreign language literacy* (pp. 40–59). New Haven, CT: Yale University Press.

Chapter 1

Pages 21–22: Hall, Joan Kelly, *Methods for teaching foreign languages: Creating a community of learners in the classroom*, 1st Ed., ©2002. Reprinted and electronically reproduced by permission of Pearson Education, Inc., Upper Saddle River, New Jersey.

Page 22: Kern, R. (2003. p. 51). Literacy as a new organizing principle for foreign language education. In P. C. Patrikis (Ed.), *Reading between the lines: Perspectives on foreign language literacy* (pp. 40–59). New Haven, CT: Yale University Press.

Page 24: Cope, C., & Kalantzis, M. (2009. p. 175, 177). 'Multiliteracies': New literacies, new learning. *Pedagogies, 4(3)*, 164–194.

Page 25: Based on Kern, R. (2000. p. 60). *Literacy and language teaching*. Oxford, England: Oxford University Press.

Page 25: Cope, C., & Kalantzis, M. (2009. p. 176). 'Multiliteracies': New literacies, new learning. *Pedagogies*, 4(3), 164–194.

Page 26: New London Group. (1996. p. 73). A pedagogy of multiliteracies: Designing social futures. *Harvard Educational Review, 66*, 60–92.

Pages 28–29: Kalantzis, M., & Cope, B. (n.d.). *Kalantzis and Cope on differentiated literacies instruction*. Retrieved from www.newlearningonline.com/literacies/chapter-14/kalantzisand-cope-on-differentiated-literacies-instruction

Page 29: Based on Kern, R. (2000. p. 68). *Literacy and language teaching*. Oxford, England: Oxford University Press.

Page 30: Kern, R. (2000. p. 17). *Literacy and language teaching*. Oxford, England: Oxford University Press.

Page 31: Swaffar, J. K., & Arens, K. (2005, p. 99). *Remapping the foreign language curriculum: An approach through multiple literacies*. New York, NY Modern Language Association of America.

Page 32: Based on Kern, R. (2000. p. 183). Literacy and language teaching. Oxford, England: Oxford University Press. Page 33: New London Group. (1996. p. 74). A pedagogy of multiliteracies: Designing social futures. *Harvard Educational Review, 66*, 60–92.

Page 35: Hammadou, J. A. (2002, p. 219). Advanced foreign language readers' inferencing. In J. A. Hammadou Sullivan (Ed.), *Literacy and the second language learner* (pp. 217–238). Greenwich, CT: Information Age Publishing.

Pages 36, 37: Kern, R. (2003. p. 49). Literacy as a new organizing principle for foreign language education. In P. C. Patrikis (Ed.), *Reading between the lines: Perspectives on foreign language literacy* (pp. 40–59). New Haven, CT: Yale University Press.

Page 38: Based on Hall, J. K. (2001). *Methods for teaching foreign languages: Creating a community of learners in the classroom*. Upper Saddle River, NJ: Prentice Hall. pp. 52–53.

Pages 38, 39: Cope, C., & Kalantzis, M. (2009, p. 18). 'Multiliteracies': New literacies, new learning. *Pedagogies, 4(3)*, 164–194.

Chapter 2

Page 50: Kramsch, C. (1988. p. 63). The cultural discourse of FL textbooks. In A. J. Singerman (Ed.), *Toward a new integration of language and culture* (pp. 63–88). Middlebury, VT: Northeast Conference on the Teaching of Foreign Languages.

Page 51: Byrnes, H., Maxim, H. H., & Norris, J. (2010. p. 4). Realizing advanced foreign language writing development in collegiate education: Curricular design, pedagogy, assessment. *Modern Language Journal*, 94, Supplement, 1–221.

Page 52: Graves, K. (1999. p. 76). *Designing language courses: A guide for teachers.* Boston: Heinle.

Pages 52–53: © Pearson Education, Inc.

Page 55: Kern, R. (2000. p. 267). *Literacy and language teaching.* Oxford, England: Oxford University Press.

Page 56: Shrum, J. L., & Glisan, E. W. (2010. p. 395). *Teacher's handbook: Contextualized language instruction* (4th ed.). Boston, MA: Heinle.

Page 58: Poehner, M. E. (2007. pp. 323–324). Beyond the test: L2 dynamic assessment and the transcendence of mediated learning. *Modern Language Journal, 91*, 323–340.

Page 60: Terrell, T. D., Rogers, M. B., Kerr, B. J., & Spielmann, G. (2009. p. 73). *Deux mondes: A communicative approach* (6th ed.). Boston, MA: McGraw Hill Higher Education.

Page 60: Kern, R. (2004. p. 7). Literacy and advanced foreign language learning: Rethinking the curriculum. In H. Byrnes & H. H. Maxim (Eds.), *Advanced foreign language learning: A challenge to college programs* (pp. 2–18). Boston, MA: Heinle.

Pages 61–62: Kern, R. (2002. p. 22). Reconciling the language–literature split through literacy. *ADFL Bulletin, 33(3)*, 20–24.

Page 62: Based on Kern, R. (2000. pp. 304–305). *Literacy and language teaching.* Oxford, England: Oxford University Press.

Page 62: Kern, R. (2003. p. 48). Literacy as a new organizing principle for foreign language education. In P. C. Patrikis (Ed.), *Reading between the lines: Perspectives on foreign language literacy* (pp. 40–59). New Haven, CT: Yale University Press.

Page 62: Based on Kern, R. (2000. p. 5). *Literacy and language teaching.* Oxford, England: Oxford University Press.

Page 63: Arens, K. (2008, p. 35, 38). Genres and the Standards: Teaching the 5 Cs through texts. *German Quarterly, 81(1)*, 35–48.

Page 63: Kern, R. (2004. p. 8). Literacy and advanced foreign language learning: Rethinking the curriculum. In H. Byrnes & H. H. Maxim (Eds.), *Advanced foreign language learning: A challenge to college programs* (pp. 2–18). Boston, MA: Heinle.

Page 64: Swaffar, J. K., & Arens, K. (2005, pp. 40–41). *Remapping the foreign language curriculum: An approach through multiple literacies.* New York, NY: Modern Language Association of America.

Page 64: Byrnes, H., Maxim, H. H., & Norris, J. (2010. p. 59). Realizing advanced foreign language writing development in collegiate education: Curricular design, pedagogy, assessment. *Modern Language Journal, 94*, Supplement, 1–221.

Page 65: Arens, K. (2010, p. 321). The field of culture: The Standards as a model for teaching culture. *Modern Language Journal, 94*, 321–324.

Page 65: Arens, K. (2008, p. 45). *Genres and the Standards: Teaching the 5 Cs through texts. German Quarterly, 81(1)*, 35–48.

Page 65: Byrnes, H., Crane, C., Maxim, H. H., & Sprang, K. (2006, p. 93). Taking text to task: Issues and choices in curriculum construction. *International Journal of Applied Linguistics, 152*, 85–110.

Page 68: Street, B. (1997, p. 84). *The implications of the "New Literacy Studies" for literacy education. English in Education, 31(3)*, 45–59.

Page 69: New London Group. (1996, p. 87). A pedagogy of multiliteracies: Designing social futures. *Harvard Educational Review, 66(1)*, 60–92.

Chapter 3

Page 77: Katz, S., & Blyth, C. (2007, p. 264). *Teaching French grammar in context: Theory and practice.* New Haven, CT: Yale University Press.

Page 77: Broady, E. (2008. p. 264). Fragmentation and consolidation: Recent articles on vocabulary acquisition. *Language Learning Journal, 36*, 259–265.

Page 78: Schmitt, N. (2010. p. 18). *Researching vocabulary: A vocabulary research manual.* New York: Palgrave Macmillan.

Page 80: Spada, N. (2011. p. 233). Beyond form-focused instruction: Reflections on past, present and future research. *Language Teaching, 44*, 225–236.

Page 80: Doughty, C., Williams, J. *Focus on Form in Classroom Second Language Acquisition.* Cambridge University Press, 1998, p. 3.

Page 82: Celce-Murcia, M. (1991, pp. 466–467). Grammar pedagogy in second and foreign language teaching. *TESOL Quarterly, 25*, 459–480.

Page 83: Celce-Murcia, M. (1991, p. 466). Grammar pedagogy in second and foreign language teaching. *TESOL Quarterly, 25*, 459–480.

Page 86: Allen, H. W. (2008, p. 21). Textbook materials and foreign language teaching: Perspectives from the classroom. *The NECTFL Review, 62*, 5–28.

Page 87: McCarthy, M. J. (1984, pp. 13–14). A new look at vocabulary in EFL. *Applied Linguistics*, 5, 12–22.

Page 89: Allen, H. W. (2008, pp. 14–15). Textbook materials and foreign language teaching: Perspectives from the classroom. *The NECTFL Review, 62*, 5–28.

Page 89: Askildon, V. (2008, p. 219). *What do teachers and students want from a foreign language textbook?* (Unpublished doctoral dissertation). University of Arizona, Tucson, AZ.

Page 90: Swaffar, J. K., & Arens, K. (2005, p. 30). *Remapping the foreign language curriculum: An approach through multiple literacies.* New York, NY: Modern Language Association of America.

Page 92: Adair-Hauck, B., & Donato, R. (2010, p. 224, 225). Using a story-based approach to teach grammar. In J. Shrum & E. Glisan (Authors), *Teachers handbook: Contextualized foreign language instruction* (4th ed.) (pp. 216–243). Boston: Heinle.

Page 92: Blyth, C., & Davis, J. (2007). Using formative evaluation in the development of learner-centered materials. *CALICO Journal, 25*, 48–68.

Page 94: Paesani, K. (2005). Literary texts and grammar instruction: Revisiting the inductive presentation. *Foreign Language Annals*, 38, 15–23; Adair-Hauck, B., & Donato, R. (2010). Using a story-based approach to teach grammar. In J. Shrum & E. Glisan (Authors), *Teachers handbook: Contextualized foreign language instruction* (4th ed.) (pp. 216–243). Boston: Heinle; Kelton, K., Guilloteau, N., & Blyth, C. (2004). *Français interactif: An online introductory French course.* Retrieved from http://www.laits.utexas.edu/fi.

Page 97: Swaffar, J. K., & Arens, K. (2005, p. 87). *Remapping the foreign language curriculum: An approach through multiple literacies.* New York, NY: Modern Language Association of America.

Page 99: Barrette, C., Paesani, K. & Vinall, K. (2010, p. 219, 220), Toward an integrated curriculum: maximising the use of TL literature. *Foreign Language Annuals, 43(2)*, 216–230.

Page 100: Based on Barrette, C., Paesani, K. & Vinall, K. (2010), Toward an integrated curriculum: maximising the use of TL literature. *Foreign Language Annuals, 43(2)*, 216–230.

Page 106: Denevi, M. *Falsificaciones*, Buenos Aires, Corregidor, 2007.

Chapter 4

Page 108: Schulz, R. A. (2006. p. 254). Reevaluating communicative competence as a major goal in postsecondary language requirement courses. *Modern Language Journal, 90*, 252–255.

Page 108: Phillips, J. K. (2008. p. 96). Foreign language standards and contexts of communication. Language Teaching, *41*, 93–102.

Page 108: Shrum, J. L., & Glisan, E. W. (2010. pp. 300–301). *Teacher's handbook: Contextualized language instruction* (4th ed.). Boston, MA: Heinle.

Page 109: McCarthy, M. (2001. p. 96). *Issues in applied linguistics.* Cambridge, England: Cambridge University Press.

Page 111: Gass, S. M., & Mackey, A. (2007. p. 176). Input, interaction, and output in second language acquisition. In B. VanPatten & J. Williams (Eds.), *Theories in second language acquisition: An introduction* (pp. 175–199). Mahwah, NJ: Lawrence Erlbaum.

Page 111: Long, M. H. (1996. p. 418). The role of the linguistic environment in second language acquisition. In w. Ritchie & T. K. Bhatia (Eds.), *Handbook of language acquisition: Vol.2. Second language acquisition* (pp. 413–468). San Diego, CA: Academic Press.

Page 112: Brooks, F. B., & Donato, R. (1994. p. 262). Vygotskian approaches to understanding foreign language learner discourse during communicative tasks. *Hispania, 77*, 262–274.

Page 113: McCarthy, M., & O'Keefe, A. (2004. p. 30). Research in the teaching of speaking. *Annual Review of Applied Linguistics, 24*, 26–43.

Page 114: Todhunter, S. (2007. p. 605). Instructional conversations in a high school Spanish class. *Foreign Language Annals, 40*, 604–621.

Page 114: Toth, P. D. (2011. p. 18). Social and cognitive factors in making teacher-led classroom discourse relevant for second language development.*Modern Language Journal, 95*, 1–25.

Page 115: Weissberg, R. (2006. p. 60). *Connecting speaking and writing in second language writing instruction*. Ann Arbor, MI: The University of Michigan Press.

Page 115: Brooks, F. B., Donato, R., & McGlone, J. V. (1997. p. 526, emphasis in the original). When are they going to say "it" right? Understanding learner talk during pair-work activity. *Foreign Language Annals, 30*, 524–541.

Pages 116, 117: Brooks, F. B., & Donato, R. (1994. p. 264, 272). Vygotskian approaches to understanding foreign language learner discourse during communicative tasks. *Hispania, 77*, 262–274.

Page 117: Burns, A. (1998. p. 106). Teaching speaking. *Annual Review of Applied Linguistics, 18*, 102–123.

Pages 118–119: Hall, J. K. *Methods for teaching foreign languages: Creating a community of learners in the classroom*, 1st Ed., ©2002. Reprinted and electronically reproduced by permission of Pearson Education, Inc., Upper Saddle River, New Jersey.

Page 119: Antón, M. (1999. p. 314). The discourse of a learner-centered classroom: Sociocultural perspectives on teacher-learner interaction in the second-language classroom. *Modern Language Journal, 83*, 303–318.

Page 123: Redmann, J. (2005. p. 136). Stationlernen: A student-centered approach to working with foreign language texts. *Die Unterichtspraxis/Teaching German, 38*, 135–142.

Page 123: Redmann, J. (2005. p. 138, 139). Stationlernen: A student-centered approach to working with foreign language texts. *Die Unterichtspraxis/Teaching German, 38*, 135–142.

Page 124: Bueno, K. (2006). Stepping out of the comfort zone: Profiles of third-year Spanish students' attempts to develop their speaking skills. *Foreign Language Annals, 39*, 451–470; Johnson, K. E. (2003). Let's make a deal: A sample project for advanced ESL learners. CALPER Pedagogical Materials Project Work, No 1. The Pennsylvania State University: Center for Advanced Proficiency Education and Research.; Redmann, J. (2005). Stationlernen: A student-centered approach to working with foreign language texts. *Die Unterichtspraxis/Teaching German, 38*, 135–142.

Pages 197–199: © Pearson Education, Inc.

Chapter 5

Page 140: Bernhardt, E. (2005. p. 140). Progress and procrastination in second language reading. *Annual Review of Applied Linguistics, 25*, 133–150.

Page 140: Kucer, S. B. (2009. p. 132). *Dimensions of literacy: A conceptual base for teaching reading and writing in school settings* (3rd ed.). New York, NY: Routledge.

Page 141: Bernhardt, E. (2005. p. 140). Progress and procrastination in second language reading. *Annual Review of Applied Linguistics, 25*, 133–150. Reprinted with the permission of Cambridge University Press.

Page 143: http://coerll.utexas.edu/methods/modules/reading/01/

Pages 143–144: Hammadou, J. A. (2002. p. 219). Advanced foreign language readers' inferencing. In J. A. Hammadou Sullivan (Ed.), *Literacy and the second language learner* (pp. 217–238). Greenwich, CT: Information Age Publishing.

Page 144: Based on Kern, R. (2000. p. 111). *Literacy and language teaching*. Oxford, England: Oxford University Press.

Page 144: Kucer, S. B., & Silva, C. (2006. p. 7). *Teaching the dimensions of literacy*. New York, NY: Routledge.

Page 146: Allen, H. W., & Paesani, K. (2010. p. 122). Exploring the feasibility of a pedagogy of multiliteracies in introductory foreign language courses. *L2 Journal, 2(1)*, 119–142.

Page 146: New London Group. (1996. p. 75). A pedagogy of multiliteracies: Designing social futures. *Harvard Educational Review, 66(1)*, 60–92.

Page 148: Maxim, H. H. (2006. p. 21). Integrating textual thinking into the introductory college-level foreign language classroom. *Modern Language Journal, 90*, 19–32.

Page 150: Hedgcock, J. S., & Ferris, D. R. (2009. p. 192, 326, 184). *Teaching readers of English: Students, texts, and contexts*. New York, NY: Routledge.

Pages 150, 151: Swaffar, J., Arens, K., & Byrnes, H. (1991. p. 78, 87). *Reading for meaning: An integrated approach to language learning*. Englewood Cliffs, NJ: Prentice Hall.

Page 151: Swaffar, J. K., & Arens, K. (2005. p. 87). *Remapping the foreign language curriculum: An approach through multiple literacies.* Reprinted by permission of the Modern Language Association. New York, NY.

Page 151: Anderson Imbert, E. (1976). *Cuento en miniature: Antología.* Caracas, Venezuela: Equinoccio, Universidad Simon Bolivar.

Pages 151, 152: Swaffar, J. K., & Arens, K. (2005. p. 81, 21). *Remapping the foreign language curriculum: An approach through multiple literacies.* New York, NY: Modern Language Association of America.

Page 152: Maxim, H. H. (2006. p. 23). Integrating textual thinking into the introductory college-level foreign language classroom. *Modern Language Journal, 90,* 19–32.

Page 154: Hedgcock, J. S., & Ferris, D. R. (2009). *Teaching readers of English: Students, texts, and contexts.* New York, NY: Routledge; Swaffar, J. K., & Arens, K. (2005). *Remapping the foreign language curriculum: An approach through multiple literacies.* New York, NY: Modern Language Association of America; Maxim, H. H. (2006). Integrating textual thinking into the introductory college-level foreign language classroom. *Modern Language Journal, 90,* 19–32.; Kern, R. (2000). *Literacy and language teaching.* Oxford, England: Oxford University Press.

Page 156: Hall, J. K. (2001). *Methods for teaching foreign languages: Creating a community of learners in the classroom.* Upper Saddle River, NJ: Prentice Hall; Kern, R. (2000). *Literacy and language teaching.* Oxford, England: Oxford University Press; Kucer, S. B., & Silva, C. (2006). *Teaching the dimensions of literacy.* New York, NY: Routledge.

Page 158: Kern, R. (2000. pp. 164–165). *Literacy and language teaching.* Oxford, England: Oxford University Press.

Page 160: Based on from Allen, H. W., & Paesani, K. (2010). Exploring the feasibility of a pedagogy of multiliteracies in introductory foreign language courses. *L2 Journal, 2(1),* 119–142.

Page 163: Based on Kern, R. (2000. p. 129, 132). *Literacy and language teaching.* Oxford, England: Oxford University Press.

Page 165: Swaffar, J. (2004, p. 19). A template for advanced learner tasks: Staging reading and cultural literacy through the précis. In H. Byrnes & H. H. Maxim (Eds.), *Advanced foreign language learning: A challenge to college programs* (pp. 19–46). Boston: Heinle & Heinle.

Page 165: Swaffar, J., Arens, K., & Byrnes, H. (1991. p. 2). *Reading for meaning: An integrated approach to language learning.* Englewood Cliffs, NJ: Prentice Hall.

Page 166: Phillipe Delerm, La Première gorgée de bière et autres plaisirs minuscules © Gallimard, 1997.

Chapter 6

Page 168: Racelis, J. V., & Matsuda, P. K. (2013. p. 384). Integrating process and genre into the second language writing classroom: Research into practice. *Language Teaching, 46,* 382–393.

Page 168: Williams, J. (2012. p. 321). The potential role(s) of writing in second language development. *Journal of Second Language Writing, 21,* 321–331.

Page 168: Byrnes, H. (2013. p. 96). Positioning writing as meaning-making in writing research: An introduction. *Journal of Second Language Writing, 22,* 95–106.

Page 169: O'Donnell, M. E. (2007. p. 651). Policies and practices in foreign language writing at the college level: Survey results and implications. *Foreign Language Annals, 40,* 650–671.

Page 171: Reichelt, M. Lefkowitz, N., Rinnert, C., & Schultz, J. M. (2012. p. 29). Key issues in foreign language writing. *Foreign Language Annals 45,* 22–41.

Page 171: Reichelt, M. (2001. p. 578, 579). A critical review of foreign language writing research on pedagogical approaches. *Modern Language Journal 85,* 578–598.

Page 172: Manchón, R. (Ed.). (2009. p. 12). *Writing in foreign language contexts: Learning, teaching, and research.* Bristol, England: Multilingual Matters.

Pages 172–173: Hyland, K. (2011). Learning to write: Issues in theory, research, and pedagogy. In R. M. Manchón, R.M. (Ed.), *Learning to Write and Writing to Learn in an Additional Language* (pp. 17–35). Amsterdam, Netherlands: John Benjamins.

Page 173: Shrum, J. L., & Glisan, E. W. (2010. p. 302). *Teacher's handbook: Contextualized language instruction* (4th ed.). Boston, MA: Heinle.

Pages 173, 174: Manchón, R. (Ed.). (2009. p. 11, 12). *Writing in foreign language contexts: Learning, teaching, and research.* Bristol, England: Multilingual Matters.

Page 175: Williams, J. (2005. p. 33). *Teaching writing in second and foreign language classrooms.* New York, NY: McGraw–Hill.

Page 176: Kern, R. (2000. p. 183, 185). *Literacy and language teaching*. Oxford, England: Oxford University Press.

Page 176: Hyland, K. (2007. p. 151). Genre pedagogy: Language, literacy and writing instruction. *Journal of Second Language Writing 16*, 148–164.

Page 177: Racelis, J. V., & Matsuda, P. K. (2013. p. 389). Integrating process and genre into the second language writing classroom: Research into practice. *Language Teaching, 46*, 382–393.

Page 178: Williams, J. (2005). *Teaching writing in second and foreign language classrooms*. New York, NY: McGraw–Hill.

Page 179: Swaffar, J. K., & Arens, K. (2005. p. 33). *Remapping the foreign language curriculum: An approach through multiple literacies*. New York, NY: Modern Language Association of America.

Page 180: Kern, R. (2000. pp. 171–172). *Literacy and language teaching*. Oxford, England: Oxford University Press.

Page 181: Maxim, H. (2005. p. 86). Articulating foreign language writing development at the collegiate level: A curriculum-based approach. In C. Barrette & K. Paesani (Eds.), *Language program articulation: Developing a theoretical foundation* (pp. 78–93). Boston: Heinle.

Page 182: Based on Kern, R. (2000). *Literacy and language teaching*. Oxford, England: Oxford University Press.

Page 184: Schulz, R. A. (2001. pp. 94–96, 99). Cultural differences in student and teacher perceptions concerning the role of grammar instruction and corrective feedback: USA–Colombia. *Modern Language Journal, 85*, 244–258.

Pages 184–185: Schulz, R. A. (2001. p. 100, 103). Cultural differences in student and teacher perceptions concerning the role of grammar instruction and corrective feedback: USA–Colombia. *Modern Language Journal, 85*, 244–258.

Pages 185–186, 186: Maxim, H. H. (2009. p. 102, 99, 100, 103, 104, 116). "It's made to match:" Linking L2 reading and writing through textual borrowing. In C. Brantmeier (Ed.), *Crossing languages and research methods* (pp. 97–122). Charlotte, NC: Information Age Publishing.

Page 187: Based on Kern, R. (2000. p. 215). *Literacy and language teaching*. Oxford, England: Oxford University Press

Page 188: Schulz, R. A. (2001). Cultural differences in student and teacher perceptions concerning the role of grammar instruction and corrective feedback: USA–Colombia. *Modern Language Journal, 85*, 244–258; Maxim, H. H. (2009). "It's made to match:" Linking L2 reading and writing through textual borrowing. In C. Brantmeier (Ed.), *Crossing languages and research methods* (pp. 97–122). Charlotte, NC: Information Age Publishing; Kern, R. (2000). *Literacy and language teaching*. Oxford, England: Oxford University Press.

Page 191: Swaffar, J. K., & Arens, K. (2005. p. 87). *Remapping the foreign language curriculum: An approach through multiple literacies*. New York, NY: Modern Language Association of America.

Page 198: Maxim, H. H. (2009. p. 97). "It's made to match:" Linking L2 reading and writing through textual borrowing. In C. Brantmeier (Ed.), *Crossing languages and research methods* (pp. 97–122). Charlotte, NC: Information Age Publishing.

Chapter 7

Page 200: Kaiser, M. (2011. p. 232). New approaches to exploiting film in the foreign language classroom. *L2 Journal, 3*, 232–249.

Page 200: MLA Ad Hoc Committee on Foreign Languages. (2007. pp. 3–4). Foreign languages and higher education: New structures for a changed world. *Profession*, 234–245.

Page 202: Joiner, E. G. (1990. p. 54). Choosing and using videotexts. *Foreign Language Annals, 23*, 53–64.

Page 202: Gruba, P. (2005. p. 9). Developing media literacy in the L2 classroom. Sydney, Australia: Macquarie University, National Centre for English Teaching and Research.

Page 204: Gruba, P. (2006. p. 77). Playing the videotext: A media literacy perspective on video-mediated L2 listening. *Language Learning & Technology, 10*, 77–92.

Page 205: Rubin, J. (1995a. p. 7). An overview to A guide for the teaching of second language listening. In D. J. Mendelsohn & J. Rubin (Eds.), *A guide for the teaching of second language listening* (pp. 7–11). San Diego, CA: Dominie Press.

Pages 208, 209, 211: Kramsch, C., & Andersen, R. (1999. p. 39, 40). Teaching text and context through multimedia. *Language Learning & Technology, 2*, 31–42.

Page 211: Hammer, J., & Swaffar, J. (2012. p. 219). Assessing strategic cultural competency: Holistic approaches to student learning through media. *Modern Language Journal, 96*, 209–233.

Page 212: Thoman, E., & Jolls, T. (2003. p. 12, 31). *Literacy for the 21st century: An overview and orientation guide to media literacy education (Part I: Theory).* Malibu, CA: Center for Media Literacy.

Page 213: © Pearson Education, Inc.

Page 214: Zhang, L. (2011. p. 213, 216, 227). Teaching Chinese cultural perspectives through film. *L2 Journal, 3,* 201–231.

Pages 215, 216, 217, 226: Swaffar, J., & Vlatten, A. (1997. p. 175, 176, 177, 179, 181). A sequential model for video viewing in the foreign language curriculum. *Modern Language Journal, 81,* 175–188.

Page 217: Thoman, E., & Jolls, T. (2003). *Literacy for the 21st century: An overview and orientation guide to media literacy education (Part I: Theory).* Malibu, CA: Center for Media Literacy; Eken, A., N (2001). *The third eye. Journal of Adolescent and Adult Literacy, 46,* 220–230; Zhang, L. (2011). Teaching Chinese cultural perspectives through film. *L2 Journal, 3,* 201–231; Swaffar, J., & Vlatten, A. (1997). A sequential model for video viewing in the foreign language curriculum. *Modern Language Journal, 81,* 175–188.

Page 221: Zhang, L. (2011. p. 228). Teaching Chinese cultural perspectives through film. *L2 Journal, 3,* 201–231.

Page 224: Stresstest, Nivea: https://www.youtube.com/watch?v=F49pS5ty7mQ&list=PLjWjZvZQn9NoVeW7M2x9HfVbwFIixnOY1]

Page 227: Gunther R. K. Theo van Leeuwen, *Reading Images: The Grammar of Visual Design* (Psychology Press, 1996). p. vii.

Page 227: Kress, G. R. (2003. p. 140). *Literacy in the new media age.* New York, NY: Routledge.

Page 228: Hammer, J., & Swaffar, J. (2012. pp. 210–211). Assessing strategic cultural competency: Holistic approaches to student learning through media. *The Modern Language Journal, 96,* 209–233.

Page 228: Zhang, L. (2011. p. 213). Teaching Chinese cultural perspectives through film. *L2 Journal, 3,* 201–231.

Pages 229–230: Stresstest, Nivea: https://www.youtube.com/watch?v=F49pS5ty7mQ&list=PLjWjZvZQn9NoVeW7M2x9HfVbwFIixnOY1

Chapter 8

Page 232: Modern Language Association. (2002, para. 1). *Guidelines for institutional support of and access to IT for faculty members and students.* Retrieved from https://www.mla.org/it_support

Page 232: MLA Ad Hoc Committee on Foreign Languages. (2007. p. 4). Foreign languages and higher education: New structures for a changed world. *Profession,* 234–245.

Page 233: Pahl, K., & Rowsell, J. (Eds). (2006. p. 8). *Travel notes from the New Literacy Studies: Instances of practice.* Clevedon, England: Multilingual Matters.

Page 233: Lotherington, H., & Jenson, J. (2011. p. 227) Teaching multimodal and digital literacy in L2 settings: New literacies, new basics, new pedagogies. *Annual Review of Applied Linguistics, 31,* 226–246.

Page 233: New London Group. (1996. p. 65). A pedagogy of multiliteracies: Designing social futures. *Harvard Educational Review, 66(1),* 60–92.

Page 236: Thorne, S. L. (2010. p. 143). The 'intercultural turn' and language learning in the crucible of new media. In F. Helm & S. Guth (Eds.), *Telecollaboration 2.0 for language and intercultural learning* (pp. 139–164). New York, NY: Peter Lang.

Page 237: Clark, J. E. (2010. p. 28). The digital imperative: Making the case for a 21st century pedagogy. *Computers and Composition, 27,* 23–35.

Page 237: Walsh, M. (2009. p. 2). Pedagogic potential of multimodal literacy. In L. T. W. Hin & R. Subramaniam (Eds.), *Handbook of research on new media literacy at the K–12 Level: Issues and challenges* (pp. 32–47). Hershey, PA: IGI Global.

Page 238: Boardman, M. (2005. p. 4). *The language of websites.* New York, NY: Routledge.

Pages 238–239: Coiro, J., & Dobler, E. (2007. p. 242). Exploring the online reading comprehension strategies used by sixth-grade skilled readers to search for and locate information on the Internet. *Reading Research Quarterly, 42,* 214–257.

Pages 239–240: Gonglewski, M. (2001. p. 116, 118, 121). Hypermedia: Enriching L2 compositions. In G. Brauer (Ed.), *Pedagogy of language learning in higher education: An introduction* (pp. 109–126). Westport, CT: Ablex Publishing.

Page 240: Kramsch, C., A'Ness, F., & Lam, E. (2000. pp. 88–89). Authenticity and authorship in the computer-mediated acquisition of l2 literacy. *Language Learning & Technology, 4*, 78–104. Retrieved from http://llt.msu.edu/vol4num2/kramsch/default.html

Page 240: Kress, G. R. (2003. p. 19) *Literacy in the new media age*. New York, NY: Routledge.

Page 241: *"Google Corporate Information"*. Google, Inc. Retrieved February 14, 2010.

Page 241: Based on Kress, G. R., & van Leeuwen, T. (2006). *Reading images: The grammar of visual design*. (2nd. ed.). New York, NY: Routledge.

Page 242: Google, Inc.

Page 243: Thorne, S. L. (2010. p. 144). The 'intercultural turn' and language learning in the crucible of new media. In F. Helm & S. Guth (Eds.), *Telecollaboration 2.0 for language and intercultural learning* (pp. 139–164). New York, NY: Peter Lang.

Page 243: Black, R. (2008. p. 174). *Adolescents and online fan fiction*. New York, NY: Peter Lang.

Page 243: Lam, W. S. E. (2000. p. 470). Second language literacy and the design of the self: A case study of a teenager writing on the Internet. *TESOL Quarterly, 34*, 457–483.

Page 244: Bakhtin, M. (1986. p. 89). *Speech genres and other late essays*. Austin, TX: University of Texas Press.

Page 244: Barthes, R. (1977. p. 146). The death of the author. In *Image, music and text: Essays selected and translated by Stephen Heath* (pp. 142–148). London, England: Fontana. Retrieved from http://www.scribd.com/doc/13270483/Barthes-ImageMusicText

Page 244: Gruber-Miller, J. (2013. p. 148). Engaging multiple literacies through remix practices: Vergil recomposed. *Teaching Classical Languages, 4*, 141–161.

Page 246: van Compernolle, R., & Abraham, L. (2009. p. 209). Interactional and discursive features of English-language weblogs for language learning and teaching. In L. Abraham & L. Williams (Eds.), *Electronic discourse in language learning and language teaching* (pp. 193–211). Amsterdam, Netherlands: John Benjamins.

Page 246: Jones, R., & Hafner, C. (2012. p. 43). *Understanding digital literacies: A practical introduction*. New York, NY: Routledge.

Page 246: Thorne, S. L. (2010. pp. 139–164). The 'intercultural turn' and language learning in the crucible of new media. In F. Helm & S. Guth (Eds.), *Telecollaboration 2.0 for language and intercultural learning*. New York, NY: Peter Lang.

Page 246: Thorne, S. L., & Black, R. (2007. p. 5). Language and literacy development in computer-mediated contexts and communities. *Annual Review of Applied Linguistics, 27*, 133–160.

Page 246: Reinhardt, J., & Sykes, J. (2012. p. 35). Conceptualizing digital game-mediated L2 learning and pedagogy: Game-enhanced and game-based research and practice. In H. Reinders (Ed.), *Digital games in language learning and teaching* (pp. 32–49). New York, NY: Palgrave Macmillan.

Pages 246–247: Thorne, S. L. (2010. p. 149). The 'intercultural turn' and language learning in the crucible of new media. In F. Helm & S. Guth (Eds.), *Telecollaboration 2.0 for language and intercultural learning* (pp. 139–164). New York, NY: Peter Lang.

Page 247: Peterson, M. (2010, p. 436). Massively multiplayer online role-playing games as arenas for second language learning.*Computer Assisted Language Learning, 23*, 429–439.

Page 247: Thorne, S., Black, R., & Sykes, J. (2009. p. 811, 815). Second language use, socialization, and learning in Internet interest communities and online gaming. *Modern Language Journal, 93(s1)*, 802–821.

Page 249: Black, R. (2005. p. 127). Access and affiliation: The literacy and composition practices of English-language learners in an online fanfiction community. *Journal of Adolescent & Adult Literacy, 48*, 118–128.

Page 249: Gee, J. (2004. p. 73). *Situated language and learning: A critique of traditional schooling*. New York, NY: Routledge.

Page 249: Gee, J. (2005. p. 228). Semiotic social spaces and affinity spaces: From the age of mythology to today's schools. In D. Barton & K. Tusting (Eds.), *Beyond communities of practice: Language, power and social context* (pp. 214–232). Cambridge, England: Cambridge University Press.

Page 251: Based on Herring, S. C. (2007). A faceted classification scheme for computer-mediated discourse. *Language@Internet, 4*, Article 1. Retrieved from http://www.languageatinternet.org/articles/2007/761/

Page 251: Reinhardt, J., & Thorne, S. L. (2011. p. 270). Beyond comparisons: Frameworks for developing digital L2 literacies. In N. Arnold & L. Ducate (Eds.), *Present and future promises of CALL: From theory and research to new directions in language teaching* (pp. 257–280). San Marcos, TX: CALICO Publications.

Page 252: van Compernolle, R., & Abraham, L. (2009. p. 206, 208). Interactional and discursive features of English-language weblogs for language learning and teaching. In L. Abraham & L. Williams (Eds.), *Electronic discourse in language learning and language teaching* (pp. 193–211). Amsterdam, Netherlands: John Benjamins.

Page 252: Hyland, K. (2001. p. 136). *Genre and second language writing*. Ann. Arbor, MI: University of Michigan Press.

Page 253: Based on van Compernolle, R., & Abraham, L. (2009. pp. 193–211). Interactional and discursive features of English-language weblogs for language learning and teaching. In L. Abraham & L. Williams (Eds.), *Electronic discourse in language learning and language teaching*. Amsterdam, Netherlands: John Benjamins.

Page 254: Based on Hyland, K. (2001). *Genre and second language writing*. Ann. Arbor, MI: University of Michigan Press.

Page 254: Reinhardt, J., & Thorne, S. L. (2011. p. 270). Beyond comparisons: Frameworks for developing digital L2 literacies. In N. Arnold & L. Ducate (Eds.), *Present and future promises of CALL: From theory and research to new directions in language teaching* (pp. 257–280). San Marcos, TX: CALICO Publications.

Page 255: Based on Reinhardt, J., & Zander, V. (2011. pp. 334–228). Social networking in an intensive English program classroom: A language socialization perspective. *CALICO Journal, 28*, 326–344.

Page 255: Reinhardt, J., & Thorne, S. L. (2011. p. 271). Beyond comparisons: Frameworks for developing digital L2 literacies. In N. Arnold & L. Ducate (Eds.), *Present and future promises of CALL: From theory and research to new directions in language teaching* (pp. 257–280). San Marcos, TX: CALICO Publications.

Page 255: Reinhardt, J., & Zander, V. (2011. p. 326). Social networking in an intensive English program classroom: A language socialization perspective. *CALICO Journal, 28*, 326–344.

Page 256: van Compernolle, R., & Abraham, L. (2009). Interactional and discursive features of English-language weblogs for language learning and teaching. In L. Abraham & L. Williams (Eds.), *Electronic discourse in language learning and language teaching* (pp. 193–211). Amsterdam, Netherlands: John Benjamins; Hyland, K. (2001). *Genre and second language writing*. Ann. Arbor, MI: University of Michigan Press; Reinhardt, J., & Thorne, S. L. (2011). Beyond comparisons: Frameworks for developing digital L2 literacies. In N. Arnold & L. Ducate (Eds.), *Present and future promises of CALL: From theory and research to new directions in language teaching* (pp. 257–280). San Marcos, TX: CALICO Publications.

Pages 259, 260: Kalantzis, M., & Cope, B. (2012) The knowledge processes. *New Learning: Transformational designs for pedagogy and assessment*. Retrieved from http://newlearningonline.com/learning-by-design/the-knowledge-processes

Page 266: Thorne, S. L., & Black, R. (2007. p. 149). Language and literacy development in computer-mediated contexts and communities. *Annual Review of Applied Linguistics, 27*, 133–160.

Pages 266–267: Sykes, J., Oskoz, A., & Thorne, S. (2008. p. 539). Web 2.0, immersive environments, and the future of language education. *CALICO Journal, 25*, 528–546.

Page 267: Lotherington, H., & Jenson, J. (2011. p. 228) Teaching multimodal and digital literacy in L2 settings: New literacies, new basics, new pedagogies. *Annual Review of Applied Linguistics, 31*, 226–246.

Afterword

Page 270: Kern, R. (2000. p. 6). *Literacy and language teaching*. Oxford, England: Oxford University Press.

Pages 271, 272: Swaffar, J. K., & Arens, K. (2005. p. 15, 29). *Remapping the foreign language curriculum: An approach through multiple literacies*. New York, NY: Modern Language Association of America.

Page 271: Paesani, K., & Allen, H. W. (2012. p. s67). Beyond the language-content divide: Research on advanced foreign language instruction at the postsecondary level. *Foreign Language Annals, 45(s1)*, s54–s75.

INDEX

M

N

O

S

T

U

V